Deleuze & Guattari

Deleuze & Guattari

NEW MAPPINGS

IN POLITICS,

PHILOSOPHY,

AND CULTURE

Eleanor Kaufman &
Kevin Jon Heller,
Editors

University of Minnesota Press
Minneapolis
London

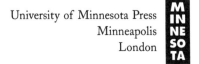

"Having an Idea in Cinema (On the Cinema of Straub-Huillet)," by Gilles Deleuze, was originally published in French in *Antigone: Revue litteraire de photographie;* reprinted with permission.
"The Withering of Civil Society," by Michael Hardt, was originally published in *Social Text* 45,
vol. 14, no. 4 (winter 1995): 27–44; copyright Duke University Press, reprinted with permission. "Requiem for Our Prospective Dead (Toward a Participatory Critique of Capitalist Power),"
by Brian Massumi, was originally published in *UTS Review* 2 (October 1990); reprinted with
permission of the author. An earlier version of *"Capital/Cinema,"* by Jonathan L. Beller, was
originally published as "Cinema, Capital of the Twentieth Century," in the electronic journal
Postmodern Culture 4, no. 3 (May 1994); reprinted with permission.

Published by the University of Minnesota Press
111 Third Avenue South, Suite 290
Minneapolis, MN 55401–2520
http://www.upress.umn.edu

Printed in the United States of America on acid-free paper

The University of Minnesota is an equal-opportunity educator and employer.

Library of Congress Cataloging-in-Publication Data

Deleuze & Guattari : new mappings in politics, philosophy, and culture
  / Eleanor Kaufman & Kevin Jon Heller, editors.
     p.   cm.
   Includes bibliographical references and index.
   ISBN 0-8166-3027-5 (hardcover : alk. paper). — ISBN 0-8166-3028-3
(pbk. : alk. paper)
     1. Deleuze, Gilles.   2. Guattari, Félix.   I. Kaufman, Eleanor.
  II. Heller, Kevin Jon.
  B2430.D454D397   1998
  194–dc21   98–14992

10 09 08 07 06 05 04 03 02 01 00 99   10 9 8 7 6 5 4 3 2

To Marvin Kaufman
— E. K.

For Stuart
— K. J. H.

Contents

Acknowledgments

At every stage of this project, all of our contributors have been extremely encouraging and patient. Gary Genosko, Michael Hardt, Brian Massumi, Tim Murphy, and Dan Smith were of invaluable assistance in putting this collection together. Tom Conley was an exceptional reader and commentator. Special thanks go to Lisa Freeman, Robin A. Moir, William Murphy, Laura Westlund, and Hank Schlau for their superb editorial guidance. Many people in the Duke Literature Program, the Duke Department of English, and the Duke Department of Romance Studies have a presence in this volume — we will here acknowledge only the ongoing support of Fredric Jameson. Gene Kuperman inspired everything. Cesare Casarino and Yonatan Touval came to bear greatly on this project. Jonathan Beller, Renu Bora, Sara Danius, Meg Gandy, Anita Gutierrez, Anna Hahn, Daniel Itzkovitz, Judith Jaffe, Stefan Jonsson, Geneviève Pruvost, Lisa Radinovsky, Brian Selsky, and Neferti Tadiar lent various kinds of support, and Hank Okazaki lent essential technical and neighborly support. Finally, this book is dedicated to two extraordinary parents: to the memory of Marion Dean Kaufman and, above all, to Marvin Kaufman.

1

Introductory Pieces

Introduction

Eleanor Kaufman

If this collection of essays were to be grouped around one image or theme, it would be that of the mythic Borgesian cartographer who charts out a map so detailed that it coincides one-to-one with real space. The map thereby produced would be an odd conjunction of the actual and the virtual: actual in that it would be drawn to real-life scale, virtual in the way that only the real can be, so real that it is no longer really a map but something other. The Borgesian map calls into question the very form of relation upon which a certain type of cartography is based. If maps are meant to be small-scale and easily decipherable plans that correspond through some given unit of proportion to a larger reality, then a map that coincides with that reality, on the one hand, retains the necessary relation of proportion but, on the other hand, transforms it and reconfigures it into a relation of equivalence. Such an alternative system of mapping would not simplify, reduce, and explain but rather complicate, expand, and question.

To use a geographically relevant analogy, one might imagine the various forms of navigation around the city of Paris. Here, we will consider only three. First, there is walking, Paris being renowned as an eminently walkable city. On foot, one might traverse several distinct neighborhoods in a relatively short space of time, perhaps with the aid of a street map or a pocket-sized guidebook that charts out the city by arrondissement. Navigating on foot would require a body capable of such movement as well as an attentiveness to traffic and other objects that might obstruct one's path. Second, one might navigate the city by bus, which affords both a panoramic view and faster movement. Here, one would chart one's course with the large, intricate bus map or with the smaller bus map that comes with the metro map or perhaps with the maps inside the bus itself, maps that show only the streets on the bus's actual route and not the other surrounding streets. A third mode of navigation involves the metro. Like the bus but more so, the metro has the attribute of speed. Unlike the bus, the metro is (usually) below ground and so presents an entirely different visual panorama, a distinct subterranean maze. The keys to this maze are contained in a system of maps that link a given metro line to other metro lines. An obsessive metro navigator not only will have internally charted the points of transfer and the layout of the various stations but will know the very car that should be entered in order to arrive as close as possible to the correct exit at the station of destination.

What does navigating around Paris have to do with the Borgesian cartographer or with Gilles Deleuze and Félix Guattari? At issue here is the relation to real space. In going from one Parisian locale to another by foot, bus, or metro, the space covered is the same, but the mode in which it is covered — and the forms of perception this mode entails, the social, physical, and economic factors that inflect it (its unique mapping system) — is radically different from the others. The Parisian or metropole navigator, like the Borgesian cartographer, charts with his or her body a map that corresponds to actual space. Yet the relation of this bodily mapping to the other forms of mapping remains perpetually virtual. The space of the metro, for example, corresponds virtually to the space of the bus or the space of walking in that these spaces are interconnected but rarely coterminous. Yet with this, each of the three spaces is no less real at any given moment. The challenge comes in trying to link these virtual spaces together (for example, using the bus as a way of connecting the perceptive space of the metro with the perceptive space of walking) and map the various virtualities with and against one another.

Such a mapping on the level of thought is at stake both in the work of Deleuze and Guattari and in the selection and arrangement of the essays in this volume. These essays, in their content and modes of expression, parallel important aspects of the content and modes of expression unique to Deleuze and Guattari, both in their jointly authored and in their separate works. Just as Deleuze and Guattari propose a system of mapping that would try to make connections or linkages between wildly different media, spaces, and social practices, so too do the essays collected here forge connections between the work of Deleuze and Guattari and topics that range from the Gulf War to *Citizen Kane* to quantum physics.

Before outlining the essays in question, it will be useful to delineate Deleuze and Guattari's shared and respective concepts of mapping and the way in which these concepts are integral to their thought as a whole. In the coauthored *A Thousand Plateaus*, the map is repeatedly linked to other central concepts in the Deleuzo-Guattarian lexicon. One such linkage is that between the map and the rhizome. In "Introduction: Rhizome," Deleuze and Guattari write:

> The rhizome is altogether different, a *map and not a tracing*. Make a map, not a tracing. The orchid does not reproduce the tracing of the wasp; it forms a map with the wasp, in a rhizome. What distinguishes the map from the tracing is that it is entirely oriented toward an experimentation in contact with the real. The map does not reproduce an unconscious closed in upon itself; it constructs the unconscious. It fosters connections between fields, the removal of blockages

on bodies without organs, the maximum opening of bodies without organs onto a plane of consistency. It is itself a part of the rhizome. The map is open and connectable in all of its dimensions; it is detachable, reversible, susceptible to constant modification. It can be torn, reversed, adapted to any kind of mounting, reworked by an individual, group, or social formation. It can be drawn on a wall, conceived of as a work of art, constructed as a political action or as a mediation.[1]

The map, then, is not an instrument of *reproduction* but rather one of *construction*. The map is not a contained model, or tracing, of something larger, but it is at all points constantly inflecting that larger thing, so that the map is not clearly distinguishable from the thing mapped. Not only is the map constantly redrawn and reconnected, but its functions are multiple, intersecting at once the realms of politics, art, and philosophy. Moreover, it is linked to the rhizome, which, in contrast to the static and arborescent tree, is mobile and nonhierarchical. Throughout *A Thousand Plateaus,* Deleuze and Guattari use the rhizome to emblematize a new form of thought and politics that is not trapped in the rigid formations of the state, the unconscious, or language. Instead, the movement of the thought in question is flexible and nomadic, transversal and nonhierarchical; this thought is able to move *between* the formations of the state, the unconscious, or language and not just exclusively within one formation. Like the navigator who in one trajectory uses the metro, the bus, and the foot in combination — thereby integrating a network of bodily and mechanic locomotion into one "assemblage" — a rhizomatic or nomadic thought would forge linkages or connections between different systems of knowledge-formation. In this fashion, Deleuze and Guattari outline an expansive cartography of living, one that is coterminous with real time and space.

Such a cartography of living is not constructed by persons and individual subjects. Rather, it is the cartographic functions that construct bodies and affects. Deleuze and Guattari link a depersonalized cartography of the body to their concept of "haecceity" in the following manner:

A body is not defined by the form that determines it nor as a determinate substance or subject nor by the organs it possesses or the functions it fulfills. On the plane of consistency, *a body is defined only by a longitude and a latitude:* in other words the sum total of the material elements belonging to it under given relations of movement and rest, speed and slowness (longitude); the sum total of the intensive affects it is capable of at a given power or degree of potential (latitude). Nothing but affects and local movements, differential speeds. The credit goes to Spinoza for calling attention to these two dimensions of the Body, and for having defined the plane of Nature as pure longitude and latitude. Latitude and longitude are the two elements of a cartography.

There is a mode of individuation very different from that of a person, subject, thing, or substance. We reserve the name *haecceity* for it. A season, a winter, a summer, an hour, a date have a perfect individuality lacking nothing, even though this individuality is different from that of a thing or a subject. They are haecceities in the sense that they consist entirely of relations of movement and rest between molecules or particles, capacities to affect and be affected.[2]

In this passage, Deleuze and Guattari show how the cartographic functions of longitude and latitude define a body rather than an individual subjecthood. Such a concept of the body as a map of variations in movement and speed relates to the Deleuzo-Guattarian concept of the "body without organs" alluded to in the previous passage (a concept that will be taken up in detail in the essays by John S. Howard and Bryan Reynolds). A body without organs is defined not by the organs it contains but rather by the forces that intersect it and the things it can do. The body is not something that harbors an interior grid of organs but is instead the temporary product of a larger exterior mapping of forces. Such a relational mapping is what Deleuze and Guattari term "haecceity." Given this desubjectified dimension of mapping, the analogy of the city navigator must also be brought into this new dimension. Here, we would reverse the perspective and look not at the person who travels from Rue Glacière in the Thirteenth Arrondissement via the 21 bus to its endpoint at Gare St. Lazare and then via line 3 of the metro to the station Pereire and finally on foot down Avenue Niel — instead we would attend to the conjunction of forces at a given moment, the fact that, say, the 21 bus was held up by the traffic at Opéra so that its rider missed a given metro train and caught the next one, which in turn led to a chance encounter of breathtaking proportions. This encounter is a haecceity, an event, that occurs not as a result of an individual's self-determined trajectory but rather due to the trajectory that maps the individual's connection to other trajectories of movement and flux. Mapping, then, is at once the act of charting out a pathway and the opening of that pathway to the event of the chance encounter. The aim of this collection is to open up the potential for such chance encounters in the realm of thought.

Indeed, the very association of Deleuze and Guattari is such an encounter, one where thought is bounced off of two entities and mapped between them in such a way as to belong precisely to neither of them. In *Dialogues*, Deleuze explains his association with Guattari as follows:

We are only two, but what was important for us was less our working together than this strange fact of working between the two of us. We stopped being "author." And these "between the twos" referred back to other people, who were different on one side from on the other....I stole Félix, and I hope he did the same for me. You know how we work — I repeat it because it seems to me to be important — we do not work together, we work between the two. In these conditions, as soon as there is this type of multiplicity, there is politics, micro-politics.[3]

One of the goals of this collection is to respect the way in which Deleuze and Guattari work between each other. To be sure, each thinker has his own distinct voice, yet each voice inflects the other to such an extent that the boundaries often blur, even in the singly authored works. Since Guattari's voice is the one usually subsumed under Deleuze's, it is our aim to bring this voice out as much as possible. While three essays focus specifically on Guattari (those by Bernardo Alexander Attias, Bruno Bosteels, and Gary Genosko), several of the others focus on Deleuze and Guattari as an ensemble.

Nonetheless, Deleuze's statement that between the two of them "there is politics, micro-politics," applies above all to Guattari. As a long-time political activist and a practicing analyst at the experimental psychiatric clinic La Borde, Guattari brought theory and practice together in a virtually unparalleled fashion. In "La Borde: A Clinic Unlike Any Other," Guattari outlines the way in which he and founder Jean Oury set up La Borde as a collective establishment, one where the customarily rigid distinctions between patients, directors, and workers were entirely rearranged, so that each sector overlapped with the others; all met regularly; and everyone shared common tasks.[4] In this fashion, schizoanalysis, as opposed to psychoanalysis, was put into practice. Schizoanalysis takes into consideration multiple forces of production. Rather than viewing the unconscious as the exclusive locus of libidinal and creative production, Deleuze and Guattari argue for an analysis of production that takes into consideration both desiring-production and social production. The residents of La Borde are thereby not relegated to the status of psychiatric patients but elevated into contributing components of the social system that encompasses them. They are positive forces in a micropolitical — or what Deleuze and Guattari term "molecular" — system. Such a combination of psychic and social productive forces constitutes what Guattari terms a "schizoanalytic cartography."[5] In "Subjectivities: For Better and for Worse," Guattari links schizoanalytic cartography with a deindividualized restructuring of subjectivity:

> [W]e do not propose our "schizoanalytic cartographies" as scientific doctrines. Just as an artist borrows elements that suit him from his precursors and contemporaries, we invite our readers to freely take and leave the concepts we advance. The important thing is not the final result but the fact that a cartographic method coexists with the process of subjectivation, and that a reappropriation, an autopoiesis of the means of production of subjectivity, [is] made possible.[6]

Cartography here corresponds to a method that dehierarchizes the building blocks of subjectivity and reassembles them in a different and more elemental state. Such an elemental state extends across social registers and is not limited to only one domain.

This analysis in turn maps back onto Deleuze's more philosophical reading of Michel Foucault in which he expands upon Foucault's construct of the diagram. In "A New Cartographer," Deleuze writes that "the *diagram* is no longer an auditory or visual archive but a map, a cartography that is coextensive with the whole social field."[7] As a map that coincides with the forces that determine its mapping function, a diagram is not representational but productive. Furthermore, it constantly intersects and transforms other maps and diagrams. As Deleuze concludes, "[A] diagram is a map, or rather several superimposed maps. And from one diagram to the next, new maps are drawn. Thus there is no diagram that does not also include, besides the points which it connects up, certain relatively free or unbound points, points of creativity, change and resistance, and it is perhaps with these that we ought to begin in order to understand the whole picture."[8] The essays that follow are just such an array of superimposed maps, maps that, when read together, work to transform one another. While these essays are ordered by general topics — which range from politics to cinema to mapping itself[9] and then finally to philosophy — many of the thematics of one grouping (for example, "societies of control" in the section on politics) return as leitmotifs in the sections that follow. The groupings therefore are not contained but spill over onto one another.

The volume begins with a previously untranslated essay by Gilles Deleuze. In "Having an Idea in Cinema," Deleuze approaches aesthetic creation as something that pushes our spatiotemporal limits rather than being explicitly communicative. "Having an idea" is therefore not a matter of communicating information or using one discipline to reflect upon another. Rather, it is a matter of engaging in solitary creation within one's proper domain. Thus Deleuze does not use philosophy as a tool to decode cinema — or any other discipline — but recognizes it as a mode in which concepts are invented. Cinema, then, has its own space of invention, which is that of movement and duration. In occupying its own space and form of invention, the work of art functions as a mode of resistance in today's information- and communication-governed society.

The first group of essays explicitly maps the work of Deleuze and Guattari onto the domain of global politics. In "The Withering of Civil Society," Michael Hardt explores the complexity of Hegel's notion of civil society, a notion that, in designating a society of abstract labor, has certain uncanny parallels to Foucault's concept of a disciplinary society. He suggests that Deleuze's concept of the "society of control" is more resonant with our postcivil society, a society that is not organized, in panopticon fashion, by rigid institutional structures but rather by the absence of fixed structures or positions. This is not to say that relations of power and force are no longer operative but that they are now constituted differently. Hardt argues that the society of control might be emblematized by shifting desert sands or the smooth surface of cyberspace, which constitutes a "whatever" space that shuns position and identity in favor of mobility and anonymity. Whereas civil society preserved labor as a category that was definitionally distinct from the larger social system, the society of control undoes any sort of dialectic between labor and capital; here, labor is no longer representationally separated from capital but is indeed the very "product of the system itself."

Brian Massumi's "Requiem for Our Prospective Dead (Toward a Participatory Critique of Capitalist Power)" provides a blow-by-blow illustration of the ways in which civil society dissolves into the dissipative structures, the ordered chaos, of a society of control in which life itself is subsumed under capital. Drawing examples from the Gulf War and the U.S. "humanitarian" mission in Somalia, Massumi details the ever-increasing "blurring of the distinction between total war and total peace." In response to this, he calls for a new "metalogics," a pure virtuality, barely thinkable, which is "the potential, contained by capitalism, for its own collapse."

Eugene W. Holland also focuses on the shift from what Foucault called sovereign and disciplinary societies to the contemporary society of control. Holland maps this shift alongside Deleuze and Guattari's varying usage of the term "schizophrenia" from *Anti-Oedipus* to *A Thousand Plateaus*. In doing this he situates these shifts in relation to a refiguring of the concept of axiomatization, which takes into consideration the interrelation of the two modes of domination (servitude and subjection) and the three types of capture (ground rent, profit, and levy). Furthermore, Holland argues that Deleuze and Guattari's analysis of capitalism in *Anti-Oedipus* is ultimately more indebted to Georges Bataille's notion of excess than to Marx or Freud in that "capitalism appears as the most complex form of organization for concentrating and dissipating excess energy."

The next set of essays uses Deleuze and Guattari to explore new strategies of perception under the society of control and new ways of inhabiting its spaces. In "*Capital/Cinema*," Jonathan L. Beller shows how cinema, or more precisely the cinematic mode of perception, is at the center of the virtual metalogic of the society of control. He puts forth the radical suggestion that cinema is not merely a product of capital but actually *is* capital. In other words, cinema is not just a form of representation but has in fact become part of consciousness itself. Thus "each body-machine interface may well be potentially productive of value." As Hardt and Massumi have argued, labor is no longer something that can be represented apart from capital, or, in this case, apart from cinema. Rather, "looking is a form of labor." Beller goes on to formulate an explicit parallel between Marx's analyses of capital and Deleuze's analyses of cinema, while nevertheless insisting that the "unthought of [Deleuze's] cinema books is production itself." Beller concludes by pointing out possibilities for channeling and retooling the labor-value of our perceptions.

While Beller's analysis suggests the revolutionary potential of cinematic perception, Bernardo Alexander Attias draws on Guattari's a-signifying semiotics to outline a project of revolutionary transformation through rhetoric. Attias begins "To Each Its Own Sexes? Toward a Rhetorical Understanding

of *Molecular Revolution*" by showing how rhetorical theory "is concerned first
and foremost with language use as a form of material action in the world."
Attias then turns to Guattari's groundbreaking contributions to rhetorical theory — his demonstration of the importance of material forces that operate
outside a straightforward logic of signifier/signified/meaning as well as the
way in which such forces allow for a space of positivity that stands apart from
certain "negative" formulations of the unconscious or of schizoanalysis. Attias
also charts the trajectory of Guattari's thought into a realm of a-signifying
temporality, one marked by "a movement toward an uncertain future anterior
of which we as yet have no rubric of understanding."

John S. Howard extends the above analyses of capitalism and materiality
into the domain of space itself. In "Subjectivity and Space: Deleuze and Guattari's BwO in the New World Order," Howard uses Deleuze and Guattari's
Anti-Oedipus and *A Thousand Plateaus* to elaborate the concept of the "city as
event." Drawing on William Blake's depiction of eighteenth-century London
and reports on the 1992 Los Angeles riots and the great Midwestern floods of
1993, Howard reveals moments where the smooth space of the city in the new
world order implodes, allowing for the advent of a space in which city and occupying subject are no longer dissociable entities but instead a nondialectical
ensemble. This coincides with the fundamental Deleuzo-Guattarian notion of
the body without organs (BwO) — a term taken from Artaud — which designates a different way of conceptualizing the body, one in which the body
is akin to a force field of differential energies rather than a self-contained
individual subject.

The relation of space to the desubjectified body is central to Samira
Kawash's "415 Men: Moving Bodies, or, The Cinematic Politics of Deportation." As in Deleuze's "Having an Idea in Cinema" and Beller's "*Capital/
Cinema,*" Kawash draws out the political and philosophical ramifications of
cinematic perception, what she calls "cinematic politics." She brings such a
cinematic politics to bear on the case of the "415" Palestinian men deported
from Israel in late 1992 but denied entrance into Lebanon, thus effectively
constituting a desubjectified and nomadic body dwelling outside state boundaries. Like the body without organs, the deported body defies representational
logic: as Palestinian, it is a body that "exists only as that which must not exist,
which must be effaced, pushed back into history, transformed into an arti-
fact"; as individual body, the deported body defies exact numeration or human
specificity apart from its abstract state as suffering materiality; as displaced
object, it is a nomadic body constantly on the move yet simultaneously re-
strained to an ever-restricted no-man's-land. In this fashion the desubjectified,
deported body accedes into a space all its own, one that functions according
to the same antirepresentational logic as Deleuze's notion of cinematic perception. As Kawash affirms, "[T]he paradox of deportation is that the same
action by which the state aims to extrude the being that is incompatible with

it produces another being that poses an even more radical challenge to the state's totalizing force."

Just as the deported body remains outside a representational system, so too does Guattarian cartography signal a breakdown of representational thinking. The next set of essays engages in such a project of nontraditional mapping. As noted above, the process of mapping marks the nonlocalizable and non-representational spatiality of the event. Bruno Bosteels provides a detailed diagram of Guattari's concept of mapping in "From Text to Territory: Félix Guattari's Cartographies of the Unconscious." Here, Bosteels charts the major focal points of Guattari's oeuvre (the reproduction of subjectivity, the social encoding of signs, and the transformation of the environment), traces his borrowings from and reworkings of Charles Sanders Peirce and Louis Hjelmslev, and explicates the key concepts of transversality and functional diagrams. He shows how the map — and in particular the proverbial map that itself coincides with the territory to be mapped — is emblematic of Guattari's pioneering work in the field of a-signifying semiotics.

In "Guattari's Schizoanalytic Semiotics: Mixing Hjelmslev and Peirce," Gary Genosko analyzes the transversal politics of Guattari's own mode of writing and borrowing. This transversality constitutes a mode, or more nearly a semiotics, of reading against the grain, of happily deviating from the thought at hand. Genosko demonstrates how Guattari reads not only Peirce against Peirce but more importantly Hjelmslev against Hjelmslev. Thus, Guattari draws upon the attention to formalism in Hjelmslevian glossematics — the way in which both expression and content are considered foremost as forms rather than as substances — but uses this to underscore the semiotic materiality of form itself, the way in which the pinnacle of abstraction is also the heart of material flux. As a result of this, Guattari develops a basis from which to conduct a micropolitical analysis of the encounters between different semiotic — and a-semiotic — systems of forms.

Bryan Reynolds also engages in a project of mapping that both draws on and contests traditional psychoanalytic interpretation. In "Becoming a Body without Organs: The Masochistic Quest of Jean-Jacques Rousseau," Reynolds provides a schizoanalytic reading of Rousseau's penchant for masochism as outlined in his *Confessions.* Eschewing the psychoanalytic notions of lack, Oedipus, and repression, Reynolds reads Rousseau's masochism as a "road map" to the endless conflictual encounter between desiring-machines and the body without organs (BwO). While the desiring-machine's desire is to keep producing more desire, the BwO is an antiproductive continuum in which "the desiring-machines no longer desire the intensity of desiring-production; there is no production; there is only the electric fervor of desire." Given this parameter, Rousseau's youthful desire to "earn" punishments reveals the mechanism of the desiring-machine that strives to postpone pleasure so as to maintain an ecstatic state of constant desire. Such a desiring-mechanism repeats itself in Rousseau's later-life manifestations of paranoia and hypochondria, intensified bodily states that enabled him to approximate or "become" a BwO. Such a practice of schizoanalysis dislocates the symptomatic body from a purely libidinal register and instead recasts it in a more expansive social field.

The final group of essays engages in a similar sort of mapping project, but one that takes Deleuzian philosophy as its starting point. In "Quantum Ontology: A Virtual Mechanics of Becoming," Timothy S. Murphy expands Deleuze's philosophical concepts to demonstrate their resonances with quantum physics, particularly the work of David Bohm. Murphy reveals the considerable overlap between Bohm's and Deleuze's conceptions of machinic perception, time, and virtuality. Both Deleuze and Bohm "treat the universe as origami," highlighting the endless capacity of matter, space, time, and subjects to fold back in upon themselves. Whether it is called "haecceity" (Deleuze) or "moment" (Bohm), such a mode of thought seeks not to construct meaning but rather to coincide with — or be — its own meaning, thereby resembling Borges's map or Leibniz's monad. Yet this does not mean that these concepts are perfectly identical. Murphy suggests that "conditioned forms must be understood in terms of transcendent virtual conditions that do not necessarily resemble the empirical forms they render actual." Similarly, the philosophy and physics of Deleuze and Bohm are not identical but more nearly resonate on the same wavelength.

The simultaneous convergence and nonconvergence, personality and impersonality, excess and restraint between and within the entity Deleuze-Foucault is the subject of my essay "Madness and Repetition: The Absence of Work in Deleuze, Foucault, and Jacques Martin." Looking in detail at the laudatory essays written by Deleuze and Foucault in praise of each other's work, I somewhat paradoxically characterize this exchange with the term "absence of work" and link it to the obscure figure of Jacques Martin. What is at stake is an ethics of thought as materiality, of thinking and being with and for a friend. The realm of this materiality of thought is indeed akin to the nonlocalizable space charted out in the previous essays.

In "The Place of Ethics in Deleuze's Philosophy: Three Questions of Immanence," Daniel W. Smith poses ethics as a mode of resistance. Rather than implying a moral code, Deleuzian ethics refigures the Kantian moral law to affirm a Nietzschean "transvaluation of values." More specifically, Deleuzian ethics draws on Spinoza in order to pose three fundamental questions regarding modes of existence: "How is a mode of existence determined? How are modes of existence to be evaluated? What are the conditions for the creation of new modes of existence?" Smith approaches these questions by posing the body as a model for ethics and linking it to Foucault's notion of subjectification in order to suggest that a mode of existence is intrinsically linked to its power of acting. Smith concludes by linking his ethical questions to a question raised by many of the preceding essays, namely: How is resistance possible under the society of control? Smith's response lies in a differential conception of ethics that joins the singular and the actual.

The concluding essay, "Another Always Thinks in Me," by Aden Evens, Mani Haghighi, Stacey Johnson, Karen Ocaña, and Gordon Thompson, is a singular actualization of ethical thought, thought coming together to pose the problem of freedom. And "in fact, the solution to the problem of freedom is its exercise." Here, freedom is exercised as a joint meditation on the question of freedom, a being-together in freedom to pose freedom as a problem, a state for which these thinkers create a playful neologism — "freedomdum." In this space of freedomdum, "Another Always Thinks in Me" both addresses and enacts many of the recurrent questions of this collection of essays — the relation of a nonspatiotemporal ideal space to actual spatiotemporal sites, the opening up of thought to movements that are outside of representation, and the creation of a form of thought so material that thought as such is no longer separable from its content and is thus beyond subjectivity. Finally, this piece addresses the problem of artistic creativity that was touched on in Deleuze's opening essay and connects aesthetics — via politics and philosophy — to the question of freedom. Having come full circle, we are left with the hope that, as the final essay suggests, such a thinking and enacting of a work in common will have at least envisioned, if not opened up, a new dimension of freedom.

Notes

1. Gilles Deleuze and Félix Guattari, *A Thousand Plateaus*, trans. Brian Massumi (Minneapolis: University of Minnesota Press, 1987), 12.

2. Ibid., 260–61.

3. Gilles Deleuze and Claire Parnet, *Dialogues*, trans. Hugh Tomlinson and Barbara Habberjam (New York: Columbia University Press, 1987), 17.

4. See Félix Guattari, "La Borde: A Clinic Unlike Any Other," in *Chaosophy*, ed. Sylvère Lotringer (New York: Semiotext[e], 1995), 187–208.

5. For an overview of Deleuzo-Guattarian schizoanalysis, see Gilles Deleuze and Félix Guattari, "Introduction to Schizoanalysis," in *Anti-Oedipus*, trans. Robert Hurley, Mark Seem, and Helen R. Lane (Minneapolis: University of Minnesota Press, 1983), 273–382. This theme is also taken up in the essay by Eugene W. Holland in the present volume.

6. Félix Guattari, "Subjectivities: For Better and for Worse," in *The Guattari Reader*, ed. Gary Genosko (Oxford: Blackwell, 1996), 198.

7. In Gilles Deleuze, *Foucault*, trans. Seán Hand (Minneapolis: University of Minnesota Press, 1988), 34.

8. Ibid., 44.

9. See Bruno Bosteels's essay on cartography in this volume; this essay pursues the question of mapping in far greater detail than this introduction and additionally links Guattari's concept of mapping to the work of other cartography theorists.

Having an Idea in Cinema

(On the Cinema of Straub-Huillet)

Gilles Deleuze

Translated by Eleanor Kaufman

I, too, would like to pose some questions. Pose them to you and to myself. They would be in this vein: What exactly do you, who do cinema, do? And for me: What exactly do I do when I do, or hope to do, philosophy?

I could pose the question otherwise: What is having an idea in cinema? If one does or wants to do cinema, what does having an idea mean? What happens when one says: "Wait, I have an idea"? For, on the one hand, everyone clearly knows that having an idea is an event that rarely takes place; it is a sort of celebration, very uncommon. And then, on the other hand, having an idea is not a general thing. One does not have an idea in general. An idea — like the one who has the idea — is already dedicated to this or that domain. It is sometimes an idea in painting, sometimes an idea in fiction, sometimes an idea in philosophy, sometimes an idea in science. And it is certainly not the same thing that can have all that. Ideas must be treated as potentials that are already engaged in this or that mode of expression and inseparable from it, so much so that I cannot say that I have an idea in general. According to the techniques that I know, I can have an idea in a given domain, an idea in cinema or rather an idea in philosophy.

What is having an idea in something?

So I begin again with the principle that I do philosophy and that you do cinema. Given this, it would be too easy to say that since philosophy is prepared to reflect on anything at all, why wouldn't it reflect on cinema? This is ridiculous. Philosophy is not made for reflecting on anything at all. In treating philosophy as a power of "reflecting on," much would seem to be accorded to it when in fact everything is taken from it. This is because no one needs philosophy for reflecting. Only filmmakers or cinema critics, or even those who like cinema, can effectively reflect on cinema. These people have no need of philosophy in order to reflect on cinema. The idea that mathematicians would need philosophy to reflect on mathematics is comical. If philosophy had to

14

serve as a means of reflecting on something, it would have no reason to exist. If philosophy exists, it is because it has its own content.

What is the content of philosophy?

It is very simple: philosophy is a discipline that is just as creative and inventive as any other discipline, and it entails creating or even inventing concepts. And concepts do not exist ready-made in the sky waiting for a philosopher to seize them. Concepts must be made. To be sure, they are not made just like that. It's not that one just says one day, "Look, I'm going to invent such and such a concept," no more than a painter says one day, "Look, I'm going to make a painting like this," or a filmmaker, "Look, I'm going to make such and such a film!" There must be a necessity, as much in philosophy as elsewhere, for if not there is nothing at all. A creator is not a being who works for pleasure. A creator does only what he or she absolutely needs to do. The fact remains that this necessity — which, if it exists, is a very complex thing — makes a philosopher (and here, I at least know what the concerns of the philosopher are) propose to invent, to create, concepts and not to concern himself or herself with reflecting, even on cinema.

I say that I do philosophy, which is to say that I try to invent concepts. What if I say, to you who do cinema: What do you do?

What you invent are not concepts — which are not your concern — but blocks of movements/duration. If one puts together a block of movements/duration, perhaps one does cinema. It is not a matter of invoking a story or of contesting one. Everything has a story. Philosophy tells stories as well. Stories with concepts. Cinema tells stories with blocks of movements/duration. Painting invents entirely different types of blocks. These are neither blocks of concepts nor blocks of movements/duration, but blocks of lines/colors. Music invents other types of blocks, equally specific. Beside all this, science is no less creative. I don't really see oppositions between the sciences and the arts.

If I ask a scientist what he or she does, the answer is that the scientist also invents. He or she does not discover — discovery exists, but it is not what defines scientific activity as such — but rather creates just as much as an artist. It is not complicated: a scientist is someone who invents or creates functions. And the scientist is the only one. A scientist as such has nothing to do with concepts. On the one hand, it is precisely — and fortunately — for this that there is philosophy. On the other hand, there is one thing that only a scientist knows how to do: invent and create functions. What is a function? There is a function as soon as at least two wholes are put into fixed correspondence. The fundamental notion of science — and not just of late but for a long time — is the notion of the whole. A whole has nothing to do with a concept. As soon as you put wholes into fixed correlation, you obtain functions and can say, "I do science."

If anyone can speak to anyone else — if a filmmaker can speak to a scientist, if a scientist can have something to say to a philosopher and vice versa —

it is according to and by function of each one's creative activity. It is not that talk of creation took place — creation, to the contrary, is something very solitary — but it is in the name of my creation that I have something to say to someone. If I lined up all these disciplines that are defined by their creative activity, I would say that there is a limit common to all of them. The limit common to all these series of inventions — inventions of functions, inventions of blocks of movements/duration, inventions of concepts — is space-time. If all the disciplines communicate together, it is on the level of that which never emerges for itself, but which is, as it were, *engaged* in every creative discipline, and this is the constitution of space-times.

An example of a cinematographic idea is the famous sight-sound dissociation in the relatively recent cinema of Hans-Jürgen Syberberg, the Straubs,[1] and Marguerite Duras, to take the best-known cases. What is common to these, and in what sense is this disjunction of the visual and the auditory a properly cinematic idea? Why could this not take place in theater? Or at least if this happened in theater, if the theater found the means, then one can say without exception that the theater borrowed it from cinema. There is nothing necessarily wrong with this, but the operation of disjunction between sight and sound, between the visual and the auditory, is just the sort of cinematographic idea that would respond to the question, What, for example, is having an idea in cinema?

A voice speaks of something. Something is spoken of. At the same time, we are made to see something else. And finally, what is spoken of is *under* what we are made to see. This third point is very important. You can tell that here is where theater cannot follow. Theater could take up the first two propositions: something is spoken of, and we are made to see something else. But at the same time what is spoken of is placed *under* what we are made to see — and this is necessary since otherwise the first two operations would have no meaning or interest whatsoever. This can be restated: speech rises into air, while the visible ground sinks farther and farther. Or rather, while this speech rises into air, what it speaks of sinks under the ground.

What is this, if only cinema can do it? I am not saying that cinema should do it but that cinema has done it two or three times; I can merely say that it was the great filmmakers who had this idea. This is a cinematographic idea. It is extraordinary in that it provides a veritable transformation of elements at the level of cinema, a cycle that in one stroke makes cinema resonate with a qualitative physics of elements. This produces a sort of transformation, a great circulation of elements in cinema, beginning with air, earth, water, and fire. All that I say does not diminish the story. The story is always there, but what strikes us is why the story is so interesting if not for the fact that all of this is behind it and with it. In this cycle that I have just defined so rapidly — where the voice rises while what it speaks of flees underground — you can recognize most of the Straubs's films, their great cycle of elements. Deserted ground is the only thing that can be seen, but this deserted ground is heavy with what lies beneath. And you respond: But what is known about what lies beneath? It is precisely of this that the voice speaks. It is as if the ground buckles with what the voice tells us, and with what comes, in its time and place, to reside underground. And if the voice speaks to us of corpses, of the whole lineage of corpses that come to reside underground, at this very moment the slightest quivering of wind on the deserted ground, on the empty space under your eyes, the slightest hollow in this ground — all of this becomes clear.

I would say that, in any case, having an idea is not on the order of communication.

This is what I'm getting at. All that we speak of is irreducible to any form of communication. This is not a problem. Which is to say what? In the first sense, communication is the transmission and the propagation of a piece of information. But what is a piece of information? As everyone knows, this is not very complicated: a piece of information is a grouping of order-words. When you are informed, you are told what you are supposed to believe. In other words, informing is circulating a keyword. Police statements are aptly called communiqués. Information is communicated to us; we are told what we are supposed to be ready or able to do or what we are supposed to believe. Not even to believe but to act as if we believed. We are not asked to believe but to behave as if we believed. That is information, communication, and apart from these order-words and their transmission, there is no information, no communication. All of which underscores that information is precisely the system of control. This is clearly of particular concern to us today.

It is true that we are entering a society that can be called a society of control. A thinker such as Michel Foucault has analyzed two types of societies that are rather close to us. He calls the former sovereign societies and the latter disciplinary societies. He locates the typical passage of a sovereign society to a disciplinary society with Napoleon. Disciplinary society is defined — and here Foucault's analyses are rightly famous — by the accumulation of structures of confinement: prisons, schools, workshops, hospitals. Disciplinary societies require this. This analysis engendered ambiguities in certain of Foucault's readers because it was believed that this was his last thought. This was certainly not the case. Foucault never believed and indeed said very precisely that disciplinary societies were not eternal. Moreover, he clearly thought that we were entering a new type of society. To be sure, there are all kinds of things left over from disciplinary societies, and this for years on end, but we know already that we are in societies of another sort that should be called, to use the term put forth by William Burroughs — whom Foucault admired greatly — societies of control. We are entering into societies of control that are defined very differently from disciplinary societies. Those who look after our interests do not need or will no longer need structures of confinement. These structures — prisons, schools, hospitals — are already sites of permanent discussion. Wouldn't it be better to spread out the treatment? To the home? Yes, this is unquestionably the future. The workshops, the factories — they are falling apart everywhere. Wouldn't systems of subcontracting and work at home be better? Aren't there means of punishing people other than prison? Societies of control will no longer pass through structures of confinement. Even the school. The themes that are surfacing, which will develop in forty or fifty years and which indicate that the most shocking thing would be to undertake school and a profession at once — these themes must be watched closely. It will be interesting to know what the identity of the school and the profession will be in the course of permanent training, which is our future and which will no longer necessarily imply the regrouping of school children in a structure of confinement. A control is not a discipline. In making highways, for example, you don't enclose people but instead multiply the means of control. I am not saying that this is the highway's exclusive purpose, but that people can drive infinitely and "freely" without being at all confined yet while still being perfectly controlled. This is our future.

So let us consider information as the controlled system of order-words that are used in a given society.

What does the work of art have to do with this?

Let us not speak of the work of art, but let us at least say that there is counterinformation. There are countries ruled by dictatorships where, under particularly cruel and difficult conditions, counterinformation exists. In the time of Hitler, the Jews who arrived from Germany, and who were the first to inform us of the existence of extermination camps, engaged in counterinformation. It must be noted that counterinformation was never sufficient to do anything. No counterinformation ever disturbed Hitler. Except in one case. What was the case? And here lies its importance. The only response would be that counterinformation only effectively becomes useful when it is — and it is this by nature — or when it becomes an act of resistance. And the act of resistance is neither information nor counterinformation. Counterinformation is effective only when it becomes an act of resistance.

What is the relation between the work of art and communication?

None whatsoever. The work of art is not an instrument of communication. The work of art has nothing to do with communication. The work of art strictly does not contain the least bit of information. To the contrary, there is a fundamental affinity between the work of art and the act of resistance. There, yes. It has something to do with information and communication as acts of resistance. What is this mysterious relation between a work of art and an act of resistance when men who resist have neither the time nor sometimes the necessary culture to have the least relation to art? I don't know. André Malraux develops a beautiful philosophical concept; he says something very simple about art; he says it is the only thing that resists death. Let's return to where we began: What does one do when one does philosophy? One invents con-

cepts. I think this is the basis of a beautiful philosophical concept. Think —
What resists death? One need only see a statuette from three thousand years
before our time to find that Malraux's response is a rather good one. From our
point of view, we could then say, rather less elegantly, that art is what resists
even if it is not the only thing that resists. Where does such a close relation
between the act of resistance and the work of art come from? Each act of
resistance is not a work of art while, in a certain sense, it is all the same. Each
work of art is not an act of resistance and yet, in a certain sense, it is.

What is having an idea in cinema?

Take the case, for example, of the Straubs when they perform this disjunction between auditory voice and visual image, which goes as follows: the
voice rises, it rises, it rises, and what it speaks about passes under the naked,
deserted ground that the visual image was showing us, a visual image that
had no direct relation to the auditory image. But what is this speech act that
rises in the air while its object passes underground? Resistance. An act of
resistance. And in all of the Straubs' oeuvre, the speech act is an act of resistance. From *Moses and Aaron* to the last Kafka film (*Class Relations*) and
passing through — now this is not in order — *Not Reconciled* or *The Chronicle
of Anna Magdalena Bach*. Bach's speech act is his music, which is an act of
resistance, an active struggle against the partitioning of the profane and the
sacred. This musical act of resistance culminates in a cry. Just as there is a cry
in *Woyzeck,* there is a cry in *Bach:* "Outside! outside! Go on, I don't want to
see you!" When the Straubs underscore the cry, that of Bach or that of the
old schizophrenic in *Not Reconciled,* this reveals a double aspect. The act of
resistance has two sides. It is human, and it is also the act of art. Only the act
of resistance resists death, whether the act is in the form of a work of art or
in the form of human struggle.

What relation is there between human struggle and the work of art?

It is the strictest and for me the most mysterious relation. Precisely what
Paul Klee wanted to say when he said: "You know, the people are missing."
The people are missing while at the same time they are not missing. The
people are missing: that means that this fundamental affinity between a work
of art and a people who do not yet exist is not, and never will be, clear. There
is no work of art that does not appeal to a people who do not yet exist.

Note

1. When Deleuze refers to the Straubs, he is actually referring to the team of
Jean-Marie Straub and Danièle Huillet. *Trans.*

2

Global Politics

The Withering of Civil Society

Michael Hardt

Gilles Deleuze claims, in a brief and enigmatic essay, "Postscript on the Societies of Control," that contemporary society has recently undergone a fundamental shift: the paradigm of rule has moved from disciplinary regimes to regimes of control.[1] Deleuze claims to read this passage as implicit in the work of Michel Foucault. In effect, Deleuze tells us that anyone who imagines himself or herself following Foucault by attempting to interpret contemporary society as a disciplinary society has read Foucault all wrong. One of the most important aspects of Foucault's definition of disciplinary regimes is that it is historical: before the predominance of disciplinary societies, societies of sovereignty were the paradigm of rule; and after disciplinary societies, the societies of control entered the scene. Today power is no longer exerted primarily through disciplinary deployments, but through networks of control.

We might understand better the nature and importance of this political passage, however, if we situate Foucault's and Deleuze's arguments in the context of traditional problematics in political philosophy. Specifically, the passage from discipline to control coincides in large part, I believe, with the withering of the institutions commonly gathered under the term "civil society." Investigating the history and fortunes of this concept and the social forms it designates will flesh out the terrain of Foucault's and Deleuze's claims. The withering of civil society may also give us useful terms for grasping more adequately what is all too often vaguely indicated by references to the end of modernity or the end of modern society. The terms "modern" and "postmodern" lack the specificity to be useful beyond a certain point. The society we are living in today, the society of control, is more properly understood as a postcivil society.

The Society of the Organization of Abstract Labor

In political philosophy, civil society is fundamentally linked to the modern notion of labor, and the thinker who made this connection clearest is G. W. F.

Hegel. The concept of civil society is perhaps Hegel's greatest contribution to political philosophy, but he was certainly not the first social theorist to employ the concept. Throughout the early modern period, from Hobbes to Rousseau at least, the distinction between natural society and civil society, or rather between the state of nature and the civil state, played a fundamental role, as the dualism that founded and justified the political order. In these early modern theories, the primary concern was that the rational order of civil society be contrasted with the irrational disorder of natural society. The movement from the natural to the civil was thus the historical and/or theoretical movement of human civilization.

By the time that Hegel developed his political theory, however, the axis of this fundamental social distinction had shifted, so that Hegel focused primarily on the contrast not between natural society and civil society but between civil society and political society, that is, between civil society and the State. When we look at Hegel's usage of the concept of civil society against the backdrop of the early modern theories, then, we have to be struck by two closely related innovations. The first, which should be credited as much to the tenor of Hegel's times as to Hegel himself, is that civil society has gained a more complex economic definition, due at least in part to the progressive spread and maturation of capitalism. Many commentators have pointed out that Hegel developed his conception of civil society on the basis of the writings of English economists of the time and that the standard German translation of the English "civil society," which Hegel used, was *bürgerliche Gesellschaft*, or "bourgeois society." This fact alone should lead us to focus on the relationship between Hegel's conception of civil society and the conceptions, which were widespread at the time, of the civilizing process contained in market exchange and capitalist relations of production. According to Hegel, through needs, work, exchange, and the pursuit of particular self-interests, the "unorganized atoms of civil society"[2] are to be ordered toward the universal — not exactly through the mysterious actions of Adam Smith's invisible hand, but rather though the competitive institutions of capitalist production and circulation. In this respect, then, the economic medium of civil society can be said to fill the role of nature, to which Hegel can contrast the rational order of the political realm.

The second innovation in Hegel's usage of the concept of civil society, which is closely tied to the first but specific to Hegel in its formulation, is the emphasis on the educative aspect of civil society. Here it should be clear that Hegel does not merely replace the earlier dualism (natural society–civil society) with another dualism (civil society–political society) but rather sets up a three-part conception (natural–civil–political). The state of nature, as a realm of needs and unrelated self-interest, has no direct relation to the political State in Hegel but must instead pass through or be mediated by civil society before becoming political. Civil society shares with natural society the fact of being a realm of needs and self-interest, Hegel emphasizes, but civil society is also a "sphere of relatedness — a sphere of education."[3] In other words, civil society takes the natural human systems of needs and particular self-interests, puts them in relation with each other through the capitalist social institutions of production and exchange, and thus, on the basis of the mediation and subsumption of the particular, poses a terrain on which the State can realize the universal interest of society in "the actuality of the ethical Idea."[4] Hegelian education in civil society is a process of formal subsumption, that is, a process whereby particular differences, foreign to the universal, are negated and preserved in unity.

Hegel combines and highlights these economic and educative aspects in his conception that civil society is primarily a society of labor. This can be our first approximation of a definition of the concept. Labor produces and labor educates. In his early writings on the State, in the Jena period, Hegel conceived the process of the abstraction of labor from its concrete instantiations as the motor driving the civilizing social institutions. "Concrete labor is the elemental, substantial conversation, the basic foundation of everything, but it is also blind and savage," that is, uneducated in the universal interest.[5] Concrete labor, which in this early period Hegel imagined as the labor of peasants, is the human activity closest to nature. Just like nature, concrete labor, since it is the foundation of all society, cannot be simply negated, but neither can it be simply integrated since it is savage and uncivilized; "like a savage beast," Hegel writes, "[it] must be constantly subjugated and tamed [*Beherrschung und Bezähmung*]."[6] Labor must be *aufgehoben,* negated and integrated, subsumed. The process of abstraction, then, from concrete labor to abstract labor, is the educative process whereby the singular is transformed into the universal by negation, by abandoning itself.[7] As a second approximation, then, we should say that civil society is not simply the society of labor but specifically the society of abstract labor.

This same educative process of abstraction is also at the center of Hegel's mature conception of civil society, which he poses in his later writings in less philosophical, more practical terms: through labor the pursuit of the satisfaction of one's particular needs is related to the pursuits of others, and thus "subjective self-seeking turns into a contribution to the satisfaction of the needs of everyone else."[8] Hegel finds this educative role of labor, the transformation to the universal, organized and made explicit in the institutional trade unions, the corporations, which structurally orient the particular interests of workers toward the universal interest of society.[9] Civil society consists of not just the unions but all the institutions of capitalist society that organize abstract labor. In its mature formulation, then, and for us as a third approximation, we should say that civil society is the society of the organization of abstract labor.

Education, Hegemony, and Discipline

The Hegelian conception of civil society persists in various forms throughout modern and contemporary social and political theory. When we survey the work of the wide variety of twentieth-century authors who in some form or another take up this notion of civil society, we quickly recognize that the social dialectic of civil society is presented in two guises, one more democratic and the other more authoritarian. Antonio Gramsci is perhaps the thinker who has gone furthest in theorizing the democratic and socialist potential of civil society. He insists repeatedly in his prison notebooks on the importance of the Hegelian distinction between civil society and political society for any liberal or progressive political theory, but in effect he inverts the relationship between these two concepts, standing the relationship, he might say, on its feet.[10] As we have seen, Hegel conceives the end of social movement and conflict, in both logical and historical terms, as gathered together, subsumed, and thus realized in the ends of the State, "the actuality of the ethical Idea." Gramsci casts the historical movement or flow in the opposite direction, proposing instead "that the State's goal is its own end, its own disappearance, in other words, the re-absorption of political society within civil society."[11] The term "re-absorption" indicates a reversal of the social flow: what according to the Hegelian process of subsumption flowed from society toward the State now is reversed from the State to civil society, as a sort of inverted subsumption. Gramsci is able to understand the process of the withering or disappearance of the State as a process of reabsorption because he conceives the State as existing only secondarily, as if it were a placeholder that fills the structural void left by a civil society that is not fully developed. When civil society does manage fully to fill its role, the State as such will no longer exist; or rather, State elements will continue to exist only as subordinated agents of civil society's hegemony. In effect, Gramsci has taken what he finds to be democratic in Hegel's conception of civil society and given those aspects the prominent position, turning the system upside down. Expanding and reinforcing the scope and powers of the various segments and institutions of civil society are thus central to a Gramscian strategy of social progress, which will eventually reverse the flow of the Hegelian process and fill the dictatorial and coercive spaces now occupied by the State with democratic forces organized in terms of social hegemony and consent. This hegemony is grounded finally on a Hegelian form of education, which gives the revolutionary class or party its ability to "absorb" or "assimilate all of society" in the name of general interests. When the State has been effectively subsumed, Gramsci claims, the reign of civil society, that is, self-government, will begin.[12]

The writings of authors who like Gramsci highlight the democratic aspects of civil society focus in general on the pluralism of the institutions of civil society and the avenues or channels they provide for input into the rule of political society, or the State. Seen in this light, the institutional labor union, to take up Hegel's prime example, provides a channel for the representation of the workers' interests in the forum of political society. Juridical reformism might point toward another example, exploiting the channel of the legal institutions and the framework of rights in order to represent diverse interests within the State. Numerous other strategies of political practice and scholarly analysis — focusing, for example, on interest-group politics, the interplay of political parties, segments of the media, church movements, and popular reform movements — all emphasize the possibilities of democratic representation available through the passages opened by the ideological, cultural, and economic institutions of civil society. From this perspective, the social dialectic activated in civil society and the possibilities of mediation make the State open to the plurality of social flows channeled through the institutions. The activation of the forces of civil society makes the State porous, destabilizing its dictatorial powers or rather "reabsorbing" them within the expanding hegemony of civil society.

In the work of other authors, however, the mediatory institutions that define the relationship between civil society and the State are shown to function not toward democratic but toward authoritarian ends. From this second perspective, then, the representation of interests through the channels of the institutions does not reveal the pluralistic effects of social forces on the State but rather highlights the State's capacities to organize, recuperate, even produce social forces. Michel Foucault's work has made clear that the institutions and *enfermements* (enclosures) of civil society — the church, the school, the prison, the family, the union, the party, and so on — constitute the paradigmatic terrain for the disciplinary deployments of power in modern society, producing normalized subjects and thus exerting hegemony through consent in a way that is perhaps more subtle but no less authoritarian than the exertion of dictatorship through coercion. The disciplinary perspective, then, might recognize the same channels passing through civil society but sees the flows moving again in the opposite direction. The institutional labor union, for example, is viewed not so much as a passage for the expression of worker interests to be represented in the plurality of rule but rather as a means to mediate and recuperate the antagonisms born of capitalist production and capitalist social relations — thus creating a worker subjectivity that is recuperable within and will actually support the order of the capitalist State. This is not only the sense in which Foucault analyzes the institutions of civil society, but also the very same way in which Hegel celebrates them. As we saw earlier, the labor union and the other institutions of civil society are to "educate" the citizens, creating within them the universal desires that are in line with the State. "Actually, therefore," Hegel writes, "the State as such is not so much the result as the beginning."[13] The social dialectic thus functions in order that antagonistic social forces be subsumed within the prior and unitary synthesis of the State.

In order to situate Foucault's work on the terrain of Hegel's civil society, however, we need to take a step back and elaborate some of the nuances of Foucault's theoretical perspective. Hegel's understanding of the historical rise of civil society and the generalization of its educative social role does correspond in several respects to the process that Michel Foucault calls the governmentalization of the State. The State of sovereignty, which according to Foucault served as the dominant form of rule in Europe approximately from the Middle Ages to the sixteenth century, positioned itself as a transcendent singularity with respect to its subjects. The transcendence of the sovereign State afforded it a certain detachment from the pressures of conflictive particular interests in society. In the passage to the modern State, however, the transcendence and singularity of the State were overturned through the rise of what Foucault calls "governmentality." The rule of the governmental State is characterized instead by its immanence to the population through a multiplicity of forms. "The art of government...," Foucault said, "must respond essentially to this question: how can it introduce the economy, in other words, the manner of adequately managing individuals, goods, and wealth, as can be done within a family, like a good father who knows how to direct his wife, his children, and his servants?"[14] The management of people and things implied by this governance involves an active engagement, exchange, or dialectic among social forces and between social forces and the State. The same educative social processes that Hegel casts in terms of abstraction and organization, Foucault recognizes in terms of training, discipline, and management. The channels, or striations, in which these processes function, recognized as social institutions by Hegel, are characterized by Foucault in terms of deployments (*dispositifs*) and enclosures (*enfermements*). Civil society, from this perspective, is the productive site of modern economy (economy understood now in the large sense); in other words, it is the site of the production of goods, desires, individual and collective identities, and so on. It is the site, finally, of the institutional dialectic of social forces, of the social dialectic that gives rise to and underwrites the State.

In his extensive work on the nature of power, however, Foucault not only refuses Gramsci's inversion of the priority between civil society and political society (that is, civil society and the State) but goes one step further and argues that we can make no analytical distinction at all between them. When Foucault argues that power cannot be isolated but is everywhere, that it comes from everywhere, that there is no outside to power, he is also denying the analytical separation of political society from civil society. In what is now a famous passage Foucault writes, "[R]elations of power are not in a position of exteriority with respect to other types of relationship (economic processes, knowledge relationships, sexual relations), but are immanent to the latter. . . . [T]hey have a directly productive role, wherever they come into play."[15] In the disciplinary and governmental society the lines of power extend throughout social space in the channels created by the institutions of civil society. The exertion of power is organized through deployments, which are at once ideological, institutional, and corporeal. This is not to say that there is no State, but rather that it cannot effectively be isolated and contested at a level separate from society. In Foucault's framework, the modern State is not properly understood as the transcendent source of power relations in society. On the contrary, the State as such is better understood as a result, the consolidation or molarization of forces of "statization" (*étatisation*) immanent to social power relations.[16] The causes and intentions that inform and order power relations are not isolated in some headquarters of rationality, but immanent to the field of forces. Foucault thus prefers to use instead of "State" the term "government," which indicates the multiplicity and immanence of the forces of statization to the social field. While this denies all the moral and teleological elements of Hegel's social theory, Foucault's understanding of the disciplinary and governmental society does in certain respects take the Hegelian notion of civil society to its logical conclusion. In particular, Foucault emphasizes the "educational" aspect of civil society whereby particular social interests are enlightened to the general interest and brought in line with the universal. Education means discipline. More accurately, Foucault reformulates the educational process of civil society in terms of production: power acts not only by training or ordering the elements of the social terrain but actually by producing them — producing desires, needs, individuals, identities, and so on. I see this not so much as a contradiction but as an extension of Hegelian theory. The State, Hegel says, is not the result but the cause; Foucault adds, not a transcendent but an immanent cause, statization, immanent to the various channels, institutions, or enclosures of social production.

Let me take a moment to summarize before moving on. Disciplinary society can be characterized as civil society seen from a different perspective, approached from underneath, from the microphysics of its power relations. While Gramsci highlighted the democratic potentials of the institutions of civil society, Foucault made clear that civil society is a society founded on discipline and that the education it offers is a diffuse network of normalization. From this perspective, Gramsci and Foucault highlight the two contrasting faces of Hegel's civil society. And in all of this what is primary is the way our labor or our social practice is organized and recuperated in social institutions and educated in the general interest of political society. In presenting the arguments this way I do not intend to charge that either Foucault or Gramsci is finally too Hegelian. Foucault's work on disciplinary societies, while of course in certain regards decisively non-Hegelian, does remain on the same terrain as Hegel's social analysis, as does Gramsci's, primarily because they are all oriented toward understanding the same social formation, the historical phase of

European civil society. As Marx said, however, neither Hegel nor anyone else should be blamed for theorizing the existing relationship between the State and society; they should be blamed only when they cast that formation as necessary and eternal, outside of history.

The Infinite Undulations of the Snake

When we look at the contemporary societies of Western Europe and North America, however, it seems that these various, rich, promising, and frightening theoretical visions of civil society, both in the Hegelian version and in the Gramscian and Foucauldian reformulations, no longer hold — they no longer grasp the dominant mechanisms or schema of social production and social ordering. The decline of the paradigm of civil society correlates to a passage in contemporary society toward a new configuration of social relations and new conditions of rule. This is not to say that the forms and structures of social exchange, participation, and domination that were identified by the concept of civil society have ceased entirely to exist, but rather that they have been displaced from the dominant position by a new configuration of apparatuses, deployments, and structures.

This is the context in which I understand Gilles Deleuze's claim that we have recently experienced a passage from a disciplinary society to a society of control. Deleuze's notion can serve us here as a first attempt to understand the decline of the rule of civil society and the rise of a new form of control. Disciplinary societies, as I said earlier, are characterized by the enclosures or institutions that serve as the skeleton or backbone of civil society; these enclosures define the striations of social space. The coordinated striations formed by the institutions of civil society branch out through social space in structured networks, as Deleuze says, like the tunnels of a mole.[17] Gramsci in fact takes this same image and casts it with a military metaphor: "The superstructures of civil society are like the trench-systems of modern warfare."[18] Lines of power or lines of resistance, the striations of civil society are the skeleton that defines and supports the figure of the social body.

Deleuze insists, however, that these social enclosures or institutions are today everywhere in crisis. One might interpret the crisis of the factory, the family, the church, and the other social enclosures as the progressive crumbling of various social walls that subsequently leave a social void, as if the striated social space of civil society had been smoothed into a vacant free space. One of the most important lessons that Foucault tried to teach us, however, is that power never leaves a vacuum, but always in some form fills social space. Deleuze suggests that it is more adequate, then, to understand the collapse of the walls defined by the enclosures not as some sort of social evacuation but rather as the generalization of the logics that previously functioned within these limited domains across the entire society, spreading like a virus. The logic of capitalist production perfected in the factory now invests all forms of social production. The same might be said also for the school, the family, the hospital, and the other disciplinary institutions. "The prison," Foucault notes, "begins well before its doors. It begins as soon as you leave your house"[19] — and even before. Social space is smooth, not in the sense that it has been cleared of the disciplinary striations but rather in the sense that those striations have been generalized across society. Social space has not been emptied of the disciplinary institutions but completely filled with the modulations of control. The relationship between society and the State no longer primarily involves the mediation and organization of the institutions for discipline and rule but rather sets the State in motion directly through the perpetual circuitry of social production.

We should be careful to point out, however, that the passage from disciplinary society to the society of control is not merely a shift in the institutional structures of rule. Foucault insisted, as we saw earlier, that the institutions do not occupy a primary position, as the sources of power relations; instead, institutions represent the consolidation or assemblage of the strategies of power. What underlies the various institutions is the diagram: the anonymous or abstract strategic machine, the unformed or nonstratified schema of power relations. The diagram transcends, or better subtends, the various institutional assemblages. Foucault's most successful attempt to grasp the diagram of disciplinary society is his analysis of the panopticon. "Is it surprising that prisons resemble factories, schools, barracks, hospitals, which all resemble prisons?"[20] The disciplinary diagram runs throughout the various institutions defining the conditions of possibility, the conditions of what can be seen, said, and known, the conditions of the exertion of power. The passage to a society of control, then, will certainly manifest symptoms at the institutional level, but it should be grasped also and above all at the diagrammatic level. If we are to follow Foucault's method, then, first we should ask: What are the diagrams that define the conditions of possibility in the societies of control? And then: In what kinds of social assemblages will these diagrammatic forces be consolidated, and how?

The metaphors available to us can at least give us an indication of the nature of this passage. We can no longer, for example, use the metaphor of structure and superstructure that was central to the conception of the mediating institutions of civil society. The image of the intersecting burrows of the mole that characterized the structures of disciplinary societies no longer holds in this new domain. Not the structured passages of the mole, Deleuze insists, but the infinite undulations of the snake are what characterize the smooth space of the societies of control.[21] Similarly, the Gramscian metaphor of a system of trenches that supported the war of position in civil society has been definitively surpassed by the contemporary techniques of warfare. Fixed positions have become a liability, not a strength, in combat; instead, monitoring, mobility, and speed have become the dominant characteristics. The Iraqi army certainly learned this lesson in the Gulf War. Iraqi soldiers were literally buried alive when their trenches were smoothed over by the U.S. war machine. The metaphorical space of the societies of control is perhaps best characterized by the shifting desert sands, where positions are continually swept away; or better, the smooth surfaces of cyberspace, with its infinitely programmable flows of codes and information.

These metaphors suggest an important shift marked by the diagram of the society of control. The panopticon, and disciplinary diagrammatics in general, functioned primarily in terms of positions, fixed points, and identities. Foucault saw the production of identities (even "oppositional" or "deviant" identities, such as the factory worker and the homosexual) as fundamental to the functions of rule in disciplinary societies. The diagram of control, however, is oriented not toward position and identity but rather toward mobility and anonymity. It functions on the basis of "the whatever,"[22] the flexible and mobile performance of contingent identities, and thus its assemblages or institutions are elaborated primarily through repetition and the production of simulacra. Fordist and Taylorist production schema elaborated long ago a model of interchangeability, but that interchangeability was based on common roles, fixed positions, and defined parts. The fixed identity of each part is precisely what made interchangeability possible. The post-Fordist productive model of "the whatever" and contingent performativity proposes a broader mobility and flexibility that fix no identities, giving repetition free rein. In this sense the societies of control preserve the anonymous character common to all diagrams and refuse the particularization that previously accompanied the translation of the diagram into molar assemblages or institutions. Elaborate controls over information flow, extensive use of polling and monitoring techniques, and innovative social use of the media thus gain prominent positions in the exertion of power. Control functions on the plane of the simulacra of society. The anonymity and whateverness of the societies of control are precisely what give them their smooth surfaces.

We should not get carried away, however, with applying these metaphors absolutely. Claiming the decline of civil society, of course, does not mean that all the mechanisms of rule and organization that characterized civil society no longer exist or function. Similarly, recognizing a passage from disciplinary societies to societies of control does not mean that disciplinary deployments and the attendant potentialities of resistance have completely disappeared. Disciplinary deployments remain, as do elements of sovereignty in the regimes of control. Even more important, the smoothing of social space does not bring an end to social striation; on the contrary, as Deleuze and Guattari are careful to point out, within this process of smoothing, elements of social striation reappear "in the most perfect and severe forms."[23] In other words, the crisis or decline of the enclosures or institutions gives rise in certain respects to a hypersegmentation of society. For example, while in recent years factory production has declined and the social striations that it defined have been smoothed, it has been at least partially replaced by forms of flexible production that have segmented the labor force in extreme forms, creating mobile, anonymous networks of home labor, part-time work, and various forms of undeclared or illegal labor. While wage labor seems to disappear, its relations are really proliferated and generalized throughout society. The shift from factory production to flexible production paradoxically combines the smoothing and the hypersegmentation of social space. Although extreme, the new segmentation is nonetheless mobile or flexible — these are flexible rigidities. What is primarily at issue, though, is not simply the existence of certain apparatuses, mechanisms, or deployments, but rather their predominance within a specific paradigm of rule. Our task is to discern the salient characteristics of the social formation that succeeds civil society; the smooth spaces of the societies of control constitute our first attempt.

We can formulate a second, complementary approach to this problematic by casting the passage not in Foucauldian but rather in Marxian terminology, which will highlight the contemporary change in the social organization of labor. Straining their periodizations a bit, we could say that Foucault's societies of sovereignty correspond to feudal relations of production; disciplinary regimes rely on what Marx calls the formal subsumption of labor under capital; and the societies of control point to the real subsumption of labor under capital. This periodization is central to both Marx's and Foucault's understandings of the historically specific relationships among the State, society, and capital. The State today has moved beyond Hegel and his dialectic, not limiting but perfecting the State's rule.

Marx recognized the passage from the formal to the real subsumption in nineteenth-century society as a tendency, but it seems to me that this passage has come to be generalized only in the most completely capitalist countries in our times.[24] Let me take a moment to explain Marx's understanding of this passage within capitalism. According to Marx, in the first of these two phases, the formal subsumption, social labor processes are subsumed under capital; that is, they are enveloped within the capitalist relations of production in such a manner that capital intervenes as the director or manager. In this arrangement capital subsumes labor the way it finds it; capital takes over existing labor processes that were developed in previous modes of production or at any rate outside of capitalist production. This subsumption is formal insofar as the labor process exists within capital, subordinated to its command as an imported foreign force, born outside of capital's domain. Actually, as Hegel clearly recognized in his early writings (in the Jena period), capital cannot directly integrate concrete labor but must first abstract it from its concrete forms. The various processes of abstraction, the resistances these give rise to, and the potential lines of social conflict between concrete labor and abstract labor are thus principal characteristics of the phase of the formal subsumption.

Capital tends, however, through the socialization of production and through scientific and technological innovation, to create new labor processes and destroy old ones, transforming the situations of the various agents of production. Capital thus sets in motion a specifically capitalist mode of production. Marx calls the subsumption of labor real, then, when the labor processes themselves are born within capital and therefore when labor is incorporated not as an external but as an internal force proper to capital itself.

As we move to the phase of the real subsumption, Marx explains, labor processes evolve so that, first of all, production is no longer a direct and individual activity but an immediately social activity. "Direct labor as such," Marx writes, "ceases to be the basis of production, since, in one respect, it is transformed more into a supervisory and regulatory activity; but then also because the product ceases to be the product of isolated direct labor, and the combination of social activity appears, rather, as the producer."[25] Furthermore, this socialized labor-power itself seems to disappear as it is displaced from its position as the source of capitalist production. "This entire development of the productive forces of socialized labor, and together with it the use of science, takes the form of the productive power of capital. It no longer appears as the productive power of labor."[26] In very brief summary, then, Marx identifies a three-stage shift in the apparent source of capitalist production, from individual labor to social labor and finally to social capital. In the specifically capitalist mode of production, that is, in the phase of the real subsumption, productive labor — or even production in general — no longer appears as the pillar that defines and sustains capitalist social organization. Production is given an objective quality, as if the capitalist system were a machine that marched forward of its own accord, without labor, a capitalist automaton.

In this light the real subsumption appears as the completion of capital's project and the fulfillment of its long-standing dream — to present itself as separate from labor and pose a capitalist society that does not look to labor as its dynamic foundation. "The political history of capital," Mario Tronti writes, is "a sequence of attempts by capital to withdraw from the class relationship"; more properly, these are "attempts of the capitalist class to emancipate itself from the working class through the medium of various forms of capital's political domination over the working class."[27] This is how we should understand the passage from the formal to the real subsumption. The society of the formal subsumption was characterized by the dialectic between capital and labor: as a foreign force subsumed within capital, labor had to be abstracted, recuperated, disciplined, and tamed within the productive processes. But labor nonetheless was continually recognized as the source of all social wealth. (Consider, for example, the opening sentence of the Italian Constitution of 1948: "Italy is a republic founded on labor.") In the society of the real subsumption this dialectic no longer holds the central role, and capital no longer needs to engage labor or represent labor at the heart of production.[28] What is subsumed, what is accepted into the process, is no longer a potentially conflictive force but a product of the system itself; the real subsumption does not extend vertically throughout the various strata of society but rather constructs a separate plane, a simulacrum of society that excludes or marginalizes social forces foreign to the system. Social capital thus appears to reproduce itself autonomously, as if it were emancipated from the working class, and labor becomes invisible in the system. The contemporary decline of labor unions in both juridical and political terms, as the right to organize and the right to strike become increasingly irrelevant, is only one symptom of this more general passage.

The State of the formal subsumption was indeed, as Hegel saw, defined by the organization of abstract labor. The State of the real subsumption is no longer interested in mediation or "education" but separation, no longer discipline but control. The State of the real subsumption operates on a separate plane, a simulacrum of the social field, abstract from labor itself. (We can recognize here, parenthetically, the utility of an investigation of Guy Debord's society of the integrated spectacle and the separateness it implies as a third approximation of this passage.) Once again, my general point here is simply that in this passage the democratic and/or disciplinary institutions of civil society, the channels of social mediation, as a particular form of the organization of social labor, have declined and been displaced from the center of the scene. Not the State but civil society has withered away! In other words, even if one were to consider civil society politically desirable — and I hope to have shown that this position is at least contestable — the social conditions necessary for civil society no longer exist.[29]

The Postcivil Condition

As I stated at the outset, I consider each of these attempts to register adequately the fundamental changes in contemporary society coherent with the various social theories of postmodernism, at least to the extent that they are all focused on the same social terrain. The difficulty with many of these discourses, however, arises from the fact that they have not defined their field accurately enough. The end of modernity is a notion too vague and abstract to be very useful. Reformulating the problematic as the analysis of not postmodern but postcivil society is already a great step forward. Civil society, as we have seen, is central to a form of rule, or government as Foucault says, that focuses, on the one hand, on the identity of the citizen and the processes of civilization and, on the other hand, on the organization of abstract labor. These processes are variously conceived as education, training, or discipline, but what remains common is the active engagement with social forces (through either mediation or production) to order social identities within the context of institutions. What has come to an end, or more accurately declined in importance in postcivil society, then, is precisely these functions of mediation or education and the institutions that gave them form.

The formulation postcivil, however, like postmodern, is finally limited by its backward gaze; it is too reactive to do justice to the new paradigm of social relations. More important than the social elements and techniques that have faded from prominence are those that have newly taken the dominant positions. The deployments of control and the social constitution of the real subsumption give us a framework to begin to grasp the novelties of our situation. Instead of disciplining the citizen as a fixed social identity, the new social regime seeks to control the citizen as a whatever identity, or rather an infinitely flexible placeholder for identity. It tends to establish an autonomous plane of rule, a simulacrum of the social — separate from the terrain of conflictive social forces. Mobility, speed, and flexibility are the qualities that characterize this separate plane of rule. The infinitely programmable machine, the ideal of cybernetics, gives us at least an approximation of the diagram of the new paradigm of rule.

Analyzing the new techniques of social control is worthwhile only to the extent that it allows us to grasp also the new potentialities for contestation and freedom emerging within this new paradigm. Foucault suggested in an interview in 1978 that we have to begin thinking politics in a society without discipline:

> In the last few years society has changed and individuals have changed too; they are more and more diverse, different, and independent. There are ever more categories of people who are not compelled by discipline ["qui ne sont pas astreints à la discipline"], so that we are obliged to imagine the development of society without discipline. The ruling class is still impregnated with the old technique. But it is clear that in the future we must separate ourselves from the society of discipline of today.[30]

I would suggest that in order to begin thinking these new potentialities we should return again to investigate the form and nature of labor, or creative social practices, in contemporary society. This is one way that we can begin to separate ourselves from the society of discipline and begin to think the lines of power and potentiality in the new society. Social practices have certainly changed and so too should our notion of what constitutes labor — not just in the sphere of wage labor (which indeed has undergone radical transformation in some sectors) but also in the sphere of desiring-production, intellectual creativity, caring labor, kin work, and so forth.[31] The phase of the real subsumption is characterized by the increasingly pervasive eclipse of labor in the production and reproduction of society, but that does not negate in any way the fact that labor is still the source of wealth and sociality. Even in the society of control, labor is still the "savage beast" that Hegel feared, refusing to be subjugated and tamed — and perhaps its potential is even greater today when it is no longer engaged, mediated, and disciplined through the institutions of civil society as it was in the previous paradigm. The networks of sociality and forms of cooperation embedded in contemporary social practices constitute the germs for a new movement, with new forms of contestation and new conceptions of liberation. This alternative community of social practices (call it, perhaps, the self-organization of concrete labor) will be the most potent challenge to the control of postcivil society and will point, perhaps, to the community of our future.

Notes

This essay was originally delivered at a conference on the work of Deleuze and Guattari at Duke University, April 1993. A version of the essay appeared in *Social Text* 45 (1995): 27–44. The principal ideas elaborated here were first developed with Antonio Negri as part of a study of the contemporary juridical formation of the capitalist State. See Michael Hardt and Antonio Negri, *The Labor of Dionysus: A Critique of the State-Form* (Minneapolis: University of Minnesota Press, 1994), esp. 257–61. I would like to thank Marianne Constable and Rebecca Karl for their comments on earlier versions of the essay.

    1. I will focus in this essay on the genealogy of civil society in the Euro-American context, but I hope that this genealogy will be relevant also for evaluating the question of civil society in other parts of the world. In nearly all countries outside of North America and Western Europe, proposals for the contemporary establishment of a civil society seem to serve only as part of an imagined re-creation of one of the stages of civilization that Europe has already passed through, specifically the historical processes of the development and consolidation of capitalism in eighteenth- and nineteenth-century Europe. As Partha Chatterjee says, "[T]he central assumption of this proposal is that it is only the concepts of European social philosophy" such as civil society "that contain within them the possibility of universalization" ("A Response to Taylor's 'Modes of Civil Society,'" *Public Culture* 3, no. 1 [1990]: 119). Hence, he continues, "the provincialism of the European experience [is] taken as the universal history of progress" (131).
    2. G. W. F. Hegel, *Philosophy of Right,* trans. T. M. Knox (Oxford: Oxford University Press, 1952), §255.
    3. Ibid., §209.
    4. Ibid., §257.
    5. G. W. F. Hegel, *Jenenser Realphilosophie*, vol. 2 (Leipzig: Meiner, 1932), 268.
    6. G. W. F. Hegel, *Jenenser Realphilosophie*, vol. 1 (Leipzig: Meiner, 1932), 240.
    7. Alexandre Kojève notes in his famous reading of the *Phenomenology of Spirit* that "labor is what 'forms or educates' man, distinguishing him from the animals" (*Introduction à la lecture de Hegel* [Paris: Gallimard, 1947], 30). The educative laboring process that Kojève recognizes, however, is one oriented toward the recognition and self-consciousness of the laborer, while the conception that interests us here is oriented instead toward the alignment of the particular interest of the laborer with the universal interest of the State.

8. Hegel, *Philosophy of Right*, §199.

9. See ibid., §251.

10. In his now-classic analysis, Norberto Bobbio makes clear the Hegelian roots of Gramsci's notion of civil society: "In fact, contrary to what is commonly believed, Gramsci does not derive his concept of civil society from Marx but is openly indebted to Hegel for it" ("Gramsci and the Conception of Civil Society," in *Which Socialism? Marxism, Socialism, and Democracy*, trans. Roger Griffin, ed. and intro. Richard Bellamy [Minneapolis: University of Minnesota Press, 1987], 149).

11. Antonio Gramsci, *Selections from Prison Notebooks*, trans. Quintin Hoare and Geoffrey Nowell Smith (New York: International Publishers, 1971), 253; Italian: *Quaderni del carcere* (Turin: Einaudi, 1975), 622.

12. Gramsci, *Quaderni del carcere*, 1020.

13. Hegel, *Philosophy of Right*, §256.

14. Michel Foucault, "La gouvernementalité," in *Dits et écrits*, vol. 3 (Paris: Gallimard, 1994), 641–42 (originally published in 1978). In the course from which this text was taken, "Sécurité, territoire et population" (given at the Collège de France, 1977–78), Foucault made a distinction between the techniques of discipline and those of governmentality, not in the sense that they pertain to different historical periods but rather in the sense that they pertain in a parallel fashion to different domains of society. "Can one speak of something like governmentality that would be to the State what the technologies of segregation were to psychiatry, what the technologies of discipline were to the penal system...?" (February 8, 1978). This quote should also indicate to us that Foucault does not deny the existence of the State (any more than he would deny the existence of the penal or psychiatric systems), but rather that he finds it more useful to formulate his problematic in terms of the technologies of governmentality that in some sense constitute the power of the State.

15. Michel Foucault, *The History of Sexuality*, vol. 1, trans. Robert Hurley (New York: Vintage Books, 1978), 94.

16. Gilles Deleuze, *Foucault* (Paris: Minuit, 1986), 84.

17. Gilles Deleuze, "Postscript on the Societies of Control," *October* 59 (1993): 5.

18. Gramsci, *Selections from Prison Notebooks*, 235 (*Quaderni del carcere*, 1615).

19. Michel Foucault, "Le prison partout," in *Dits et écrits*, vol. 2 (Paris: Gallimard, 1994), 194 (originally published in 1971).

20. Michel Foucault, *Discipline and Punish*, trans. Alan Sheridan (New York: Vintage Books, 1977), 228.

21. Deleuze, "Postscript on the Societies of Control," 7.

22. I use the term "whatever" to translate what Giorgio Agamben refers to in Italian as *il qualunque* and what Deleuze and Foucault indicate in French with *le quelconque*. See Giorgio Agamben, *The Coming Community*, trans. Michael Hardt (Minneapolis: University of Minnesota Press, 1993).

23. Gilles Deleuze and Félix Guattari, *A Thousand Plateaus*, trans. Brian Massumi (Minneapolis: University of Minnesota Press, 1987), 492.

24. See Antonio Negri, *Marx beyond Marx*, trans. Harry Cleaver, Michael Ryan, and Maurizio Viano (South Hadley, Mass.: Bergin and Garvey, 1984), 113–23.

25. Karl Marx, *Grundrisse*, trans. Martin Nicolaus (New York: Vintage Books, 1973), 709.

26. Karl Marx, *Capital*, vol. 1, trans. Ben Fowkes (New York: Vintage Books, 1977), 1024.

27. Mario Tronti, "The Strategy of Refusal," *Autonomia*, special issue of *Semio-text(e)* 3, no. 3 (1980): 32.

28. This eclipse of labor in the society of the real subsumption is very close to Fredric Jameson's claim of the heightened role of commodity fetishism in post-modernity, or rather, in the era of late capitalism (see his essay "Actually Existing Marxism," *Polygraph* 6, no. 7 [1993]: 170–95). Commodity fetishism, after all, refers to the fact that in capitalist society commodities seem to present themselves and relate to each other autonomously, without revealing the various forms of labor and the social circuits of laboring cooperation that went into their production.

29. Once again, I am arguing here that the social conditions for civil society no longer exist in Western Europe and North America. In order to consider the question of civil society outside the Euro-American context, one would first have to look to its primary condition of possibility, that is, the organization of abstract labor in the institutions of a specific phase of capitalist society.

30. Michel Foucault, "La société disciplinaire en crise," in *Dits et écrits*, 3:533.

31. Antonio Negri and I have proposed in *The Labor of Dionysus: A Critique of the State-Form* (Minneapolis: University of Minnesota Press, 1994) that the concept "labor" be considered a site of social contestation that depends in large part on the way that value is produced in a given social context (7–11). In the course of our investigation of the contemporary nature, forms, and organization of labor we individuate a series of "prerequisites of communism" already existing in our postcivil society (275–83).

Requiem for Our Prospective Dead
(Toward a Participatory Critique of Capitalist Power)
Brian Massumi

Shoot to Feed

In the beginning, was a screen. Dead center, a figure. It is black. And shriveled, as if shrinking from its surroundings, the menacing emptiness of which is attenuated only by a sprinkling of crumbs. Is it an ant, at the extremities of exhaustion, foraging far from the safety of the nest? Concentric circles ring the end of an outstretched limb. A target. No, an insect wouldn't be worth the ammunition. Now we see. It's not an ant — it's a Somali. "Aim for the bowl," says a corpulent figure standing beside the screen, pinpointing the spot with his confident baton. It is none other than General Schwarzkopf. The "hero of Desert Storm" himself. He has returned from retirement to make a fantasy appearance in another desert "theater" whose unforgiving sun will now have to compete with the caring afterimage of his shining glory. Your *life* is in my sights, the fantasy knight-errant of the new world disorder seems to be saying. What is "life," in a world in crisis, but an armed stay of execution? Your human potential is beggary gone ballistic. My philanthropic bullet delivers the coup de grâce.

The political cartoon described above appeared in North American newspapers on New Year's Day 1993, two weeks after U.S. Marines arrived on Mogadishu beach to begin what would be the most heavily publicized humanitarian mission in U.S. military history and two weeks before President George Bush went out with a bang, resuming his bombing of Iraq on the eve of Bill Clinton's inauguration in a fond farewell to his relished role as commander in chief. The legitimation of state violence in those early days of post-Soviet America hovered in the air midway between Mogadishu and Baghdad, and in the airwaves between "terrorist," "thug," and starving child, straddling the transition between Reagan Republican and "New Democrat."

These images belong to a particular moment in recent American self-fashioning in the world theater (the rest of the world figuring, in the accustomed American way, as an indistinct backdrop for the drama of the country's reassertion of its official self-image, primarily for domestic consumption, toward home-front political ends).

According to a self-congratulatory formula widely circulated at the time in the U.S. press, under American leadership the world was on the verge of making the old call to arms obsolete: henceforth, "thugs" aside, the armed forces would no longer "shoot to kill" but "shoot to *feed*." It is nothing new for the military to justify itself with the claim that it slaughters in the service of life. What is more remarkable is the tendency to blur the very boundary between life and death, even between the organic and the inorganic — and with it the distinctions between war and peace, civilian and combatant. The Gulf War, Jean Baudrillard tells us with characteristic overkill, did not take place.[1] He is obviously not speaking from the obliterated point of view of the estimated 350,000 Iraqis — two-thirds of whom were civilians — who died in the live-feed "spectacle."[2] He is speaking as a Westerner watching on television from a safe distance. From that vantage point, it was in fact easy to come away with the impression that the Allied forces, self-proclaimed upholders of international law, had taught the "criminally insane" "butcher of Baghdad" a lesson he would remember, without shedding real blood. It played in the media as a clean war. Military censorship tightly controlled reporters' access to the front and for the most part successfully discouraged transmitting images of dead or wounded Americans. Coverage was limited as much as possible to Department of Defense footage of fireworks and hardware and polished PR performances by baton-wielding top brass supported by the latest in business presentation equipment. It looked from a distance as though the only combatants were remote-controlled ballistic automatons who were not, however, without social graces. At least on "our" side. American missiles "serviced" their counterparts. The enemy was a scofflaw client who needed a bit of "punishment" in order to recognize the benefits of rejoining the international "community," on its terms. For "community," read "marketplace." Everyone knew on some level that the "crime" for which Saddam Hussein was being punished was not against "humanity." His gassing of Kurdish civilians before the war was passed over in silence by Western governments, as would be his postwar cruelty to the Shi'ites in the south.[3] The crime that fit the punishment was against the economic status quo. No one pretended the war was not over the oil that fueled the proudly displayed military machinery. The human suffering on the Iraqi side disappeared into the geopolitical relay circuits automatically connecting, among others, the oil market and the weapons market and into the automatic feedback circuit of Western opinion polling, which installed the launch button for the missiles abroad into television remote controls at home. The most haunting images of destruction entered America's living rooms at the end of the war. The miles of burned-out Iraqi vehicles, serviced into immobility along the "highway of death" as they attempted a panicked return from Kuwait, contained charred human remains. These were graphically displayed. But the uniform color of soot clothed the organic and inorganic in a surface sameness. The aerial pans showed a still: one automatic feedback that had dead-ended, dry as the desert, no more flow, any blood that may have warmed the veins of the vehicle operators boiled away in the blasts. In that stillness, the blackened ex-human became visibly a part of the circuitry.

American suffering, for its part, was not lost from view. But neither did it splash in liquid abandon on the antiseptic battlefield (American casualties were counted in the low hundreds). It skipped over the actual conflict. This was not just because the high-tech hardware of war was made to stand in, as much as possible, for flesh-and-blood fighters. Human presence on the Allied war front had not simply been replaced with machinic body-doubles. The warring present, the time of human suffering, had been translated from a haunting past directly into a function of futurity.

The dead have always played an active role in American politics. During the 1980s, they came to be one of the most powerful political constituencies in the country. This is not because they voted, as they had done in an earlier era of American democracy, and are still rumored to do from time to time in Chicago. It was because they had felt. The constant reminder of their death agonies made them a potent lobby. By the 1988 presidential election, it had became difficult, if not impossible, for a politician on the national scene to admit to having had doubts about the U.S. role in Vietnam. Draft-dodging or antiwar activism, or in the case of the older generation failure to serve in Korea or World War II, meant political suicide if combined with anything approaching a peaceful outlook on U.S. international relations or with softness toward designated internal enemies (in particular, terrorists, thugs, drug-users, and welfare recipients, fused into the figure of the criminal or social cheat, which in turn overlapped with any number of figures of "deviance," most of which were dark of skin but could range anywhere from women exercising their constitutional right to reproductive freedom to anyone implicating their organs in unauthorized couplings). The taint of pacifism was a disqualifier for national service because it indicated an unworthiness or unwillingness to authorize the casual use of force to protect American interests (read "markets") in crisis-prone overseas locations and, domestically, to extend police powers in response to the growing chaos of what was perceived to be a disintegrating social order in North America. Being "soft" on "crime" or insufficiently aggressive toward third world "thugs" (read "otherly complexioned heads of state") was itself portrayed to be a violent crime. It was violence against the dead. It retrospectively sullied the purity of fallen heroes. "Our boys" in Vietnam did not die in vain, even though that war was lost. Their angelic sacrifice would be in vain only if the lessons of Vietnam went unheeded and the next wars — including the "wars" on crime and drugs — were lost as well. As Sylvester Stallone had established in *Rambo,* the boys in uniform didn't lose the war in Vietnam. It was lost by pusillanimous bureaucrats in Washington who didn't have the right stuff to cheerfully blow the Vietnamese away, as Bush would do with the Iraqis to near universal acclaim from the U.S. electorate. The U.S. soldiers in Vietnam were killed by their own leaders, as surely as if they had pulled the trigger. Their bureaucratic successors kill them all over again every time they go soft, heaping a cross-generational accumulation of shame on their warmly remembered stone-cold memorials. The U.S. soldiers in Vietnam died less from their wounds than from a lack of resolve and pride that was passed like a plague from grassroots pacifists to politicians. Antiwar activists were serial-killers-at-a-distance whose attacks were relayed through the mass media to the battlefield, in the form of protest-motivated bureaucratic inaction. They killed fifty thousand in Nam and would doubtless kill again, barring preemptive measures. "Can we win next time?" "Ronbo" Reagan had asked plaintively, echoing that other bad actor.

Throughout the 1980s, this necromantic legitimation of state violence functioned primarily in retrospect. By the time of the Gulf War, the constant appeals to remember the lessons of Vietnam for the future well-being of the country had given it prospective force. The preemptive measure was to accuse any potential critic of the eventual use of armed force by the U.S. government of signing and sealing a death sentence against the "boys" at the theoretical front. Commemoration of sacrifice had buckled into anticipation of risk. Now premeditated slaughter by high command was justifiable as the prevention of death.

This weapon was used so effectively in the buildup to the hostilities in Iraq that expressions of dissent when the war did come were muffled. It is not that there were no protests; rather, the surprisingly widespread protest that did occur (including spontaneous walkouts by high school students across North America, and in San Francisco an organized blockade of the Bay Bridge and rioting downtown) was downplayed or passed over in silence by the press. Media coverage of protest had been reclassified as accessory to murder. After the war, doubts would emerge about the wisdom of the violence or the truth-value of government claims and statistics. But before and during, mum was the word. The popular wisdom that *was* picked up by the press, in interminable person-on-the-street interviews, was a chorus of "we *have* to support our boys," regardless — 'cause their lives depend on it. They're ready to make the supreme sacrifice, and we're duty-bound to support them. Bring out the yellow ribbons.

The Vietnam War–era slogan, "America Right or Wrong," had been personalized as "Our Boys Right or Wrong." The moral imperative of the state no longer needed to be grounded in an assertion of the innate superiority of the American way of life — a claim that had long since deconstructed itself in economic stagnation and endless social strife. Now there was an easier way to access moral rectitude for reasons of state. You needn't think or assert a claim that you might be called upon to support with an argument. All you need do is feel — a oneness with the prospective dead hero, and based on that, hostility for the hypothetical enemy. The legitimation of state violence would now operate preferentially on an affective register, through the mass media. Both moral reasoning and critical thinking would fall out, in favor of the mutual amplification of empathy-based aggressiveness and government policy in a direct feedback loop between formal and informal opinion polling and military strikes. The legitimation of state violence would no longer ground itself in the originary rectitude of founding fathers or even in a clear and present danger faced by their sons. Legitimation was now up and moving. It hinges on an affective circulation centering on a vague eventuality blurring the difference between politics and crime, past and future, protest and social de-generacy, accessory and first-degree, action and inaction, even life and death, as being in this world is reduced to a stay of execution selectively granted by nonparticipants by dint of not judging. What of those with no reprieve? At this distance, it all seems so hypothetical. We don't have to dwell on the mess, let alone dwell in it. We'll just enjoy the light shows over Baghdad. End of story. Moral and political reasoning are short-circuited, along with collective memory, by a kind of magical thought by default. The punctual, hierarchical, command-based exercise of power is enabled by horizontal mass-media flows of necromantic not-doing. The Zen of state slaughter. Legitimate violence is now more ritualistic than reasoned.

The indistinction between life and death brings us back to the starving Somali. The death of the enemy has been visually absented in the theater of war by the link-up of high-tech imaging and weapons circuitry and dis-placed from thought through the mass-media-exorcised suffering of the hero. The emptiness of that death twice-removed goes to Somalia and dons civvies. Rags. In peacetime, the unseen of war — the legitimated boiling of blood and morally color-corrected body rot — assumes the figure of a rapidly disappear-ing life force that is nevertheless plainly visible as a blot on the evening news. The marine's bullet aims for this well-publicized vanishing point of humanity. Now it is the bullet that is hypothetical, and it gives life back its substance and at the same time its dignity, instead of taking them away. Biopower scoops up the commander's baton, as grain showers the bottom of the bowl. Shoot to feed. Bull's-eye.

In spite of the (at best) implicit racism of this postcolonial revival of the theme of the white man's burden, a certain complicity is produced between the white Americans who make up the television target audience and the black Africans in the soldiers' humanitarian sights. The war-time television viewer has accorded the soldier a stay of execution, which is now peacefully trans-mitted to the Somali. The deficit of those who do not not-do, the a priori guilt of government critics, comes out the other side of the media relay as a surplus of virtue positively expressed by soldiers as life-affirming action in the civil sphere. The threat of death becomes fully visible as armed force af-

firms life, and the imminence of death reenters thought, after a fashion. Both
the misery of the famine victims and the risk run by their brave saviors are
lavishly screened for contemplation. Not analysis: contemplation. It won't be
asked too loudly what role Cold War–era U.S. foreign policy played in creating the crisis in Somalia by propping up a brutal dictator until all-out civil
war forced him into exile. There will be no questions about the consequences
of the UN's decision to arrive in Somalia under the auspices of a long-time
adversary of the exiled Said Barre, one General Aideed, whose power base at
the time of the UN operation was clan-based in a country breaking at the
seams with ethnic rivalries.

Rather, it will be marveled: how tenuous is life! Mortal danger is the
great leveler. It makes an empathetic "us" of the soldier (white or black),
the famished black African, and the riot-stunned white American viewer
more or less explicitly targeted by television programmers and advertisers (and
who may well have difficulty mustering the same measure of sympathy for
black heroism and black suffering closer to home). An implied community
of victimization overshadows the obvious political and economic differential
signaled by the fact that it is the philanthropy of the fantasy white knight,
represented in the opening cartoon by a now-mythic General Schwarzkopf,
that seems to give the black American soldier the potential for heroism and
purports to put the black African's very humanity back on the menu. Whether
in the famine-stricken Horn of Africa or opulent LA, "we" are scurrying
about as helplessly as ants under the glare of a panoply of life-threatening
forces. These may be natural or social or, increasingly, a combination of
both,[4] and run in both directions in infinite regress from the human scale: the
ever-present specter of the "terrorist" and the "thug" stands at the scalar intersection between AIDS and global warming, threats microscopic and cosmic.[5]
The variety and unpredictability of the threats seem to place them outside the
control of ordinary mortals.

For a moment, however, the omnipresent threat of death appeared to have
been localized in Somalia and neutralized. If it could be neutralized once
there, the operation could be repeated elsewhere. A promise of life begins to
circulate through the media. Why can't civilians on the home front be given
the same promise? Done. When there's a riot in LA, who you gonna call? The
army. A hurricane hit? Who you gonna call? The army. The drug war getting
you down? Why not call the army? There are cultists prowling around your
schools conspiring to steal your children? Incite a gun battle, and then call any
one of a number of rapid-response paramilitary shock troops available on the
state and federal level for high-profile special assignment.

War and nonwar are getting harder and harder to tell apart, as the provocative title of Baudrillard's Gulf War book points out and as Paul Virilio, writing
two decades earlier, predicted would happen.[6] The mass-media circulation of
violence-legitimating affect conditions a seriality that makes questions of ori-

gin and sequence moot points. Whichever came first, war or nonwar, hot war or cold, shooting peace or peacetime war, whatever it is, it is here, and it is now, in our anticipatory present, transported from the trauma of a reconstructed collective past directly into the insistent here-now futurity of "our" implied community at risk. "We" seem to be in a new world reorder that has shuffled not only "our" feelings and contemplations but "our" very temporality, henceforth nonlinear. With the fall of the Soviet Union, Virilio's "total peace" is already upon us. "Total peace," also known as "pure war," is history deprived of the teleological frameworks once assured by now-exhausted mythologies of democratic progress and ideological macrobattles between power blocs in dialectical embrace. The blurring of the distinction between war and peace to the extreme squeezes out any possibility of mediation.

Command and Control

The mass "media" do anything but mediate. They directly instill and effectively circulate politically and morally operative affect. Electoral politics no longer represents the will of an actual community, if it ever did. It functions to attach legitimating affect to caricatural personalities carefully shaped with the help of marketing expertise, in a way that enables the entrenched machinery of government to continue its autonomic functioning. The end of the Cold War has coincided with a rapid decline in the ability of Western legislatures to govern. In the United States, a wave of popular referenda is attempting to limit many legislators' terms in office. The president is valued most as commander in chief, and there is a popular expectation (not always satisfied) that at least in the early months of his tenure the Congress is duty-bound to pass his legislative initiatives largely unmodified, in what amounts to electorally sanctioned rule by decree. The passage of the line-item veto is another expression of the trend to push the presidency's civil rule in an autocratic direction reminiscent of military leadership. In spite of the long-term trend toward strengthening of the executive branch, neither the commander in chief nor the legislature can accurately be said to govern. It is more that their periodic replacement through the electoral process gives an entire landscape of collective autonomic apparatuses participating in political legitimation and decision making a chance to readjust themselves to one another. These include all governmental branches at every level (the military services, the intelligence agencies, the many layers of administrative bureaucracy, the regulatory agencies, the foreign service and diplomatic corps, the state legislatures vis-à-vis the federal government, the courts); paragovernmental bodies (not-for-profit organizations, think tanks, lobbies); supposedly nongovernmental technological apparatuses such as communications systems (including but in no way limited to the mass media) and weapons systems; and even apparently nongovernmental, nontechnological apparatuses, such as commercial markets.

Each of these can be seen as a self-reproducing system hermetically sealed from the would-be expression of "popular will" by decades of accumulated procedure, giving it a vested center of gravity. Each self-reproducing collective apparatus is an orbit caught in an inconceivably complicated web of multilateral alliances and antagonisms implicating every other apparatus. Each apparatus implants command centers that radiate spheres of influence and patrol jurisdictions, sinking control basins into the collective landscape. The command centers multiply and disseminate foci of autocratic decision, in other words of "negative" power, the power over life, modeled on the right to kill. Every command is a little death because its interdictions subtract a potential from life. The control basins are eddies of "positive" power, the power to target life and reinforce or even produce certain of its potentials.

The ever-complexifying web of orbit-obeying powers over life and powers to enliven automatically readjusts itself at election time. The election is a forced interruption of the continuous functioning of this interlinking of self-reproducing systems. It is a rigged event injecting a measure of contingency into the web. That contingency becomes the focus of a mutual readjustment of a system that is so complicated that it cannot be described as a structure, but only as a metastable, self-organizing system of systems in a continual struggle to integrate interruptions, planned and unplanned, ranging from the relatively minor to the catastrophic, into periodicities or regularized rhythms of functionings. All of the periodicities generated by the system of systems revolve around the periodicity of the electoral process in various ways. Elections are the periodicity of general reference.

If all this adds up to a structure, it is a dissipative structure combining a multiplicity of periodicities in a fluctuating set of highly complex differentiations that are locally implanted following divergent patterns, but resonate globally. This is chaos. Each self-reproducing system in this generalized production of order out of chaos combines modulations of what could be called, broadly, the "political" dimension (command, in its relation with control) with the "economic" dimension (all submit in one way or another to monetary criteria of productivity and efficiency), and contributes in a way that could be called "cultural" to the binding of selected affect sequences to more or less predictable pathways of thought assigned a territorial base (what is commonly referred to as an "identity"). For lack of a better word, the chaotic cofunctioning of the political, economic, and cultural dimensions could be dubbed the "social" — although all of these designations are fairly arbitrary at this point.

What happens to "civil society" in this chaotic social landscape? It falls into the cracks between command and control. Between command and control, as between the systems implanting and perpetuating them, there can be no mediation, only resonance and autonomic readjustment. That *is* "communication": *interference* between autonomic systems and the modes of power they accrete, not exchange between autonomous individuals. The possibility of unweighted negotiation between equal civil entities is lost in the web of vested procedural power. When control procedure hits a snag, a specialized autocratic function rises up from the horizontal web and swoops down on the problem in a sometimes spectacular command-center assault. If well orchestrated with the mass media, this does produce a consensus of sorts, but not of the Habermasian variety: it is an affective consensus that legitimates the premeditated but unmediated application of state violence in a way that can only be qualified as innocently but thoroughly sadistic. Civil society disappears in the rhythmic rumble of self-reproducing autonomic systems going about their daily business, punctuated by impatient outbursts of excessive violence. Life and death on Ranch Apocalypse. In Waco, negotiation went up in smoke, for once and for "next."[7]

It would be a mistake to make too much of the fondness in the mass media, and in some theoretical circles, for apocalyptic imagery. The conflagrations accompanying disproportionate deployments of state violence are spectacularized versions of the modest command decisions percolating the social on a daily basis. The power of death, the power over life, is utterly mundane. It is tripped into operation a thousand times a day on any number of levels, to varying degrees of intensity, any time the autonomic functioning of a self-reproducing system is jolted by a temporarily unassimilable event requiring it to readjust itself. Excessive displays of the power over life occur when interruptions affect more than one autonomic system, the mass media among them. Interruptions that cut across several of the semiautonomous levels, or strata, composing the social threaten to send amplifying shock waves through the resonating network. This is especially so when the interruption of the day-to-day calls into question the generalized affective legitimation of state violence operated by the mass media. For example, when large numbers of "ordinary" Americans find themselves sympathizing, in spite of themselves, with gun-toting, child-molesting cultists under siege. The disproportion of the response, the excessiveness of the sudden state violence, its overflow of all reasonable bounds, changes the status of the situation. It lifts it entirely out of the sphere of the mundane, elevating it to the level of ritual. This trips the mechanisms of exorcistic affective legitimation into operation. The force of the conflagration is funneled toward normative ends.

What stands out is less the rupture of apocalypse, but rather its periodicity, its seriality. State violence has the ability to leap from one outburst to the next, as if its excess was transported directly from the past into the future without bothering to detour through the present, understood as a continuous flow of time providing the duration necessary for processes of mediation to run their course. Negotiation short-circuits in a burst of sparks, or it is never even undertaken with any expectation of a successful outcome. The delay between exercises of state violence is less a present than a suspense, a dramatic tension running a tightrope over the void between the past and future, on which nothing can be sustainably grounded.

The suspension of linear time characteristic of state violence short-circuits not only negotiation but apparatuses of ideological mediation as well. Bill Clinton's first presidential election aroused hopes in some quarters that U.S. foreign policy might follow a less interventionist course. Those hopes were destined to be disappointed. What are one man's personal convictions against his public conviction — for mass murder? Clinton was among those guilty of nonviolent homicide. The stigma of his student activities against the Vietnam War nearly derailed his presidential campaign and haunted him during his crucial first four months in office. He was unworthy, it was argued, of the all-important role of commander in chief. The heckling that greeted him at a visit to the Vietnam War Memorial in Washington seriously undermined him, contributing to his record low showing in the polls at the four-month mark and prompting a *Time* magazine cover story entitled "The Incredible Shrinking President" (7 June 1993). Only a military adventure would save him. The Gulf War had worked wonders for Bush, taking him from some of the lowest poll ratings ever recorded for an American president to some of the highest in a matter of weeks. Clinton made a go at Bosnia but was rebuffed by fears in Europe and in his own administration of a prolonged Vietnam-style engagement. Somalia afforded some short-term relief when victim status rebounded on the UN forces and "shoot to feed" reverted to "shoot to kill," "peacekeeping" to war-making, in another demonstration of the convertibility of these functions.[8] But what really did the trick was that trusty standby, Saddam Hussein, all over again. George Bush's nonassassination (the alleged Iraqi plot to kill him during a visit to Kuwait) provided the perfect exorcistic pretext. A majority of the American public declared through the polls that they would have supported the punitive strike ordered by Clinton in retaliation for a crime not committed even if it had been known in advance that there would be civilian casualties, thus confirming — if more confirmation were needed — that blurring the line between civilians and combatants, action and inaction, life and death, participant and onlooker, guilt and innocence, was a perfectly legitimate state-function.[9] The light show resumed in the sky over Baghdad (or was that replay footage?). Clinton's ratings recovered enough to put his domestic agenda back on track. According to a *New York Times*/CNN poll (30 June 1993), Clinton's ratings jumped eleven points to 50 percent in the week following the attack. This placed him in the strongest position of any of the G-7 leaders for the 1993 Tokyo trade summit held two weeks after the attack. Clinton's Tokyo performance in turn strengthened his hand with Congress in the debate over his domestic economic package and saved an ambitious education reform, unveiled three weeks after, from the oblivion to which it might otherwise have been consigned. Clinton had paid for domestic reform in the currency of displaced death. In spite of his ideological differences with his predecessors, when it came to neocolonial violence he had taken up exactly where George Bush left off.[10] Bush had continued the Reagan series, adding Panama and Iraq to Grenada and Libya. The series will doubtless be prolonged long into the future, regardless of whether it is the Democrats or Republicans who hold the White House. This in spite of the short-lived success of Clinton's Bushification. By the second half of Clinton's term, his ability to direct domestic policy had been almost completely undermined by a Republican sweep of the 1994 legislative elections, won on a campaign highlighting his "waffling," or the lack of affective constancy in his media image. His ability to generate legitimating foreign adventures had withered under the combined weight of television images of dead American soldiers dragged through the streets of Mogadishu, an uncelebrated withdrawal from Somalia that left the country in worse shape than the American troops found it in, frustration over the failure of the UN forces in Bosnia to prevent continued hostilities, a mysterious illness affecting Gulf War veterans that in its concrete incomprehensibility resembled nothing more than the virtuality of risk made flesh, and the new visibility in Congress of conservative politicians with more convincing militarist credentials than Clinton could ever muster. Bosnia gave Clinton a fleeting, gun-related feel-good incident when a downed American pilot was rescued in Bosnia by American forces in the northern spring of 1995. However, the sheen of the occasion was soon entomologically tarnished. The relish with which Captain O'Grady related how he had survived by eating insects didn't go down easily. Bugs are not what comes first to Americans' minds when they hear the television slogan the "breakfast of champions." Subsequent revelations that the culinary "hero" had made every mistake in the book, and that his own incompetence as a flyer was what landed him in his predicament in the first place, did not help.[11] Clinton and heroism just didn't mix. The president was left to pursue nonwar by other, more mundane means (trade war with Japan). What had started in Kuwait with a well-oiled bang ended with a whine heard round the world, emanating from the general direction of Detroit: from crude to cars.

Perhaps most significantly, the Waco incident had incubated in American grassroots populism. The existence of a widespread local militia movement allied with the gun lobby, and nurtured on racial hatred and resentment against welfare, burst into public view in the media follow-up of the bombing of the Oklahoma federal building on the anniversary of the Waco conflagration in April 1995. The disproportion of the government response to the Branch Davidians had become a potent symbol for a significant minority of mostly white, mostly rural, and mostly male Americans. Far from affectively legitimating the head of state, for this segment of the population any muscled government action only stoked an already growing disaffection from centralized government in any form. Waco began to be ritually invoked at cross-purposes to its mainstream function, in a spontaneous combustion of affective attachment to the government. The excess that was Waco changed signs. The command-and-control legitimation loop that had been in continuous, virtually unopposed operation from at least the beginning of the Reagan years through the first half of Clinton's term was now under contestation from a radical movement for whom, fantastically, the highest legitimatable level of collective organization was the county. The militias' combination of traditional right-wing elements (isolationism, vigilantism, international conspiracy theories targeting Jews, a general scapegoating of racial and ethnic minorities, a focus on moral issues, a defense of the patriarchal family) with orientations that in recent American experience have been associated with the far left (an anarchistic rhetoric of direct democracy; volatile, decentralized forms of sometimes clandestine organization) was a shock to the system. In the lead-up to the 1996 presidential campaign, the most active political tension was no longer between Clinton and the Republicans, but between two wings of the Republican Party: statesmanlike political veterans invoking, yet again, the hallowed name of Ronald Reagan (who for many was now on the liberal end of the political spectrum!) and upstarts trying to ride the wave of radical populism. The center of political imbalance had shifted markedly to the right and beyond, threatening to leave Clinton out of the loop. Only a Dole candidacy was able to save him.

Although the affective legitimation of command, in its articulation with control, has fallen into relative quiescence, it is not a political "moment" in the sense of a simple phase in a linear development that is now past. Social time is nonlinear time. It is the *non*functioning of the Baghdad-Mogadishu legitimation mechanisms described above that is the political moment in the sense of a present that will pass. Command and control are woven in the social fabric as the pervasive mode of power. The system's fortunes do not hinge on any one political figure or election. Its macrolevel ability to legitimate itself may have been interrupted for a time, but it will take more than a bomb to dislodge it from its pervasive microimplantation in the social field. Baghdad-Mogadishu legitimation is quiescent, not obsolescent. It takes no soothsayer to predict its return. The difference is that the next time it happens, its renascent statism will most likely be warding off a threat from the grassroots right rather than from the liberal left. The main point is that the seriality of the command attacks is the product of an autonomic repetition-compulsion embedded in the political machinery of government as a dimension of the social — not the continuity of a personally invested ideological framework, on the part of the leader or the voters. Although nothing prevents the commander in chief or a mere civilian from investing in the violence ideologically, command and its legitimation are currently produced by means that are fundamentally nonideological, in the sense that belief does not necessarily enter into the equation at any stage, either on the part of the perpetrators of the violence or on the part of their domestic audience. Affective concurrence suffices. Subsequent to the fall of the Soviet Union, the eternal recurrence of state violence has all but lost its pretense of serving ideological ends. It no longer presents itself as a principled defense of a well-grounded totality with an a priori right to survive. It presents itself as a life-giving "service" to a community that is not a people, and is not actually unified. The operative "community" is a fractious and fissile global market, upon which the well-being of the national home audience is seen to hang. The attacks do not always have a well-defined geopolitical objective over and above their legitimating aim (even if they always have a geopolitical *effect* in their area of application). When they do have a geopolitical objective, it is now more decidedly than ever economic. The army doesn't fight; it does market maintenance work using cruise missiles as a grocery store janitor would a broom. It is all part of the balancing act among and within trade blocs that is now the primary concern of foreign policy.[12] To say that the mediations of civil society have disappeared is to say that every aspect of life and death, at home and abroad, is now directly capitalized. The "radical right-wing" militias earn the "radical" of their media label, even if the "right-wing" may be open to assessment, by dimly opposing the world capitalist order embraced by every other media-visible political tendency, taking as their weapons delirious international conspiracy theories and an isolationist survivalism whose utopianism is as economically unformed as its resurgent ideology is politically anomalous. Reagan Republican and "New Democrat" vie to steer the same, prevailing social dynamic (as if a self-organizing system were really steerable). The militias opt out. The countervailing movement of which they are a part is too embryonic to say what precise mode of power it would grow into, given the chance to develop the social dynamic it envelops. One thing that is certain is that the resulting sociality would hardly qualify as "civil."

The Singular-Generic

This account has come full circle, several times, just as Clinton, Bush, and Reagan did. There is a limit as to how far the kind of analysis set in motion here can go. The emphasis in the analysis of affective legitimation was on blurrings, reversals, repetitions, disappearances, displacements, fusions: mutual convertibilities. This strategy was not followed in order to reach a sublime evocation of postmodern implosion or deconstructive aporia. Quite the contrary, it is meant to preface an appeal for the construction of theoretical tools tuned to levels of complexity to which cultural theory as a whole has not yet adapted. The mutual convertibilities are not negativities, and while they operate on the representational level in mass-media imaging, they are not confined to that level. They are rhetorical figures, and more: they are positive *operators* of the self-reproducing system of systems that is contemporary capitalist sociality. The figures we see on television are distilled enactments on the level of representation of processes occurring at all levels, through-out the social field. The autonomic supersystem of global capitalism works by making ever-finer *differentiations* as part of a continuing, generalized pro-cess of adaptational recomposition that reshuffles the cards and changes the rules of the game at every turn, in response to frictions arising from its own functioning (trade-related nonwars) as well as to perturbations from without (antigovernment isolationism). The "implosions" and "aporias" are real, super-systemic elasticities enabling the recomposition and mutual readjustment of constituent subsystems. Contemporary capitalist power is metaconstructivist, as must be its critique. And all critique of power must participate, directly or indirectly, lucidly or deliriously, in the critique of capitalism, or risk falling into instant obsolescence in the ever-changing landscape it governs.

The following are a few tentative principles for a capitalist critique of a kind, it is hoped, that no populist militia would ever think to embrace.

1. Capitalism, following Marx's metaphor, is vampiric. It sucks value from preexisting formations but in killing them endows them with an eternal after-life. In Deleuze and Guattari's words, capitalism is the "motley collection of everything that has ever existed." Tribal societies, for example, are relegated to reserves, which then become bases for the expansion of the burgeoning worldwide tourism market. Elements of their art, music, and dress are ex-tracted from their ghettoized societies to circulate indefinitely through the periodicities of the entertainment and fashion industries. The strategy is one of circulatory stratification: shreds of a precapitalist formation are conserved by the institutionalization of a vested territory, which may or may not corre-spond to a tract of land but is always legally or procedurally formalized as a distinct social stratum. That stratum is then completely subsumed by processes of capitalist valorization involving deterritorialized circulations ("representa-tion"). The level of deterritorialized circulations itself constitutes a stratum, that of communication, defined as extractive interference. All of this might be called the principle of capitalist *additivity*.

2. You can't shuffle without cutting. This is the principle of *separation*. Every convertibility that is produced through communication, on the level of deterritorialized circulation, is predicated on a transformative separation (an extraction). For example, the figure of the "thug" is extracted from the civil sphere and imported into diplomacy, producing a fusion of "enemy" and "third world head of state" under the sign of the generic "criminal." This feeds, on the one hand, into codifications of punitive international law and, on the other hand, into a mass-media borne backwash of the new composite figure into the domestic civil sphere from which it was extracted. Domestic political enemies will now tend to be filed under "criminal," feeding into a preexisting tendency to reinforce police powers. This produces further fusions between the "crimi-nal" and "drug addict" or "welfare recipient" or "terrorist" — the latter being a word that gained currency at the beginning of the century in connection with

ideologically motivated anarchist "propagandists by the deed" but that is now an all-purpose term for those practicing nonlegitimated, stateless violence. A new stratum is produced: that of generic criminality, which migrates between strata. On each stratum it fuses a different mix of already functioning figures. These figures do not disappear. They continue to function parallel to the generic, but more suggestively they are also stockpiled in the generic figure, from which they can always be reextracted as needed. The enemy is still lurking and can always be called upon or reassigned. Each of the constituent figures of the generic overfigure is available for reactivation at new sites at any time and thus can be swiftly adapted to changing circumstances. The fusion of figures in the generic is less a confusion than the production of a generative matrix composed of fissionable atoms of figurability. The generic is not an absence of determination but the continuity and coexistence of *determinabilities* defining a virtual range of sociality. Each determined figure that is reextracted from the generic mix serves as a point of subjectification (in other words, a gravitational pull around which competing orbits of affect and thought are organized) and at the same time as a nucleus of power (a gravitational pull for competing bureaucratic bodies of control procedure and political command centers). Once again, communication — in this case the circulatory production of generic figures of sociality in the mass media — is more concerned with the creation of interference patterns than with either transparencies or black holes. Baudrillardian "implosions" are in fact productive interweavings that can be analyzed functionally in terms of convergences, bifurcations, and resonations (interference patterns) that are auto-generated within an expanding and complexifying chaotic supersystem. Any of the "confusions" evoked earlier can be approached in this way. It would be absurd, for instance, to argue that linear time has become extinct, replaced by a nonlinear temporality based on recursive causality between past and future. Linear time is very much with us. But now so is nonlinear time. The question is: In what mix, to what effect, at what levels?

   3. The principle of separation brought us, through the generic, to the next principle, that of *determination*. The object of capitalist power does not preexist the exercise of that power. Productive power is exercised on points of indeterminacy: on molecules of genericness fusing singular atoms of sociality in an unstable primal soup of power. The figures are determined enough to be perceived and to attract the attention of autonomic apparatuses of power. But they are not determined enough to fall unambiguously into an already codified procedural or political category. They are unqualified, nonspecified. They are not yet determinations, but determinabilities.[13] The exercise of control-and-command power qualifies, specifies, determines: in other words, it extracts a codifiable figure from the generic soup and attaches it to a territory. The territory is less a tract of land or an individual body than a *class* defining possible sites and embodied objects of power. The virtual singularity of the generic

is classified as a particularized possibility for the exercise of power. Newly emergent social sites and embodiments, or mutations of already existing ones, will not be immediately classifiable and will fall under unclear jurisdiction. They will be competed over. In the end, they will be determined as belonging to a given class or as requiring the creation of a new class. Once classified, they fall under the auspices of one or more apparatuses of power. Productive capitalist power operates on the supersystemic level as an *apparatus of capture* feeding social escapes back into the web of interacting power systems. The determined sites and embodiments also form the basis for claims of freedom or privilege on the part of the bodies to which the class or category is applied. Negotiation has not become entirely extinct, any more than linear time has. It has been reshuffled. It has been internalized into the supersystem's mechanisms of expansion and adaptational self-reproduction. Forces of existence that coalesce enough to begin to define new social sites or embodiments are perceived by the supersystem as indeterminacies that are then competitively determined by the supersystem's constituent systems in a way that assimilates them into the existing social landscape with minimal disruption. Ontological emergence is hijacked. Emergences creating the conditions for serious conflict are funneled into normative channels setting carefully controlled parameters of negotiation. Not only do these emergences not disrupt the supersystem — they feed it. Every socially recognized class is a potential market. Productive capitalist power is directly a market-expansion tool; and conversely, every market-expansion tool is directly a form of capitalist power. The creation of a niche market through advertising is the creation of a niche power-object that is also a potential political constituency. Social emergence, the irruption of new forces of existence, are precapitalized. In other words, *the power to exist has been transformed into an internal variable of the capitalist supersystem.* This subsumption of life itself under capital is expressed in different ways on many levels. Biotechnology and the Human Genome Project are the most literal examples. On the level of capitalist diplomacy, this subsumption involves the singular-generic "humanity" that enters into mass-media circulation, disappearing and reappearing following a complicated rhythm. We saw earlier how the "humanity" of the Iraqi war dead disappeared into the machinic circuitry. We also saw how "humanity" reappeared in Somalia thanks to the philanthropic gesture of the military white knight who shot to feed. Life and death are fused in the generic figure of "humanity" in crisis, then are reparticularized, reimplanted, proceduralized, and valorized in a variety of ways. This vastly increases the reach of power but also expands the potential for negotiation and advocacy under the banner of "human rights" and "humanitarian aid." The stakes are real. The importance of human-rights advocacy cannot be underestimated and should not be seen to be belittled by critiques of "humanism." But by the same token, it is not in itself a site of resistance. It is a site of adaptational capture — which is a far better option for the starving

Somali than obliteration, which is the only other option open in the absence
of conditions for resistance. Resistance, if it is still at all possible (and I think
it is), will take a different, most likely posthuman, route. Critiques of humanism could very well prove useful in opening that path. This is an argument for
an additivity of political strategies on the part of those who desire to change
the capitalist supersystem, to match the additivity of capitalism itself. It is
crucial to begin thinking in terms of nonmutually exclusive strata of political action (including identitarian politics) and how they may be coalesced into
supersystemic contestation.

   4. It is as artificial to separate *command* from *control* as it is to separate
death from life. Command (power over life, power of death) and control
(power to enliven), though really distinct, cofunction. They are interwoven
into the fabric of everyday life, and their uneasy ground-level mixes can be
seen to lie along the same continuum of power. On that continuum, the
quality of their respective effects converge. On the one hand, the command
subtraction of a potential provokes a reflexive evasion or adaptive alteration:
command is also productive of life; control is its by-product. On the other
hand, the field of operation of noncoercive, incitative, power-of-control channelings is punctuated and porously delimited by command attacks, to which
it regularly appeals in self-defense. Command and control are reciprocal by-
products, as are life and death. "Death becomes multiplied and differentiated,
endowing life with the singularities, and thus the truths, from which life believes its resistance arises . . . , death as coextensive with life, and as composed
of a multiplicity of partial and singular deaths."[14] The interpenetration of life
and death, of course, is a characteristic of all modes of power, even the "negative" power of absolutist command, the evocation of which opens Foucault's
Discipline and Punish, and whose object is *sovereignty.* Foucault's disciplinary
institutions can be seen as normative command centers radiating control, productive less of sovereignty than of eddies of social *order.* Biopower takes the
interpenetration of life and death, control and command, to a new level. It
integrates disciplinary power into a new social landscape marshaling the par-
tiality of death, subdivided and multiplied, toward the goal of enlivenment,
the multiplication of life's productive powers. Unleashed *production* replaces
order as the object of power (in Marxist terms, this coincides with the "formal subsumption of labor" under capital). Deleuze suggests that contemporary
capitalism must be seen to function under yet another regime. A "crisis of enclosure" has occurred (the "crises" long heralded in the media, among which
the "breakdowns" of the family, of the judicial and prison subsystems, and of
the school subsystem figure prominently). When the walls come down, disciplinary command functions are not dismantled, but rather released. They
disseminate and vary, coming to be even more finely distributed throughout
the social field, bringing death, subdivided and multiplied, and life channelings into even more intimate embrace. Deleuze applies the name "control"

to the regime of power growing out of the ultimate fine-meshing of command and control, because the overall tenor of the system is one of positive channeling and incitement. In spite of its "productive" nature, he *contrasts* this mode of power with "biopower." This is because it actually bears more directly on circulation than production — to the extent that this distinction still holds. The society of control corresponds, in Marxist terms, to the "real subsumption of society" under capital. Real subsumption is characterized by a blurring of the boundary between circulation and production (every deterritorialized circulation expressing and creating a surplus value). "Control" is best taken in a sense close to its cybernetic sense: systems' control of input, output, and the transformative operations effected in the autonomic machine — applied to bodies (defined as broadly as possible, to include images) rather than to information. In this view, input and output combine into one function, as a channeling across a threshold (a residual wall that came down). The threshold is not between an inside and an outside but between two juxtaposed outsides in an open field. The transformative operation does not follow the crossing of the threshold; it *is* the threshold. Emergence is serialized in successive passages. It is processed. The object of this mode of power is not sovereignty, order, production, or even circulation per se; rather, it is the circulatory *modulation* of all of these (and more).[15] Control involves the assimilation of powers of existence, at the moment of their emergence (their phased passing), into a classificatory schema determining normative orbits around which procedural parameters for negotiation and advocacy are set. It has to do with the production of socially valorized normative entities. The normative undergoes rapid inflation, as classificatory and regulative mechanisms are elaborated for every socially recognizable state of being, including illness (support and advocacy groups for people living with particular health conditions: the socialization of disease) and death (euthanasia: the properly social, as opposed to political, production of death). "Normal" is now free-standing, no longer the opposite and necessary complement of "abnormal," "deviant," or "dysfunctional," as it was under disciplinary power, except in limit-cases. The meaning of normative has changed. Normativity becomes synonymous with collective visibility and social operativity — with living itself (and with illness and death "with dignity," in other words actively transformed into an affirmation of life). Command, for its part, is a militarized police function that is activated in the limit-case by a transgression of an existing norm (that is, by a failure or refusal to be assimilated to a new norm). Command takes over at the point at which the normal re-binarizes with the "abnormal," "deviant," and "dysfunctional." That point is fluid, under constant renegotiation. The mass circulation of figures of criminality, and their police-figure complements, applied to heads of state as well as their subjects, is not as gratuitous as it might have seemed.[16] Crime is itself the figure of the limit-case (particularly crimes "against the community" and "against humanity," which by their generic nature tend to subsume all other varieties). It is in the domain of crime that the continually displaced parameters of command are constantly reset. The vagueness of the generic figures of crime, criminal, and cop clearly expresses a general function of the capitalist supersystem. Command and control are the fissionable and fusionable atoms of capitalist power (the singular-generics proper to it). They reciprocally generate each other and disappear and reappear into each other following a complicated and fundamentally unpredictable rhythm covering the totality of social space. The principle of modulation states that the capitalist supersystem must be characterized, globally, as a modulatory social control system conditioned by and conditioning command (the "political" defined narrowly as autocratic decision backed by effective force).

5. Normative control systems and command centers are collective autonomic apparatuses, as are their interlinkages. So although humanized intentionality, as expressed through negotiation and advocacy, also appears and reappears and disseminates throughout the social fabric, it does not characterize the system as a whole. Like life itself, human intentionality has become an internal variable of capitalist power. What mediations continue to function are incapable of founding anything approaching a civil society that could ground a consensus-based decision-making power. The dream of a civil society that could serve as an equilibrium-seeking, democratic counterpull to the profoundly undemocratic, crisis-ridden, creative chaos of the capitalist supersystem is just that: a dream. This is the principle of *complicity,* or untranscendable control. Mediation-based strategies, whether of reform or of dialectical struggle, are now bit players on the global scene of power (which does not preclude their retaining important roles locally). If the human disappears and reappears locally and primarily affectively, globally it is relegated to the status of a reflexive machinic relay. For example, instant opinion polling elicits human reflex responses that are relayed via the autonomic apparatus of the mass media to other apparatuses, where they legitimate or enable certain autonomic operations.[17] In the case of the Gulf War, human response was relayed through the executive branch to military command centers, where it was translated into decisions to shoot, this time to kill. In such autonomic surroundings, it is vain to mourn the passing of moral reasoning and philosophies of right. Our social existence is affective and reflexive, and it serves little purpose to deny it. Any movement aiming to breathe new life into ideological power mechanisms in the name of humanity, or even a county-sized portion of it, is working against an enormous posthuman tide.

6. Although capitalist control endlessly produces norms and normativity, although capitalist command polices them, although controlled assimilations of sociality give rise to codifications and recodifications, although the generic figures it circulates may give grist for symbolic orderings, the contemporary capitalist supersystem as such is neither normative, codifying, nor structural-symbolic. This is what distinguishes it from earlier regimes of power. On

the formal level, contemporary capitalism's constituent elements are indeterminacies that are determinabilities that are singular-generics — the very
convertibilities that were argued above to constitute positivities. They are the
positivity of the supersystem in its formal dimension. This amounts to saying that the system is formally undetermined but gives rise to determinations;
that it is ungrounded yet grounds. Capitalist power is determining (of norms,
codes, and symbolic structures) in *effect*. But its every ground-effect is no
sooner implanted than uprooted. Deviance, decoding, and structural escape
are also, in effect, determined (as channeled transformative passage, captive
social fluidity productive of new norms, codes, symbolic structures). The emphasis on multiplication and fluidity should not be taken to imply that formal
analysis of contemporary capitalism is impossible, that its formal dimension
is unthinkable. All that it means is that contemporary capitalism is not defin-
able in the framework of traditional logic. Fortunately, there exist new logics,
as well as *metalogics*. The latter are formal supersystems not averse to productive paradox whose constituent elements are, precisely, the excluded middles
of indeterminacy, determinability, and the singular-generic. Although the formal expression of such *axiomatics* is of little value to cultural theory, their
conceptual scaffolding may well have contributions to make to a metalogical
description of capitalism.[18] Mainstream social sciences are already employ-
ing axiomatic method. The open-systems theory of Niklas Luhmann can be
seen as an axiomatic conceptualization of the self-reproduction of social systems. Luhmann's analyses of "autopoietic" self-referential systems describe the
formal dimension of what are being called here "autonomic apparatuses of
power."[19] In the deregulatory environment of contemporary capitalism, every
apparatus of government power is under intense pressure to reinvent itself
as a self-reflective, self-reproducing system subordinated less to the will of
a "people" than to measurable output criteria defined in directly capitalist
terms ("productivity" and "profitability"). Metatheoretical approaches to cultural studies often attempt to map possibilities for global contestation. Their
problem is not that they are too "meta" but that they are not "meta" enough.
Cultural theory has to be raised to an entirely new level of abstraction in
order to be able to grasp the utter and increasing concreteness of capitalist
power. Because the reality of that power is in flux. The supersystem has no
constants. It is a field of continual variation, each modulation of which combines a superabstractness with an infra-empirical concreteness, at the border
between life and death: once again, the fickle figure of "humanity" and the
marketable mapping of the human gene provide suggestive examples. Enlightenment "Man" has deterritorialized and bifurcated. Torn from its metaphysical
mooring in any putative human essence, uprooted from any stable existential territory, it enters circulation. Ex-"Man" circulates, on the one hand, as a
singular-generic "humanity" that can be shot to be fed or shot to be killed, can
become a military staging ground, as ant or enemy, or a machinic disappear-

ance. This is a "humanity" that, as a collective, affective, generative matrix, is too essentially changeable, too multiply determinable, to be attributed the pallid integrity of "moral personhood" that is the presumption of any enlightened ideology of emancipation. On the other hand, ex-"Man" circulates as a generative (genetic) matrix embedded in the materiality of the human. The singular-generic human genome lies at the point of capital indistinction between the biological and the chemical, where the "human" is more closely akin to a salable virus, neither dead nor alive, than a reasonable animal standing at the pinnacle of earthly life-forms, one step below the divine on a ladder of perfection. Moral-rational integrity is lost in a human self-concept struck with the metalogical mutability of affect; species integrity is lost in a biochemical code expressing the mutability of human matter. Capitalist power operates on that double-edged mutability. Its preferential domain can be said to be where the far side of abstraction meets the underneath of the concrete — where concept becomes affect (and thus returns to the body as seat of affective actualization); where body becomes code (and thus conceptual); where the conceptual becomes corporeal (where reflection becomes reflex), and vice versa, in a double becoming no sooner splintering "Man" into singular-generics than fusing these in a shared capitalization on a global scale; and no sooner fusing them than launching them into differential circulation on distinct empirical levels (the mass media and biotechnology). Only an axiomatic can grasp this super-infra-mutability, this systemic capacity for differential fluctuation, as a positivity, rather than an aporia. The *axiomatic* principle holds that the thinking of late capitalist power as autopoiesis should not be left to state apologists such as Luhmann but redirected with a view to resistance.

7. Resistance, if it is possible (and again, I think it is), needs to be reinscribed in the generic. As it is usually conceived, resistance starts from a particularity and either defends or deepens that particularity. But particularity is an effect of the very system of determination that resistance is meant to resist. It is a reductive embodiment of the singular-generic in a serially determinate, normatively specifiable entity. Resistance must be reconceptualized as an operation on *the generic:* its direct embodiment *as multiply singular.*[20] The tactical embodiment of the groundless ground of capitalist power would short-circuit its channelings. It would dephase controlled emergence: in other words, envelop locally the globality of its phasings (this is the technical definition of "singularity" in chaos theory). Resistance would be the condensation of vital powers of emergence — and multiple deaths. In other words, it would define itself less as an oppositional practice than as a pragmatics of intensified *ontogenesis:* at life's edge. This is the countercapitalist principle of *vitalist metaconstructivism.* This principle can only be fully theorized through its own pragmatic application. In other words, through experimentation.

8. A final principle might be dubbed the *autonomy of affect.* Affect constitutes a social stratum. It is no less a social automaton than any other apparatus

of capitalist power. And apparatus of power it is: the circulation of affect through the mass media is in and of itself a normative control mechanism (a channeling of attention). It feeds into other control systems operating on other levels and is directly convertible into fuel for command systems. It must be borne in mind that affect, in the continually varying capitalist landscape, is an impersonal *flow* before it is a subjective content. That is why the sadism of affective legitimation was earlier characterized as "innocent." It is everyone's, but no one's in particular. If there is criminal guilt here, it is fluid and generic. Affect is an internal variable of the system. Like every such variable, its variability is predicated on a deterritorialization, but its determination involves a reterritorialization. It is a crucial task of capitalist critique to redefine affect, to reconceptualize the processes by which affect is deterritorialized from its historical territory (the supposedly autonomous subject) and reterritorialized in a variety of autonomic apparatuses — including but not limited to innocently complicit bodies. Such a redefinition of affect would have to find a way of describing deterritorialized circulation in terms of forces and movement (forces of existence, intensive movement), retaining a derivative role for signification (coding and symbolization).[21] This done, there is no reason why complicit collectivities could not or should not intervene pragmatically on what then appears as an eminently pragmatic register. Affective intervention could take place on the level of capitalist communication, perhaps even through the mass media. This insider, or immanent, resistance might play on the nature of communication as productive interference. Productive interference patterns that fail to resonate with capitalist legitimation, either by excess or by deficiency or with humor, are at least momentarily unassimilable by the supersystem and seem, from its point of view, to be simple negativities, "vacuoles of noncommunication," to quote Deleuze.[22] Tactical noncommunication might take a ritualistic form, mimicking the ritual legitimation of capitalist power, to very different effect — and affect. For it would not be sadistic but joyful; not exorcistic but invocational, calling forth what are, again from the point of view of the supersystem, vague and alien powers of collective existence whose determinations escape.

This essay itself is meant to be such an invocation, however hesitant and unformed. It began with what was essentially an expression of *my* complicity, my involvement in the Gulf War and Somalia, as an American television viewer with intensely ambivalent reactions to what I saw. For there was no option simply to step outside the Reagan-Bush/Clinton legitimation of state violence. The only "outside" my Gulf War television experience admits of is a criminalized Saddam Hussein-General Aideed: so evidently an outwardly projected, distorted image of the "inside" in which I find myself. This "outside" is a relative outside that is the inside's own creation (through the mass media, through foreign aid). No, I am in, and the only way out is through to an absolute outside, an as yet barely thinkable, still inexistent outside that would amount to an immanent conversion of capitalism. Critique is not an abstract distancing of the self *from* its concrete "object"; it is a superabstract, infraconcrete distance *to* — to an outside, of the self *and* its system of objects (capitalism). That outside is the potential, contained by capitalism, for its own collapse. It is a pure virtuality. I do not affirm the opposite of Reagan-Bush/Clinton (Hussein-Aideed). I affirm the extinction of that opposition as a mode of capitalist power. The "principles" outlined above were affectively inflected concepts taking faltering steps toward the threshold, in a manner meant to match the mode of operation of capitalist power, without buying into it. They are less "principles" in any strict sense than pragmatic "pointers" in which I invest not my "self" — but my affect, my body (my thought as affect-body). This is an investment in a future money can't buy. It is complicity — but not toward retirement.

Notes

1. Jean Baudrillard, *The Gulf War Did Not Take Place,* trans. Paul Patton (Sydney: Power Publications, 1995).

2. These are Pentagon estimates, as reported in the news media (*Montreal Gazette,* 9 May 1992, B3).

3. Iraqi violations of the southern "no-fly zone," declared by the UN and policed primarily by the United States, received high-profile international attention. Relatively insignificant air flight and radar violations (for example, on 30 June 1993) made high-profile news as affronts to the world community, while Saddam Hussein's relentless ground operations against the southern Iraqi populations supposedly protected by the no-fly zone were hardly featured. These operations included wholesale ecological warfare: the systematic destruction by fire and drainage of the wetlands ecosystem that was the traditional home of the "Marsh Arabs" of the Tigris-Euphrates delta.

4. On "hybrid objects" combining the social and the natural, see Bruno Latour, *We Have Never Been Modern* (Cambridge, Mass.: Harvard University Press, 1993).

5. François Ewald, "Two Infinities of Risk," in *The Politics of Everyday Fear,* ed. Brian Massumi (Minneapolis: University of Minnesota Press, 1993), 221–28.

6. Paul Virilio, *L'insécurité du territoire* (Paris: Stock, 1976).

7. On the fate of civil society under contemporary capitalism, see Antonio Negri and Michael Hardt, *Labor of Dionysus: A Critique of the State-Form* (Minneapolis: University of Minnesota Press, 1994), 217–61, and Michael Hardt, "The Withering of Civil Society" (in this volume).

8. The UN has encountered embarrassing difficulties patrolling its official "peacekeeping" vocabulary. All copies of a glossy Australian Department of Defence booklet entitled *Peacekeeping Policy: The Future Australian Defence Force Role* had to be recalled because the authors had used the word "peace*making*" in several passages referring to operations in Somalia. The problem wasn't that "peacemaking" recalled its etymological model, "warmaking." "Peacemaking" is in fact approved UN vocabulary, but it is carefully distinguished from "peacekeeping" and "peace enforcement" (the correct term for the Somali case). The authors of the booklet had failed to appreciate the subtleties of this array of neologisms, the effect of which is to annex mediation, military action,

and police enforcement into a continuum subsumed by the concept of "peace" (see "Defence Gaffe Leads to Recall of Booklet," *Australian*, 1 July 1993).

9. The evidence of the plot against George Bush's life would not hold up in court. Iraq's ambassador to the UN accused the United States, quite accurately, of acting as "prosecution, judge, jury and executioner in its own case" ("Missiles Cannot Plug Holes in Evidence," *Guardian Weekly*, 4 July 1993). Saddam Hussein had a simpler defense, stating that George Bush, already political deadwood, would not be worth the explosives.

10. Clinton said after his election that he would do "precisely what the Bush administration has done" in relation to Saddam Hussein. And that is precisely what he did — to the audible relief of many media military analysts. "Clinton has comprehensively embraced the U.S. military's view of security" (a doctrine of military deterrence known as "forward deployment"), cooed the *Australian*'s foreign editor, Greg Sheridan (15 July 1993), in response to the Iraqi attack and Clinton's post-Tokyo summit statement in Seoul that North Korea would "cease to exist" if it attacked the South.

11. "Pilot Shot Down over Bosnia Broke Rules on the Ground Too," *Australian*, 8–9 July 1995.

12. This has entailed a post–Cold War adaptation of intelligence agencies. Revelations in June 1993 that the French intelligence agency, after the collapse of the Soviet Union, its old nemesis and reason for being, had turned its attention to the high-tech secrets of political allies have led to a general recognition that industrial spying is the new priority in international intelligence across the board. See, for example, "A New World for Spies," *Newsweek*, 5 July 1993.

13. On determinability, see Gilles Deleuze, *Difference and Repetition* (New York: Columbia University Press, 1994), 168–76.

14. Gilles Deleuze, *Foucault*, trans. Seán Hand (Minneapolis: University of Minnesota Press, 1988), 95 (translation modified).

15. See Gilles Deleuze, "Post-script on the Societies of Control," *Negotiations 1972–1990*, trans. Martin Joughin (New York: Columbia University Press, 1995), 177–182. On Deleuze's updating of Foucault in the context of the Marxist theory of real subsumption, see Negri and Hardt, *Labor of Dionysus*.

16. On the current convergence between the figure of the statesman and that of the criminal, see Giorgio Agamben, "The Sovereign Police," in Massumi, ed., *The Politics of Everyday Fear*, 61–63.

17. This is what Deleuze-Guattari call "machinic enslavement." See Gilles Deleuze and Félix Guattari, *A Thousand Plateaus*, trans. Brian Massumi (Minneapolis: University of Minneapolis Press, 1987), 456–58.

18. Deleuze and Guattari develop the theory of capitalism as axiomatic in *A Thousand Plateaus*, 460–73. They base their analysis on Robert Blanché's overview of axiomatic method in *L'axiomatique* (Paris: PUF, 1955).

19. Félix Guattari, in *Chaosmosis*, trans. Julian Pefanis and Paul Bains (Sydney: Power Publications, 1995), elaborates from the work of Francisco Varela to develop an ontological model of "autopoiesis" that should not be confused with Niklas Luhmann's communicational model of "self-referential systems" as "autopoietic." See in particular 6–7 and 38–42 of *Chaosmosis*. For Luhmann's use of the term, see *Essays in Self-Reference* (New York: Columbia University Press, 1990), 1–20 and passim.

20. On the singular as multiple, see Gilles Deleuze, *The Logic of Sense* (New York:

Columbia University Press, 1990), 58–65, 100–108. On the singular-multiple as generic, see Giorgio Agamben, *The Coming Community* (Minneapolis: University of
Minnesota Press, 1993), passim.

21. For an attempt to carry out a redefinition of affect along these lines, see Brian
Massumi, "The Autonomy of Affect," in *Deleuze: A Critical Reader*, ed. Paul Patton
(London: Blackwell, 1996), 217–39.

22. Deleuze, "Post-script on the Societies of Control."

From Schizophrenia to Social Control

Eugene W. Holland

What happened "in-between" (to use one of Deleuze's favorites expressions) the first and second volumes of *Capitalism and Schizophrenia*?[1] Is the second volume an advance or a retreat relative to the first? Does the plateau format of volume 2 explode the vestiges of "arborescence" informing the—finally quite conventional—linear format and argument of volume 1? Or does the second volume represent a retreat from the uncompromising militancy of the first into political caution or quiescence? Rather than hazard a global judgment on this issue, I propose to consider here the evolution of Deleuze and Guattari's thought on one relatively circumscribed topic: the interplay of prospects for freedom and pressures of constraint within capitalist social formations. My title indicates the overall direction their thought takes from volume 1 to volume 2 and beyond[2]—from schizophrenia to social control—but I intend to return nonetheless to the topic of schizophrenia, if only briefly, at the end of the essay.

We start, then, with volume 1, *Anti-Oedipus*. Three topics need to be addressed: where the concept of schizophrenia comes from and how and why Deleuze-Guattari transform it; how the forces and dynamics of social control opposed to schizophrenia are conceived; and what kind of prognosis is given regarding the opposition between schizophrenia and social control.

The term "schizophrenia" comes from Lacan's linguistic-existentialist version of psychoanalysis, where it designates a purely metonymic form of desire untrammeled by the metaphoric associations of equivalence and meaning imposed on desire by social and/or linguistic codes operating in the name of the father. These codes in effect rivet desire onto socially sanctioned objects. While the metaphoric axis of discourse submits desire to social coding in the symbolic order, the metonymic axis—what Lacan calls the metonymy of desire—fuels the vain attempt to restore an immediate connection to the realm of being and the body, a connection forever lost (in Lacan's version of existialism) with the acquisition of language and entry into the symbolic order.[3]

Of all this, Deleuze-Guattari retain only the semiosis of Lacanian schizophrenia, its definition as a spontaneous or unpredictable form of desire freed from social coding. And what frees desire, according to Deleuze-Guattari, is capitalism rather than anything psychological or therapeutic: schizophrenia arises from the decoding processes characteristic of capitalism. But capitalist decoding in turn only expresses to a historically unprecedented extent a universal tendency inherent in all human societies and indeed in all forms of life: the tendency to expend energy on either growth or dilapidation, or some combination of both. Deleuze-Guattari's work is what we might call Marx-informed rather than Marx*ist,* and here they draw on Bataille and on the second law of thermodynamics more than on any Marxian-dialectical view of society and history.[4] Indeed, *Anti-Oedipus* represents a kind of "natural history" of human societies (see *AO* 4–5, 24–25), according to which social forms — like all other life-forms — are understood as contradictory dissipative structures: they are antientropically and irreversibly organized, but only in order to dissipate that much more of the practically infinite supply of energy provided to the planet by light and heat radiation from the sun. The predatory life-form of the tiger, for Bataille, is the epitome of complex biological organization devoted purely to the consumption of as much incarnated energy as it can eat. The even more complexly organized life-form that is capitalist society, Bataille argues, logarithmically increases the pressure to dissipate surplus energy, since it perversely concentrates the already excessive energy coming from the sun in endlessly accumulated means of further production, rather than devoting itself to glorious expenditure, as do all other life-forms (including all other human social forms in history). Decoding responds to or expresses that pressure to dissipate excess accumulated energy; indeed, schizophrenia can be understood as the release of that pressure or as a kind of accelerated entropy applied to overaccumulated codes. (John Coltrane takes a nicely coded song like "My Favorite Things" from *The Sound of Music* and decodes it — puts it to flight.) Applied to capitalist institutions as well as to codes, schizophrenic deterritorialization is the entropic principle and motive force of revolution.

What is most immediately opposed to revolutionary schizophrenia is paranoia, even though it derives from the structure of precapitalist social formations. Whereas schizophrenia designates the affirmation of the signifying process itself without stable codes or familiar meaning (John Coltrane), in paranoia not only is everything coded and meaningful, but it all means the same thing — whatever the terrifying god or despot says it means. Whereas in schizophrenia there is no source of meaning outside the process of improvisation, there is in paranoia a single and supreme source of all codes and meaning: god the despot (*AO* 192–94). At the same time, but in sociohistorical rather than strictly psychological terms, the despot is the imperial sovereign to whom all subjects owe an infinite debt, including their very lives. (Only the "psychological" paranoid personality actually believes the despot is doing everything imaginable to collect it from him personally.) All meaning arises *from* the sovereign because it is *to* him that all debt is owed, and vice versa.

But capitalism is crucially not a form of sovereignty, and its modes of social control are not sovereign ones: capital succeeds in occupying the position of the sovereign without generally dispensing meaning.[5] Capital is thus owed an infinite debt, but what is owed is merely one's work, one's quantified labor-power rather than one's life; and so capital sits mute on the deposed sovereign's throne, without offering any stable meaning in return. Indeed, capitalist decoding tends instead to systematically strip the halo of meaning from all aspects of social life (as Marx put it) and organizes society as a cash nexus for the sake of surplus-accumulation alone rather than in any meaningful way. Deleuze-Guattari call this market-based capitalist process of social organization "axiomatization";[6] and what sets it apart from other social forms is that capitalist axioms conjoin completely undetermined flows of matter/energy, flows that become determinate — take on content, quality, even local meaning — only *after* they have been conjoined. The emergence of capitalism depended, of course, on the conjunction of flows of wealth in liquid form (money rather than land) and of labor-power, such as the mass of serfs that had been forcibly "freed" from its previous determination as peasant labor by the Enclosure Acts. This process of deterritorialization — detaching labor-power from means of production so that it becomes indeterminate "labor-power in general" — is accompanied by a process of reterritorialization, which reattaches former peasants to new means of production: the looms of the nascent textile industry. Many other axioms have since been added, needless to say, in the course of capitalist development: technologies of production, of demand-stimulation and taste-management, and so forth.

These processes of detaching and reattaching indeterminate labor-power to means of production that are in constant technological flux themselves constitute the basic rhythms of capitalist development, according to Deleuze-Guattari (*AO* 257–60). The fundamental form of social control under capitalism is thus forced reterritorialization due to generalized deterritorialization — forced in the sense that since labor is divorced from any means of life, it must sell its power to owners of means of production just to survive. Capitalist axiomatization is thus ambivalent (not to say contradictory): through deterritorialization and decoding, it frees people from determinate conditions of existence and codes of meaning (thereby releasing schizophrenia), only to force them by necessity to accept new and increasingly exploitative conditions of existence through reterritorialization. Note the asymmetry: Deleuze-Guattari rarely mention "recoding" in connection with reterritorialization. This is because capitalist axiomatization is essentially a meaningless calculus: capitalism offers no stable code valid for the market it ceaselessly revolutionizes and expands: the belief in any general meaning under these conditions is "paranoid." If it weren't for the unavoidable inconvenience of managing workers and consumers, capitalism would do very nicely without meaning altogether.[7] What temporary, local meanings capitalism does provide are derivatives of whatever axioms happen to be in place: job-training and retraining through education systems, taste-management through advertising and marketing systems, and so on. What is remarkable is that in all these specific domains, recoding as an aftereffect of deterritorialization takes the general form of the Oedipus complex, based on the pattern of separation from means of life (the mother) followed by subjection to an external authority (not merely the father, but also the boss, priest, teacher, rock or sports star, politician, whomever). The Oedipus complex, in other words, derives directly from capitalist axiomatization before becoming the model of subjectivation characteristic of the nuclear family. In connection with reterritorialization, then, oedipal recoding is the other major form of social control under capitalism — and this includes Freudian psychoanalysis, which by means of transference merely reproduces the local meanings and pattern-of-subjectivation established by the nuclear family in an intimate form of recoding perfectly suited to (and indeed derived from) capitalist axiomatization.

So that is how Deleuze-Guattari rewrite the psychoanalytic Oedipus complex in Marxist terms. But it is Bataille (and ultimately Nietzsche) who has the last word in *Anti-Oedipus,* over and against Marx as well as Freud. It may appear, to the contrary, that Freud or Lacan has the last word: after all, the most striking political judgment in *Anti-Oedipus* is that unconscious investments of desire always count for more than conscious investments of interest; the pursuit of rational self-interest, even when defined in terms of class interest, is nothing more than a rationalization for pursuing whatever desire finds desirable (*AO* 257, 343–48). But recall how Deleuze-Guattari have redefined desire: it is not a question of wanting to sleep with the mother and murder the father; nor is it Lacan's metonymy of desire, a vain striving for fusion with being: it is the entropic desire for maximum dissipation or expenditure of energy, what Deleuze-Guattari call "antiproduction" (and illustrate with reference to the military-industrial complex and the nuclear arms race, among other things). In the "natural history" of human society, capitalism appears as the most complex form of organization for concentrating and dissipating excess energy; it is thus not the level of capitalist productivity but the level of capitalist antiproduction that serves as the primary (and usually sinister) attractor for desire, regardless of and even contrary to any conceivable rational interest. Given this important Bataille-Nietzsche strain, it is no surprise that *Anti-Oedipus* adamantly refuses to enunciate a political program, for the prospect of transferring the investment of desire from capital to another, even more intensely dissipative attractor for desire, to what Deleuze-Guattari only allude to as the "new earth" (*AO* 35, 321–22, 382), seems quite remote (not to say simply utopian), and *Capitalism and Schizophrenia,* volume 1 — for all its insight and rigor — doesn't pretend to map a strategy to accomplish it.

To which it must be added that volume 2 doesn't either: *A Thousand Plateaus* accomplishes many other things, but not that. It is much broader in scope, and the references to Freud and Lacan that focused the first volume almost entirely disappear (even in the "Wolf-Man" plateau!). Something different happens to the concept of axiomatization, which as we have seen lay at the heart of volume 1: it doesn't disappear but gets resituated in a larger conceptual matrix that analyzes social formations in terms of three criteria — forms of power, modes of domination, and types of what Deleuze-Guattari call "capture."[8] There are three forms of social power: sovereign, disciplinary, and control. There are two modes of domination: servitude and subjection. And there are three types of "capture" — that is, three ways of establishing and appropriating value: they are ground rent, profit, and what I'll call "levy" (to translate *prélèvement*), which is most recognizable in the forms of taxes and interest (as distinct from profit). A recurrent narrative trope seems to organize these categories, a kind of perverse return to origins: the most advanced capitalism is seen as rejoining the most archaic forms of barbarism.

I'll start by resituating axiomatization among the forms of capture. Axiomatization is what formally distinguishes profit from ground rent as types of capture and what historically distinguishes capitalism from feudalism at its emergence in Europe. Unlike axiomatization, which as we saw conjoins decoded flows (for example, of wealth and labor), ground rent captures the product of specifically landed wealth: it is based on directly personal (rather than market-mediated) relations of obligation, and it can be (and often was) paid in kind rather than in currency. But this last feature (the possibility of payment in kind) distinguishes ground rent from the levy form of capture as much as from axiomatization and the profit-form. For imperial tax levies involve large-scale, long-distance dominion where directly personal relations do not obtain and money is an absolute necessity: payments in kind would too quickly become redundant (if they didn't simply spoil en route) to be of any interest to an emperor. Indeed Deleuze-Guattari insist quite strenuously — against the conventional Marxist view — that the social origin of money was not in commerce (not in a dialectical surpassing of barter destined to result in the commodification of labor-power as the source of all value and especially of surplus value) but in the levy of imperial taxes (*A Thousand Plateaus* [*ATP*] 442–44). Imperial capture was based on the monopoly-power to mint money and to put it into circulation in ways that consistently enhanced the emperor's dominion and constantly swelled his own coffers. In Deleuze-Guattari's view, finance capital today plays precisely the same role and (*pace* Marx) has achieved dominion over industrial capital. The levy on circulating capital known as interest is thus no longer to be understood as a portion of the total sum of surplus value produced by labor-power but as an appropriation deriving from the power to "issue" or "invent" capital itself and to put it in circulation in ways that enhance its dominion and its ability to issue more capital.[9] We have a perverse return to origins, then, which sees capital not as really a social relation disguised as a monetary relation among things but as a social illusion or fiction that only involves things — the production and consumption of things — as a kind of epicycle of the predominant movement that is that of money begetting money.

The return of levy as the dominant type of capture does not, however, entail a return to the imperial state itself as the contemporary form of power, largely because the tax levies of the state are now subordinate to the interest levies of finance and speculative capital, with which they nonetheless continue to coexist (as we all know). What happened to the state? How did it succumb to capital? That history is of course a long and complicated one, but its logic is less so: because capitalist axioms operate on decoded flows, the capture of profit has proven far more flexible, innovative, and powerful than anything the sovereign state could muster, based as it was on merely overcoding existing codes through raw domination and capturing whatever surplus was produced far below it. The power of sovereignty demanded only obedience and held only the power of death over its members, whereas disciplinary power operating in the service of capitalism seeks power over life as a productive resource (biopower) and insinuates itself directly into the production process to demand constantly enhanced efficiency rather than mere obedience, as Foucault has shown.[10]

At the same time, by forcibly separating labor from its means of life through deterritorialization, capitalism increases the quotient of subjectivation of its workers: under capitalism, a whole new mode of domination, a whole new form of subjectivity — including new practical skills obtained through increasingly long-term training or education, but also new attitudes toward what comes to be known as "work," self-control, the deferral of gratification, the mediation of money, the impersonality of the market, the disintegration of community, and so on — is required: Deleuze-Guattari call it "subjection" and define it in opposition to "servitude," which requires mere obedience. Exemplary of servitude is what Lewis Mumford calls the "megamachine" that built the pyramids:[11] here the labor force consisted of raw manpower whose physical capacities were utilized strictly as a factor of production like that of any other beast of burden, without regard to or any need for subjectivity. Under capitalism, by contrast, workers aren't mere disposable parts of the megamachine; they are formally independent, self-reliant agents who train for and then contract to work at or alongside machines; capitalism, after all, maintains a clear distinction between technologized constant capital and subjectivized variable capital — a distinction that simply doesn't obtain in despotic state-forms whose mode of domination is servitude.

But disciplinary power is not coterminous with domination by subjection, even if capitalist work-discipline represents a first historical quantum leap in the quotient of subjectivation. For as capitalism develops, retail buying power becomes at least as important a locus of subjectivation as labor-power, as advertising and marketing produce subjectivities that define themselves by what they consume more than what they produce.

Many public school systems in the United States today have allowed corporate sponsors to install television sets in the classrooms to show ersatz news programs for an hour or more each day. (Needless to say, the accompanying advertisements and often enough the "news" stories themselves shamelessly promote the corporate sponsor and the fast-food products a corporate subsidiary is probably selling in the school cafeteria.) Schools are targeted for programming of this kind not so much to degrade skills and thus depreciate in advance the value of labor-power (though this happens too) as to capture consumer power both at school and in the future.

When Deleuze-Guattari insist that states today serve as little more than "models of realization" for capital, this includes furnishing modes of subjectivation that mold citizens into producers and consumers appropriate for various regimes of capitalist axiomatization, ranging from the advanced to the underdeveloped and everything in-between; states also provide necessary legal and infrastructural frameworks (labor laws, the information superhighway) necessary for capturing profit and for levying interest on capital placed in circulation — whether in speculative investment, retail trade, or good old-fashioned production.

As levies on all kinds of circulating capital surpass the capture of profit in magnitude and importance, disciplinary society gives way to what Deleuze called "control society" in an article that summarizes and develops the conclusions reached in the final plateaus of *Capitalism and Schizophrenia,* volume 2.[12] High-tech, niche-targeted advertising and computer-managed, high-speed speculation in stocks, commodities, and currencies make marketing consultants and program traders rather than factory bosses the "impudent masters" of control society, as Deleuze puts it. Whereas disciplinary power was exercised in loci of enclosure — in the factory, in the schools, in the military, in the asylum — control is exercised virtually everywhere: marketing information, for example, is collected wherever and whenever people shop, travel, pay taxes, register to vote, and so on.

It used to be, for example, that marketing campaigns (political as well as commercial) would ask prospective voters or consumers in so-called focus groups to fill out questionnaires to rate an advertisement or campaign speech; this was domination by *subjection,* inasmuch as subjective responses were solicited and interpreted. Increasingly, however, focus-group participants are hooked instead to biofeedback devices that measure galvanic skin response, heartbeat, pulse, and breathing rates: subjection has given way to high-tech *servitude,* inasmuch as these participants are a-subjective parts of a megamachine.

In control society, disciplinary subjection is losing ground and making way for a perverse return to servitude as the prevailing mode of domination. To be sure, profit is still captured from the subjection of work, but even here, wage levels are determined increasingly through high-tech individual performance measures wherever and whenever work is performed, rather than by collective labor-time spent in the factory. And even more widespread, shoppers, voters, travelers, investors, home owners, and so forth all become parts of a vast cybernetic megamachine that instantaneously registers every decision and feeds it back into control mechanisms operating in the service of the levies that "pure" finance capital captures from virtually all moments of circulation throughout the market.

Social control today, then (in what is sometimes called a regime of flexible accumulation), operates through a combination of long-term discipline and high-speed control, while the mode of subjection and enclosure associated with the former loses ground to a pervasive cybernetic servitude in connection with the latter. And it is the high-speed control feature of advanced capitalism — to return to our point of departure — that casts doubt on the viability of schizophrenia as a potentially revolutionary line of flight. As long as the relative fixity of social codes — codes of labor discipline, codes of collective fashion preference, and so on — was crucial to axioms of mass production, schizophrenic decoding had a point (a *point d'appui*) and a disruptive effect. But as soon as the cybernetic megamachine can almost instantaneously capture the slightest shifts in consumer taste or lifestyle (like those of currency differentials or stock and bond prices), and can program them into its system, the dazzling semiotics of schizophrenia become pointless, all too easily recaptured by the axiomatics of high-speed marketing. This is not to say that Deleuze-Guattari simply give up on the value of schizophrenia, for they don't; but they do try to assess its risks: rates of decoding fast enough to outpace today's high-speed marketing technologies may well accelerate into black holes of solitary subjectivity, ranging from "anomie" to catatonia. Hence the importance that *A Thousand Plateaus* ascribes to devising planes of consistency or composition where lines of flight can intersect and become productive instead of spinning off into the void.[13]

And the best instance, to my mind, of a plane of consistency composing schizophrenic lines of flight in productive (not to say revolutionary) ways is still improvisational jazz — one of "My Favorite Things."[14]

Notes

1. See the special issue of *SubStance* on this question, *SubStance* 66 (1991).

2. Gilles Deleuze and Félix Guattari, *Capitalism and Schizophrenia*, 2 vols. (Minneapolis: University of Minnesota Press, 1983 and 1987) (original French editions, Paris: Minuit, 1972 and 1980). Page references to the English editions of vol. 1, *Anti-Oedipus* (*AO*), and vol. 2, *A Thousand Plateaus* (*ATP*), appear parenthetically in the

text. I also draw on Deleuze's essay "Postscript on the Societies of Control," which appeared in English translation in *October* 59 (1992): 3–8 (originally published in *L'autre journal* 1 [May 1990] as "Postscriptum sur les sociétés de contrôle"; it also appeared in *Pourparlers* [Paris: Minuit, 1990], 240–47).

3. On metaphor and metonymy in Lacan, see Kaja Silverman, *The Subject of Semiotics* (New York: Oxford University Press, 1983), and my "Schizoanalysis and Baudelaire: Some Illustrations of Decoding at Work," in *Deleuze: A Critical Reader,* ed. Paul Patton (Oxford: Basil Blackwell, 1996), 240–56.

4. See especially Georges Bataille, *The Accursed Share,* trans. Robert Hurley (New York: Zone Books, 1988) (original French edition, *La part maudite* [1949; Paris: Minuit, 1967]). Deleuze and Guattari's notion of "antiproduction" in *Anti-Oedipus* derives from Bataille's notion of "expenditure" (see *AO* 4, 190).

5. "[U]nlike previous social machines, the capitalist machine is incapable of providing a code that will apply to the whole of the social field" (*AO* 33).

6. On the concept of axiomatization, see *AO* 33, 224–34.

7. But see John Carlos Rowe, "The Writing Class," in *Politics, Theory, and Contemporary Culture,* ed. Mark Poster (New York: Columbia University Press, 1993), 41–82.

8. On the forms of social power, see "Postscript on the Societies of Control"; on the modes of domination, see *ATP,* Plateau 5, "On Several Regimes of Signs"; on the types of capture, see *ATP,* Plateau 13, "Apparatus of Capture."

9. On the role of narrative in the generation and circulation of capital, see Rowe, "Writing Class."

10. See in particular Michel Foucault's *History of Sexuality,* vol. 1, trans. Robert Hurley (New York: Vintage Books, 1980) (original French edition, *Histoire de la sexualité* [Paris: Gallimard, 1976]); and idem, *Discipline and Punish,* trans. Alan Sheridan (New York: Pantheon, 1977) (original French edition, *Surveillir et punir* [Paris: Gallimard, 1975]).

11. See Lewis Mumford, *The Myth of the Machine* (New York: Harcourt, Brace and World, 1967), and idem, *Technics and Civilization* (New York: Harcourt, Brace and Co., 1934).

12. Deleuze, "Postscript on the Societies of Control."

13. See especially *ATP,* Plateau 6, "How to Make Yourself a Body-without-Organs."

14. For a discussion of the nonhierarchical social relations embodied in jazz bands compared to those of symphony orchestras, see my " 'Introduction to the Non-fascist Life': Deleuze and Guattari's 'Revolutionary' Semiotics," *L'esprit créateur* 27, no. 2 (1987): 19–29.

3

Cinema, Perception, and Space

Capital/Cinema
Jonathan L. Beller

The exact development of the concept of capital [is] necessary, because it is the basic concept of modern political economy, just as capital itself, of which it is the abstract reflected image, is the basis of bourgeois society.

Karl Marx, Grundrisse

The spectacle is *capital* to such a degree of accumulation that it becomes an image.

Guy Debord, Society of the Spectacle

The following is an extract from a larger work in progress entitled *The Cinematic Mode of Production,* the purpose of which is at once to show that all of cinema, no matter what else it is, is an extension of capital-logic's colonization of the body and to imagine new ways to oppose capital's violations.

The argument is as follows: cinema develops a completely new method of value production and extraction by projecting the dynamics of political economy into the visual arena and by colonizing bodies by inducing them to labor in what amounts to a deterritorialized factory — mass media. In other words, (1) cinematic movement is an extension of capital circulation: the cinematic image develops out of the commodity-form; and (2) cinema becomes directly involved in the process of social production and reproduction by occupying human time and converting visual attention to labor-power — in short, the labor theory of value is a special case of what I call *the theory of the productive value of human attention.*[1]

From the function of movement and time indicated above, one might intuit the zones of intersection for my disagreements with the principal categories of the cinema books of Gilles Deleuze: *Cinema 1: The Movement-Image* and *Cinema 2: The Time-Image.* In this essay I argue that the cinema books, hereafter referred to as *Cinema,* might have been for the twentieth century what Karl Marx's *Capital* was for the nineteenth — that is, Deleuze's books might have been a development of the concepts of capital as it colonizes the visual through and as cinema.[2] However, *Cinema* fails to achieve what might provocatively be identified as its predestined stature because of Deleuze's refusal to theorize political economy. As a result, the cinema books at once consolidate Deleuze's extraordinary erudition and are a means for cognitive production by a rigorous traversal of his associations, without, as it were, managing to give an account of the significance of cinema. Such of course is his intention and his practice (production without reterritorialization), but I want to here suggest the cost of this practice.

My argument with respect to Deleuze is that the cinematic mode of production as a world historical moment is already implicit in his work; it is immanent. However, in the name of a "nonfascist politics," Deleuze represses the concept of the mode of production generally in and as the concept of "the machinic assemblage," in works such as *Anti-Oedipus* and *A Thousand Plateaus,* and *Cinema,* via the tropes he utilizes to articulate his concepts. Therefore, as my very deployment of the term "repression" betrays, I have found it necessary to systematically misread him, paying less attention to what he says and more to certain things he does not, will not, or cannot say. Though it is always immanent in *Cinema,* Deleuze refuses to think cinema in *dialectical* relation to capital.[3]

It is important to think for a moment that cinema is to our period what capital was to Marx's.[4] For Marx, capital itself posited a universal history of which capital the idea was a culminating moment in that it allowed the apprehension of universal process. The name of the work, *Capital,* is the hypostatization of the machinic logic that had the world in its grip: a process as a thing (capital), which, when actualized as process (movement), unlocked the secret dynamics between the historical construction of the world and of consciousness. Capital the idea, with its ability to deploy the concepts developed in *Capital,* was precisely the consciousness of capitalism, at once the realization and representation of the material and conscious processes of capital itself; its specter, if you will. *Cinema,* like *Capital,* can also be taken as designating a mode of production; the works consist of spectral projections of cinematic circulation in the discourse of philosophy.

Positing cinema as the process and the sign for the dominant mode of production argues that cinematic relations are an extension of capitalist relations — the development of culture as a sphere of the production line. Thus cinema is at once a sign for itself as a phenomenon and its process, as well as a sign for capital as a phenomenon and its processes. Cinema in my usage here marks a phase in the development of capitalism and capital's utter modification (metamorphosis) of all things social, perceptual, material. To grasp this idea, the very term "cinema" must be cut loose from the archive of films and network of institutions that are so well documented in order to signify the emergence of a new cultural logic — a coordination of spectacular production.[5]

The cinema for Deleuze is nothing if it is not a force of deterritorialization. So too, we must remember, was capital for Marx: simultaneously the most productive and destructive force unleashed in human history. The cinema, for Deleuze, is an industrial-strength modifier of consciousness capable, in its strong form, of unweaving the most arborescent and solidified of thought-formations, the most reified of perceptions — it annihilates traditional thought-forms as well as tradition itself. Hence its attraction for philosophy, its valorization as the good kind of consciousness. Cinema, like capital, is also a relentlessly material practice that can be recapitulated in the movement of concepts. Deleuze works "alongside" the cinema, producing cinema's concepts in order to deploy cinema's deterritorializing forces within the discourse of philosophy. This way of working is to be taken at once as a kind of representational verisimilitude and a performance of cinematic movement/time in the discourse of concepts. In the cinema books, Deleuze is interested neither in ideology critique nor in psychoanalysis, the two dominant modes of film theory at the time of their writing; he builds his assemblages around the work of *auteurs,* whom he takes as machines who produce certain distinct kinds of forms.

To write cinema as an agent of deterritorialization, Deleuze eliminates most of it. He makes a distinction at the beginning of *Cinema 1* between the work of the great directors — who are to be compared "not merely with painters, architects, and musicians, but also with thinkers" — and all the rest of cinema's products, what he calls "the vast proportion of rubbish in cinematic production."[6] For an adequate theory of cinema, we will have to consider, in principle at least, all of cinema, but for Deleuze, "We are talking only of masterpieces to which no hierarchy of value applies."[7] This leaves him one or two hundred directors at most, and their commentators. We are left to assume that the rest, the producers of "rubbish," recapitulate state-forms.

The translators of *Cinema 1* say that "[t]he book can . . . be seen as a kind of intercutting of cinema and philosophy," but even given that cinema is a force for the unweaving of existing structures, conceptual and otherwise, Deleuze must keep philosophy itself from arborescence, that is, from becoming a reterritorializing practice that would undo the cinema and put the brakes on desire.[8] However, this means that Deleuze must write, as it were, without history. As I have noted, to accomplish this unweaving he conceptualizes filmmakers as other great philosophers, painters, and writers have been conceptualized by the New Critics and their legacy, that is, as *auteurs,* geniuses. Desire, the animus of movement and deterritorialization, is to Deleuze what Power, the animus of immobilization and discursive production, is to Foucault: the name for productive praxis, the ether of relations, the field of the event. The release of desire (that is, the becoming molecular of the molar, the destratification of the stratified) and weaving by unweaving are precisely the desire of Deleuze. How then but through a kind of close-reading, text-in-itself debunking of history to keep philosophy from producing a field of stratification, from undoing the work Deleuze sees performed by cinema and that he would himself perform in the force field of philosophy (and again in the world) by filming cinema with his numerous and extraordinary descriptions/abstractions of its decontextualized relations? In short, how but through a studied myopia to keep philosophy from becoming a state-form?

The difficulty of the cinema books is a partial answer to these questions. The fact that there is only one periodization in the books provides another answer. Their concepts are neither hierarchized nor even serialized. Although the concepts emerge from each other and draw on each other, they are not locked into any strict array. Yet, for all that, they have the aura of a profound interdependence. Just as with the films Deleuze writes about, the movement of his concepts sets up alternate economies of forces. These alternate economies are economies of movement, of time, of knowing that are not/*have not yet been* produced on a massive scale. This refusal of stratification, the refusal of concepts to become knowledge in Foucault's sense of the word, makes Deleuze's concepts of the cinema as difficult to understand within their "system" as it is to understand the "system" itself. His "system," if one had but world enough and time, would, I fear, end up like the proverbial Chinese emperor's map of the kingdom that is as big as the kingdom itself — not much of a map for the Chinese emperor, not much of a system for the philosopher. The system is manifest rather as a mode of production — one learns one's way around by following a path and by wandering about. Deleuze is not building a system; he is making pieces, pieces for us to use in our own constructions, pieces at once so delicately, precisely, and *precariously* placed that as soon as we touch them, they become something else. Cinema is for Deleuze a machine that makes machines. Deleuze machines concepts from cinema's flows. The consistency of the flow of Deleuze's concepts one from the other, their complex yet ultimately undecidable relations to an unconceptualizable whole of cinema, is a negation of what for Deleuze is fascistic understanding, an understanding that takes the form of recognition, of history. This recognition, which for Deleuze and Guattari confirms the clichés of prefabricated thought, prevents the encounter.[9] It is not that Deleuze does not recognize questions of political economy and the development of the forces of production; he writes to preclude these modes of analysis because he considers them dead-ends. The ostensible consistency of method in the cinema books, a consistency that withstands a thousand variations of angle, illumination, and content without cohering as an object, is here at once the sign of the game of philosophy and its undoing as a state-form in Deleuze's terms.

This fluidity then is very much like the *Grundrisse*, the first draft of *Capital*, with one important (historical) difference: it is "postdialectical," nonhierarchical, and nontotalizing. Yet the question of dialectics persists; the concerns of the economic as a determinant of production remain. Like the cinema books, the *Grundrisse* is also not a solid; it is as well precisely a representation of production *process.* In the *Grundrisse* one cannot understand the commodity-form without understanding the entire process of exchange. One cannot understand exchange without understanding circulation and production. One cannot understand circulation and production without understanding money. One cannot understand money without understanding wage labor. One cannot understand wage labor without understanding necessary labor-time and surplus labor-time. One cannot understand these without understanding the falling rate of profit and so on until one can see the grand functioning of all aspects of Marx's great mimetic model with each mutually interactive, dialectical concept spinning into and from the others, mutually defined. Deleuze's concepts, in contrast, all precisely defined and interactive, create discrete images of a totality, the totality of cinema. These image-concepts are individuated and noninterdependent, yet another thousand plateaus. As with Marx, the process of this totality occurs offscreen, as it were (as "metaphysics"), but unlike Marx, Deleuze's conceptual architecture cannot, even in theory, be grasped in its entirety — totality for Deleuze is not, strictly speaking, a concept. For Deleuze the process of consciousness is unremittingly material but can never be fully posited conceptually. This is in part because the concepts abstracted from the materials that make up a filmic thought arise from the way the elements combine with each other but then fall away to be replaced with a seemingly ceaseless stream of new formations, and in so doing, necessarily posit a world outside. However, unlike dialectics, the logic embedded in the concept (the abstraction of the material articulation of form) tells us nothing final about what *is* beyond the frame: hence the plateau, the *auteur*, the assem blage, and Deleuze himself. *Deleuze* makes the link, not history or necessity, or any such narrator. The method here is not differentiation and sublation but differentiation and *transgression*. One moves across, not through and beyond. But the necessity of moving across the infinity of proliferations, the tireless press of movement, becomes a beyond — quantity becomes quality — even for Deleuze. This beyond is precisely the condition of possibility for the time-image. Even though he does not write "in the name of an outside," an outside appears. The precision of Deleuzian concepts taken together with the impossibility of finding an underlying logic that explains them in their totality make them figurations of the fact of an unconceptualizable beyond; they become intimations of an unconceptualizable immensity, an infinity of movement, in short, sublime.

Recall the way each of the sections in the cinema books ends: phrases like "the three time-images all break with indirect representation, but also shatter the empirical continuation of time, the chronological succession, the separation of the before and after. They are thus connected with each other and interpenetrate . . . but allow the distinction of their signs to subsist in a particular work";[10] or, "It is these three aspects, topological, of probabilistic [*sic*], and irrational which constitute the new image of thought. Each is easily inferred from the others, and forms with the others a circulation: the noosphere."[11] What I am interested in here, aside from the fact that the meaning of cinema for Deleuze is ultimately thought, is the motion of the phrasing. In the cinema books a summary of what came before is already a going after. These are examples of the Deleuzian cut, which as it finishes something off begins it anew in another key. Always leaving something behind, always moving on to something else, the Deleuzian cut is always, infinitely in-between.

The mode of production in the cinema books is well described in *A Thousand Plateaus*. In the chapter entitled "How Do You Make Yourself a Body without Organs?" Deleuze and Guattari say:

> This is how it should be done: Lodge yourself on a stratum, experiment with the opportunities it offers, find an advantageous place on it, find potential movements of deterritorialization, possible lines of flight, experience them, produce flow conjunctions here and there, try out continuums of intensities segment by segment, have a small plot of new land at all times. It is through meticulous relation with the strata that one succeeds in freeing the lines of flight, causing conjugated flows to pass and escape and bringing forth continuous intensities for a BwO. Connect, conjugate, continue: a whole "diagram," as opposed to still signifying and subjective formations. We are in a social formation; first see how it is stratified for us and in us and at the place where we are; then descend from the strata to the deeper assemblage within which we are held; gently tip the assemblage, making it pass over to the plane of consistency.[12]

Deleuze understands such occupation and tipping as characteristic of the cinema. Whether in the dialectical yearning of the image he elaborates in Sergei Eisenstein, the interval he expostulates in Dziga Vertov, the free and indirect discourse of Pier Paolo Pasolini, the duration of the time-images from the films of Yasujirō Ozu, the effect present in the masterpiece is one of an actual retreading of perception and hence of thought. Cinema connects, conjugates, and continues, making us pass over into something else. For as Deleuze says, "Cinema's concepts are not given in cinema.... Cinema itself is a new practice of images and signs whose theory philosophy must produce as a conceptual practice."[13] For Deleuze, this practice checkmates prefabricated thought and releases desire, either pushing thought beyond itself into its own unthought or, as Deleuze puts it by paraphrasing Antonin Artaud, making thought aware that it is *"not yet thinking."*[14] As the body undergoes new forms of viscerality, new forms of thought are produced.

I am suggesting that the encounter with the paralysis of thought, the encounter with the immensity of the not-yet thought that results for Deleuze in an encounter with the sublime, marks at once a moment in the retooling of our sensoriums and cinema's encounter with the immensity of, for lack of a better term, the world-system. The retooling of the sensorium that occurs in the encounters with the unrepresentable occasions in the work of Deleuze a retooling of philosophy. Though I can only suggest it here, it should turn out that the experiences of events in the cinema are, from the standpoint of capital, experiments about what can be done with the body by machines and by the circulation of capital. Not all of these visceral events turn out to be equal. The structures and intensities of surrealism, for example, seem thus far to have had greater possibilities for capital expansion (for example, MTV) than those of Russian suprematism, but perhaps that too will change. Deleuze's conceptualization of these events (the encounters between machines, value, and minds) is, as he himself states, a finding of concepts for forms. The cinema books, it seems to me, grapple in the language of concepts with the *darstellung* of cinema in a manner similar to the way in which Marx's *Capital*, or better, the *Grundrisse* (because there one sees the thought happening), grapples with the *darstellung* of capital. Deleuze's books are at once an attempt to translate the logic of cinema into an explicitly conceptual language and an excrescence of cinema. Philosophy endeavors to film the thought of cinema — its thinking — just as Marx endeavored to make the film of capital in which capital is the screen across which each moment of production passes. If capital realizes itself as cinema, that is, if industrial capital gives way to the society of the spectacle, one might well imagine cinema, with respect to the body, geography, labor, raw material, and time, to have become the most radically deterritorializing force since capital itself. As production itself moves into the visual, the visceral, the sensual, the cultural, cinema emerges as a higher form of capital — a form capable of coordinating all of the (dialectically) prior moments.

To show the relevance of Deleuze's cinema to the visual economy and the cinematic mode of production, I have noted that there is really only one explicitly historical thesis in the cinema books, a thesis that at once unifies and divides the two volumes. "Why," asks Deleuze, "is the Second World War taken as a break [between the movement-image and the time-image, between *Cinema 1* and *Cinema 2*]?"

> The fact is that in Europe, the post-war period has greatly increased the situations which we no longer know how to react to, in spaces which we no longer know how to describe.... [These] situations could be extremes, or, on the contrary, those of everyday banality, or both at once [Deleuze's exhibit A is the neorealism of Rossellini]: what tends to collapse is the sensory-motor schema which constituted the action-image of the old cinema. And thanks to this loosening of the sensory-motor linkage, it is time, "a little time in the pure state," which rises up to the surface of the screen. Time ceases to be derived from the movement, it appears in itself.[15]

The emergence of what Deleuze calls the time-image is a result of the increase in the number of situations to which we do not know how to respond. For Deleuze it leads directly to the sublime, and he produces it as such. That the time-image is also a response to the informatics of culture and to informatics itself, to what Benjamin called in "The Storyteller" a decline of experience, should also be clear: "Was it not noticeable after the war [that is, World War I] that men returned from the battlefield grown silent —

not richer, but poorer in communicable experience?"[16] Shock, whether from war, from modern life in the metropolis, or from the profusion of information, severs organic (low-speed, traditional, nonmetropolitan) human relationships. In fact the organization of warfare, metropolitan life, and information is functionally a continuum. The tendency toward the severing of experience and language is manifest in the development of this organizational continuum.

Deleuze notes that "the life or afterlife of cinema depends upon its internal struggle with informatics."[17] Here in *Cinema 2*, Deleuze, again very close to the Benjamin of "The Storyteller," writes with the desire to ward off the categoricality of capital-thought, that is, the degradation (reification) of thought and experience that comes with the mass-communicational regime — information's procrustean bed. For Deleuze the category of the time-image with its attendant sublimity, its ability to cancel or bully thought and identification, names a multiplex of forms that cinema (the ultimate body without organs) as contemporary consciousness actualizes as resistance to molarity, to the field of stratification, to the plane of organization of which the overarching force is capitalism and its spatial, temporal, and perceptual orders. But the question arises regarding just what is being made — schizophrenia, understood as the breaking up of old identities, temporalities, and metaphysical conceits, is without doubt essential to capitalist production today. The fields of stratification destroyed by Deleuze's masterpieces are marked by the reification endemic to capital process, but many of the social forms first broken up and decoded by the masterpieces of cinema are being broken up in and for capitalist society by dominant culture (the culture of dominance) today. Their overcoming *as well as their recoding* must be taken as forms of labor. Indeed such overcomings and recodings take place all the time in the practice of everyday life. In the social sciences such work, when it exists in an unofficial and hence unaccounted for economic form, is referred to as informal economy or disguised wage labor.[18] I am attempting to figure such unofficial, unrecognized labor practices as a cultural activity necessary, among other things, to bridge the gap between the noncorrespondence of language and experience.

Elsewhere in *Cinema 2*, cinema's struggle with the informatics of capitalism is made more explicit:

> The cinema as art lives in direct relation with a permanent plot, an international conspiracy that conditions it from within, as the most intimate and indispensable enemy. This conspiracy is that of money; what defines industrial art is not mechanical reproduction but the internalized relation with money. The only rejoinder to the harsh law of cinema — a minute of image which costs a day of collective work is Fellini's: "When there is no more money left, the film will be finished." Money is the obverse of all images that the cinema shows and sets in place so that films about money are already, if implicitly, films within the film or about the film.[19]

Deleuze argues that the film within the film is in one way or another a film about the film's economic conditions of possibility. One should take the citation from Fellini at once literally (when the filmmaker runs out of money his film is finished) and absolutely (when and if the money-form becomes obsolete, film will be outmoded, which in a way it is). Though Deleuze says disappointingly little about film's direct relation with "a permanent plot, an international conspiracy that conditions it from within," it is clear that for him cinema as forms of thought is locked into a dire struggle with capitalism. The cinema of masterpieces is at once enabled and threatened by the schizophrenia of capital. For Deleuze the criteria of the masterpiece is the schizophrenic relation to hegemony — its adherence to and its deviations from the law of money.

After writing that "the cinema confronts its most internal presupposition, money," Deleuze goes on to claim that in cinema "we are giving image for money, giving time for image, converting time, the transparent side, and money, the opaque side, like a spinning top on its end."[20] I suggest that this statement is, for Deleuze, an implicit recognition of the dialectical relationship between cinema and money, despite the fact that Deleuze wants to subtend the dialectic and recognize only a moment in its iterative shape. He says that the relationship between time and money, with respect to cinema, is one of reciprocal presupposition, but a reciprocal relationship that is not dialectical but as Deleuze emphasizes, merely "dissymmetrical." Deleuze's example to illustrate the dissymmetricality of the relationship between cinema and money is Marx's expression M-C-M (money-commodity-money), which Marx contrasts to C-M-C (commodity-money-commodity), the symmetrical exchange of equivalents. The formulation C-M-C, Deleuze writes, "is that of equivalence, but M-C-M is that of impossible equivalence or tricked dissymmetrical exchange."[21] Though for Marx it is the very mystery of the dissymmetrical relationship money-commodity-money that produces for him a critique of political economy (the second "money" being greater than the first "money" raises the whole question of the production of value), for Deleuze this dissymmetricality produces the category of the unthought, "money as the totality of the film."[22] Though totality is the conceptual zone for the emergence of a theory of social production, Deleuze strikes a somewhat more ontological note here: "This is the old curse which undermines the cinema: time is money. If it is true that movement maintains a set of exchanges or an equivalence, a symmetry as an invariant, time is by nature the conspiracy of unequal change or the impossibility of equivalence."[23] Even here, however, one could read Deleuze allegorically: the movement-image is circulation; the time-image is production.

"It is this unthought element which haunts the cinema of the time-image (e.g., *Citizen Kane* and the unthought and unthinkable Rosebud which conditions the chrono-logical unfolding of the film)."[24] This unthought is, for me,

precisely political economy, and though Deleuze sees the *formal* struggle of
cinema with money, he does not read this M-C-M of cinema as part of a
continuing circuit of flow; that is, he reads the struggle as primarily formal
(that is, impacting on the film-form) and, once the film is made, complete
(the film is finished), rather than actual and ongoing. But this is like imag-
ining the function of a bomb is at an end when it leaves the factory. The
film is an expressive machine, yes, but for Deleuze it remains primarily an expression. Rather, the film as an M-C-M relation will be bound by this logic
of profit (and unseen work), both as a particular individual production and
as part of an institution. The codification of the M-C-M progression is the
condition of the film, and it is in vain to imagine that its existence in the
world will not somehow be bound to it — that the film and its product, "time"
for Deleuze, will have to play by the rules of money throughout its life span
and across the entire range of its function. The aesthetic and visceral zones
nascent in film-spectator cybernesis are the new arenas of production for a
new order of industrialization. The individual film will have to ratify capital
both at the level of immediate profit for investors in what is recognizable as
standard financial exchange but also in the other transaction I have been trying to articulate, the dissymmetrical exchange, that is, the exchange without
equivalent. At a first level of analysis, the former, that is, the cash transaction,
is part of what Marx refers to as simple circulation, the exchange of equivalents. One use value is given for another: coin is given for the modicum of
pleasure (and whatever else) the film promises. The latter, in contrast, the extraction of surplus value through attention, is altogether different from paying
for a ticket. However, though different from the actual sale of tickets and
fees for distribution, and so on, by which a film directly and obviously recoups
a part of its investment, the production of value via attention is inseparable
from even this ostensibly transparent form of exchange. First, the social form
of film as cult value, what brings people into the theaters in the first place,
comes from the perception of others' perception — the gazes of others accrete on the image and increase its value. In addition, films pave the roads
for future films (building theaters, projectors, sound systems, and desires) and
for capital in general, meaning bourgeois/first-world popular culture and its
fallout (imperialism/neocolonialism). In short, spectators simultaneously ratify the image (valorize it) and retool themselves for the changing demands of
social life. Both activities are socially productive labor.

By putting spectators to work in their machines, films produce batteries of
psychosocial possibilities that exist as standing reserve for future deployment.
Each libidinal vector, each attracting pose, is created within the constraints
of the money system and, depending upon the attention it garners, attains a
certain specific gravity in the ocean of forms lying in wait for future attrac-
tions. Spectators are rewarded with pleasure and a little time, but this is the
commodity they purchased in the first place. It is a means to life, bus fare

in the image of the linguistic sign) under the referential function of the sign: a denoted real and a representational image.

The sign, Guattari specifies,[32] is cut off from the real because it must pass through the mental world of representations. To be cut off from material intensities is to be trapped in a "signifying ghetto" lorded over by a despotic signifier whose goal is to "treat everything that appears in order to represent it through a process of repetition which refers only to itself."[33] Signification echoes to infinity because it is supremely redundant. The subjectivity produced in the world of signification is a shut-in, a semiological shipwreck. Enunciative polyvocity is crushed by being split between a subject of enunciation and the subject of the statement: "The subject of the statement has become the respondent of the subject of enunciation by the effect of a sort of reductive echolalia."[34] This splitting effectively accomplishes the individuation, personalization, and gender specification of the subject of the statement bound to *je–tu–il–elle*. Polyvocity becomes bi(uni)vocity. In all of this, Guattari's goal remains the discovery of "the residual traces, the transversal flights of a collective assemblage of enunciation which constitutes the real productive insistence of all semiotic machinism."[35] In order to reach this schizoanalytic goal, Guattari requires a third category.

The third category is that of a-signifying semiotics. There is a circular connection, skirting around signifying semiologies, between form and matter but without leaving — unlike a-semiotic encodings — the expression and content planes. It is this circularity that allows a-signifying semiotics to remain independent of, and in a nonhierarchical relation with, signifying semiologies and language. Guattari specifies that a-signifying semiotics retain, however, a partial use for signifying semiologies. The polysemiotic connections established between the abstract machines (form) and material intensities escape, then, the overcoding functions of signifying semiological systems. But they are neither completely deterritorialized nor reterritorialized. Consider an example from linguistics such as idioms. Idioms jump over denotation and form assemblages by grouping existing words together, giving them new connotations. Idioms even focus on what are called "prone words" (such as, in English, "take" and "get") and hijack them. The a-signifying semiotic potential of idiom formation is constantly threatened by paranoiac recodings of signifying semiologies (respectable academic grammar) that want to reduce them to a single proper, formal, substance. A-signifying semiotics leave behind significative redundancies for the production of nonredundant, even improbable, and original conjunctions of signs and material fluxes. Such conjunctions between semiotic and real material machines, which create a-signifying collective assemblages, do not imply that the semiotic machines are less real than the material machines, nor that the material machines are less semiotic. On the contrary, they share these attributes. The conjunctions between signs and fluxes, between abstract machines and material intensities, between form and matter, are all unmediated by representation; they are, in other words, in constant and direct contact. There is no need for recourse to representative structures. Guattari describes the shift from signifying semiologies to a-signifying semiotics in terms of the de-localization, de-privatization, an-oedipalization of the individuated subject of enunciation to a collective assemblage of enunciation. He correlates the individual with signification and the collective with machinic assemblage, adding that the signifier plus the signified and form plus substance equals signification (individuation of phantasms belonging to subjugated groups) and that collective assemblages of enunciation consisting of conjunctions of abstract machines and material fluxes belong to the phantasms of subject groups. Guattari then enumerates dialectically negative and positive attributes of the individual-collective relation: signification involves self-reference and thus the rupture of machinic conjunctions, whereas collective assemblages give up comprehension, being in some instance without signification for anyone, for the sake of creating meaning directly from the fluxes.[36] Signification thus has no machinic meaning because of the absence of conjunctions with the real fluxes.

The collective assemblages composed by creative machinic connections of semiotic and material fluxes cannot be individuated, having left the field of representation. A-signifying semiotic machines free desiring-production, the singularities of desire, from the signifiers of national, familial, personal, racial, humanist, and transcendent values (including the semiotic myth of a return to nature, to the presignifying world of a-semiotic encodings); in short, desiring-production is freed from all "territorializing alienations" and set coordinates.[37] But this freedom must not be exaggerated. Signifying semiologies are only tools to be employed in semiotics of schizoanalytic practice in and outside of the psychiatric institution. Assemblages are not, then, groups composed of individuals. Schizoanalytic mixed-semiotics has the task of "furthering the formation of relatively autonomous and untranslatable semiotic substances, by accommodating the sense and non-sense of desire as they are, by not attempting to adapt the modes of subjectification to signification and to dominant social laws. Its objective is not at all to recuperate facts and acts that are outside the norm; on the contrary, it is to make a place for the singularity traits of subjects who, for one reason or another, escape the common law."[38] For Guattari, this is the task of a genuine analytic practice. One of the important elements of this practice concerns the recognition that the subject in contact with desiring-machines in a-signifying semiotics oscillates between reterritorializations on signification and deterritorializations into new machinic conjunctions. This oscillation helps to explain why signifying semiologies still have a role to play. Guattari's semiotics is always, it needs to be emphasized, mixed. Further, on this point Guattari writes: "[I]n schizoanalysis free rein will be given to oedipalizing representations and paranoid-fascist fantasms in order to better plot the effects of their blockage of the fluxes, and to relaunch the process in a sort of machinic forward flight."[39] Indeed, one of the trademarks of Guattari's schizoanalysis is his focus on subjective redundancies (refrains, black holes, and so on).[40]

These technical details should not obscure the more general issue of whether or not the detour solves more problems for schizoanalysis than it creates. By the time Guattari published *L'inconscient machinique* in 1979, his reasons for turning to Hjelmslev had become more explicit. Guattari's opening salvos are directed against linguistic imperialists because they attempt to annex both semiotics and pragmatics and use structural analysis to depoliticize their domains of inquiry; these salvos lead at once to the choice of Hjelmslev as an alternative while running against the grain of glossematics. For if there is no language in itself (unified and autonomous), and if, on the contrary, language "always remains open to other modes of semioticization," as Guattari thinks,[41] then Hjelmslev's efforts to establish the truth of Saussure's linguistics must be counterbalanced (to say the least) in some manner. Guattari detours since he does not continue the Hjelmslevian project; instead, he takes up certain categories because they "appear to be the only ones resulting from a truly rigorous examination of the whole of the semiotic problematic, by drawing out, in particular, all of the consequences of calling into question the status of content and expression."[42] Guattari had, however, two regrets about glossematics: (1) "le bi-face hjelmslevien" of expression and content coincided with other "binarist reductions"; (2) Hjelmslev seemed to willingly participate in the sovereign overcoding of language when he wrote "in practice, a language is a semiotic into which all other semiotics may be translated,"[43] thus leaving ample room for the Barthesean reversal of Saussure's statement concerning the place of linguistics in semiology. Guattari wanted nothing to do with this dogma cherished by linguists.

Guattari's attention to the semiotic formation of substances on the planes of expression and content is nevertheless modeled on Hjelmslev's interpretation of the formation of linguistically unformed matter into substance. A language casts a shadow like a net over the amorphous thought-mass of purport and lays down boundaries in this sand; purport is continually reworked in different ways by different languages. The French word *car* (for, because) and the English word *car* (automobile) have the same expression-purport but different content-purport; the French *dix* (10) and the English *ten* (10) have the same content-purport but a different expression-purport. Guattari makes light of Hjelmslev's metaphors of the "net" and of "sand" by arguing that there are not, on the one side, "little building blocks of semiological construction and, on the other side, the amorphous mass of possibility."[44] For Guattari, the Hjelmslevian sand is already "as differentiated as the most material of matters." Anyone who has been to a beach would recognize this under foot.

There are, then, several species of signs and semiotic connections involved in the formation of matter and the conjugations of unformed material fluxes, and many of these are borrowed from the work of Charles Sanders Peirce. Although some semionauts hold that semiology lifted off under Hjelmslev from the Saussurean launching pad, it is Peirce, as Deleuze and Guattari write, who "is the true inventor of semiotics. That is why we can borrow his terms, even while changing their connotations." Deleuze and Guattari regret that Peircean icons, indexes, and symbols "are based on signifier-signified relations (contiguity for the index, similitude for the icon, conventional rule for the symbol); this leads him to make the 'diagram' a special case of the icon (the icon of relation)."[45] In order to liberate the diagram from the supposed yoke of the Saussureanism that infects icons, for example, Guattari in particular has developed the semiotic category of diagrammatism through the division of icon and diagrams along the lines of signifying semiotics and a-signifying semiotics, the latter involving signs that are more deterritorialized than icons.

Diagrammatic machines of signs elude the territorializing systems of symbolic and signifying semiologies by displaying a kind of reserve in relation to their referents, forgoing polysemy and eschewing lateral signifying effects. Although they have meaning for me, most of my scribbles concerning this notion did not make their way into this essay because they could not be translated into a communicable semiology. Still, such scribbles function independently "of the fact that they signify or fail to signify something for someone," which is only to say that they do not behave like well-formed signs in a universal system of signification and fail to pass smoothly through the simulacral dialogism of ideal models of communication.[46]

For Peirce, diagrammatic reasoning is iconic: "A Diagram is mainly an Icon, and an icon of intelligible relations in the constitution of its Object."[47] In Guattari's terminology, a diagram connects deterritorialized material fluxes without the authority of a signifying semiology. Returning to Peirce, a diagram is mainly but not exclusively an icon. It incorporates certain habits involved in the creation of graphic abstractions (in geometry and syllogistics); it also has the indexical feature of pointing "There!"[48] without, however, describing or providing any insight into its object. Since a diagram displays in itself the formal features of its object, it may be said to take the place of its object: "[T]he distinction of the real and the copy disappears, and it is for the moment a pure dream."[49] This simulation defies, Guattari specifies, the territorializing effects of representation and denotation. In Peirce's work, too, diagrams can be deterritorializing because they are iconic — icons do not lead one away from themselves to their objects; rather, they exhibit their object's characteristics in themselves. Icons can be indifferent to the demands of dominant semiotic formalizations. While a Peircean could rightly claim that Deleuze and Guattari have engaged in acts of interpretive violence by playing favorites with iconic phenomena, their approach to Peirce is, I think, uncannily Peircean. It needs to be recalled that Deleuze and Guattari feel no compulsion to honor the concepts that they borrow from their semiotic masters.

In their reading of this American master, Deleuze and Guattari adopt a Peircean attitude toward Peirce. They read him against himself by extending interpretation beyond his conventional definitions. This is precisely the approach Guattari adopted in his use of Hjelmslevian categories, and it is what Peirce called critical-philosophical thinking since it requires that one observe an author's line of thought, from which one then extrapolates imaginatively. Take, for example, Deleuze and Guattari's phrase: "Look at mathematics: it's not a science, it's a monster slang, it's nomadic."[50] This glance at mathematics is Peircean. An active mathematical mind is, according to Peirce, necessary for interpreting signs. The ability of mathematics to travel is part of its dynamic character. Peirce held that mathematical practice or what he called theorematic reasoning bears little relation to the semimechanical deductive inferences and demonstrations of logical calculus. A monster slang is not limited to a class or profession or generation. It is a playful practice involving active and creative experimentation. In his discussion of theorematic reasoning,[51] Peirce wrote: "It is necessary that something be DONE." An a-signifying abstract machine is diagrammatic. So too is theorematic reasoning. What was a necessary question for Lenin and Jerry Rubin was a question of necessity for Peirce. Points are made and stretched. Hypotheses are advanced. Algebraic relations pour forth. Pins are stuck in maps. Pages are covered in scribbles. Living mathematical thought involves the construction of diagrams and experiments with points, surfaces, lines, and so on. Deleuze and Guattari's diagram is also constructive. It conjugates physically and semiotically unformed matter; in Hjelmslev's linguistics, functives contract (draw together) their function. A diagram is a pure matter-function machine joining together and changing the shape of semio-chips — edges, points, particles, degrees of intensity, and so on. In short, the diagram facilitates connections between the most deterritorialized particles of expression and content. Diagrams are irreducible to icons, Guattari contends, because icons remain encysted in preestablished semiotic coordinates.[52] Guattari adds that semiotically formed substances may be diagrammaticized by being emptied as if pieces of them were flung centrifugally along certain vectors toward new spaces to which they cling.

Let's revisit Hjelmslev's metaphor of the net. Hjelmslevian purport is like sand that can be put into different molds (that is, the formal molds of different languages). In the formation of purport into a content-substance and expression-substance by content-form and expression-form, form lays down lines like a net casting its shadow onto an "undivided surface." For Guattari, this sand is already differentiated and in some ways formed, but not as a linguistic substance or even as semiotic substance. Is this net a diagram? The idea of this net throwing its shadow and "netting" purport is antithetical to certain aspects of Guattari's polysemiotic typology; the idea suggests that diagrammatic, a-signifying semiotic productions of meaning have not escaped the signifying machines of semiological authority. A-signifying semiotics establishes connections between material fluxes that have not been semiotically formed as substances, but these connections mix with signifying semiological substances, even of the most despotic types driven by signifier fetishism and the demands of structural isomorphism. The net is a signifying semiology driven by the linguistic domination of purport, but it is also full of a-signifying holes irreducible to the ties that bind it.

My own "prolegomenon" to an understanding of how Guattari does things with Hjelmslev in the end required a brief investigation of the semiotic of Peirce since Guattari enlivened the form-substance relation with the sign particles of a diagrammatic function borrowed and adapted from him. It would be necessary to examine in detail the schizoanalytic cartographies of Guattari (by which I mean literally his map- and diagram-making) in order to trace the subtleties of his brand of political polysemiotics.

Hjelmslev puts the linguist on guard against substance and warns of the extralinguistic seductions of purport. Guattari puts the glossematician on guard against formed substances. Hjelmslev's sand became substance for new linguistic forms, to which substance was inferior and upon which it depended. But Guattari thought that this kind of study of substance occluded the mapping of purport (unformed matter) about which linguistics, Hjelmslev believed, would not concern itself and, even if it did, could only come to know purport to the extent that it was formed. Guattari deviates from Hjelmslev on this point by deviating from Peirce and opening up the categories of a-semiotic encodings and a-signifying semiotics. It was clearly not a deviation from Deleuze and Guattari for Brian Massumi to begin his *User's Guide* with an analysis of a complex substance (woodworker-tools-wood) in order to develop the interrelations at play in its formation and to identify, among other things, its Hjelmslevian components. I have taken a different approach to a similar goal by reading Deleuze and Guattari (primarily the latter) through the problems inherent in glossematics. This is not so much a deviation as a study of how, programmatically at least, the vicissitudes of glossematics can serve schizoanalysis.

Notes

1. See Giulio C. Lepschy, "European Structuralism: Post-Saussurean Schools," in *Current Trends in Linguistics*, vol. 13, ed. T. A. Sebeok (The Hague: Mouton, 1975), 189; and idem, *La linguistique structurale*, trans. Louis-Jean Calvet (Paris: Payot, 1968), 81–98; see also Umberto Eco, *A Theory of Semiotics* (Bloomington: Indiana University Press, 1976), 54, and idem, "The Influence of Roman Jakobson on the Development of Semiotics," in *Classics of Semiotics*, ed. Martin Krampen, Klaus Oehler, Roland Posner, T. A. Sebeok, and Thure von Uexküll (New York: Plenum Press, 1981), 111.

2. Bertha Siertsema, *A Study Of Glossematics: Critical Survey of Its Fundamental Concepts*, 2d ed. (The Hague: Martinus Nijhoff, 1965 [1955]). See also the review of Siertsema by W. Haas, "Concerning Glossematics," *Archivum Linguisticum* 8, no. 2 (1956): 105.

3. André Martinet, "Au sujet des fondements de la théorie linguistique de Louis Hjelmslev," *Bulletin de la Société de Linguistique de Paris* 42 (1942–45): 19–43; for a later but no less influential paper, see idem, "La double articulation linguistique," in *Recherches structurales 1949: Interventions dans le débat glossématique: Publiée à l'occasion du cinquantenaire de M. L. Hjelmslev* (Copenhagen: Nordisk sprog-og kultur-forlag, 1970); Louis Hjelmslev, *Prolegomena to a Theory of Language*, trans. Francis J. Whitfield (Madison: University of Wisconsin Press, 1969 [1961]) (original: *Omkring Sprogteoriens Grundlaeggelse*, 1943).

4. Nicolas Ruwet, *An Introduction to Generative Grammar*, trans. Norval S. H. Smith (Amsterdam: North-Holland Publishing, 1973); idem, "La linguistique générale aujourd'hui," *Archives européennes de sociologie* 5 (1964): 277–310.

5. Louis Hjelmslev, *Le langage*, preface by A. J. Greimas (Paris: Minuit, 1966) (original: 1963); idem, *Prolégomènes à une théorie du langage* (Paris: Minuit, 1968) (English translation: *Language: An Introduction*, trans. Francis J. Whitfield [Madison: University of Wisconsin Press, 1970]); see the review by Nicole Gueunier for a general contextualization of the impact of the *Prolégomènes*, "Expression et contenu," *La quinzaine littéraire* 71 (16–30 April 1969): 24.

6. See especially Roland Barthes, "Eléments de sémiologie," *Communications* 4 (1964): 1–27 (English translation: *Elements of Semiology*, trans. Annette Lavers and Colin Smith [New York: Hill and Wang, 1968]). Barthes popularized what was already "in a sense" a popularization of glossematics (the *Prolegomena*), according to Francis Whitfield in the "editor's introduction" to Louis Hjelmslev, *Résumé of a Theory of Language* (Madison: University of Wisconsin Press, 1975).

7. Jean Baudrillard, *For a Critique of the Political Economy of the Sign*, trans. Charles Levin (St. Louis: Telos, 1981), 162ff. (original: 1972); see also my *Baudrillard and Signs* (London: Routledge, 1994), 1–27.

8. Gilles Deleuze and Félix Guattari, *Anti-Oedipus: Capitalism and Schizophrenia*, trans. Robert Hurley, Mark Seem, and Helen R. Lane (New York: Viking Press, 1977), 242 (original: 1972).

9. For a further clarification of this point see Brian Massumi, *A User's Guide to Capitalism and Schizophrenia: Deviations from Deleuze and Guattari* (Cambridge, Mass.: MIT Press, 1992), 154–55n. 45.

10. Louis Hjelmslev, "L'analyse structurale de langage," in *Essais linguistiques* (Paris: Minuit, 1971), 39.

11. Ferdinand de Saussure, *Course in General Linguistics*, trans. Wade Baskin (New York: McGraw-Hill, 1966), 232 (ms. 1906–11).

12. Paul L. Garvin, "Review of *Prolegomena to a Theory of Language*," *Language* 30, no. 1 (1954): 90.

13. Hjelmslev, "Linguistique structurale," in *Essais*, 31–32.

14. Deleuze and Guattari, *Anti-Oedipus*, 243, with slight changes from the English translation in accordance with the original text, *L'anti-oedipe*, new expanded edition (Paris: Minuit, 1975 [1972]), 288–89. See also Deleuze and Guattari, *A Thousand*

Plateaus, trans. Brian Massumi (Minneapolis: University of Minnesota Press, 1987 [1980]), 66ff. and 98ff.

15. Hjelmslev, *Prolegomena,* 57.

16. Ibid., 75.

17. Siertsema, *Study,* 61–63.

18. Ruwet, *Introduction,* 30.

19. Deleuze and Guattari, *Anti-Oedipus,* 242–43 and note.

20. Ruwet, *Introduction,* 293–94.

21. Félix Guattari, *La révolution moléculaire* (Fontenay-sous-Bois: Recherches, 1977), 307ff.

22. Ibid., 242.

23. Guattari, *L'inconscient machinique* (Fontenay-sous-Bois: Recherches, 1979), 39ff (English translation: "Semiological Subjection, Semiotic Enslavement," trans. Peter Trnka, in *The Guattari Reader* [Oxford: Blackwell, 1996], 145ff.).

24. Hjelmslev, *Prolegomena,* 52.

25. Jürgen Trabant, "Louis Hjelmslev: Glossematics as General Semiotics," trans. Ian Boyd Whyte, in *Classics of Semiotics,* ed. Martin Krampen et al. (New York: Plenum Press, 1981), 94.

26. Hjelmslev, *Prolegomena,* 57; Guattari, *Révolution moléculaire,* 278.

27. Hjelmslev, *Prolegomena,* 79.

28. Ibid., 106.

29. Ibid., 39.

30. Guattari, *Révolution moléculaire,* 279; see also idem, "The Place of the Signifier in the Institution," trans. Gary Genosko, in *The Guattari Reader,* 149.

31. Guattari, *Révolution moléculaire,* 253.

32. Ibid., 255.

33. Ibid., 256.

34. Ibid.

35. Ibid., 256–57.

36. Ibid., 260.

37. Ibid., 263.

38. Ibid., 284; see also idem, "The Place of the Signifier," 153.

39. Guattari, *Révolution moléculaire,* 269.

40. Massumi, *User's Guide,* 151n. 33.

41. Guattari, *L'inconscient machinique,* 25.

42. Ibid., 40; Guattari, "Semiological Subject," 145.

43. Hjelmslev, *Prolegomena,* 109.

44. Guattari, *L'inconscient machinique,* 205.

45. Deleuze and Guattari, *A Thousand Plateaus,* 531n. 41.

46. Guattari, *Révolution moléculaire,* 310–11.

47. Charles Sanders Peirce, *The Collected Papers,* ed. Charles Hartshorne and Paul Weiss (Cambridge, Mass.: Harvard University Press, 1935–1966), 4.531.

48. Ibid., 3.361.

49. Ibid., 3.362.

50. Deleuze and Guattari, *A Thousand Plateaus,* 24.

51. Peirce, *Collected Papers,* 4.233.

52. Ibid., 141ff.; Guattari, *L'inconscient machinique,* 224.

Becoming a Body without Organs

The Masochistic Quest of Jean-Jacques Rousseau

Bryan Reynolds

Jean-Jacques Rousseau sweated, urinated, defecated, and ejaculated. He produced and reproduced. Like all human beings, according to the "schizo-analytic" theory of Gilles Deleuze and Félix Guattari, Rousseau was a desiring-machine; he was desiring-production, desiring because of desire's natural desire to produce desire. For Deleuze and Guattari, desire is both the subject and object of desire; it is not about acquisition or lack but rather about production and a process of desiring-production; it cannot be defined as the lack of a real object. This is not to assert that one cannot feel the lack of a real object and therefore direct one's desire toward that real object, but that one does not desire simply as a result of feeling the lack of a real object — or anything else. To comprehend desire as only lack is to disregard "the intrinsic power of desire to create its own object — if only in an unreal, hallucinatory, or delirious form — or from representing this causality as stemming from within desire itself."[1]

For the myth of desire-as-lack to achieve axiomatic status, the material world would have to lack at least one real object, a paradoxically missing yet known object that desire experiences as lack. This out-of-this-world object would have to account for the desire and production of things not modeled on things already existent in this world. It would have to account for such phenomena as innovation, invention, and science fiction. But inasmuch as the probability of an imagined and existent out-of-this-world reality is an overwhelming impossibility, so is the desire-as-lack formulation. Deleuze and Guattari point out that if we were to accept the notion of desire as the lack of the real object and that its existence as a real entity thus depends upon an essence of lack (as explained by psychoanalysis), desire would still have to produce, at some point, a fantasized or symbolic object that functions as a double of reality. Hence, it is illogical to insist that feelings of lack or an imaginary object are requisite to the inspiration, conception, and actuality of desire.

Deleuze and Guattari maintain that desire is only a machine producing the

191

desire for production, a condition perpetuated by additional desiring-machines as the by-products of the desire for production. This process of desiring-production necessitates a chain of desiring-machines that is continuous and generative. Rousseau was a desiring-machine, and he was comprised of various desiring-machines connected to other desiring-machines, both inside and outside of his own body:

> [O]ne machine is always coupled with another.... [T]here is always a flow-producing machine, and another machine connected to it that interrupts or draws off part of this flow (the breast — the mouth). And because the first machine is in turn connected to another whose flow it interrupts or partially drains off, the binary series is linear in every direction.[2]

Desiring-machines never constitute a whole, but rather each is a component of a universal continuum of ceaseless production and consumption. In other words, desire is an innate psychic force that is always already compelled to create/produce. This force in effect produces stimuli, real (progeny, dry goods, businesses) or unreal (fictions, dreams, hallucinations), which in turn stimulate its congenital yearning to create (desiring-production), causing it to create more stimuli, and so on. Desire is a desiring-machine that manufactures, in every way possible and with any available materials, the desire to produce. As parts of a psychic mechanism, desiring-machines are not merely thought-machines or dream-machines. They are machines that work to elevate, ultimately, the intensity of desiring-production. Unless there is repression, desiring-machines have no fixed object of desire other than desiring-production. If there is repression, which is almost always the case, the desiring-machines become disorganized and wayward; they desire not only desiring-production but also other usually exterior and real objects, and their subjects are other desiring-machines connected to the repressed desiring-machines. Desiring-machines subsequently produce a reality of desiring-production that parallels the vast social production that is itself a collective result of the similar desiring-machines of numerous individuals.

For Deleuze and Guattari, need is derived from desiring-machines. It is the counterproduct within the real that is manufactured by desire, and lack is a countereffect of desiring-production within this real that is natural and socially constructed. Desiring-machines create voids that they need to fill. Ergo they search for the materials that their bodies and minds, the communal products of other bodies, have determined to be lacking. Lack is never primary to production because production is never organized on the basis of a preexisting need or lack. Both need and lack develop and operate in the social realm of the real created by desiring-machines. As a counterproduct of the pressures of antiproductivity, lack is founded, designed, and instituted by the business of social production: "This involves deliberately organizing wants and needs (*manque*) amid an abundance of production; making all fall victim to the

great fear of not having one's needs satisfied; and making the object dependent upon a real production that is supposedly exterior to desire (the demands
of rationality), while at the same time the production of desire is categorized
as fantasy and nothing but fantasy."[3] Deleuze and Guattari claim that psychoanalysis stifles and besmirches the favorable processes of desiring-production
and social production by speciously shunting them into a conception of unconscious representation that associates, reduces, and comprehends everything
(the productive unconscious, desiring-machines, desiring-production) as an
expression of the unconscious. "The unconscious ceases to be what it is — a
factory, a workshop — to become a theater, a scene and its staging"; it becomes
a theatrical representation of the oedipal familial romance, and "the psychoanalyst becomes a director for a private theater, rather than the engineer or
mechanic who sets up units of production, and grapples with collective agents
of production and antiproduction."[4] This idea of the unconscious marks from
the beginning psychoanalysis's own bankruptcy or abnegation: an unconscious
(or preconscious) that no longer produces but is content to believe. It believes
in its own theatricality; it believes in desire-as-lack; it believes in Oedipus, in
castration, in the law. In short, it can be brainwashed to believe in just about
anything. Once the unconscious has been forced to bow down to psychoanalysis, it is easy for the conscious individual to be deluded and controlled.
This person is now forever vulnerable to the uncertainty, guilt, shame, and
anxiety instituted by oedipalization.[5]

Deleuze and Guattari's theory of the productive unconscious attempts to
explain irregularities and unconventionalities in human thought and behavior
in relation to the antiproductivity with which they are commonly associated.
The oedipal paradigm is displaced by a paradigm of constant struggle between the desire for the intensity of desiring-production and the desire for
the plane of consistency proper to desire on which desire is immanent and
pure intensities flow free from the impulse to produce. Existing alongside the
connective syntheses achieved by the desiring-machines are the disjunctive
syntheses achieved on this plane. Deleuze and Guattari call these disjunctive syntheses "the body without organs (BwO)." The desiring-machines and
the BwO coexist as two separate yet interrelated constituents of the psychic
process of repulsion and attraction, antiproduction and production, deterritorialization and reterritorialization, that extends beyond the individual and into
the social world. Freud has a somewhat similar theory known as the "pleasure principle," in which the "mental apparatus endeavors to keep the quantity
of excitation present in it as low as possible or at least to keep it constant"
in an effort to attenuate or avoid "unpleasurable tension."[6] The main difference between Deleuze and Guattari's and Freud's theories lies in the greater
degree to which the BwO theory is seen as critical to the interpretation of
all psychic phenomena. The BwO theory maintains that there is an ideal to
which all human beings continually aspire, whether consciously or not. This

ideal is the psychic state in which we experience ourselves as nothing other than a deterritorialized, antiproductive, and uninterrupted continuum of excitant desire. In this state, the desiring-machines no longer desire the intensity of desiring-production: there is no production; there is only the electric fervor of desire. Simply put, all human beings wish to become a body without organs: no brain, no ears, no eyes, no stomach, no heart, no lungs, no kidneys, no clitoris, no penis, and so on. "The BwO is what remains when you take everything away."[7]

The totalized BwO, according to Deleuze and Guattari, possesses neither awareness of needs or lacks nor burdensome organs. To possess organs is, by nature of their accessibility, to attract persistent harassment from desiring-production. In the words of Antonin Artaud, "When you will have made him a body without organs, then you will have delivered him from all his automatic reactions and restored him to his true freedom."[8] The human-being/desiring-machines is a battlefield. The psychic mechanisms of desiring-production strive to cross over, break into, and utilize the always already desiring to be static BwO. In no way a docile body, the BwO repels and represses the desiring-machines since it experiences them as enemies of its ecstatic, antiproductive existence. According to Artaud,

> The body is the body
> it is all by itself
> and has no need of organs
> the body is never an organism
> organisms are the enemies of the body.[9]

However, the repulsion and repression of desiring-machines by the BwO is not enough to prevent desiring-production. The conflict between the desiring-machines and the BwO is an inherently never-ending one. As mentioned above, the BwO's repression of the desiring-machines encourages desiring-production as attention is deflected away from the BwO; this causes the designation of external objects of desire and creates the desire to produce these objects. Pursuit of these objects by the desiring-machines serves to defer a complete takeover of the BwO. Yet the BwO also limits its own potentiality of ever fully inhabiting the deterritorialized ideal. The strenuousness of the endless tussle between the desiring-machines and the BwO causes the BwO to respond paranoically to a counterinside or counteroutside in the form of a persecuting organ or some exterior agent of persecution. Ultimately, both the BwO and the desiring-machines locate something external on which to demonstrate their redirected desires, misdirected retaliations, and persistent frustrations. The outside, outer-body world becomes the virtual battlefield and recording surface for the internal struggle.

Hence, there is no certain or easy way to become a BwO. In fact, Deleuze and Guattari claim that "you never reach the Body without Organs, you can't reach it, you are forever attaining it, it is a limit.... But you're already on it, scurrying like a vermin, groping like a blind person, or running like a lunatic: desert traveller and nomad of the steppes."[10] Nevertheless, according to Deleuze and Guattari's schizoanalytic theory, at least five types of bodies can come close to realizing the BwO, even though their proximity to it can be encumbering, expensive, and perhaps fatal: (1) the hypochondriac body, which disorganizes and eventually destroys its own organs through neglect and drug-abuse; (2) the paranoid body, which though delightfully preoccupied, must always be under attack; (3) the schizophrenic body, waging its own personal war against the organs, at the cost of catatonia; (4) the drugged body, which is depressingly ephemeral and afflicted sporadically by withdrawal; and (5) the masochist body, which usually suffers unforeseen and frequently destabilizing side effects and almost always requires the assistance of a sadist.

For the purpose of this "schizoanalysis," as coined by Deleuze and Guattari, I will examine the masochistic, hypochondriac, and paranoiac Jean-Jacques Rousseau. Intelligibly revealing Rousseau's struggle to make himself a BwO, and not yet muddled by the ideology of psychoanalysis and capitalism, the exemplary self-conscious, autobiographical writings of Rousseau seem to invite a schizoanalytic investigation. This essay is therefore an attempt to present a schizoanalytic literary-critical model from which we can better understand both the theory of the body without organs as well as the rich experiences of Jean-Jacques Rousseau.

The joy of steady pain was discovered by Rousseau at the youthful age of eight. Deleuze and Guattari explain that this type of joy is fundamentally different from pleasure. They point out that it is commonly and erroneously asserted that the masochist, like everybody else, quests for pleasure, but can only attain it via pain and fantasized humiliations, which function to alleviate or deflect deep anxiety. Instead, Deleuze and Guattari maintain that

> the masochist's suffering is the price he must pay, not to achieve pleasure, but to untie the pseudobond between desire and pleasure as an extrinsic measure. Pleasure is in no way something that can be attained only by a detour through suffering; it is something that must be delayed as long as possible because it interrupts the continuous process of positive desire. There is, in fact, a joy that is immanent to desire as though desire were filled by itself and its contemplations, a joy that implies no lack or impossibility and is not measured by pleasure since it is what distributes intensities of pleasure and prevents them from being suffused by anxiety, shame, and guilt. In short, a masochist uses suffering as a way of constituting a body without organs and bringing forth a plane of consistency of desire.[11]

Rousseau's description of his earliest encounter with pain, punitively inflicted upon him by his surrogate mother, Mlle Lambercier, illustrates Deleuze

and Guattari's idea of the necessary postponement of pleasure.[12] It shows
how pleasure-postponement operates on both individual and social levels as
a means of control and a way of approaching the BwO. Unlike Freud's
"reality principle," which "does not abandon the intention of ultimately attaining pleasure, but it nevertheless demands and carries into effect the
postponement of satisfaction, the abandonment of a number of possibilities
of gaining satisfaction and the temporary toleration of unpleasure as a step
on the long indirect road to pleasure,"[13] Deleuze and Guattari's understanding
of pleasure-postponement is not really about "toleration" or "unpleasure" or
"postponement of satisfaction." For the most part, it is about precisely the opposite. By postponing pleasure, say Deleuze and Guattari, the joy of constant
desire is strongly intensified, and it is from this intensity of joyful desire, and
not from the vitality of pleasure, that a profound satisfaction is derived.

Rousseau recalls that Mlle Lambercier initially "confined herself to threats,
and the threat of a punishment entirely unknown to me frightened me sufficiently" (25). But what does Rousseau mean by "frightened me sufficiently"?
Inasmuch as the terrorizing threats of a mysterious castigation did not prevent Rousseau from pursuing and eventually receiving this castigation, it is
difficult to determine in what way he was sufficiently frightened or why he
relates the circumstances in a positive tone. Rousseau's affirmative reading of
the situation is further revealed when he declares that he "earned," rather than,
say, "received" or "suffered," the chastisements that were finally inflicted upon
him. Rousseau seems to have found Mlle Lambercier's threats sufficient because he actually enjoyed the terror effected and perpetuated by them. After
all, it was this original experience with the intensity of this terror that induced him to seek, consciously or not, the unknown punishment. It is not
surprising, then, that Rousseau says, "when in the end I was beaten I found
the experience less dreadful in fact than in anticipation; and the very strange
thing was that this punishment increased my affection for the inflicter" (25).
Rousseau's comprehension of his "anticipation" is comparable to Deleuze and
Guattari's notion of the joy that is immanent to desire. That is, when "in
anticipation," Rousseau was in the impassioned and uninterrupted state of
desiring-alleviation from the terror, which, in his case, required the realization of the feared punishment. Yet, like pleasure, the punishment had to be
delayed as long as possible since it would interrupt the continuous process of
positive desire necessitated by the duration and intensity of the terror, unless,
of course, the punishment itself was to be administered continuously. In this
case, the joyful process of positive desire, the desire for alleviation from the
punishment, would be ceaseless.

Whereas, as Rousseau acknowledges, there might have been "some degree
of precocious sexuality" in his increased affection for the inflicter (25), Deleuze and Guattari would assert that it was primarily the joyful effects of
the beating that caused Rousseau to contemplate deliberately earning more

beatings. Nevertheless, Rousseau did not intentionally earn more beatings: "It required all the strength of my devotion and all my natural gentleness to prevent me from deliberately earning another beating; I had discovered in the shame and pain of the punishment an admixture of sensuality which had left me rather eager than otherwise for a repetition by the same hand" (25). However unconsciously, Rousseau behaved in such a way as to keep himself on the verge of being punished; he lingered on the very brink of punishment, and he did this to sustain the fervor of positive desire brought about by the terror and anticipation that such circumstances forced him to endure. However consciously, Rousseau avoided the blatantly masochistic joy of his population by intensities of what Deleuze and Guattari call "pain-waves."[14] He declares, "[I]f I refrained from earning a fresh punishment, it was only out of fear of annoying Mlle Lambercier" (26). Although Rousseau opted for the more socially acceptable joy that is immanent to the process of positive desire connected to his "fear of annoying Mlle Lambercier," which is probably less intense than the joy connected to the corporeal punishment, he did not allow his masochistic quest for the supreme intensity of BwO status to be tempered or led astray so easily, at least not during this callow and eager stage of his life.

After putting it off presumably as long as possible, to reap fully the benefits of the socially imposed terror (anxiety, shame, and guilt) that was associated with his conventionally aberrant and "strange taste" for pain-waves (27–28), Rousseau acquired another punishment: "[T]he next occasion, which I postponed, although not through fear [of the punishment], occurred through no fault of mine — that is to say I did not act deliberately" (26). Aware that this beating would probably be his last because he would not respond to it as Mlle Lambercier would expect, since "Mlle Lambercier had no doubt detected signs that this punishment was not having the desired effect" (26), for he enjoyed the beatings, therefore giving her no reason to persist with this kind of punishment, Rousseau chose to remain in the state of desiring-pain-waves ("I did not act deliberately"). In other words, because it was likely that Mlle Lambercier would discover that he enjoyed the beatings and thus cease to administer them, Rousseau avoided the beatings in order to prolong his painful craving for them; that is, he wanted to prolong the intense state of desiring-pain-waves caused by his desperate longing for the beatings. The intensity of this painful craving was potentially longer lasting, more economically painful, than the pain-intensities of any final beating. Insofar as the longevity of this desiring-condition would probably prove more rewarding than either the state of desiring-alleviation from the fear of punishment or the short-lived intensity of the punishment, the state of desiring-pain-waves (the painful craving) is most practical for the masochist striving to become a BwO. Rousseau admits of the situation without recognizing the full implications of his confession: "But I may say that I took advantage of it with an easy conscience" (26).

Rousseau interpreted what, according to the theories of Deleuze and Guattari, was really a common and perfectly natural manifestation of the reaction of his desiring-machines to their repression as an unfortunate and formative incident in the development of his psychology, one with which he would forever have to cope: "Who could have supposed that this childish punishment, received at the age of eight at the hands of a woman of thirty, would determine my tastes and desires, my passions, my very self for the rest of my life, and in a sense diametrically opposed to the one in which they should normally have developed" (26). Freud seems to concur with Rousseau's interpretation:

> Ever since Jean-Jacques Rousseau's *Confessions*, it has been well-known to all educationalists that the painful stimulation of the skin of the buttocks is one of the erotogenic zones of the *passive* instinct of cruelty (masochism). The conclusion has rightly been drawn by them that corporal punishment, which is usually applied to this part of the body, should not be inflicted upon any children whose libido is liable to be forced into collateral channels by the later demands of cultural education.[15]

If the interpretations of Rousseau and Freud are compatible with popular conceptions of sexual normality and psychological development, and I think they are, are we to passively accept their accuracy? Maybe we are ready to do so because such an act of acceptance is in conjunction with what we have been taught or because the common, passive, and masochistic acceptance of these traditionally informed perceptions contributes to the psychosexual frustration we all already (unconsciously) enjoy. Was, as Deleuze and Guattari might argue, Rousseau's experience merely the result of an instinctive yet culturally repressed desire for pain-waves? If Freud is correct in claiming that the purportedly detrimental potentialities of corporal punishment were well known to educationalists, then why does corporeal punishment remain a principal form of punishment for them?

On the conscious level, nevertheless, Rousseau's experience does seem unfortunate for three major reasons: (1) the known and unknown ways in which it made his life more difficult at the time; (2) the various negative effects it may have had on him (such as contributing to his dread of women or by teaching him that violence is an appropriate tool for teaching children); and (3) because it acquainted him with a natural but socially unacceptable form of deriving pleasure, one that he was never again able to relish and thus ostensibly tormented him psychologically throughout his lifetime. As the product of a culture fashioned inadvertently to prevent the realization of any BwO, Rousseau could not help from misunderstanding his congenital inclination toward making himself one; he perceived himself as peculiarly adulterated by his newfangled masochism: "My morals might well have been impaired by these strange tastes, which persisted with a depraved and insane intensity" (26). What is curious, however, is that he was aware of the "insane

intensity" of his desiring-condition, his apparent schizophrenia or schizo-
thymia, which exposes itself more and more as his hypochondria and general
paranoia increasingly overshadow his narrative. The blank pages on which
Rousseau wrote his story were clearly the recording surfaces, the products of
his desiring-production, the discursive representation of an intuitive intellect
investigating retrospectively his own displaced struggle to totalize his BwO.

When one is having difficulties performing or when one is not producing the
prescribed quota for production, there must be something wrong. If the problem is not obvious, it must be invented. A problem must be produced from
within, or one must be produced from without. In any case, something or
someone else is inevitably to blame. Call the police! Bring in the psychoanalysts! Let's begin the oedipalization process! Who done it — mommy, daddy,
or me? Psychoanalysis informs us: if you do not internalize the Oedipus myth
so as to better rediscover it on the outside, in social authority, where it will
be made to proliferate and be passed on to future generations, if you do
not follow the demarcated configuration of differentiation — daddy(the law)-
mommy-me — and the exclusive alternatives that delineate it, and thereby
"resolve" Oedipus, then you will be marginalized and bewildered in the neurotic darkness of the imaginary identifications of the undifferentiated.[16] The
oedipal theory is designed to weed the bad eggs from the good; it must
separate the "abnormal" and cryptic people from the "normal" and readily
categorized. But it is just a theory, a now very powerful and suspiciously
all-encompassing phallocentric theory founded primarily on conjecture and a
false model (Sophocles' Laius tried to kill Oedipus first, not the other way
around).[17]

To avoid such neurotic categorization, Deleuze and Guattari argue that
when attempting to construct a genealogy of one's psychology we must refrain
from relying on Freud's oedipal paradigm. We must follow Artaud:

> I don't believe in father
> in mother,
> got no
> papamummy[18]

Indeed, according to Deleuze and Guattari, we must not attempt to construct a genealogy of one's psychology in the language of psychoanalysis at
all. We must not attempt, like psychoanalysis, to "understand BwO phenomena as regressions, progressions, phantasies, in terms of an *image* of the
body.... [Psychoanalysis] only grasps the flipside of the BwO and immediately substitutes family photos, childhood memories, and part-objects for a
worldwide intensity map."[19] This does not mean that we should not analyze
what appear to have been formative events in the development of an individual's psychology but that we must examine those events with respect to the

underlying conflict between the BwO and the desiring-machines. There is no psychological chronology or narrative, but only arbitrary stratification and a road map rife with potholes and roadblocks. Simply put, Deleuze and Guattari assert that we must consider all psychological phenomena in relation to the egg:

> We treat the BwO as the full egg before the extension of the organism and the organization of the organs, before the formation of the strata; as the intense egg defined by axes and vectors, gradients and thresholds, by dynamic tendencies involving energy transformation and kinematic movements involving group displacement, by migrations: all independent of *accessory forms* because the organs appear and function here only as pure intensities.[20]

The egg, as principal of production, is the milieu of pure intensity and zero intensity. The BwO is the egg. The BwO does not exist before the organism; "it is adjacent to it and is continually in the process of constructing itself."[21]

"My heart pounded with joy on the road," exclaims Rousseau of his 1737 journey back to his beloved Mme de Warens (known to him as "Mamma") (234). This summer, Rousseau says, was one of the happiest periods of his life. Again, as with his recollection of the beatings, it is peculiar and paradoxical that Rousseau has such a positive memory of what was really a very difficult period for him. This summer marked the culmination of Rousseau's hypochondria: his exaggerated anxiety over his bodily health and the various psychosomatic manifestations of this anxiety. In conjunction with his hypochondria, either as sources or as symptoms, Rousseau's capacity for satisfying his own quota for self-productivity and his standard for self-reliance were at an all-time low:

> Meanwhile my health was far from recovering; on the contrary I was visibly wasting away. I was deathly pale and as thin as a skeleton; the throbbing in my arteries was terrible, and my heart palpitations more frequent. I was continually short of breath, and finally I became so weak that I found it difficult to move.... I could not lift a small weight, and was reduced to an inactivity most painful to a man as restless as I am. No doubt their was a great deal of *vapours* mixed up in all this. The *vapours*, being the malady of happy people, was therefore mine.... When I might have been enjoying the delights of life, my decaying physique prevented me, though no one could make out the true seat or cause of the disease. (235)

Rousseau apparently came closest to totalizing his BwO at this time more than at any other point during his life. The intensities of pain-waves, zero productivity, and desiring-production expressed in this passage are emphatic and revealing. Rousseau was practically immobilized by his maladies, all of which were symptoms allegedly caused by an unknown disease. Compelled to research the possible origins of his ailments, and after much investigation, Rousseau deduced: "Since I found in every disease some symptoms of my own, I believed I had them all" (235). Rousseau had unconsciously launched a full-scale, pro-BwO attack against his organs.

Somewhat aware of his hypochondriacal anxiety and the deep relationship between this anxiety and his inner masochistic drive for desiring-pain-waves, Rousseau refers paranoically to the mysterious *"vapours"* (an eighteenth-century word meaning hypochondria or hysteria) "mixed up in all this." He even makes the meaningful connection, albeit probably a slip of the pen (as Freud would put it), between the necessity for physical fitness and his body as an effective surface for recording the contention between his desiring-machines and BwO. He does these things without questioning the rationale behind his suffering; he simply presupposes that he must suffer, and he seems to take pride in this idea: "[D]espite my declining years and very real and serious maladies, my body seems to have regained its strength, the better to feel my suffering.... [R]acked by pains of every description, I feel more strength and life in me with which to suffer than I had for enjoyment when I was in the flower of my youth" (235). For Rousseau, suffering was an ambiguous and unavoidable reality, or was it?

Of course, Rousseau's desiring-machines' continual desire for desiring-production and the never-ending effort of his BwO to repress their desire and deterritorialize itself were unidentified and thus incomprehensible to Rousseau. However, the overall effects of the conflicts were not entirely removed from his conscious regulation. Evidently, his suffering could be lessened or averted, and this happened when his desiring-production subverted its repression by the BwO and was realized and encoded externally, like his pain-waves, on some object (such as his own body), in a creation of his (such as his writings) and/or by impregnating the complexities of a social situation. Freud observes that "hypochondria, like organic disease, manifests itself in distressing and painful bodily sensations, and it has the same effect as organic disease on the distribution of the libido. The hypochondriac withdraws both interest and libido — the latter specially markedly — from the objects of the external world and concentrates both of them upon the organ that is engaging his attention."[22] Accordingly, Rousseau's hypochondriac affliction and antiproductivity were diminished as his libidinal energy was augmented. For instance, when Mme de Larnage took an interest in him, Rousseau declares: "So she undertook my conquest, and it was good-bye to poor Jean-Jacques, or rather to his fever, his *vapours*, and his polypus. It was good-bye to everything when in her company, except certain palpitations which remained and of which she did not wish to cure me" (237). Rousseau's desiring-production temporarily eclipsed or blocked the progress made by his BwO.

"It was clear," admits Rousseau, "that my doctors, who had discovered nothing about my illness, regarded me as a hypochondriac" (245). Freud, like Rousseau's doctors, would have also considered him someone suffering from the "phenomena of hypochondria."[23] Freud treats hypochondria as a slippery and obscure disorder, one that he could not easily explain or distinguish. In contrast, Deleuze and Guattari offer a sensible explanation for hypochondria as a probable consequence of the BwO tussle: plagued by the nervous and often painful intensities of imaginary diseases, the hypochondriac body is one of the body-types capable of coming close to realizing the BwO; hypochondria is a common manifestation of any body desperately seeking BwO status. Therefore the schizoanalyst would not consider Rousseau's hypochondria a mental disorder per se; Rousseau would not be perceived or treated as strange, abnormal, or enigmatic. Thus, under the influence of schizoanalytic theory, it is unlikely that Rousseau would have internalized the pejorative implications of these sentiments; it is less likely that his contemplation of the illness would have resulted in a negative self-concept.

Rousseau's encounter with the prostitute Giulietta is a conspicuous external, social manifestation of his internal predicament. Rousseau states that his rendezvous with Giulietta was the "one incident in my life which plainly reveals my character" and that it will provide his readers with "complete knowledge of Jean-Jacques Rousseau" (300). For him to recount this incident and accomplish "the purpose of my book" (300), which is, says Rousseau, "to reveal my inner thoughts exactly in all situations of my life" and give "a history of my soul" (262), Rousseau maintains that he "shall" possess the necessary "strength to despise the false modesty which might prevent my fulfilling it" (300). Once more, in his introduction to the incident, we are confronted with Rousseau's pleasure-postponement: the repressive forces of his BwO emerge in what he terms his "false modesty," that idiosyncrasy that still "might prevent" the pleasurable fulfillment of his self-proclaimed "purpose." This "purpose," according to Deleuze and Guattari, could have been predominantly inspired by (1) Rousseau's desiring-production; (2) the symptomatic paranoia of his BwO (the desire to rationalize publicly the nature of his character and thus defend himself and his BwO against their imaginary "enemies" — as Rousseau himself frequently calls them);[24] and/or (3) the desiring-recording inadvertently inaugurated by the fierceness of the war between Rousseau's BwO and desiring-machines. Whether Rousseau's "false modesty" was victorious in impeding or distorting his account of his meeting with Giulietta, even partially so, is something that we can never know for certain. As schizoanalytical material, however, the "two or three pages" (300) that Rousseau does proffer on the topic are very informative.

"Never was such sweet pleasure offered to mortal heart and senses," says Rousseau regretfully of his brief relationship with Giulietta: "Alas, had I only known how to enjoy it fully and completely for a single second....I dulled all its delights. I killed them as if on purpose" (300). But why did Rousseau kill its delights "as if on purpose"? And if he did not do it on purpose, then how and why might he have done it? Rousseau himself divulges that he "has always had a disgust for prostitutes" (296). Yet if he truly had such a "disgust for prostitutes," why did he visit them? According to a Freudian interpretation, Rousseau's meetings with prostitutes could plausibly be explained as stemming from a common male precondition for loving. At an early age, claims Freud, the boy child "tells himself with cynical logic that the difference between his mother and a whore is not after all so very great, since basically they do the same thing": they welcome the penis; they copulate.[25] Inasmuch as the boy child combines traditionally antithetical stereotypes, and since conscious binary oppositions such as this Madonna/whore dichotomy often exist in the unconscious as a unity, Freud asserts that the prostitute is a likely "object-choice" for a man because she functions as a replacement for his now-repressed childhood object of sexual desire: his mother.[26] While for Freud, of course, this explanation is directly related to his theory of the Oedipus complex, Deleuze and Guattari would understand Rousseau's motivation to visit prostitutes as predominantly masochistic, as a psychological procedure for the realization of his suppressed masochism; his "disgust" would be considered a phobia, an aspect of his paranoia or hypochondria: his deep craving for anxiety-intensities.

When speaking of an earlier rendezvous with a different prostitute, Rousseau confesses: "I was so strangely stupid as to give in to her scruple," and after the sexual interaction, "so certain that I had caught the pox that the first thing I did on my return was to send for the surgeon and ask for some medicines" (297). Not surprisingly, the medicines were apparently ineffective: "Nothing can equal the uneasiness I felt for a whole three weeks," says Rousseau, "without any real discomfort or any obvious symptom to justify it" (297). Rousseau's intense dread of disease, his view of prostitutes as insidious transmitters of disease, and the subsequent anxiety he experienced after being with prostitutes all seem to indicate that his engagements with them were certainly masochistic. For the unconscious or preconscious Rousseau, the prostitutes constituted the female torturers or sadists for whom he had longed since childhood. His voluntary and repeated meetings with them caused him to suffer from a variety of invented ailments, as well as from guilt and shame, all of which successfully tormented him for a long time, maybe for the rest of his life.

Rousseau was so overcome by the "value" of Giulietta's "charms and caresses" that, "fearing to lose the fruit prematurely," he "tried to make haste and pluck it" (300). Nevertheless, his venture was thwarted: "Suddenly," recalls Rousseau, "I felt a deathly cold flow through my veins; my legs trembled; I sat down on the point of fainting, and wept like a child" (300). What happened to poor Jean-Jacques? "It is true," acknowledges Freud, "that psychoanalysis puts forward absence of sexual satisfaction as the cause of nervous disorders."[27] Central to this premise, and rather analogous to the nervous characteristics commonly stimulated by the contention between the desiring-machines and the BwO, is Freud's claim that "nervous symptoms arise from a conflict between two forces — on the one hand, the libido (which has as a rule become excessive), and on the other, a rejection of sexuality, or a repression which is over-severe."[28] In comparison to schizoanalytic theory, the "libido" of psychoanalysis functions similarly to desiring-production, and psychoanalysis's ideas of "rejection of sexuality" and "repression" could easily be seen as antiproductive symptoms and integral aspects of the BwO struggle. When psychoanalysis and schizoanalysis are applied, however, these parallels in their structures yield very different conclusions.

For psychoanalysis, on the one hand, Rousseau's temporary breakdown and later scrutiny of Giulietta's body are primarily results of his nervous disorders: they are unconsciously motivated denunciations of Giulietta as a mother-replacement/love-object and thus as an acceptable commodity fetish; and, if Rousseau was suffering from a prolonged castration complex, they could represent his fear of castration by the terrifying and devouring female genitalia. Accordingly, Rousseau's scrutiny necessarily discovers on Giulietta's body the "secret flaw" (301) that confirms for him biologically that she is a being of inferior and unworthy status, "some kind of monster, rejected by Nature, men and love" (301).

Schizoanalysis, on the other hand, might perceive Rousseau's breakdown as an obvious external manifestation of his BwO's success in ephemerally vanquishing his conscious intention to mollify with sexual activity the consciously felt pressures of his desiring-production. Or the breakdown itself could indicate that it was masochistic enough simply for Rousseau to have visited Giulietta (a prostitute) without ever needing to consummate the endeavor. In the long run, Rousseau's obstruction of the presumed purpose of the meeting (copulation/orgasm) may have been even more masochistically rewarding for him than he unconsciously anticipated. Unable to "repair my mistakes" during the next scheduled appointment because Giulietta did not show, Rousseau laments, "[M]y insane regret has never left me" (302). Rousseau's hypochondria and paranoia are explicitly illustrated in his representation of the encounter. Again a prostitute has become for him an infectious threat ("it did not so much as occur to me that the pox might have something to do with it" — her "secret flaw" [301]) and the administer of pain-waves, and now also the external object on which to project his internal conflict: on her breast he "perceived that she had a malformed nipple" (301).

In addition to the differences already highlighted, there are some general differences between psychoanalytic and schizoanalytic theory that are apparent even within the confines of this application. Whereas psychoanalysis presupposes and privileges the libido as the biological origin and principal catalyst in the development of human psychology, schizoanalysis understands libidi-nal energy as only one of several primary side effects brought about by the interaction of two profound psychic processes (the desiring-machines and the BwO) that contribute capriciously and in a variety of ways to psychological formation. The libido is neither determined centrally nor centrally located by schizoanalysis but seen as forever suffusing different assemblages of machines within which we are caught up at different times; Rousseau was caught up in an assemblage with Giulietta. Libidinal assemblages invest and are invested by the social field, with all the machineries they bring into play, all the multiple love-subjects and love-objects. Any libidinal investment is necessarily a collec-tive statement, since in any social field "there are no individual statements, only statement-producing mechanic assemblages."[29] For Freud, "the libido must be desexualized and sublimated in order to invest society and its flows," but for Deleuze and Guattari, "it is love, desire, and their flows that man-ifest the directly social character of the nonsublimated libido and its sexual investments."[30] Every assemblage is fundamentally libidinal and unconsciously motivated, and every libido or unconscious is fundamentally associated with certain assemblages. Nothing exists independently. Everything is plugged in everywhere.

Psychoanalysis is a sociopolitical apparatus with an ideological investment in the distribution of power within the social field. Striving both to rep-resent the interests of the dominant classes and distinguish itself from all assemblages, it imagines and presents itself as the master decoder and inter-polator of psychological meaning. To accomplish this, psychoanalysis "subjects the unconscious to arborescent structures, hierarchical graphs, recapitulatory memories, central organs, the phallus, the phallus-tree — not only in its theory but also in its practice of calculation and treatment" and "bases its own dictatorial power on a dictatorial conception of the unconscious."[31] The psychoanalyst conveniently explains the unconscious in such a way that all psychological phenomena can be understood according to a phallocentric for-mula, a patriarchal, heterosexist credo: in the final analysis, psychological whole(some)ness is an ideal only attainable for heterosexual men. The psycho-analyst does what it takes to perpetuate the order of things, simultaneously using and reinforcing the privileged position of psychoanalysis within that order: this entails molding the patient's unconscious to the predetermined model, neuroticizing the thought-patterns of the patient if necessary, subju-gating the patient through a diagnostic process of classification. To be sure, psychoanalysis is a despotic theory: "[T]here is always a general, always a leader (General Freud)."[32] But since psychoanalysis depends on and is cir-cumscribed by this hermeneutic and authoritative arrangement, one that is reductive and absolute, it is necessarily limited in maneuverability and scope.

Like psychoanalysis, schizoanalysis is also a sociopolitical apparatus with an ideological investment in the distribution of power within the social field.

However, schizoanalysis strives to complicate, redefine, and equilibrate the existing order of things rather than consolidate it. To accomplish this, schizoanalysis reformulates the unconscious of psychoanalysis and transforms it into an a-centered system, a machinic network, that cannot be reduced or interpreted according to a tree model. Schizoanalysis's unconscious is in no way an obstacle, a key, or a mysterious thing that must be revealed, reckoned with, and adopted: "[T]he unconscious no longer designates the hidden principle of the transcendent plane of organization, but the process of the immanent plane of consistency as it appears on itself in the course of its construction. For the unconscious must be constructed, not rediscovered. There is no longer a conscious-unconscious dualism machine, because the unconscious is, or rather is produced, there where consciousness goes, carried by the plane."[33] Schizoanalysis comprehends the unconscious not as a symbolic structure but as an informative process always already particular, arbitrary, and produced (with new statements, different desires) within a totality of historical determinations within which the related conscious operates.

"The task of schizoanalysis," as Deleuze and Guattari emphasize, "therefore is to reach the investments of unconscious desire of the social field, insofar as they are differentiated from the preconscious investments of interest, and insofar as they are not merely capable of counteracting them, but also of coexisting with them in opposite modes."[34] Instead of attempting, like psychoanalysis, to appropriate and solidify egos under the auspices of a certain idea and hierarchical scale of normality, schizoanalysis takes apart egos and their presuppositions; it liberates the prepersonal psychological singularities that they contain and repress; it mobilizes the ideational flows they would be capable of transmitting, receiving, or intercepting; it establishes further and more sharply the ambiguities, slippages, and fractures well beneath conditions of identity; it assembles the desiring-machines that countersect everyone and group everyone with others.[35] In effect, schizoanalysis posits an understanding of difference that is dependent on neither negation nor opposition but on the positive recognition of intersections; mutual, parallel, and disjunctive flows and desires; and assemblage-statements — the infinite network to which we are all connected. Schizoanalysis acknowledges, encourages, and accepts difference as an affirmative movement and actuality: it seeks only a community of positive differences.

Notes

My thanks to Leo Damrosch, Kim Savelson, and James Intriligator for their many helpful suggestions throughout the writing of this essay.

1. Gilles Deleuze and Félix Guattari, *Anti-Oedipus: Capitalism and Schizophrenia*, trans. Robert Hurley, Mark Seem, and Helen R. Lane (Minneapolis: University of Minnesota Press, 1983), 25.

2. Ibid., 5.

3. Ibid., 28.

4. Ibid., 55.

5. See ibid., 296–322.

6. Sigmund Freud, "Beyond the Pleasure Principle," in *The Freud Reader*, ed. Peter Gay (New York: Norton, 1989), 595.

7. Gilles Deleuze and Félix Guattari, *A Thousand Plateaus: Capitalism and Schizophrenia*, trans. Brian Massumi (Minneapolis: University of Minnesota Press, 1987), 151.

8. Antonin Artaud, *Selected Writings*, ed. and intro. Susan Sontag (Berkeley: University of California Press, 1976), 571.

9. Artaud cited in Deleuze and Guattari, *Anti-Oedipus*, 9.

10. Deleuze and Guattari, *A Thousand Plateaus*, 150.

11. Ibid., 155. See Gilles Deleuze, *Coldness and Cruelty*, published with Leopold von Sacher-Masoch's *Venus in Furs* (New York: Zone Books, 1991), for a discussion of masochism's relationship to sadism and the law and of the relationship between psychoanalysis and the state. Central to this discussion is Deleuze's assertion that "a close examination of masochistic fantasies or rites reveals that while they bring into play the very strictest application of the law, the result in every case is the opposite of what might be expected (thus whipping, far from punishing or preventing an erection, provokes and ensures it). It is a demonstration of the law's absurdity. The masochist regards the law as a punitive process and therefore begins by having the punishment inflicted upon himself; once he has undergone the punishment, he feels that he is allowed or indeed commanded to experience the pleasure that the law was supposed to forbid" (88). For Deleuze, masochism becomes a process of subverting and mocking the law; masochism locates the masochist beyond the law.

12. In *The Confessions*, Rousseau does inform us that he did, at some earlier point in his life, "receive blows intended" for his brother, but does not mention any pain related to this incident (*The Confessions*, trans. and intro. J. M. Cohen [London: Penguin, 1953], 21). I am not including the original French since the English translation in no way problematizes my reading. All subsequent references to *The Confessions* will be included parenthetically in the text.

13. Sigmund Freud, "Beyond the Pleasure Principle," 596.

14. Deleuze and Guattari, *A Thousand Plateaus*, 152.

15. Sigmund Freud, "Three Essays on the Theory of Sexuality," in *The Freud Reader*, 270.

16. Deleuze and Guattari, *Anti-Oedipus*, 78–79.

17. Psychoanalysis does not account for the fact that in Sophocles' *Oedipus the King*, the literary model from which Freud derived the name "Oedipus" for his fundamental complex/theory, Oedipus killed his father (Laius) only after Laius attempted to kill him: Oedipus killed his father in self-defense (see lines 885–98). Freud does indicate that a father might be jealous of his son's close relationship with the mother, but, according to Freud, this jealousy does not necessarily imply that the father wants the son removed from the picture; nor does it occur at any regular period in the oedipal process.

18. Antonin Artaud, *Artaud Anthology*, trans. F. Teri Wehn and Jack Hirschman (San Francisco: City Lights, 1965), 247.

19. Deleuze and Guattari, *A Thousand Plateaus*, 165.

20. Ibid., 153.

21. Ibid., 164.

22. Sigmund Freud, "On Narcissism: An Introduction," in *The Freud Reader*, 551.

23. Ibid., 552.

24. See, for example, Rousseau, *Confessions*, 590.

25. Sigmund Freud, "A Special Type of Choice of Object Made by Men," in *The Freud Reader*, 391–92.

26. Ibid., 389–91.

27. Sigmund Freud, "'Wild' Psycho-analysis," in *The Freud Reader*, 353.

28. Ibid.

29. Deleuze and Guattari, *A Thousand Plateaus*, 36.

30. Deleuze and Guattari, *Anti-Oedipus*, 353.

31. Deleuze and Guattari, *A Thousand Plateaus*, 17.

32. Ibid., 18.

33. Ibid., 284.

34. Deleuze and Guattari, *Anti-Oedipus*, 350.

35. Ibid., 362.

5

Philosophy and Ethics

Quantum Ontology
A Virtual Mechanics of Becoming
Timothy S. Murphy

"Ontology" and "metaphysics" have become dirty words in philosophy, as they have in physics. This is not a recent development; in the preface to the first edition of the *Critique of Pure Reason*, Kant notes the disrepute into which "higher physics" had fallen in his day and promises to rescue it, but in so doing he displaces the "science of being" in the direction of "phenomena" — that is, being is displaced into its representation for consciousness. Hegel, the next man in the relay, formalizes the displacement by raising phenomena to the level of "science" and subsuming all being within a phenomenology of mind or spirit. From this "science" arise most of the dominant forms of Continental philosophy and its competitors: Husserlian and Heideggerian phenomenology, Freudian and Lacanian psychoanalysis, structural anthropology and sociology, even some forms of Marxism. They are all marked by the refusal of ontology and the critique of metaphysics inaugurated by the Kantian displacement of being into its representation for consciousness. It is no coincidence that Kant, the historical point of displacement, is the first and last philosopher in this phenomenological line to act as a consistent point of reference for the physical sciences. But the philosophy of science eventually manifests the representational mediation that it has repressed. Philosophies of science share what Werner Heisenberg calls "realism": "We 'objectivate' a statement if we claim that its content does not depend on the conditions under which it can be verified."[1] For Heisenberg, there are three types of realism: practical, in which we assume that *most* of our experience consists of statements that can be objectivated; dogmatic, in which we assume that *all* of our experience consists of such statements; and metaphysical, in which we make the additional, unverifiable assumption that "the things [about which we make statements] really exist."[2] Materialist ontology is metaphysical, and classical Newtonian mechanics is dogmatic, while quantum physics, for Heisenberg, requires a practical-realist point of view in that its results cannot be separated from the devices that measure them and the statistical formalism that expresses them.

211

In the Copenhagen interpretation of quantum physics, buttressed by Heisenberg's own indeterminacy principle,[3] the statistical structure of the equations makes it meaningless to ask what happens to a particle or field between observations; therefore it is meaningless to claim that the particle or field exists when it is not being observed. All that *is*, all that has meaning, is the mathematical expression of probabilities. In this way, the Kantian phenomenal displacement is ultimately repeated by physics, but as an objective phenomenality, depending on technical measuring instruments, rather than a subjective phenomenology, relying on self-consciousness. "Things" can be known only through the formalism of representational mediation, which means that only the mediation itself can be known in any way.

Yet there are physics other than phenomenality, and philosophies other than phenomenology. Gilles Deleuze's philosophy is one of the latter, so he makes no attempt to suspend metaphysical realism, that is, ontological speculation. As the principles of Deleuze's ontology have come to light, it has become clear that it does not fit into the dominant phenomenological line of descent of Western philosophy. This lack of connection with the dominant strains of thought in the human sciences has slowed and distorted the reception of Deleuze's ontology in anglophone circles; his work appears as an odd mixture of precision, reduction, and omission to critics schooled in derivations of phenomenology. This is because his problems, the encounters with the unthought that give his thought its impetus, are not the problems of phenomenology, and in order to understand his work, "the conditions under which the problem acquires a maximum of comprehension and extension must be determined, conditions capable of communicating to a given case of solution the ideal continuity appropriate to it."[4] In order to follow Deleuze's lines of flight, one must move onto the terrain that his work has defined and engage with the tradition that he has created for himself, a tradition that intersects phenomenology at only a few points. Rather, Deleuze's work finds its antecedents in materialist and rationalist philosophy, primarily Spinoza and Nietzsche. On the contemporary scene, his work resonates not so much with the human sciences as with the physical sciences. Manuel De Landa has shown the important connections that link Deleuze to recent work in cybernetics and information theory, while Brian Massumi has demonstrated the lines of flight that link Deleuze's work to the biochemical and thermodynamic work of Ilya Prigogine, one of the primary theorists of complex dissipative systems or "chaos";[5] Prigogine has named Deleuze one of the contemporary thinkers in whom he has "found inspiration" for his work on self-organizing complex systems, such as living organisms.[6] If this "extension of the conditions of the problem" is necessary to reveal the full scope of Deleuze's work, then the most important task that remains in this area is to link Deleuze's thought to contemporary work in physics.

Among the physical sciences, physics is the most abstract discourse that

claims material reference for its statements, even though the Copenhagen interpretation of quantum physics has restored the hegemony of representational
mediation and post-Kantian phenomenality that physics had long ignored.
That hegemony has been challenged in much the same way that Deleuze has
implicitly challenged phenomenology. A number of contemporary physicists,
including Roger Penrose, J. S. Bell, and David Bohm, have attempted to formulate a consistent and useful method of treating quantum mechanical events
as actual occurrences rather than as probabilities that fulfill formal equations
(and nothing else); chief among these was the late David Bohm, who made
a concerted effort to formulate not only a new method of treating quantum
equations but also a realist ontological framework into which to contextualize
the mathematics. His attempt to go beyond Bohr's principle of wave-particle
complementarity to found new models for thought in physics finds its relay
in Deleuze's attempt to create new images for philosophical thought; an articulation of the two produces an ontological mechanics, not of static being
but dynamic becoming.

   That such new images and models are necessary may not be admitted, and
the suggestion that they could be constructed in the precritical tradition of
metaphysics will almost certainly meet great skepticism. The first argument
that will no doubt be raised against this return to ontology is the self-evident
one of its necessary textual articulation: an ontology that purports to explain
the material world is a representational structure, expressed in logical arguments contained in books and seminars. These books and seminars would
be constantly susceptible to the disseminative power of their own rhetoric,
and that rhetoric would be the only materiality with which the theory could
deal. Positivist or pragmatist philosophies of physics would express this criticism in the language of mathematical formalism and thought-pictures, but
the logic is the same. Neither Bohm nor Deleuze accepts the epistemologi-
cal assumptions that underlie such criticism. Neither science nor philosophy,
in their view, is concerned with knowledge or truth as the representation of
an extrarepresentational reality or the accumulation of absolute referential information. Theory does not take on a representational function, but rather
an active, practical one: it is a "box of tools" having "nothing to do with the
signifier."[7] Every theory, then, is a "mechanics" in that it is such a toolbox,
filled not with instruments teleologically designed for given functions but with
bizarre instruments that make possible unprecedented functions. Theoretical
tools must unsettle and disturb those who would use them in order to bring
new objects and events within range of thought. If they cannot do so, the
theory must be altered or abandoned in favor of different tools.

   For Bohm, "it is the fate of all theories eventually to be falsified[;] they
are relative truths, adequate in certain domains.... But if this is the case then
the accumulation of knowledge cannot be regarded as the *essential* purpose of
scientific research, simply because the validity of all knowledge is relative to

something that is not in the knowledge itself."[8] Validity is a function of use, of efficacy in extending the field of the problem (rather than in the pragmatic or utilitarian sense, which accepts preestablished ends). Realist science is instead an extension of active human perception, not a storehouse of truth, and in this way the theories that are constructed and proposed in science are no different from the mechanical apparatuses that allow scientists to "perceive" sensations that are beyond the range of their organic senses. Theories for Bohm "are now science's major link with reality. Theories determine not only the design of scientific instruments but also the kinds of questions that are posed in the experiments themselves.... Perception in modern science, particularly in physics, takes place essentially through the mind."[9] We must be careful not to reintroduce the phenomenal subject here, however; perception as Bohm conceives it does not require a subject. Plants and animals perceive, in that they cause and respond materially to changes in their environments, but they do so without subjectivity (at least in the normative phenomenological sense); so too do micro-organisms, as well as inorganic structures like crystals. Machines perceive in this way. The mind, Deleuze notes, is not a space of subjective representation but a sensorimotor interval, a gap that allows difference to intervene between stimulus and response.[10] The mind is the interval of freedom and creativity, but it is not fundamentally human or limited to humans; perception is an aspect of the "machinic phylum" that cuts across the organic/inorganic and subject/object antinomies.

A scientific theory is a box of tools, to be used in conjunction with machines in order to intervene in a physical system, so that its behavior can be assessed. A metaphysical or ontological theory is a box of tools also, provided that its metaphysical aspects lead to new experimental arrangements that produce definite, differentiable effects. This is what Deleuze insists marks the new relationship between theory and practice inaugurated by the critique of the phenomenological subject: "Practice is a set of relays from one theoretical point to another, and theory is a relay from one practice to another."[11] Theories are always local and nonrepresentational forms of action and must escape their constitutive impasses by moving through other, practical forms of action. Thus both are essentially social. Theory functions as an intensifying fantasy that can "invest all of an existing social field, including the latter's most repressive forms," or "launch a counterinvestment whereby revolutionary desire is plugged into the existing social field as a source of energy."[12] A theory produces certain actions, which produce certain effects and reactions that extend the theory or alter it; a realist ontology does not describe or double the world except as a residual effect of directing, damping, or amplifying an action in the world.

The ontologies in question, Bohm's and Deleuze's, arise in different disciplines and extend themselves through different contexts, but they share a surprisingly large amount of terminology, logic, and operational structure, beginning with a common point of departure. This point of departure is a very singular dissatisfaction, a "problem," with the conceptual structure and operations of phenomenal thought. For Bohm, this dissatisfaction takes the form of a critique of the intuitive models of contemporary physics, the wave model and the particle model, as well as the principles that demonstrate them to be unsurpassable (Bohr's complementarity, Heisenberg's indeterminacy principle, and von Neumann's proof of them). Matter and energy, which are interchangeable according to Einstein's equation $E=mc^2$, behave in different ways depending on the ways in which they are observed; sometimes they appear as waves moving through fields of force, and sometimes they appear as discrete particles interacting with one another. Both forms of behavior cannot be observed at the same time, because the two forms of behavior require different apparatuses to measure them; nevertheless, both must be taken into account in order to explain and predict the overall "properties" of matter and energy. Matter has wave-like properties, while fields of waves have particle-like ones.

This ambiguity in the nature of the "object" of quantum mechanics confused many physicists, and Bohr proposed the complementarity principle to avoid this. In essence, complementarity suggests that the attribution of existence in any form, wave or particle or something else, to quantum objects is a metaphysical gesture that has no measurable effects, since the object only exhibits properties when it interacts with the experimental apparatus, at which point the object and the apparatus form an unanalyzable whole. "Event" would thus be a better term than "object." All that the physicist should do is juxtapose the wave and particle models to obtain as precise a statistical picture of the measured event as possible. Bohr suggested that "the description of the experimental arrangement and the recording of observations . . . be given in plain language, suitably refined by the usual physical terminology" and *no language at all be used to refer to the quantum event* because "plain language," with its analytical form and causal ordering of events and times, cannot adequately deal with the wholeness and indeterminism of quantum events. Their mode of existence can only be described analogically by probability. The proposal of other models is ruled out a priori: "[A]ll departures from common language and ordinary logic are entirely avoided by reserving the word 'phenomenon' solely for reference to unambiguously communicable information."[13] The only alternatives for physical thought are the historically given language and concepts of classical mechanics, wave and particle, or no concepts whatsoever; these limits to analysis and inquiry are phenomenal, in that they are imposed on thought arbitrarily, on the basis of the *possibility of representation* of that thought at one moment in history. Heisenberg seconded this Copenhagen interpretation through his indeterminacy principle. To the antinomian symmetries of the wave/particle models and event/observer languages, he added the symmetry of position and momentum: at a certain level of scale, one of the two can be measured precisely only at the expense of increasing imprecision in the measurement of the other.[14] The mathematician Johann von Neumann then produced a proof that purported to demonstrate that, in essence, the Copenhagen interpretation could not be superseded by the addition of levels of activity below the Heisenberg indeterminacy limit, which amounts to a demonstration that the assumption of a physical reality below that limit could only be a useless gesture, a "metaphysical" one in the derogatory sense. The subtle veneer of formal mathematical representation is all that remains of the physical world below this threshold.

Bohm's response to this foreclosure of the event in favor of its representation in the phenomenon is characteristically nondialectical: he questions the adequacy of the existing representational models, particularly the principle that no alternative could be constructed. Using the wave model to correct the inadequacies of the particle model and the particle model to correct the wave model seems imprecise, reductive, and static. Could there not be a theory that could account for the statistical accuracy of quantum calculation and yet offer new experimental opportunities? The theory Bohm proposed has been called variously a "hidden variable" interpretation, in that it postulates the existence of subquantum factors that affect events (the sort that von Neumann had ruled out), and a "pilot wave" model of quantum events, in that it requires the assumption of an infinitesimal wave pattern that simultaneously links all aspects of an extended field of forces. The immediate importance of this proposal, from the point of view of experimental physics and materialist ontology, is double: it allows the physicist to "describe the *experimental results themselves* (and, more generally, the experimental conditions as well) in terms of a new language form that is neither 'classical' nor 'quantum,'"[15] and it eliminates the "need for a vague division of the world into 'system' on the one hand and 'apparatus' or 'observer' on the other"[16] by positing the reality of the system under consideration *independent* of observation.

Bohm adduces strong logical arguments in favor of his "hidden variable" interpretation and against the Copenhagen interpretation, particularly against von Neumann's purported "proof." Bohm points out that, like all mathematical proofs, von Neumann's is based on a number of theorems that are themselves based on the "assumption . . . that certain features associated with the current formulation of the theory are absolute and final, in the sense that they will never be contradicted in future theories and will never be discovered to be approximations."[17] Bohm's own method treats theorems as tools, to be systematically varied in order to discover new forms of intervention, to extend the range of perception and define new problems for research. The mathematical formalism must be explained, contextualized, and not simply reified. In the same way, Deleuze will characterize his own work as "problematic" and explicitly criticize the "theorematic conception of geometry" as follows: he defines the "problem by means of the events which come to affect a logical subject matter (sections, ablations, adjunctions, etc.), whereas the theorem deals with the properties which are deduced from an essence."[18] Theorems are static and dogmatic, while problems are dynamic and flexible.

Deleuze begins with guiding principles similar to Bohm's in his attempt to evade the symmetry of the mind/matter split and the phenomenological "resolution" or "suspension" that has traditionally rendered it interminable. The first principle is a critique of the dialectic drawn from Bergson. Like Bohm's criticism of complementarity, it questions the adequacy of antinomian concepts in attaining the specificity of concrete singularity: "[O]f what use is a dialectic that believes itself to be reunited with the real when it compensates for the inadequacy of a concept that is too broad or too general by invoking the opposite concept, which is no less broad and general?"[19] Abstract and general ideas, like mathematical theorems, do not explain anything, but rather must be explained; a more precise approach must be created. Along with this, Deleuze articulates a critique of the phenomenological method much like Bohm's objection to the phenomenalist imprecision in Bohr's holistic model of quantum events, but derived from Nietzsche and Sartre:

> The error of all efforts to determine the transcendental as consciousness is that they think of the transcendental in the image of, and in the resemblance to, that which it is supposed to ground. In this case, either we give ourselves ready-made, in the "originary" sense presumed to belong to the constitutive consciousness, whatever we were trying to generate through a transcendental method, or, in agreement with Kant, we give up genesis and constitution and limit ourselves to a simple transcendental conditioning.[20]

In other words, Deleuze attempts to avoid placing the human subject at the beginning or center of his investigations. To assume the subject as transcendentally given is to assume what you would explain; to transfer a conditioned empirical figure onto the transcendental conditions that render it actual is to invert their true relation. This is not to suggest that the subject is not a problem; on the contrary, an account of the constitution of the subject will be one of the minimal criteria for a more adequate theory. The subject will be constituted, but as one of many possible effects that can arise from the principles of Deleuze's ontology. The subject's representational structure must be explained, as the formalism of quantum mathematics must be explained; neither can be raised to the level of a priori principle.

If one does not begin thinking with the fact of the thinking subject, as Descartes and Kant (and their followers) did, with what does one begin? One cannot pretend to begin at something that would be an origin or at some regulative idea that would be an end or a telos. The phenomenal tradition is correct in its assumption that one must begin where and when one is, in a moment that is not present because it is continually divided against itself; the tradition goes wrong, Bohm and Deleuze argue, when it assumes that this moment is necessarily represented by and to a mediate consciousness. The problem of the transcendental subject is a false problem, a badly analyzed composite. Rather, the moment is a moment because it is asymmetrically divided and moving, because it becomes without being, certainly without being the synthesis of the dialectic being/nonbeing. The division and the movement are the faces of time, the true problem: "The future is not yet. The present *is*, but it cannot be specified in words or in thoughts, without its slipping into the past. When a future moment comes, a similar situation will prevail. Therefore, from the past of the present we may be able to predict, at most, the past of the future. The actual immediate present is always the unknown."[21] But this description of time remains phenomenal, and its constitutive division must be extended to provide a direction for intervention. We must investigate the paradoxes of pure becoming.

To do so, Deleuze identifies three syntheses of time that coexist. The first is the passive synthesis of the living present that contracts all of the past and the future, allowing time to pass unidirectionally; from this perspective, the past and future are modalities always contained in the conditioned present, which alone exists. The second is the active synthesis of the pure past, the memory that represents the old past and the current representation of that past; the pure past is the past that is a priori, that was never present and is necessary to found the past as memory. Deleuze's second synthesis relies on Bergson's intensive theory of memory, which asks us to treat the past as a virtual space into which we project ourselves in order to find the appropriate level of the past that we seek. This is a complex operation, since each level of the past contains the whole of the past, in virtual coexistence but at different degrees of dilation and intensity.[22] Similarly, Bohm's model proposes that

> each moment of time is a projection...[that] must contain further projections of earlier moments, which constitute a kind of nested sequence of enfolded images of the past. These may take the form of memories. More generally, however, they may be the enfolded "reverberations" of earlier moments within the moment in question.... Such projection is still to be thought of primarily as a kind of creativity, but here we are discussing *the creation of a moment that is related to its past in a definite way*.... Of course, all these projections into any given moment will have the past of the entire universe as their potential content, which is thus enfolded into the moment in question.[23]

The moments of the past, for both Deleuze and Bohm, are like Leibniz's monads or Borges's aleph, reflecting obscurely the entire universe of which they are parts. They constitute an intensive subspace or prespace that determines, in part, the structure of time itself.

The third synthesis is the static synthesis of the pure and empty form of time that, according to Deleuze, displaces the relation between the others to create the future; like the pure past, it is a conditioning, rather than a conditioned, time, but one capable of breaking the repetitive symmetry between living present and pure past.[24] How would such a "pure and empty form of time" create the future? How does it relate to space, to the extended events it would measure and relate? Bohm has proposed, on the basis of contemporary field theory, a model of space-time as a set of dynamic fields of force. This would be the first level of his "implicate order": "When these fields are treated quantum-mechanically, we find that even in what is called a vacuum there are 'zero-point' fluctuations, giving 'empty space' an energy that is immensely beyond that contained in what is recognized as matter. . . . [M]atter may then be compared to a set of small waves on the immense 'ocean' of the vacuum state."[25] "Empty" space is not empty but rather is constituted of different forms of energy that produce matter as one of their residual effects. Similarly, Deleuze has postulated that the universe is "chaos," enfolding in each point infinite speed and energy: "It is not even sufficient to say that intense and moving particles pass through holes; a hole is just as much a particle as what passes through it. Physicists say that holes are not the absence of particles but particles traveling faster than the speed of light."[26] Bohm explains that this vacuum state has no classically meaningful notion of time because its "'state-function' (which represents the whole of space and time) oscillates uniformly at a frequency so high that it is utterly beyond any known physical interpretation," so "[a]ll the physically significant properties of these states are then completely independent of this 'zero-point' oscillation." This means that if time is an abstraction from an ordered sequence of events, "we would be justified in saying that the vacuum state is, in a certain sense, 'timeless'"[27] because its oscillation renders all our notions of succession and simultancity useless.

To read this "timelessness" as "eternity" would be to give "the pure and empty form of time" a sense, but this sense would be a bad analysis of the composite. The term "timelessness" refers to a reality "'beyond time' at least as time is now known, measured, and experienced."[28] For Bohm, the rapid, energetic "zero-point" fluctuations mean that the small-scale structure of space-time, the vacuum state, can give rise to phenomena like particles and fields, which appear to be discrete and separable but which are really only relatively stable structures that can be abstracted from their contexts for experimental purposes. These stable structures are Deleuze's problems, which must be extended as far as possible to determine their limits, their uses. The traditional notion of time is just such a stable structure, just such a problem, but one that is fixed only within the limited contexts of absolute classical temporality and convertible relativistic temporality.

Bohm defines this stability of the problem in a very Deleuzian way, in terms of difference. He claims that "information is a difference that makes a difference. . . . A little reflection will show that our ability to abstract a limited context out of a universe of immense size . . . arises in a very simple way[:] . . . the differences in the essentially infinite context that has been left out make no significant difference in the context that has been selected for investigation."[29] When the differences in infinite context begin to make a difference in the limited context, it is necessary to change the context and hence the problem. The state-function oscillations of the vacuum state begin to make a difference in the traditional context of time at the level of the quantum interactions of particles and fields: these oscillations may affect the movements of the constituent parts of things, but at present the oscillations can only be treated statistically. Under the Copenhagen interpretation, these oscillations have no experimental use value; they are merely "metaphysical" and have no effect on the equations. But in Bohm's theory, they suggest that other structures of time may be implicit in normal space-time.

If we extend the traditional idea of time, we reach its limit in the state-function oscillations, and we must displace the problem to find a new way to proceed. There is no reason to privilege a frame of reference, an ultimate level of reality that would determine all the lower ones; on the contrary, the process of space-time production seems to move in both directions, from smaller contexts out into relatively larger orders and back from the larger context into the smaller levels of implication. The "time" of the vacuum state requires an extension of the original problem of time to allow it to function in the different context. Deleuze's third synthesis is such an extension; he suggests that every stable context-structure "has a purely logical, ideal or dialectical time. However, this virtual time itself determines a time of differenciation, or rather rhythms or different times of actualization which correspond to the relations and singularities of the structure and, for their part, measure the passage from virtual to actual."[30] Within each structure there are multiple times, subsisting in a virtual state, waiting to be actualized through the movement of the structure. The unimaginable time of the zero-point oscillations "opens the way for a new kind of time, which has primarily to do with the vacuum state.... A new system of time will have been introduced that is both very fast and very slow compared with ordinary physical times."[31] In this sense, the vacuum state would be an enfolded virtual generator of times (and spaces) yet unknown and unmeasured. Bohm's ideas would thus seem to provide much-needed specification to Deleuze's rather abstract "virtual times" and would lay the foundation for a mechanics of the generation of space-times and for what we might call, provisionally, a taxonomy of them. The present state of experimental technology prevents these hypotheses, these virtual times, from being directly testable; however, some problem-solving techniques in physics, particularly the interaction diagrams and "sum over histories" method introduced by Richard Feynman,[32] suggest that a multiple form of time is already a useful tool.

Once we have a useful transformative theory of extension and duration, space and time, to orient our interventions, we can begin to postulate logics that could account for the manifestations of matter and energy that "become" at the scale of particles, of the subject and other levels of scale. Deleuze proposes his logic in the traditional languages of ontology, mathematics, and the physical sciences, derived not only from his early work on Bergson but also, more significantly, from his studies of Spinoza's and Leibniz's anti-Cartesian rationalism, studies that analyze logics of folding — *complicatio, explicatio,* and *implicatio.* Bohm too presents his "implicate order" in a mélange of discursive registers, juxtaposing quantum field theory with analogies from Freud; his vocabulary is derived from his etymological reflections on the same term, folding, in relation to Bohr's holistic model of quantum events. Both treat the universe as origami. This common choice of terminology, which is surprising in light of the distinct intellectual itineraries followed by its expositors and the apparent lack of familiarity of each with the other's work, prefigures the form that these ontologies will take. The first problem addressed in the terminology is the issue of generality, the subsumption of individual events under general categories. Deleuze chooses the term "singularity" to specify that the events are not strictly subsumable under general categories. The object subsumed under a general category is a "particular," whose dialectic operates through the paradox known as the hermeneutic circle. This does not mean that Deleuze refuses all "categorization," for want of a better term. Instead of generalization, he offers a displaced use of the concept. For Deleuze, the concept does not abstract the common properties of things subsumed beneath it, but rather "the concept itself has become the thing. It is a universal thing, if you like, since objects sketch it out like so many degrees, but a concretion, not a genre or a generality."[33] In *Difference and Repetition,* he renames this displaced notion of the concept "Idea." Bohm echoes this when he insists that "the general is now seen to be present *concretely,* as the activity of the generative principle within the generative order."[34]

Recall that the basic unit or quantum of quantum mechanics *and* philosophy is no longer the particle or the subject but the singularity, the differential event, which Bohm calls "moment"[35] and Deleuze calls "haecceity."[36] These are the "categorical" forms of individuation. The "moment" and the "haecceity" are concrete, metaphysically real, but this does not mean that they have been "realized" on the basis of some broader idealist structure that might be called "possibility." For Bohm and Deleuze, the antithesis of possibility and reality must also be displaced, into the couple virtuality/actuality (Bohm, on the basis of precedent uses in physics, prefers the term "potentiality" to "virtuality," but his use of the term is the same as Deleuze's use of "virtuality"). Deleuze explains:

> The possible is opposed to the real; the process undergone by the possible is therefore a "realization." By contrast, the virtual is not opposed to the real; it possesses a full reality by itself. The process it undergoes is that of actualization. [In realization,] [d]ifference can no longer be anything but the negative determined by the concept: either the limitation imposed by possibles . . . in order to be realized, or the opposition of the possible to the reality of the real. The virtual, by contrast, is the characteristic state of Ideas; it is on the basis of its reality

that existence is produced, in accordance with a time and a space immanent in the Idea.[37]

Hecceities and moments are virtual events in this sense, that they themselves do not so much exist as *insist* or *subsist* in an enfolded form of space-time that is real despite its apparent ideality or abstraction: "The reality of the virtual is structure,"[38] the context-structure defined above in terms of significant difference, which we have been discussing as the extended space-time of the problem. Hecceities and moments are also virtual *in sense;* the French word *sens,* signifying "sense," "direction," or "meaning," is one of Deleuze's terms for the abstract plane of consistency on which is constituted the reality of the virtual. Bohm also prefers to deal with forces that are potential yet real, and his model of the quantum world relies on the postulate of the "quantum potential" or "pilot wave" that, like the magnetic potential, has very real effects separate from the classically real fields that measure the rates of change of the potential in classical electrodynamics.[39]

But the difference between the duality possible/real and the duality virtual/actual does not end with the postulate of complete reality. If the "realization of the possible" is a process of limitation, it is also a process of similarity that "refers to the form of identity in the concept." It is thus a static, deterministic process. The "actualization of the virtual," in contrast, "always takes place by difference, divergence or differenciation.... Actual terms never resemble the singularities they incarnate. In this sense, actualization or differenciation is always a genuine creation"[40] rather than a predetermined procedure. Bohm as well recognizes this disjunction between the virtual/potential and the actual when he explains that the "projection [of explicate orders from implicate ones] can be described as creative, rather than mechanical, for by creativity one means just the inception of new content, which unfolds into a sequence of moments that is not completely derivable from what came earlier in this sequence or set of such sequences."[41] Thus the singularities that form energy and matter, including the subject and its variants, are produced in the same way that our previous discussion showed times and spaces to be produced. Henceforth it will be more precise to speak of Deleuze's and Bohm's positions as "metaphysical actuality" rather than "realism."

Deleuze models the virtual or conceptual assemblage of these unsubsumable singularities in terms of a logic of series but ultimately arrives at a logic of folding. In *The Logic of Sense,* he gives three conditions for the creation of a structure, applying them to what we have been calling "context-structures," which amount to a virtual mechanics of becoming:

1. "There must be at least two heterogeneous series ... (a single series never suffices to form a structure)." (Heterogeneous series are disjunct, until they are traversed by the paradoxical element that conjoins and explicates them.)

2. "Each of these series is constituted by terms which exist only through the relations they maintain with one another. To these relations, or rather to the values of these relations, there correspond very particular events, that is, *singularities* which are assignable within the structure." (The formation of series is a process of connection, enfolding, or *implication*.)

3. "The two heterogeneous series converge toward a paradoxical element, which is their 'differentiator.' This is the principle of the emission of singularities" (which is the moment of conjunction, unfolding, or *explication*).[42]

These field-series produce, through their convergence, the singular events that constitute, at a larger level of scale, the objects of materialist ontology. The convergence and resultant events form a "world," a context-structure that is "metastable, endowed with a potential energy wherein the differences between series are distributed."[43] The structures emit or explicate differences, singular events, according to the singular form of their convergence. Other "worlds" begin where these series diverge to form other singularities, other context-structures, at other levels of scale and in relation to other series.

Bohm's "generative" or "implicate order," as its name implies, enfolds within itself a variety of context-structures that also explicate themselves at different levels of scale. His simplest analogy for this process is the holographic image, which is created by recording on a suitable glass plate the reflections of a laser off a three-dimensional object; the image can be reconstructed from the glass plate just as a photograph can be re-created from a film negative, but the holographic plate differs from film in that it encodes the entire three-dimensional image onto every part of the plate. If you break up a holographic plate, you can reconstruct a complete three-dimensional image from all of the separate pieces, though the parts will produce slightly different images (again, in the manner of Leibniz's monads).[44] To apply this idea to the universe, one must imagine each point, like each moment in time, to condense within itself the entire shifting structure of that universe, viewed from different perspectives; in fact, the same operation of implication/explication applies to both time and space. Bohm labels this differential omnipresence the "holomovement," since its one consistent characteristic is transformation or becoming.

But exactly how, beyond the analogy, does this constant enfolding and unfolding take place? If we recall that every point in the holomovement, even empty space, contains "zero-point" field fluctuations with tremendous energy, we can begin to work out the logic. According to Bohm's theory, a field model is more versatile than a particle one in describing the folding process, because Bohm's novel solutions to the quantum equations deprive particles of movement. The fluctuations of empty space contain an infinite number of immanent orders or fields that interact with one another; in Deleuze's terminology, Bohm's fields are series of intensities, forces that are differential and exist only as relations: *"Quantity itself is therefore inseparable from difference in quantity.* Difference in quantity is the essence of force and of the relation of force to force."[45] In interacting at the subquantum level, the fields produce effects at the larger level of scale that our measuring instruments (and ultimately our subjective structures) occupy; in other words, the fields emit singularities. These singular large-scale effects, which are relatively stable energetic structures in themselves, propagate along the force gradients of the various interacting fields and produce yet more larger-scale effects as they unfold out of the nested orders that produce them. Thus, a particle like an electron would be a stable structure of the interaction of fields, a singularity that propagates along a differential force gradient; this energy structure would behave, in the large-scale frame of reference, like a material particle, but it would have no continuous material existence. Rather, it would be made and unmade at every instant, below the threshold of measurability.[46]

The constant making and unmaking of the "particle" along the wave front deprives it of traditional being or essence, and it also cleaves the causal relation between material particles. Interactions between such particles can no longer take the form of physical collisions that transfer energy but must be understood as varieties of virtual co-creation that explicate many simultaneous field-orders. Causality is not a direct relation but is mediated by the totality of the virtual field or plane of consistency.[47] In Deleuze's terms, "cause" and "effect" belong to two disjunct series momentarily articulated or explicated by the singularity, which itself exceeds both series; the event is creative to the extent that it is an "effect" that cannot be fully determined by its "cause."[48]

This discontinuous "existence" (or "subsistence" or "insistence"), this continual becoming whose mechanics Bohm describes, accounts for the discontinuous nature of energy intervals observed in all quantum interactions: the emission and absorption of energy do not happen continuously, at a smoothly linear rate, but rather happen in discrete units that are never observed to decompose into smaller units. These discrete units are the "quanta" from which "quantum" physics takes its name. One of their most peculiar properties, unprecedented in classical science, is their ability to move from one position to another without passing through any of the points between; this is the quantum "jump," which Bohm's theory explains well with the model described above. The progressive unfolding and enfolding of the convergent fields provide contours of potential, a differential "wave" that Bohm calls the "quantum potential" or "pilot wave," along which the singularity flickers into and out of existence. Like Deleuze's *sens,* this potential or virtuality is a form of implicit, a-signifying meaning that Bohm calls "active information,"[49] which, like the attractors of chaos theory, directs the form of the entire field convergence without being a directly measurable quantity itself. Active information, however, is not signification; Bohm insists that to speak of information, difference that makes difference, in this sense is "not to say *that it has* a meaning, *but it is* its meaning."[50] This plane of consistency is an-entropic in the sense that its infinitesimal energy gives order to the much greater energies of the converging fields, and it does not diminish in intensity with distance. These features of the quantum potential account, in Bohm's model, for both the interference observed in the famous double-slit interference experiment (that shows the wave/particle duality of matter and energy) and the phenomenon of "nonlocality," the apparently instantaneous linkage of regions separated by distances that are large with respect to the speed of light (and thus that could not communicate unless signals could move faster than light). The potential registers the whole configuration of field-becomings and interactions and communicates this constantly shifting configuration to all of the constituent fields and singularities. These parts act to conserve forms of virtual and actual motion, as if they "know" the changing state of the whole system before they could physically be "informed" of its flux by waves or particles moving at the speed of light.[51] On these questions, as on so many others, the Copenhagen interpretation is necessarily silent.

The potential is both the process of implication/explication and the wholeness of the interacting fields; the two concepts are inseparable. In Bohm's model, no particle or individual field is indivisible or basic because all are just measurable manifestations of higher-dimensional resonances, unfoldings of the enfolded potentialities implicit in every point of space-time. In this sense the implicate order model resonates with the geometry of fractals, objects that occupy fractional numbers of dimensions (between one dimensional lines and two-dimensional planes, or between two-dimensional planes and three-dimensional bodies, and so on).[52] Like fractals, the implicate order generates complex structures on the basis of very simple implicate conditions, which Deleuze would call transcendental conditions or Ideas. If the quantum principle of nonlocality, which links particles according to motion-conservation laws, is extended to the largest imaginable scale, then the universe itself would appear as a giant fractal with as many implicit dimensions as it has particle- or field-structures. Since these structures only "exist" discontinuously, the dimensionality of the universe would change discontinuously; different times and spaces, as we saw above, would explicate and implicate themselves. Also like fractals (and monads and the aleph), the implicate order repeats, in every individuated point of its infinite levels, the implicit structure of the whole, from different perspectives and on different scales. This "new notion of hierarchy in which the more general principle is immanent, that is, actively pervading and indwelling,"[53] requires that creativity move from the concept/Idea to the conditioned empirical object and also the other way; the conditioned is capable of producing new conditions; the explicate order can alter the implicate order in unpredictable ways. Bohm insists that the process is always moving in two directions at every moment, just as Deleuze recognizes that conjunction is always simultaneously disjunction, and vice versa.

The subject, finally, is a structure that supervenes only at a very high level of explication; it is what Deleuze, in *The Logic of Sense,* calls a "surface effect" of the interaction of series or fields. It is determined by the same transcendental conditions that determine all other structures, but the subject resembles its conditions no more than does any other structure. The subject's representational form is not privileged in any way, and therefore the transformation of this form does not lead to a crisis in thought; the death of God is old news. The subject is a complex fold in the infinite surface of times and spaces that, like origami, can be unfolded and refolded into different shapes. For Bohm too, consciousness and the unconscious are merely moments that enfold the whole, in the same way that a fractal like the Mandelbrot set repeats its largest-scale structure at every smaller level of scale, or the way the aleph in Borges's story contains the entire universe and another aleph, which contains the universe and another aleph, to infinity. As the first letter in the Hebrew alphabet, the aleph, like the fold, also represents "Man."

These conclusions return us to our point of departure, our proposition that conditioned forms must be understood in terms of transcendental virtual conditions that do not necessarily resemble the empirical forms they render actual, whether those forms are waves, particles, or subjects. These structures are problems at a higher level of scale and as such are relatively autonomous of the lower levels of implication; thus classical physics approximates the implicate order for massive objects like planets or pendulums, just as phenomenological methods can approximate serial syntheses for certain determined subjectivities. At the limits of these structures, however, autonomy breaks down and new operations become important, at both higher and lower levels of scale. Other theories must be constructed to intervene and produce effects once the traditional models reach their limits. These new effects are not completely determinable; the theories that produce them are a bit like Mallarmé's throws of the dice that will not abolish chance but rather affirm it, or like Nietzsche's transvaluation of all values. Creativity is again possible, and it is only through creation that we may escape the crises of the old forms of thought.

This essay is not an attempt to demonstrate the existence of an extra-representational actuality; it is rather an argument in favor of a return to ontological thought under the new image given it by Deleuze and Bohm. The true problem is not Is there a reality beyond representation? but rather How can a theory have effects? How can it literally *make* a difference? I do not wish to overstate the case for Bohm's theory, which remains a minority view in the physics community; but the small yet significant number of experimental successes attributable to Bohm's physical models, like the magnetic potential and quantum nonlocality, demonstrate that such a theory can make such a difference, can have material consequences that follow from its ontological speculations. These material successes, like those of Prigogine in thermodynamics, provide the relays that extend Deleuze's problematics to their maximum comprehension and actualize the virtual mechanics of becoming.

Notes

1. Werner Heisenberg, *Physics and Philosophy* (New York: Harper, 1958), 81–82.

2. Ibid., 83.

3. I follow David Bohm in referring to Heisenberg's principle as one of indeterminacy rather than one of uncertainty: "[I]t is not to be supposed that [physically observable variables] are just 'uncertain' to us, because we are not able to measure them with complete precision. Rather, one assumes that their very mode of being requires them to be indeterminate" (*Causality and Chance in Modern Physics* [London: Routledge and Kegan Paul, 1957], n. 85). See also the discussion in David Bohm and F. David Peat, *Science, Order, and Creativity* (New York: Bantam, 1987), 76–84.

4. Gilles Deleuze, *Difference and Repetition*, trans. Paul Patton (New York: Columbia University Press, 1994), 162.

5. Manuel De Landa, *War in the Age of Intelligent Machines* (New York: Zone, 1991); and Brian Massumi, *A User's Guide to Capitalism and Schizophrenia* (Cambridge, Mass.: MIT Press, 1992).

6. Ilya Prigogine and Isabelle Stengers, *La nouvelle alliance* (Paris: Gallimard, 1979), 291–93.

7. Gilles Deleuze and Michel Foucault, "Intellectuals and Power," in Foucault, *Language, Counter-memory, Practice*, ed. and trans. Donald Bouchard (Ithaca, N.Y.: Cornell University Press, 1977), 208.

8. David Bohm, *The Special Theory of Relativity* (1965; reprint, Redwood City, Calif.: Addison-Wesley, 1989), 227.

9. Bohm and Peat, *Science, Order, and Creativity*, 65–66.

10. Gilles Deleuze, *Bergsonism*, trans. Hugh Tomlinson and Barbara Habberjam (New York: Zone, 1988), 107–10.

11. Deleuze and Foucault, "Intellectuals and Power," 206.

12. Gilles Deleuze and Félix Guattari, *Anti-Oedipus*, trans. Robert Hurley, Mark Seem, and Helen Lane (New York: Viking, 1977), 30.

13. Niels Bohr, *The Philosophical Writings*, vol. 3 (1963; reprint, Woodbridge, Conn.: Ox Box Press, 1987), 3, 6.

14. See Heisenberg, *Physics and Philosophy*, chaps. 3 and 8.

15. David Bohm, "Bohr's View concerning the Quantum Theory," in *Quantum Theory and Beyond*, ed. Ted Bastin (Cambridge: Cambridge University Press, 1971), 40.

16. J. S. Bell, *Speakable and Unspeakable in Quantum Mechanics* (Cambridge: Cambridge University Press, 1987), 173.

17. Bohm, *Causality and Chance in Modern Physics*, 96.

18. Gilles Deleuze, *The Logic of Sense*, trans. Mark Lester with Charles Stivale (New York: Columbia University Press, 1990), 54.

19. Deleuze, *Bergsonism*, 44.

20. Deleuze, *Logic of Sense*, 105.

21. David Bohm, "Time, the Implicate Order and Pre-space," in *Physics and the Ultimate Significance of Time: Bohm, Prigogine, and Process Philosophy*, ed. David Ray Griffin (Albany: State University of New York Press, 1986), 182.

22. See Deleuze, *Bergsonism*, chap. 3.

23. Bohm, "Time, the Implicate Order and Pre-space," 189–91.

24. Deleuze, *Difference and Repetition*, 70–71, 79–80, 88–89.

25. Bohm, "Time, the Implicate Order and Pre-space," 187.

26. Deleuze and Guattari, *A Thousand Plateaus*, 32.

27. Bohm, "Time, the Implicate Order and Pre-space," 189.

28. Ibid.

29. Ibid., 180.

30. Deleuze, *Difference and Repetition*, 211.

31. Bohm, "Time, the Implicate Order and Pre-space," 197.

32. Feynman's diagrams graph the interactions of subatomic particles, but they also allow the solution of problems involving antiparticles if the antiparticles are treated as normal particles *moving backward in time;* see Gary Zukav, *The Dancing Wu Li Masters* (New York: Bantam, 1979), 214–22. The "sum over histories" method involves equations that integrate all of the possible alternate histories of the particles involved.

33. Gilles Deleuze, "La conception de la différence chez Bergson," *Les etudes bergsoniennes* 4 (1956): 98, my translation.

34. Bohm and Peat, *Science, Order, and Creativity*, 164.

35. David Bohm, *Wholeness and the Implicate Order* (New York: Routledge, 1980), 207.

36. Gilles Deleuze and Claire Parnet, *Dialogues*, trans. Hugh Tomlinson and Barbara Habberjam (New York: Columbia University Press), 92, 151n. 9.

37. Deleuze, *Difference and Repetition*, 211.

38. Ibid., 209.

39. See David Bohm and Yakir Aharonov, "Significance of Electromagnetic Potentials in the Quantum Theory," *Physical Review* 115 (1959): 485–91, on the real effects of magnetic potential. They proved that electrons moving through a metal circlet would produce interference with the potential of a magnetic field, even if they were physically isolated from the field itself. Thus the potential, which had been treated as a mathematical expedient in classical electrodynamics, must now be treated as real. I would like to thank Laurence S. Hordon for bringing this point to my attention.

40. Deleuze, *Difference and Repetition*, 211–12.

41. Bohm, *Wholeness and the Implicate Order*, 212.

42. Deleuze, *Logic of Sense*, 50–51.

43. Ibid., 103.

44. Bohm, *Wholeness and the Implicate Order*, 144–47.

45. Gilles Deleuze, *Nietzsche and Philosophy*, trans. Hugh Tomlinson (New York: Columbia University Press, 1983), 43.

46. Bohm, *Wholeness and the Implicate Order*, 152.

47. Ibid., 126–27.

48. Deleuze, *Logic of Sense*, 6–7.

49. Bohm and Peat, *Science, Order, and Creativity*, 93.

50. David Bohm and Renée Weber, "Meaning as Being in the Implicate Order Philosophy of David Bohm: A Conversation," in *Quantum Implications: Essays in Honour of David Bohm*, ed. Basil J. Hiley and F. David Peat (New York: Routledge and Kegan Paul, 1987), 438.

51. This is the crux of J. S. Bell's theorem: the behavior of quantum systems demands that the actuality of these systems can only be maintained (as Bohm wishes to do) if we give up the classical idea that all interactions take place over very short distances. This has been tested experimentally by Alain Aspect, who determined that

interactions can in fact take place over very large distances (though many physicists dispute the adequacy of his experimental arrangement). On Aspect, see Bell, *Speakable and Unspeakable in Quantum Mechanics,* 139–58, and Zukav, *Dancing Wu Li Masters,* 294–95.

52. Deleuze and Guattari, *A Thousand Plateaus,* 486–88.

53. Bohm and Peat, *Science, Order, and Creativity,* 164.

Madness and Repetition

The Absence of Work in Deleuze,
Foucault, and Jacques Martin

Eleanor Kaufman

These pages are dedicated to the memory of Jacques Martin, the friend who, in the most terrible ordeal alone discovered the road to Marx's philosophy — and guided me onto it.

This dedication, which prefaces Louis Althusser's *For Marx*,[1] appeared two years after the suicide of Jacques Martin in 1963. Jacques Martin, placed in the middle between Althusser and Foucault at the École Normale Supérieure — four years younger than Althusser and four years older than Foucault — appears to have been an enigmatic and exceedingly brilliant man, in Althusser's words, "a sad yet warm homosexual, even in the distance of his latent schizophrenia, an incomparable friend."[2] Aside from short prefaces to his translations from the German and a highly acclaimed thesis "Mémoire de DES" on the notion of the individual in Hegel, Jacques Martin produced no work and ceased to advance in the French educational system, often relying on money loaned to him by Althusser and Foucault for his very subsistence.[3] Preoccupied with the idea of madness, Martin was apparently the first to equate madness with the absence of work (*l'absence d'oeuvre*), an association that was taken up by both Althusser and Foucault.

Althusser makes frequent and poignant references to Martin in his autobiographical work *L'avenir dure longtemps* (The future lasts a long time).[4] This work is punctuated with the refrain "thanks to Jacques Martin..."[5] It is Martin to whom Althusser owes his coming to philosophy and, in particular, his coming to Marx. He writes, "[T]he only one who gave me an idea (and a true one) about philosophy was Martin. Thanks to him, I was able to have an overall strategic idea of the philosophical situation, and several absolutely essential theoretical landmarks for getting my *bearings* in it."[6] Althusser credits Martin with more than bringing him to philosophy — according to Althusser, it was Martin who taught him how to *think*, and to think otherwise:

media on the scene in the first week, little is reported regarding the deportees themselves. News accounts and analysis are dominated by the pronouncements and polemic of state representatives, voices volleying over the heads of those whose lives are most immediately at stake. Deportees are directly quoted only rarely. Most often, it is in the anonymous, indirect reportorial voice that we learn of the condition of the deportees themselves. The deportees do not speak of the lives from which they were separated, of their political or personal aspirations or fears, of their opinions regarding their role in the political war of position and will being waged over their heads and on their bodies. Rather, they speak only to give voice to their transformed being as organic materiality: sickness, hunger, cold, injury.

This body's being is something other than the summing of its parts, the individual men; in fact, as a mass, it no longer has parts. The individuals that would make up a divisible group disintegrate when the group is transformed into mass. We might consider in this regard the Israeli announcement of December 28 that ten men had been deported in error and would be allowed to return to Israel. The mass of deportees is divided: ten are no longer deportees; they have returned to their previous status as individuals with rights and liberties. But the resubjectification of these ten is to make them disappear for a second time (they melt away into the interior) and simultaneously to strengthen the desubjectified condition of the remaining mass of deportees. As a rhetorical strategy, to single out ten deportees as a mistake is to insist that, as far as concerns the remainder, there has been no mistake.[19] But from the perspective of the mass, we discover paradoxically that the resubjectification of particular bodies within the mass body, the representation of individual subjects, in fact reinforces the desubjectification of the mass as a whole. We see here the limitations of a politics of representation: representation can only be the representation of the subject within the state, while the mass, as the state's excess that it can neither assimilate nor efface, cannot be represented.

The difficulty in coming to terms with this mass remains one of representation: if the mass body cannot be represented because it is not the body of the subject, on what grounds can we know it as body, and how might we conceive of such a body's appearance? Here, Deleuze makes a helpful distinction between *representation* and *perception*. There is a gap between the two: while the body in excess of the subject cannot be represented, it can in fact be perceived under particular circumstances. Leaving aside cinema's practices of representation, Deleuze analyzes cinema as a technology of perception. When the practical requirements of action have been removed, as in the cinema, Deleuze suggests that the being of the world as continual change and movement becomes perceptible. Cinema thus resists the reifying logic of natural perception: "[I]t affects the visible with a fundamental disturbance, and the world with a suspension, which contradicts all natural perception."[20] Cinema in effect makes visible a body that "I," mired in the illusions of action, cannot know: "What [cinema] produces in this way is the genesis of an 'unknown body' which we have in the back of our heads, like the unthought in thought, the birth of the visible which is still hidden from view."[21] The unknown body cannot be represented but perhaps can be perceived at the edges or limits of representation. Recognizing and confronting this body necessarily transforms thought by exposing thought to its "unthought." In *Cinema 2* the "unknown body" as it emerges in cinematic perception is the nodal point for thought's turning, from an ontological idealism that posits thought as the correlate to the state as universal, rational, and individualized, to the "counterthought" of *A Thousand Plateaus*, the thought that confronts "state-thought." Thus, the perception of this body outside representation is political insofar as it demands a transformed thought, a transformed relation to the orders and logics of state-thought.

The power of the cinematic perception of deportation lies in the connection it creates between the body and the outside, a connection that exposes a fissure in the totalizing edifice of state and subject. The outside is not a location but rather a condition, a state of being. To think the outside of the state, we need to think not only bodies without subjects but bodies without places or locations. Deportation makes this clear: on being expulsed from Israel, the deportees are transported to a "no-man's-land," the Israeli-controlled "security zone" in southern Lebanon. This expulsion takes a purely negative form. It is not the transportation from point A, where one is no longer welcome, to point B, where perhaps one can be in peace. Rather, the "you cannot be at point A" becomes a "you cannot be in any place."

This metaphysical placelessness is enacted as a drama of dislocation in the first days of the deportation. As the busses cross the official Israel-Lebanon border and approach the northern end of the security zone, Lebanese troops block the roads, refusing the deportees entry into Lebanon. The Associated Press reports, "When the deportees walked back to the Zommaraya gateway to re-enter Israel's security zone, the passage was closed.... Israeli troops fired over their heads to send them away."[22] The 415 deportees spend the first night "stranded in the snow and mud of southern Lebanon, in a desolate buffer strip that lies between the nearest Lebanese and Israeli army checkpoints."[23] Two days later, Lebanese soldiers order the deportees to leave their makeshift camp and march toward the Israeli checkpoint. Each attempt to approach the checkpoint is repulsed by shelling and machine-gun fire. One cannot dwell in this aptly described "no-man's-land." Rather, one is in a state of a perpetual movement that goes nowhere, shuttling between blocked passageways. The nowhere of these bodies is a fissure, a break that cannot be reconciled with representational notions of subjectified bodies in localizable places.

Moving Bodies

I have been considering the state not as formal government or codified law but as a system that produces spatial relationships and regulates the relations between individuals and the space of the state. In this framework the political centrality of movement becomes apparent. The state mediates the relations between individuals and places through the regulation and control of movement and property. Society is ordered around the assignation of appropriate places for each. Even the most marginal or deviant have their proper place in modern society: the homeless shelter, the insane asylum, the prison. Not only does the state aim to control movement; but it is through the enforcement of movement that the state exerts control over its subjects. Voluntarily or involuntarily, the body subject to the state conforms to movements as regulated by the state.[24]

This is the mechanism at work in Israel's most frequently employed methods of collective punishment of Palestinians living under occupation: curfew and house demolition. The curfew, deemed necessary to maintain order, is the denial of the right to free movement to the Arab populations of the occupied territories. In its most extreme form, Arab inhabitants of towns under curfew are not permitted to leave their houses under any circumstances. But even the house is at best a fragile, tenuous space in which to be when all other spaces have been refused. Occupation forces may forcibly enter and search any house and destroy the houses of those suspected of promoting any form of resistance. Homelessness is an immanent possibility for every Palestinian tenuously inhabiting this space.

Deportation becomes the negative doubling of this ordering and restriction of movement and place within the ordering structure of the state. Where each subject within the state has a proper place, the inaccessibility of place to certain individuals becomes the impossibility of subjectivity within the state: silence, invisibility, disappearance, death. This desubjectification as placelessness occurs in two modes: on one side, the body in perpetual movement, and on the other, the progressive constriction of the space of the body. Deportation enacts both these bodily effects. Under these circumstances, wandering is the condition of placelessness and, as such, is the sign not of nomadic freedom but of a body squeezed out of the surface of the social, forced into motion as the only state of being that does not require the occupation of space. At the same time, the body's extension is minimized. The body is constricted in its ability to affect and be affected, such that its reach, its sphere of activity, is brought closer and closer to zero. The body that resists total obliteration is constrained to occupy the smallest possible space and to consume the least possible substance. For this reason, such a body cannot be represented as a positive presence. From the point of view of representation, the condition of desubjectified placelessness does not exist, for there is no way to represent a not-subject that is in no-place. Only a perception that is not predicated on truthfulness as presence can account for such a body.

The paradox of deportation is that the same action by which the state aims to extrude the being that is incompatible with it produces another being that poses an even more radical challenge to the state's totalizing force. But we should note that it is only because of the extreme suffering of the deportees, the continued deprivations of the flesh, that this effect persists. Had Lebanon accepted the deportees, as it had others in the past, there would have been no crisis. Had it not been dead winter, had the men more clothing and food, had there been shelter and medical facilities, it is unlikely that the deportation would have been more than a minor, evanescent affair. Indeed, as the deportees settled in to the routines of no-man's-land weeks after their expulsion, affairs returned to "normal," that is, this event could be returned to the circuit of state meanings. Eventually, the deportees established a governing body and representatives, gained access to food and medical supplies, and replaced their flimsy tents with more permanent barracks. The deportees responded to their expulsion by the state with the creation of a new state, both as internally organized and as externally recognized. But while the narrative of deportation, as crisis followed by negotiation followed by resolution, returns us quickly to the regime of truthful narration, this does not entirely diffuse the nonnarrative force of deportation that exposes the excess of state and subject: bodies, forces, and movements that resist the identities of state and subject and of truth and justice.[25]

Politics: State, Subject, and the Outside

The recuperation of the deportees as political subjects prefigured the historic Israel-PLO accords of August 1993, in which Israel recognized the PLO as the legitimate representative of the Palestinian people in exchange for the PLO's acceptance of Israel's right to exist. While these accords seemed to promise an eventual resolution in favor of the Palestinians' demands for self-rule and self-determination, there is little beyond diplomatic posturing that would suggest that any such outcome is on the horizon. Several aspects of this situation bear remarking: the continual deferral of negotiations that would lead to meaningful Palestinian autonomy (economic and political); Israeli intervention in so-called limited-autonomy zones whenever the state deems necessary, including deploying of troops, imposing curfews, limiting movement, intervening in police activities when Palestinian police are "ineffective," and demolishing houses of suspected "terrorists"; ongoing Israeli settlement in the territories accompanied with the development of an Israeli-only infrastructure. In this context, Palestinian autonomy is a sham, allowed only to the extent that it is convenient. Political recognition and the external trappings of state-formation may soothe the conscience of international observers increasingly uncomfortable with Israel's politics of occupation and repression but will do little to address the fundamental dispossession of place, that is, of land, history, and a future, that the Palestinians have suffered.

In the "cinematic politics" of deportation, there is the possibility of a perception of a positive force that might serve as a resource for alternative futures. Deportation as I have read it here opens onto an outside that troubles the smooth orders of state and subject. In the extreme circumstance of deportation, we discover a being not as subject or identity but as an unindividuated body of movement. The case of deportation shows both the necessity of place to political being and the power of placelessness to expose the fundamental violence whereby places come into being. On the outside of these places is an *other* body that is not the body of a politically recognized subject, what I have called here the body of deportation. This body can be neither effaced nor assimilated. In its material persistence it challenges the closed system of subject and state that has produced "the Palestinian" as a threat or an impossibility. I have suggested that this body might be seen as the "war machine" of *A Thousand Plateaus*, a creative force that resists the state's drive toward destruction. We should not forget, however, that even in *A Thousand Plateaus* the war machine (like aligned figures such as nomadism) is extremely ambivalent. The war machine promises transformation, but as Paul Virilio reminds us, sometimes the line between becoming a war machine and being dead is difficult to distinguish: "[I]f 'to be is to inhabit,' . . . not to inhabit is no longer to exist. Sudden death is preferable to the slow death of he who is no longer welcome, of the reject, of the man deprived of a specific place *and thus of his identity*."[26] If the radical homelessness of the Palestinian is the condition for the emergence of a war machine that disrupts the smooth orderings of place, it is nevertheless a crisis for those bodies denied identity and excluded from any place.

What would be the political force of refusing state and subject? What might be the productive power of a body that cannot be placed? Something else emerges with these questions, something that cannot be contained by either history or politics insofar as history and politics are determined in advance to be about and for the state and the subject. In Deleuze's relentless insistence on the productive possibilities of the outside, the unthought, the unknown, he challenges us to probe for what does not appear, what cannot or is not allowed to appear in the received versions of history and politics. Cinematic politics brings into perception something that cannot be, a Palestinian body that is not already defined and delimited by its (material or political) opposition to Israel. How do we respond to this body? What alternative futures does this body demand? These are the questions that bring us back into politics and history, perhaps transformed by some effort to account for, and take account of, the productive powers of the outside.

Notes

1. Gilles Deleuze, *Cinema 2: The Time-Image,* trans. Hugh Tomlinson and Robert Galeta (Minneapolis: University of Minnesota Press, 1989), 217.

2. As Prime Minister Golda Meir put it, "Who are the Palestinians? There are no Palestinians."

3. Deleuze, *Cinema 2,* 133.

4. I am focusing here on the narratives surrounding a particular event. But as I remarked at the outset, this event repeats in signal ways the basic elements of the ongoing conflict. As regards the role of truthful narration, for example, since the founding of the Zionist movement on one side and the emergence of Palestinian nationalism on the other, both sides have attempted to use the authority of history as truthful narration to justify or necessitate a particular political outcome. Nevertheless, the amassing of authoritative histories on both sides has done little to contribute to an actual resolution, suggesting that the "truthfulness" of Israeli or Palestinian claims to the land is not itself at issue but is rather one of the ways in which the conflict is expressed.

5. "Israel Expels 400 from Occupied Lands," *New York Times,* 18 December 1992, 1(A), national edition.

6. Ibid.

7. "Palestinians Stranded in No Man's Land," *San Jose Mercury News,* 19 December 1992, 1(A).

8. "Leftists Tell an Unreceptive Rabin the P.L.O. Beckons," *New York Times,* 21 December 1992, 3(A), national edition.

9. "Ousted Arabs Shiver and Wait in Lebanese Limbo," *New York Times,* 24 December 1992, 3(A), national edition.

10. The Arab inhabitants and citizens of Israel, as well as Palestinians living as refugees or temporary residents in other countries, have fallen from sight in the discussions of Palestinian autonomy.

11. For an extended analysis of this effacement of the Palestinian, see Edward W. Said, "Zionism from the Standpoint of Its Victims," in *The Question of Palestine* (New York: Vintage Books, 1992).

12. Deleuze, *Cinema 2,* 133.

13. Gilles Deleuze, *Nietzsche and Philosophy,* trans. Hugh Tomlinson (New York: Columbia University Press, 1983), 39.

14. On the power of the false and the simulacrum, see also Gilles Deleuze, "Plato and the Simulacrum," trans. Rosalind Krauss, *October* 27 (1983): 45–56.

15. Deleuze, *Cinema 2,* 139.

16. Ibid.

17. Deleuze, *Nietzsche,* 40.

18. On counting and naming numbers, see Gilles Deleuze, *Bergsonism,* trans. Hugh Tomlinson and Barbara Habberjam (New York: Zone Books, 1991), 41–42.

19. A similar logic appeared to govern Israel's offer on 1 February 1993 to repatriate approximately one-quarter of the deportees. The group decided collectively to reject this offer, arguing that to accept would be to grant legitimacy to the continued exile of the remainder.

20. Deleuze, *Cinema 2,* 201.

21. Ibid., 210.

22. "Lebanese Troops Block Palestinian Deportees," *San Jose Mercury News*, 18 December 1992, 21(A).

23. "Palestinians Stranded in No Man's Land," 1(A).

24. See, for example, Kenneth Dean and Brian Massumi's analysis of the importance of control over movement in the Chinese empire in *First and Last Emperors: The Absolute State and the Body of the Despot* (Brooklyn, N.Y.: Autonomedia, 1992).

25. The importance of recognizing the contingency and limitations of state-determined outcomes has become especially urgent in light of the increasing collusion of the Palestinian Authority in enforcing Israeli policy and law. The Palestinian people will gain little if the result of so much struggle is a Palestinian police state no less repressive than the Israeli occupying forces.

26. Paul Virilio, *Speed and Politics: An Essay on Dromology*, trans. Mark Polizzotti (New York: Semiotext[e], 1986), 78.

4

Mapping against the Grain

From Text to Territory

Félix Guattari's Cartographies of the Unconscious

Bruno Bosteels

In their last cooperative project, *What Is Philosophy?*, Gilles Deleuze and Félix Guattari expose the sizable stakes raised in opening a new field for "geo-philosophy" around the twin notions of earth and territory. "Subject and object give a poor approximation of thought," they postulate in answer to the basic framework behind nearly all modern philosophy, to which they add: "Thinking is neither a line drawn between subject and object nor a revolving of one around the other. Rather, thinking takes place in the relationship of territory and the earth."[1] This statement is best read as the symptom of a global change that has already been occurring in the theoretical vanguards of the last decades. Such a change emerges not only in the growing circle of authors who are becoming acutely aware of the ecological problems that beset our earth today but also among numerous critics who, long after the heydays of structuralism and poststructuralism in the 1960s and 1970s, persist in questioning the discourse of the modern human sciences, of which traditionally the anthropological subject at one and the same time constitutes the privileged object. As is well known, Michel Foucault fatefully diagnoses the principal modern variants of this phenomenon in "Man and His Doubles," in *The Order of Things: An Archaeology of the Human Sciences*. More recently, the alternative to this characteristic redoubling of subject and object is no longer the continuous flow of experience cherished by both phenomenologists and philosophers of life alike, nor is it just the radical free play of difference celebrated by some poststructuralists and deconstructive philosophers of language. Instead, without automatically denying these results of previous criticisms, the answer would lie in the multifarious spaces opening up between the expanses of the earth and the territorial universes of existence. Apart from a thinly disguised nostalgic return "from text to work," what thus currently is taking place after or besides poststructuralism in some of the most fertile fields of literary, cultural, and philosophical studies can perhaps be summarized following the newly spun guiding thread of geophilosophy as a gradual yet thorough displacement "from text to territory."[2]

145

While resolutely sidestepping the rhetoric of temporality most typical of deconstruction, critical and theoretical inquiries today increasingly seem to be moving toward a general politics of spatiality. From the textual analysis of writing as much as from an ethical discussion of acting, both still evidently modeled upon the ontological analysis of being, the emphasis is shifting to the cultural study of literary, artistic, and ideological forms of mapping. In other words, rather than the "event" of temporality in the Heideggerian sense dear to Jacques Derrida, Paul de Man, or Reiner Schürmann, what is at stake becomes the "locus" of an event, in a Foucauldian (if not Sartrean) sense arguably shared by thinkers such as Deleuze and Alain Badiou. The practical and theoretical differences between these positions should be taken as indices of two apparently antagonistic but at bottom perhaps reconcilable tendencies within a general philosophy of the event, seen from a more transcendental vantage point, in the first case, and from a genealogical perspective, in the second. "What is significant," Foucault suggests about the latter, "is that history does not consider an event without seeking out the regularity of phenomena and the probable limits of their occurrence, without enquiring about variations, inflexions and the slope of the curve, without desiring to know the conditions on which these depend."[3] Anyone even remotely familiar with recent titles, if nothing else, in the humanities must in this regard have been struck by the astonishing appeal of topological and specifically cartographic images that serve, I believe, to mark out such conditions of existence. On the one hand, Deleuze and Guattari for example clarify: "The concept is the contour, the configuration, the constellation of an event to come"; on the other: "The concept is not object but territory."[4]

Across the board, in fact, all kinds of places, spaces, sites, fields, maps, and charts both real and metaphorical are fast becoming tiresomely ubiquitous. Aside from what is undoubtedly just another passing fad, the fresh allure of such images and metaphors also hides an unfinished task, perhaps even an unconsciously avoided one of conceptual elaboration. By paraphrasing an argument from Rosalind E. Krauss about the comparable advent of abstract grids earlier in modern art, I would thus like to submit the following thought as a working hypothesis: Behind almost every recent use and abuse of the cartographic metaphor there lies — like a trauma that must be repressed — an unspoken theory of articulation, more specifically a critical social theory of causality, parading in the guise of a generic statement about the current fashion of cultural studies.[5] Unless this missing link with theories of causality somehow becomes conceptually explicit, what could mark the onset of a veritable cartographic turn will only have been just another lost opportunity to guide the contemporary debates along a welcome sweep of hitherto unbeaten paths.

❖

Let me begin by explaining how the possible move from time to space and from textuality to cartography marks a gradual strategic shift rather than a radical epistemic break. First, the spatial and cartographic turn in contemporary criticism, theory, and philosophy continues to presuppose several of the familiar tenets behind poststructuralism, particularly the unremitting deconstruction of representational thinking. This first continuity at the outset excludes a metaphysical definition of mapping in the classical mimetic sense.

A map, then, is never just a mirror of nature. It is neither an adequate imitation nor a transparent reflection of a stable territory already existing elsewhere. This insight, though perhaps comfortingly obvious to literary critics and their more congenial philosophical colleagues, is nonetheless only recently becoming common knowledge among theorists and historians of cartography, who in fact most often continue to face stubborn mimetic prejudices of transparency and immediacy as so many dominant features of their field. As a result maps are still frequently evaluated in terms of their referential and scientific accuracy in relation to the represented objects, instead of being judged like works of art for their ontological and pragmatic efficacy in making and unmaking the environment, setting up existential territories, or bringing forth entire worlds from the uneven surface of the earth. Only in recent years has this situation dramatically begun to change. "Maps have entered the age of suspicion," as Christian Jacob explains: "Today one would do well to apply to maps the strategies of 'deconstruction' so as to break the exclusive and constraining link between reality and representation which has dominated cartographic thinking and constitutes the implicit epistemology of its history."[6]

Contrary to what some might reasonably expect, however, the main alternative point of reference for the cartographic turn is most often Foucault's "discourse" rather than the "texts" of Derrida, Roland Barthes, or Julia Kristeva. To be more precise, within Foucault's own body of writings a sharp displacement occurs analogous to the shift from textuality to territoriality. This is what Deleuze in a breathtaking study about his colleague translates as the passage from the "archive" (the forms and strata of discursive knowledge, which variously define both what is visible and what is expressible in a specific domain and at a precise moment in history) to the "map" or "diagram" (the forces and strategies of microphysical power, which in each case imbricate the visible and the sayable according to variable institutional relations of acting and being acted upon). Such a passage allows Deleuze to present Foucault's critical labor primarily from *Discipline and Punish: The Birth of the Prison* onward as the work of "a new cartographer," whereas his friend's lifelong project in general, from *Madness and Civilization: A History of Insanity in the Age of Reason* all the way to include the unfinished *History of Sexuality,* would contain the blueprint for a whole "topology" of being as a mode of "thinking otherwise."[7] At least for the moment this brief summary should suffice to

highlight the powerful impulse hidden just below the surface in the mean-
ders of poststructuralist cartographies to develop a thorough social theory of
articulation.

A second, Marxist line of continuing development behind the current transition from writing to mapping emerges earlier, especially in the context of the
Situationist International. There are, however, already remarkable antecedents
for this trend toward cartography to be found not only in texts such as Georg
Lukács' well-known opening lines to *The Theory of the Novel* but also in some
pedagogical ideas behind the Communist International. In articles for *Pravda*
later included in *Problems of Everyday Life,* for instance, Leon Trotsky states:
"The question of maps in our situation — that is, in a situation of imperialist
encirclement and the growth of the world revolution — is a very important
question of general education," to the point where "propaganda in favor of
political-geographical maps" becomes imperative at least if from below the
cry resounds: "Give us maps!"[8] Taken up differently among later revolution-
aries, this second current excludes an idealist definition of cartography, while
obliging dialectical materialism to become at once historical and geographical.

Most tangible particularly in the period leading up to the events of May
'68 in France is the impact of the field of psychogeography for what Guy
Debord considers the task of a unitary "critique of urban geography," which
allots a pivotal place to the invention of "a renovated cartography" so as to
bring out, for example, the "sum of possibilities" hidden in a Paris metro map.
In "Theory of the Dérive," Debord thus suggests: "With the aid of old maps,
aerial photographs and experimental dérives, one can draw up hitherto lacking
maps of influences, maps whose inevitable imprecision at this early stage is no
worse than that of the first navigational charts; the only difference is that it is
a matter no longer of delineating stable continents, but of changing architecture and urbanism."[9] Examples of this transformative and diversionary kind
of cartographic montage, such as Debord's *The Naked City,* can be found in
several anthologies from the Situationist International.

Situationists, to be sure, often provocatively scoff at what they at the
time label the modernist studies of their academic counterparts; and yet their
cartographic project at least partially overlaps with the research interests of
Marxists such as Henri Lefebvre regarding the spatial practices of everyday
life, later taken up and expanded by authors such as Michel de Certeau. Not
coincidentally, the aim to construct "situations" as distinct from Lefebvre's
earlier theory of "moments" then already entails inflecting concrete revolutionary practice in the sense of a renewed creative investment of spaces and
places, instead of seeking true liberty only in the lived thickness of historical
time. "The 'moment' is primarily temporal, it belongs to an impure but dominant zone of temporality," Debord specifies in his polemic, and he adds: "The
situation, closely articulated to the locus, is entirely spatio-temporal."[10]

The turn toward spatiality is a rare development in an emancipatory tradition usually prejudiced in favor of the time of authentic experience, against the spatial reification of life — "space" and "things" for most older critics of society being near synonyms. "At any rate," to use Ernst Bloch's exemplary words from the early 1930s, "the primacy of space over time is an infallible sign of reactionary language," a judgment with which Max Horkheimer and Theodor Adorno little more than a decade later would have no real disagreement since for them too "[s]pace is absolute alienation."[11] Some readers perhaps will take this to be an old-fashioned stance of either utopians or revolutionary pessimists, typical of heavy times other than our own seemingly free-floating context of global geopolitical drift. Consider then one of the latest avatars of such prejudice in *New Reflections on the Revolution of Our Time,* where Ernesto Laclau boldly reasserts: "Politics and space are antinomic terms. Politics only exist insofar as the spatial eludes us."[12] Inasmuch as the deconstruction of metaphysics, including Marxism, similarly presupposes an authentic temporality and a hyped-up historicity irreducible to any stable presence, there is much in the thought of difference to corroborate this dated aversion against spatiality. Whatever their personal and intellectual contentions may be, to counter this long-standing but nevertheless misguided and somewhat baffling tradition, both Debord and Lefebvre have been essential players in the process leading up to the recent spatial turn and, at least in the first case, the subversive turn to cartography.

Lefebvre's monumental study *The Production of Space,* for instance, has provided Edward Soja with a major springboard for his *Postmodern Geographies* and, more recently, *Thirdspace,* in which the author convincingly pleads for a spatial ontology. What is more, unlike his mentor, who rarely fails to lash out at any sign even vaguely reminiscent of a semiotic turn in the theory of social practice, Soja with real urgency requests original forms of cartography. In his words: "A new 'cognitive mapping' must be developed, a new way of seeing through the gratuitous veils of both reactionary postmodernism and late modern historicism to encourage the creation of a politicized spatial consciousness and a radical spatial praxis."[13] Together with Kevin Lynch's *The Image of the City,* finally, Lefebvre and Soja in turn inspire and further encourage Fredric Jameson's quest for an updated socialist political agenda to answer the postmodern culture of late capitalism with a utopian aesthetic of cognitive mapping.

On top of continuing a generous dialogue in coded form with Lukács's *History and Class-consciousness* and *The Theory of the Novel,* Jameson's platform remains perhaps the most faithful heir to the hitherto unsurpassed project from the Situationist International to figure and reappropriate the total social territory through novel forms of class consciousness. Roughly put, the argument follows a three-step program as if to constitute a perfect syllogism: "Without a conception of the social totality (and the possibility of transforming a whole social system), no properly socialist politics is possible"; "The project of cognitive mapping obviously stands or falls with the conception of some (unrepresentable, imaginary) global social totality that was to have been mapped"; hence: "An aesthetic of cognitive mapping in this sense is an integral part of any social political project."[14] Whoever is inclined to accept both premises admittedly will have a difficult time rejecting this conclusion as anything else but astute and to the point. Cartography thereby once again seeks to accomplish the daunting philosophical task of tracing "the transcendental topography of the mind," in Lukács's words. "For what," the author of *The Theory of the Novel* asks, "is the task of true philosophy if not to draw that archetypal map?"[15] Whether this type of map, in keeping with the aims of geophilosophy, is capable of avoiding the representational pitfalls lurking in the philosophy and political theory of the modern subject is of course precisely what remains to be seen.

An effective map of the social territory, in sum, shall be neither idealistic nor mimetic. Aside from listing these mostly negative characteristics, though, few of the writers above formulate a specific theoretical frame to underpin the ways in which they interpret either historical or utopian cartographies. At best there are the multiple remarks about "transcoding" scattered throughout Jameson's publications, from the last page of *The Prison-house of Language* to the numerous references in *Postmodernism, or, The Cultural Logic of Late Capitalism*, which would warrant a separate study to be taken up elsewhere. As Colin MacCabe observes in his preface to Jameson's *The Geopolitical Aesthetic: Cinema and Space in the World System:* "Theoretically speaking, cognitive mapping needs more than mere development — it is fundamentally a metaphor which needs to be unpacked into a series of concepts which would link the psychic and the social."[16] A constructive project of such ambitious range, however, is essential to the works of Guattari, who in this sense assembles the basic scaffolding for a formal and political theory of cartography. This conceptual framework, which hinges on the innovative possibility of diagrammatic modes of sign production, to a large extent dominates not only the latter half of Deleuze and Guattari's cooperative efforts, especially *Kafka* and *A Thousand Plateaus,* but also some of the works that Deleuze signs alone, including his magnificent *Foucault.*

The following presentation of Guattari's theory of cartography therefore has a double purpose: first, to counterbalance the wide variety of existing definitions of the "text" with a few guidelines for a possible conceptual definition of the "map," both as an object and as a method of contemporary cultural studies in the largest sense; and, second, to give due credit while offering a minor homage to the forceful creativity of Guattari's thinking by considering his works alone rather than only those volumes cosigned with Deleuze. To anticipate, throughout this study the aim is to follow Guattari's answers to the most persistent task haunting all of his writings in the face of an increasingly expansive and insidious form of capitalism:

How to reenact a de-alienated subjectivity without seriality, a subject I name "processual" because it produces its own existence through a process of singularization, because it engenders itself as existential territory to the extent that it constitutes itself as an analytic cartography? There you have the damn problem that I have circled for a couple of decades. Against the fashions and retreats to orthodoxies, the postmodernisms and neoconservatisms, nothing appears to me more urgent![17]

The itinerary of Guattari's entire thinking spirals around three focal points: the production of subjectivity, the social codification of signs, and the global transformation of the environment. In this order, the enumeration at once sketches out a chronological overview of Guattari's intellectual trajectory. And if his works draw three entwining spirals rather than either a single line or a set of circles, they also proceed through the thick accumulation of layers rather than through a mere succession of stages. At each time the earlier topic not only generates but also implicates the later one, with neither a rigid closure into insular regions nor a strict causality between separate levels of interest. In fact, one of the defining gestures of Guattari's thinking precisely consists in refusing to establish mere parallelisms between autonomous strata, since this segmentary kind of thinking quickly leads to the positing of a transitive causality directly grounded in one block of elements as the infrastructure, or essential core, while reducing the other to the status of a mere beyond (*un au-delà*) or after effect (*un par-après*) of some superstructure, or surrounding shell.

In Guattari's writing the refusal of segmentarity takes the form of a number of recurrent phrases that translate his explorations into a different logic of social practice, an intensive and affective logic of the included middle that would neither strictly obey the principles of identity and noncontradiction of classical reason nor merely seek to resolve and sublate opposites in the manner of dialectical reason. This critical strategy is especially poignant in regard to two traditions with which Guattari's theoretical work interacts most intensely, that is, Freudianism and Marxism, insofar as they tend to define the subject and society through such forms of causality: for example, by reducing sociopolitical relationships directly to the personal unconscious, in one case, or by interpreting cultural productions as being overcoded by the material environment, in the other. "The first thing to acknowledge is that models which propose the notion of a causal hierarchy between these various semiotic regimes are out of step with reality," Guattari concludes about the codes of capitalism. "In this domain as in many others, the influences are not unilateral, nor are we ever in the presence of a one-way causality."[18]

Only in this larger practical and theoretical context do the alternative definitions of cartography acquire their full meaning. Mapping, in other words, is Guattari's answer to the overarching question of articulation. The same is in fact true not only for Deleuze and Foucault but also for Jameson and de Certeau. A theory of cartography in this context has to account for the multiple articulations of the social and the subjective, the material and the semiotic, between map and territory; it has to detect models to imagine how desire and production, madness and work, connect or intersect while cutting in and out of one another; it has to find ways to plot the lines of entwinement — both dense and ethereal, opaque and in your face for everyone to see — between knowledge and power, discourses and practices, between ways to see, to tell, and to make do, while scrupulously disentangling the tiniest knots; and it has to conjecture how, between the real and the imaginary, or between the real and the symbolical, a precarious suture can take hold across the empty interstices, whereas in other instances a fissure rends apart the social surface all of a sudden to break the blissful spell of ready-made totalities. Meanwhile, at least for Guattari, one of the encompassing tasks of cartography is to cancel out the rigid segmentarity of these well-entrenched dualisms without having recourse only to representational mediations, be they mental (the spirit, or the universals and transcendental signifieds of thought, to which one should perhaps add the narrow cognitivist definition of cartography) or political (the party avant-garde, the council, or the wider definition of cognitive mapping as a code word for class consciousness).

Does this not perhaps strain the concept beyond recognition, forcing cartography to perform too many tasks all at once? The least one can say is that the problems that it is supposed to solve for sure will continue to pose themselves long after the talk of maps has ceased to be fashionable. Until then, what is better than to stretch the image, to strain the words to the point where they split asunder, perhaps so as to extract the components of an original concept?

Casting his long shadow over this scene, I should add, is the imposing figure of Louis Althusser. Not only does Jameson often compare his cognitive mapping to Althusser's definition of ideology as a representation of the imaginary relationship of individuals to their real conditions of existence, but perhaps less apparently so in the works of Guattari, Deleuze, and Foucault, cartography also emerges in response to the theory of reflection and to Althusser's discussion of the various types of causality between parts and whole in a social formation, whether mechanical or transitive, expressive or structural. This impact is particularly evident in a passage where, just prior to quoting Foucault's term *repérage*, which a cartographic image usually renders in Alan Sheridan's translations, Deleuze speaks of alternative diagonal connections between discursive and nondiscursive formations as an encounter between statements and institutions that takes place in a "map" or "diagram" in opposition both to "a vertical parallelism," or "primary relations of expression," and to "a horizontal causality," or "secondary relations of reflection."[19] As an indirect alternative for Althusser's structural causality, Deleuze then repeatedly has recourse to the principle of transversality, which like a flash of lightning traverses all of Guattari's writings, striking each one of the aforementioned focal points. Says Deleuze: "One must pursue the different series, travel along the different levels, and cross all thresholds; instead of simply displaying phenomena or statements in their vertical or horizontal dimensions, one must form a transversal or mobile line."[20]

Guattari and Deleuze's transversal cartographies would thus displace, if not replace, Althusser's structural topography of the social whole. Perhaps, though, the distinction hides more profound resemblances than the texts reveal at first sight. Whereas Guattari often rejects any structure as being a mechanism irreconcilable with his own notion of a machine, Deleuze for his part only in a footnote rather superficially opposes Althusser's structural approach with Foucault's serial one. There are, to be sure, signs that confirm these terminological oppositions, such as when Foucault himself observes:

> History has long since abandoned its attempts to understand events in terms of cause and effect in the formless unity of some great revolutionary process, whether vaguely homogeneous or rigidly hierarchized. It did not do this in order to seek out structures anterior to, alien or hostile to the event. It was rather in order to establish those diverse converging, and sometimes divergent, but never autonomous series that enable us to circumscribe the "locus" of an event, the limits to its fluidity and the conditions of its emergence.[21]

In terms of effective philosophical concepts, however, how can the reader of Deleuze's *Foucault* fail to recognize not only the shared logic of absent causes immanent to their effects, which both Deleuze and Althusser borrow from Spinoza, but even the related notion of the event as an unforeseeable encounter, which would seem to coincide with the latest writings by the author of *Reading Capital* about a materialism of the aleatory? In one of these notes published posthumously, in fact, Althusser himself had already applied the notion of transversality as a principle of articulation between theoretical modes of production and the sciences in general.[22] I can only surmise that Deleuze's sadly unfinished last book, announced under the title *Marx's Grandeur*, would have told the story of this family romance in much greater detail — without lapsing in the logorrhea of Derrida's *Spectres of Marx*.

Guattari's first problematic of modes of subjectivation and their analysis orients the entirety of his work starting with *Psychoanalysis and Transversality: Essays in Institutional Analysis*. This collection of essays describes the practical, theoretical, and political tasks of what the author at this point still labels institutional group analysis, which is the breeding ground for schizoanalysis. With hindsight, Guattari explains: "The aim was to render discernible a field which was neither that of institutional therapy, nor institutional pedagogy, nor finally that of the struggle for social emancipation, but which would imply an analytic method capable of traversing these multiple domains (from which came the theme of 'transversality')."[23] What already stands out from this early theoretical labor is the attempt to circumscribe the unconscious in terms radically different from the personological theses of traditional psycho-analysis — an attempt that will of course culminate in the virulent attacks of *Anti-Oedipus* against Freudianism and Lacanianism. "The unconscious, I repeat, is not something graspable only in itself, thanks to the discourse of intimacy. In fact, it is nothing else but the rhizome of machinic interactions through which we are articulated to the systems of force and the formations of power that surround us."[24] Instead of relying on the identity of individuals and their family complexes, or even groups and institutions, analytic practice will ever more decisively take flight from collective agencies or assemblages of enunciation as the site of the unconscious. Guattari explains: "The term 'collective' should be understood in the sense of a multiplicity that deploys itself as much beyond the individual, on the side of the socius, as beneath the person, on the side of preverbal intensities, indicating a logic of affects rather than a logic of delimited sets."[25] The next task is then to describe the many forms and functions of such collective semiotic assemblages.

This second question regarding various modes of sign production is properly taken up only in the collections of essays *Molecular Revolution* and *The Machinic Unconscious: Essays in Schizoanalysis*. The concept of "a map of the unconscious," for example, appears for the first time in the latter book, as does the idea for "a schizoanalytic cartography."[26] Several semiotic concepts from both volumes, moreover, will reappear with only slight modifications in the third, fourth, and fifth plateaus of *A Thousand Plateaus*. If, among the late duo Deleuze-Guattari, the reader knew the former as a singular academic philosopher at Vincennes, then the latter not only was an institutional psychotherapist at the clinic of La Borde but also profiled himself as the more radically materialist semiotician of the two. "Where Guattari is immediately radical," as an early critic remarks, "is when he talks of semiology, the productive processes of signs, in a materialist fashion."[27] Against the grain of an overly formalistic and apolitical scientific discipline, the theory of signs thereby branches out onto concrete social practices of all kinds. In fact, at La Borde as well, Guattari's pivotal role seems to have been to link the activity of clinical analysis and social sign production to the political forces coming from a possible outside. In the words of colleague Jean Oury: "Félix had this function, while being present on the spot at certain moments, not to lose footing during practice; the function of concretely exploring the political space, not in order to bring back any product whatsoever, but so as to be able to 'articulate.'"[28]

To a large extent what still drives all of the essays in Guattari's first three volumes, published in the period between *Anti-Oedipus* and *A Thousand Plateaus,* is the same creative impulse behind the events of May '68 in France, which as a boundless source of energy underlies the two-volume magnum opus written with Deleuze. In stark contrast with this surging "springtide" of the 1960s overflowing into the 1970s, the period following *A Thousand Pla-*

teaus for Guattari represents the somber "winter years" of the early 1980s. Marked by the rapidly spreading disenchantment with French socialism, the growing threats of racism, nationalism, and fundamentalism, as well as the melancholy atmosphere of postmodern intellectual resignation if not outright reaction amid the consolidation of what the author dubs "integrated world capitalism," these are the years of lead reflected upon in the short journalistic notes, interviews, and conferences of *The Winter Years 1980–1985*. In response to this hapless state of affairs, Guattari and Antonio Negri propose "to rescue 'communism' from its own disrepute" through a politics of new alliances in their tempestuous little book *Communists like Us: New Spaces of Liberty, New Lines of Alliance* (in French, this book, *Les nouveaux espaces de liberté*, was indeed first to be titled *Les nouvelles alliances*, as if to echo *La nouvelle alliance* published a few years earlier by Ilya Prigogine and Isabelle Stengers). Affirmative as ever: "Reuniting with the human roots of communism, we want to return to the sources of hope, that is, to a 'being-for,' to a collective intentionality, turned toward doing rather than toward 'being against,' secured to impotent catchphrases of resentment." They conclude with a militant call to life: "We are still far from emerging from the storm; everything suggests that the end of the 'leaden years' will still be marked by difficult tests; but it is with lucidity, and without any messianism, that we envisage the reconstruction of a movement of revolution and liberation, more effective, more intelligent, more human, more happy than it has ever been."[29]

The collection of essays *Schizoanalytical Cartographies* ends the relative hiatus in Guattari's conceptual production with what is without a doubt his most hermetic attempt to articulate a diagrammatic theory of social sign production with the larger institutional aims of schizoanalysis. Mapping the unconscious now involves the interlocking of four abstract domains, or ontological functors: machinic phylums, energetic fluxes, incorporeal universes, and existential territories. "In our perspective," Guattari insists, "the cartographies of the unconscious would have to become indispensable complements to the current systems of rationality of the sciences, politics, and all other regions of knowledge and human activity."[30] The same year the third focal point — the environment — emerges in an easily accessible shorter book, *The Three Ecologies*, which is Guattari's idiosyncratic rejoinder and answer to the Green Movement. Brought together under the heading of a new "ecosophy" inspired by Gregory Bateson, the three ecologies in question in a complementary way relate to the subject, the society, and the environment. In fact, they offer a fair summary of the key points of interest behind Guattari's entire work.

To Guattari's eclectic body of writings, finally, the dense pages of *Chaosmosis* add an involuntary testament in the form of an invitation to create singular and heterogeneous pathways onto the forces of novelty, mobility, and alterity. Guattari thereby follows an aesthetic and ethico-political rather than a scientistic paradigm of "autopoiesis," in an enlarged sense different from Francisco

Varela's biological use of the original term. "What is at stake here," he says, "is the finality of the ensemble of human activities. Beyond material and political demands, what emerges is an aspiration individually and collectively to reappropriate the production of subjectivity."[31] In this book, published only a few months before his sudden death at the age of sixty-two, Guattari once more fervently appeals to artists, intellectuals, scientists, analysts, social workers, and political activists to invent new transversal passages at the myriad points of intersection between the overlapping zones of emergent subjectivity, the social production of signs, and the natural and machinic environment. These are the book's last words: "Psychoanalysis, institutional analysis, film, literature, poetry, innovative pedagogies, town planning and architecture — all the disciplines will have to combine their creativity to ward off the ordeals of barbarism, the mental implosion and chaosmic spasms looming on the horizon, and transform them into riches and unforeseen pleasures, the promises of which, for all that, are all too tangible."[32]

First imported into the philosophical domain by Jean-Paul Sartre in a critique of Husserlian phenomenology, the idea of transversality is the mainspring of Guattari's prolific conceptual machine, and it offers a tool to understand his whole thinking, including the theory of cartographic practice, in answer to the question of articulation. The topic of one of Guattari's earliest essays, transversality in the strict sense reworks the traditional psychoanalytical notions of transference and countertransference for the purposes of institutional analysis.[33] In a larger sense, the notion also pervades the entirety of his work as the ideal limit of all activity, whether analytic, philosophical, scientific, political, or artistic: a limit where strong dividing lines and disciplinary categories of this sort should be the first to yield to diagonal crossings and reciprocal connections. At one point, in *Chaosmosis*, Guattari will thus propose no less than "an ontological transversality" especially appropriate for the present times, as he already suggests in *The Three Ecologies*: "More than ever today nature has become inseparable from culture and we have to learn 'transversally' to think the interactions between ecosystems, the mecanosphere, and social and individual universes of reference."[34] Transversality in this wider sense forms the general machinic dimension of an ontological and ethico-political "creationism,"[35] which operates prior to and across the separations of subject and object, discourse and practice, the material and the semiotic. Above all, in the specific setting of institutional group analysis, transversality aims to create the conditions favorable to the self-positing of subject groups, as distinct from subjugated groups. Since a group's desire bears no strict resemblance to an individual's libido, however, the entire theoretical and therapeutic framework of analysis will have to be readapted to achieve this aim. Rather than a mere change of scale, therefore, Guattari proposes broadly to reformulate some of the most basic presuppositions behind both Freudian and Lacanian psychoanalysis.

First, Guattari seeks to replace the dual transferential relationship between analyst and analysand in the office with a collective transversal dimension emerging around a group analyzer in the institution. In a psychiatric clinic, for instance, the official hierarchy and structural distribution of roles among doctors, nurses, administrative staff, and patients define the institution's manifest coefficient of transversality. The real institutional subject, however, implies a latent and unconscious coefficient in the extent to which the group's effective desire has been obliterated, overcoded, or reduced to formulaic modeling patterns. The analytic practice then tries to change the various coefficients of transversality at the different levels of an institution. A group analysis, in other words, must entail both more and less than transferential interpreting, talking cures, or psychodramatic role-playing, since the true site of the unconscious lies on this side and on the other side of the territorial interpretation, transmission, and readaptation of stable codes and official role models. The aim is rather to foment a group's desire there where "it could have spoken," favoring expressions to take form "at the level from which the group's potential creativity springs"; only at this juncture where the various territories and strata are about to take shape will Guattari initiate his analytic practice so as to effectuate the highest possible latent coefficient of transversality, to accelerate the processes of autoproduction, as he later writes, at "the ontological root of creativity."[36]

Transversality must thus be understood in a tense opposition to both vertical hierarchies and horizontal structures. Examples of the first would include the pyramidal organigram of an institution; of the second, the compartmental separation of wards in a hospital, but the issue is of course not limited to physical environments. In the original essay from *Psychoanalysis and Transversality*, Guattari defines the term as follows: "Transversality is a dimension that tries to overcome both the impasses of pure verticality and mere horizontality: it tends to be achieved when there is maximum communication among the different levels and, above all, in the different directions. This is the very object of the quest of a subject group."[37] Beyond the specific context of institutional analysis, this definition is large enough to encompass the subsequent uses of the term. In *Molecular Revolution*, for example, Guattari presents schizoanalysis as "a political struggle on all the 'fronts' of desiring-production," to which he adds: "Transversality is nothing else but this nomadism of 'fronts.'"[38] Such would be the sense of all effective social practices today, when the strict antagonisms of the older class struggle no longer hold: "Gone are the traditional dualist oppositions which have guided our social thought and geopolitical cartographies."[39] Henceforth, as the author suggests in *The Winter Years:* "The new social practices of liberation will not establish hierarchical relations among one another; their development will respond to a principle of transversality that allows them to sit 'astride,' in a 'rhizome,' between heterogeneous social groups and interests."[40] Likewise, in a glossary for the same book, after opposing molar strata (objects, subjects, and representations with their systems of reference) and molecular flows (becomings, transitions, intensities), Guattari writes: "This molecular traversing of strata and levels, operated by the various sorts of assemblages, will be called 'transversality.'"[41] Perhaps the most concise formula, then, is to define transversality as the principle of n-1 articulations at the core of both theory and practice. Any multiplicity whatsoever thereby seeks to cohere along the tortuous lines of a cause immanent to its effects, without expressing or reflecting a given unity as either inherent or adherent to the whole; instead, the process will continue to operate adjacent to the active forces of alterity that, from an aleatory outside folding inwards, at all times threaten to destroy the assemblage in its precarious movement back and forth between complexity and chaos.

Second, following this principle of multiple articulation, Guattari also seeks to substitute the processual cartographies of schizoanalysis for the universal topologies of psychoanalysis. He is less antagonistic, though, to Freud's first energetic topology (unconscious, preconscious, conscious) than to his second anthropomorphic triad (id, ego, super-ego), while he most strongly rejects Lacan's reduction of the unconscious to the play of a chain of signifiers within a structural topology (real, imaginary, symbolical).[42] To operate effectively in a transversal setting then means that the analytic procedures themselves undergo a thorough practical and theoretical transformation. A pivotal opposition thereby distinguishes "interpreting" or "tracing" a case in retrospect according to either universal complexes or structural mathemes from "mapping" a process in action following a functional diagram.

Aside from explicit occurrences of the concept in French, beginning with *The Machinic Unconscious,* the cartographic image indeed is an effective way to translate *repérer,* a term that Guattari like Foucault uses throughout his work to describe his own analytic activity. Here are two samples, for instance, from *Molecular Revolution* and *The Winter Years,* in which the verb has a cartographic value. The first speaks of the treatment of schizophrenia: "Rather than to look at schizophrenics as people who are paralyzed inside their own body and need tutelage, one might seek to map (and not interpret) how they function in the social domain in which they struggle, and what are the transversal, diagrammatic questions they address to us."[43] The second refers to the objects and indices most typical of psychoanalysis: "Lapses, parapraxes, symptoms are like birds knocking on the window with their beak. The point is not to interpret them. It is rather a question of mapping their trajectory to see whether they can serve as indicators of new universes of reference capable of acquiring enough consistency to turn around a situation."[44]

To interpret means to look back upon the grand theater of an individual's traumatic psychogenesis; a map, on the contrary, hooks up with the smallest possible traits of a virtual and as yet undreamed-of heterogenesis. An analytic cartography of the unconscious in this sense radically changes the aim of time's arrow as well. "In this conception of analysis, time is not something to be endured; it is activated, orientated, the object of qualitative change." Guattari sums up in *Chaosmosis:* "Analysis is no longer the transferential interpretation of symptoms as a function of a preexisting, latent content, but the invention of new catalytic nuclei capable of bifurcating existence."[45]

Similar to this opposition between two concepts of analysis, one interpretive and the other cartographic, in Guattari's writing as in much French theory and philosophy, once again especially in the works of Foucault, another contrast that is often lost in translation opposes the two operations of *quadrillage* and *repérage*. To confuse the matter, sometimes both terms are even rendered with a single cartographic image in English. The former, however, has the molar and reactive power of an orthogonal grid, a perspectival lattice or hermeneutic frame of reference, whereas the latter has the molecular and active potential of an experimental assemblage or pragmatic diagram, a way of marking out the territory on the road. As mentioned before, these functional differences coincide with the distinction that first emerges in *The Machinic Unconscious* prior to being taken over in *A Thousand Plateaus*, between a "tracing" (*un calque*) and a "map" (*une carte*). Guattari thus indicates in his earlier book: "A schizoanalytic cartography, rather than indefinitely tracing off the same complexes or the same universal mathemes, will explore and experiment with an unconscious in action."[46] Schematically speaking, the formal and political regime of an interpretive tracing or replica is mimetic and panoptic, whereas a performative map sets in motion a regime that is both autopoietic and rhizomatic. One masterfully looks backward and from above to the traumatic past of repression; the other throws a furtive glance sideways into an undecidable future of desire. "What is now on the agenda is a 'futurist' or 'constructivist' freeing-up of fields of virtuality," Guattari argues in *The Three Ecologies*, and he continues: "The unconscious remains bound to archaic fixations only as long as no engagement orients it towards the future."[47] As Deleuze remarks in his last published work just before using his friend's example of birds at the window: "There is not only a reversal of directions, but also a difference in nature: the unconscious no longer deals with persons and objects, but with trajectories and becomings; it is no longer an unconscious of commemoration but one of mobilization, an unconscious whose objects take flight rather than remaining buried in the ground."[48]

Finally, to map out rather than to interpret multiple transversal connections between several levels and in several directions of an assemblage, Guattari's schizoanalysis presupposes a different theory of the sign than the one Lacan brings to psychoanalysis. The essays from the early volume *Psychoanalysis and Transversality* in this respect remain modestly canonical. In "Transversality," for example, Guattari still adopts the notion of a therapeutic transition from the imaginary to the symbolic through a type of castration complex, whereby the signifying chain of the group would serve as a mirror for the individuals. Already at this point, however, Guattari's institutional analysis departs from Lacanianism: first, of course, by considering the larger semiotic or even machinic experimentation of collective agencies rather than the linguistic expression of individual persons; second, by heralding a possible overcoming of the idea of a successful Oedipus complex; and, finally, by breaking the axiomatic universality of the signifier and the name of the father.

Rather than "the instance of the letter," what matters to Guattari is "the incidence of the social signifier on the individual," while to gauge "the instance of this social reality," institutional analysis will have to define "a 'signifying logic' specific to the social level under consideration."[49] This project of describing the historical regime of signs for each social formation will be taken up in the third part of *Anti-Oedipus*. A radical break with Lacanianism, though, occurs only at the point where Guattari provides a classification of modes of encoding and abandons the framework of "signifying semiologies" in favor of what he terms "a-signifying semiotics." The essays from *Molecular Revolution* and *The Machinic Unconscious* in this sense clear the path to innovate the theory of signs in a drastic way. At the lofty heights of poststructuralism, Guattari in fact is one of a few figures who stand out in the landscape of European theory and philosophy for demanding more than a masterful deconstruction of the semiology of Ferdinand de Saussure. Entirely bypassing this hegemonic tradition in which, he later jokes, semiology is only a "suburb" of linguistics, Guattari prefers to shore up the scaffoldings for his alternative construct with the aid of materials stolen from two other toolboxes: the semiotics of Charles Sanders Peirce and the glossematics of Louis Hjelmslev.[50]

❖

From Peircean semiotics, Guattari freely appropriates the enormous range of "phaneroscopy," as an encyclopedic science of phenomena of expression, and the specific concept of the "diagram," which he situates outside of Peirce's typology of iconic signs to turn "diagrammatism" into a separate category of "a-signifying semiotics."[51] Schizoanalysis is more profoundly indebted, though, to the glossematics of Hjelmslev, from whom Guattari adopts a purely immanentist perspective of the sign and an inclusive model of semiotic stratification, irreducible to the hackneyed opposition of signifier and signified.

A long paragraph in *Anti-Oedipus* already hints at the potential of glossematics for "the concerted destruction of the signifier," when Deleuze and Guattari present Hjelmslev's algebraic model as "the only linguistics adapted to the nature of *both* the capitalist *and* the schizophrenic flows: until now, the only modern — and not archaic — theory of language."[52] What they treasure above all in glossematics is, first, the premise of a reciprocal presupposition between content and expression, both having their form and their substance, rather than a hierarchical subordination either between signifier and signified or between form and content; second, the intervention of abstract *figurae*, which they label points-signs or schizzes breaking through the wall of the signifier from the outside, rather than the double articulation of morphemes and phonemes within a system; and, finally, the possibility to formulate a theory of differential flows, rather than of minimal identities. From a semiotic point of view, though, *Anti-Oedipus* remains at this level of flows between substances and forms of content, on the one hand, and substances and forms of expression, on the other, both shot through with glossematic figures.

Guattari's subsequent elaborations of a cartography of the unconscious in *Molecular Revolution* and *The Machinic Unconscious* take Hjelmslev's model of stratification a step further in the direction of a-signifying, or diagrammatic machines. Beneath the double articulation of formed substances, which concretely stratifies both the plane of content and the plane of expression, Guattari's diagrams then work with the singular traits of matter, which destratify an abstract machine, or plane of consistency. Without this inclusion of matter, Hjelmslev's model threatens quickly to reinstate the Saussurean binary of signifier and signified, whereby Guattari's a-signifying semiotics risk to slide back into signifying semiologies.

Here "matter" or "purport" corresponds to Hjelmslev's *mening*, which French translators alternatively render as *sens* (meaning or sense) and as *matière* (matter). Both the plane of content and the plane of expression, then, unfold according to three layers, separable only through analysis: form, substance, and purport. For Hjelmslev, the purport is an "amorphous continuum, on which boundaries are laid by the formative action of the languages," a view that the glossematician in fact derives from Saussure, who speaks of language as a form combining thoughts and sounds, the famous recto and verso of language as a single sheet of paper: "There is thus neither materialization of thoughts nor spiritualization of sounds, but the question concerns this somewhat mysterious fact that 'thought-sound' implies divisions and that language elaborates its unities by constituting itself between two amorphous masses."[53] According to Hjelmslev, these two masses do not precede language either in time or in hierarchical order; on the contrary, they are undissociable from the formative action that turns them into formed substances. Different languages and cultures thus arbitrarily order the matter of content-purport or the sense of expression-purport into the substances for a series of forms, without which the purport is unknowable and has no possible existence. A cultural assemblage, for example, in one way lays out the color spectrum into a specific set of color zones, while another articulates the continuum of food matter to produce the various possible menus of a specific cuisine, just as language structures the phonetic continuum according to a system of significant phonological distinctions. To use Hjelmslev's metaphor, language thus widely understood in each case turns matter into formed substances "by the form's being projected on to the purport, just as an open net casts its shadow down on an undivided surface,"[54] a process that a cartographic approach might wish to reuse by transcoding the undivided surface into the earth, the open net into the maps and legends, and the projected shadow into the resulting territories.

Selectively following this model of stratification and interaction between the forms, substances, and matter or sense of content and expression, Guattari then elaborates his own classification of various modes of sign production. The most important distinction here is between signifying semiologies and a-signifying semiotics, but to break the despotism of the signifier, schizoanalysis also embraces a-semiotic and symbolical modes.

1. *A-semiotic encoding* functions without constituting an autonomous and translatable, semiotically formed substance, and thus operates outside of the strata of glossematics (for example, RNA and DNA in the genetic code, although this example is much debated).

2. *Semiologies of signification* operate with systems of signs already ordered into semiotically formed substances along the two planes of content and expression. They are of two kinds:

   a. *presignifying, symbolical semiologies* work with a polyphony of substances of expression, none of which overcodes the others (gestures, mime, rites, tattoos, images, icons, and so on, as they appear side by side for instance in so-called archaic societies and in the worlds of art, childhood, and madness);

   b. *signifying semiologies* subordinate the content to the expression, while overcoding the latter in the name of the sole expression-substance of the linguistic signifier (for example, the instance of the letter, the signifying chain in structuralism, textuality in early poststructuralism).

3. *A-signifying, diagrammatic semiotics* exceed the double articulation of already semiotically formed substances into content and expression: they work flush with the real, beneath the representational functions of signification and designation, and they have direct purchase on the continuum of material flows in the purport (for example, musical transcriptions, technological plans, scientific descriptions, to which Guattari in his last book adds the example of hypertexts).

What are some of the other differences between a-signifying and signifying regimes of signs, to stick to this most fundamental opposition? Signifying semiologies primarily concatenate a chain of actually formed substances, of either content or expression, along the horizontal syntagmatic axis, to which only secondarily corresponds a virtual set of formed substances along the vertical paradigmatic axis. Signification and interpretation along these two axes, moreover, go hand in hand with an individuation of subjectivity, divided into the subject of enunciation (*je*) and the subject of the enunciated (*moi*), both of which are subjugated to the signifying chain. "[A] signifier," as Lacan writes, "is that which represents the subject for another signifier."[55] Except of course for the shift from knowledge and thought to desire and the unconscious, this framework in fact rather faithfully replicates the redoubling of the subject in modern thought as both empirical and transcendental. A-signifying semiotics, to the contrary, are not restricted to the double bind of a horizontal proliferation of syntagms and a vertical interpretation of paradigms, nor can they be reduced to the aporetic alternative between metonymic displacement and metaphorical condensation, to which early deconstructive readings like to apply an endless amount of critical rigor; instead, they proceed along a transversal dimension that fans out in all directions to involve the dynamic sense-matter of purport. In this manner, Guattari seems to add a diagrammatic line of flight to the syntagmatic and paradigmatic axes, just as he opposes a plea for experimentation to both signification and interpretation. What interests him is no longer the play between metaphor and metonymy, nor the conflict between symbol and allegory, but the protocols of metamorphosis. In his ontological pragmatics the aporias of syntax and semantics or hermeneutics are slightly beside the point. Finally, rather than a divided subject lodged into the ellipses of the signifying chain (the personal or linguistic *moi-je*), the agencies behind diagrammatic experiments are subject groups and, more generally, collective assemblages of enunciation (an impersonal or machinic *il*). They no longer depend on the hierarchical double of a subject that seems to be both empirical and transcendental, but emerge along the diagonal curvatures in a field of immanence; rather than punctual holes or lacunae within the discursive ensemble of language, they are processual habits or inclinations across an unformed continuum.

Collective assemblages, then, effectuate diagrammatic conjunctions between semiotic flows and material flows, between machines of the real and machines of signs; they make sense without the mediation of ready-made mental representations necessary to assure signification and designation. This excludes any strictly cognitivist definition of cartography in which the symbolical realm would form an autonomous dimension. Whereas signifying practices produce useful redundancies within the sphere of semiotically formed substances of content and expression, a-signifying practices generate original interactions all across the intensive continuum of matter. At this chaosmotic level, the distinction between content and expression increasingly grows blurred or is deterritorialized, as the ambivalent French translation of *mening* with both *matière* and *sens* appropriately suggests. Between otherwise stable formations there emerges a reversible link; a transversal bridge is thrown as informal traits shuttle back and forth between virtual forms of content and expression. Animated by infinite velocities, a flux cuts across and at the same time articulates other comparable antagonisms — production and representation, labor and desire, practices and discourses, the material and the semiotic — without presupposing a higher dialectical unity. The purport remains a destratified plane of consistency, or plane of immanence, in opposition to the stratified planes of content and expression. Rather than speak of an amorphous mass, however, Guattari considers the plane of consistency a hyperactive continuum of machinic intensities, a chaosmotic field of tensions that incessantly emits multiple particles or points-signs, abstract figures of content and expression at their highest degree of deterritorialization. A-signifying semiotics then activate and accelerate diagrammatic conjunctions, or abstract machines, between the matter of content-purport and the sense of expression-purport, between material intensities and sign particles. Collective assemblages of enunciation, or concrete machines, stratify this multidimensional plane of consistency into a double articulation of formed substances.

The brief sketch of an example from *A Thousand Plateaus,* which Deleuze later expands in his *Foucault,* might help in understanding the role of diagrammatic assemblages. Take delinquency and the prison as they appear in *Discipline and Punish:* the former constitutes a complex form of expression, that is, a discursive set of statements that defines the field of what can be said about crime or illegality at this particular moment in time; the latter is a complex form of content, that is, an institutional environment that defines the field of visibility capable of keeping a peculiar watchful eye over criminal subjects in a circumscribed space. Both the regime of signs defining delinquency and the regime of light defining the prison are stratified historical systems in a tenuous and unstable balance. In this sense they correspond to an "open net" of forms of expression and content whose "shadows" could include the court sentence and subsequent incarceration imposed upon an individual person. However, to form, for example, a whole disciplinary social formation, statements and environments (the legends and territories) fit together only to the extent to which they participate in a destratified plane of consistency (the chaosmotic earth) from which they jointly emerge in the event of an unforeseeable encounter. Such a plane corresponds to the "undivided surface" of the purport. This multiplicity — a jumble of semiotic traits, facial and gestural features, particles of matter, splinters of the flesh, senseless indices, light flashes, and so on — will cohere only at the instance of a collective throw of the dice. For every historical formation of strata, there is always an aleatory conjunction of forces: an abstract machine connecting singular traits and loose figures of content and expression into an informal diagram, which a concrete machine assembles into applicable forms and strata, including the subjects, citizens both ruly and unruly, and the objects, common truths and white lies of a given social order. Finally, just as a disciplinary formation for Foucault is the locus of an unrelenting microphysics of power, diagrammatic cartographies for Guattari constitute the fronts of a micropolitics of desire, haunted by an endless potential for resistance.

For other examples, including a detailed rereading of the child's play of *Fort/Da* against the reductive dogmas of Freud and Lacan, the English-speaking reader may consult *Chaosmosis,* especially the chapter "Schizoanalytic Metamodelizations."[56] More so than in dissections of this kind, however, Guattari is at bottom always interested in the pragmatic intervention and creative production of new subjective cartographies. Clever though it may be, a diagnosis alone is not enough; nor is it the aim to reach a catharsis as a passive spectator so much as it is to produce a catalysis of emergent processes, to the point where the patient or the analyst, for instance, becomes at once the creator, the interpreter, and the admirer of a work of art. Guattari, loosely following ideas from Mikhail Bakhtin, believes in a privileging of art inasmuch as the production of emergent subjectivities involves a dimension of autonomy of an aesthetic nature. This occurs, for example, when singular traits of faciality, rhythm, or corporeality are diverted from their signifying tasks and instead are freely put to work in the bringing into existence of a motif, a refrain or ritornello capable of sustaining a tentative process of self-positing. This process is akin to an artistic experiment with the seeming chaos of a-significance. "The artist — and more generally aesthetic perception — detach and deterritorialize a segment of the real in such a way as to make it play the role of a partial enunciator," Guattari explains. He continues: "A singularity, a rupture of sense, a cut, a fragmentation, a detachment of a semiotic content — in a dadaist or surrealist manner — can originate mutant nuclei of subjectivation."[57] Everything revolves around the effective extraction of such diagrammatic nodes from the networks of signification and denotation — two functions that thereby yield to the ruptures of a pragmatic function of existentialization. Inchoate points of singularity are to become the triggering keys, the dark attractors, and the partial analyzers capable of crystallizing unexpected virtual universes of reference adjacent to the actual territories of existence. Other cartographies of subjectivation then become possible in "an infinite play of interface" between the actual and the virtual as well as between the discursive and the nondiscursive: "Machinic subjectivity," Guattari remarks, "agglomerates these different partial enunciations and installs itself, as it were, before and alongside the subject-object relation."[58]

Autopoiesis, the process of bringing into existence autonomous nuclei of subjectivation capable of reproducing themselves while constantly opening onto the so-called outside world, forms the alpha and omega of this new cartography of the unconscious. "It is a force for seizing the creative potentiality at the root of sensible finitude — 'before' it is applied to works, philosophical concepts, scientific functions and mental and social objects — which founds the new aesthetic paradigm," Guattari concludes in *Chaosmosis,* to which he adds: "The decisive threshold constituting this new aesthetic paradigm lies in the aptitude of these processes of creation to auto-affirm themselves as existential nuclei or autopoietic machines."[59] Such self-creative processes obviously cannot be limited by the superior attitude of an uninvolved observer. Rather than allowing an analyst to hide at all costs behind the blank shield of scientific objectivity, or, even more authoritatively, in the name of an originary lack, every cartographic task involves the risk of becoming immersed in the very same transformative processes that bring into existence new constellations of universes of value.

Instead of Lacan's nonintervention (*non-agir*), autopoiesis in the somewhat larger sense embraced by Guattari would seem to require the circularity of action and interpretation that in Francisco Varela's recent work becomes enaction (*faire-émerger*). "To enact" in fact seems far more appropriate than "to assemble," to render the verb that next to the principle of transversality constitutes Guattari's favorite but otherwise untranslatable concept (*agencer*). In *Cognitive Science: A Cartography of Current Ideas*, Varela describes the process as a way of bringing forth and mapping out a territory at the same time: "The fundamental idea therefore is that cognitive faculties are inextricably linked to the history of what is lived, just as a hitherto inexistent path appears in the walking."[60] What is thereby dropped entirely is the idea of language or any other form of cognition as a representation adequate to a preexisting world or at least capable of solving a fixed set of problems. Even between reality and representation, between a problem and its solution, the strong distinction collapses — not to implode, however, in the closed vacuum of postmodern simulation but rather to give way to creative processes of autoproduction. Guattari refers to this fact in *Cartographies schizoanalytiques*: "Not only does the map start to refer indefinitely to its own cartography, as Alfred Korzybski has well noted, but it is the distinction between the map and the territory (the map and 'the thing mapped') which tends to disappear."[61]

A process of autopoiesis rather than of mimesis, cartography actively enacts, assembles, and brings forth concrete existential territories as well as incorporeal universes of reference, without presupposing any static image of the earth to begin with. For a logic of the excluded middle, the fields of cartography offer maddening paradoxes: "Domains of incorporeal entities which one detects at the same time as one produces them, and which are already there, always, as soon as one engenders them." Guattari insists: "I repeat, the analytic map in that case can no longer be distinguished from the existential territory that it engenders! The object of knowledge and the subject of enunciation coincide in this kind of assemblage."[62]

Once the dice are thrown, in the event of a fortuitous encounter, both the map and the itinerary are in the walking. During this process, they bring forth a constellation of fields of virtuality, incorporeal universes of value that, unlike the universals of scholastic reason, fit neither a realist conception of

language and the world nor a nominalist one. "But," adds Guattari, "maybe
it's necessary to affirm both these positions concurrently: the domain of virtual intensities establishing itself prior to distinctions being made between the
semiotic machine, the referred object, and the enunciative subject."[63] Perhaps,
then, the cartographies at issue require a view of incorporeal events that are
neither already given in advance as is the case for realism (*ante rem* or *in re*) nor
generalized after the observation of numerous facts in the manner of nomi-
nalism or terminism (*post rem* or *in voce*), but instead are constantly in the
making as pragmatism holds (*in rebus*)? Neither deductive nor inductive, they
would primarily be in a process of enaction, or, to use Peirce's term, abduction.
Their relation to the things mapped would be existential rather than representational, based on principles of efficacy and inference instead of adequacy and
correspondence. In sum: "A schizo-analytic cartography is not 'second' with
regard to the existential territories it brings forth; one cannot even say, properly speaking, that it represents them, since here it is the map that, somehow,
engenders the territories in question."[64] Further to elaborate this possibility
today in a renewed dialogue with pragmatism constitutes, I believe, one of
the most compelling tasks facing any reader of Guattari and Deleuze, especially given the latter's brief but extraordinary reevaluation of North American
philosophy in his final book. No longer would the reader then have to sub-
scribe exclusively to the common deconstructive view condensed in a lapidary
statement by Michel de Certeau: "The journey is not the map."[65] Instead, a
constructive response would begin to emerge, a perspective capable of grafting
itself onto the processes of cartographic subjectivation. When what is happening is perpetual movement, to use Deleuze's words one more time, then
the cartographies of the unconscious indeed become the territory: "The map
expresses the identity of the journey and what one journeys through. It merges
with its object, when the object itself is movement."[66]

Capitalist societies today on a global scale use plenty of prefabricated systems of signification to assure the general translatability of dominant contents
and expressions, from the most uniformly vacuous news items to the latest
opinion polls brought to you live and ready to go. The really permanent revolution, however, takes place within the apparent nonsense of a-significant
practices, at the level of our informal maps and diagrams of everyday existence. Merely to substitute a bewildering experience for the hegemonic order
of reference is insufficient, except as a useful preliminary step to draw the attention away from the stable identity of subjects and objects toward a more
freely procedural intentionality. "This involves taking the relation between
subject and object by the middle and foregrounding the enunciating instance
(or the interpretant of the Peircean triad)," Guattari suggests. "It is in this
zone of intersection that subject and object are confused and find their common ground. It concerns a given that phenomenologists have addressed when
they show that intentionality is inseparable from its object and involves a 'be-

neath' of the discursive subject-object relation."[67] The more practical issue concerns that which happens at the intersection along the diagonal lines of transversality before any strong representational scheme is set in place. How do cartographic legends and interpretants of all kinds transform the dynamic plane of the earth in each case to produce a variety of concrete existential territories? To answer this question with the signifying practice of writing over and against interpreting is plainly insufficient, unless of course the processes are mutually redefinable as so many hidden forms of mapmaking. As Tom Conley has shown in *The Self-Made Map: Cartographic Writing in Early Modern France:* "Writings can be called 'cartographic' insofar as tensions of space and of figuration inhere in fields of printed discourse."[68] Other social practices and theories are necessary, however, both to locate and refine the analysis of events, in printed discourse as much as elsewhere in a global material and incorporeal environment, and to define appropriate geopolitical strategies in response. Different cartographies of the unconscious should develop new modes of producing subjectivity on a whole range of scales at the unstable middle ground between territory and the earth. "Like artists and writers, the cartographers of subjectivity should seek, then, with each performance, to develop and innovate, to create new perspectives, without prior recourse to assured theoretical foundations or the authority of a group, school, conservatory, or academy," Guattari conjectures in *The Three Ecologies* — as always with an eye on the contiguous future and an ear finely tuned in to the nervous twitter of birds knocking at the window: "Work in progress!"[69]

Notes

I am grateful to Eleanor Kaufman, York Gunther, Gabriela S. Basterra, Trees Cloostermans, and Verena Andermatt Conley for their critical observations; special thanks also to the members of my seminar, "Cartographic Fictions," at Harvard University, which led me to reformulate several of the ideas in this article: Susan Antebi, Mark Burns, Maruja García-Padilla, Elisabeth Hodges, Tobias Kasper, Ricardo Padrón, and Simone Pinet.

1. Gilles Deleuze and Félix Guattari, "Geophilosophy," in *What Is Philosophy?* trans. Hugh Tomlinson and Graham Burchell (New York: Columbia University Press, 1994), 85. Compare Massimo Cacciari, *Geo-filosofia dell'Europa* (Milan: Adelphi, 1994). I have dealt in more bibliographical detail with the success of this model in "A Misreading of Maps: The Politics of Cartography in Marxism and Poststructuralism," *Signs of Change,* ed. Stephen Barker (Albany, N.Y.: State University of New York Press, 1996), 109–39. To the references in that earlier article, I would add *Cartes et figures de la terre* (Paris: Centre Georges Pompidou, 1980); *Territories of Difference,* ed. Renee Baert (Alberta: Walter Phillips Gallery, 1993); *Cartographies variables,* ed. Francine Paul (Montreal: Galerie de l'UQAM, 1993); and *Le lieu de l'être: Lieux de passage et portraits d'être,* ed. Guy Mercier (Quebec: Musée du Québec, 1994).

2. Paisley Livingston, "From Text to Work," in *After Poststructuralism: Inter-*

disciplinarity and Literary Theory, ed. Nancy Easterlin and Barbara Riebling (Evanston, Ill.: Northwestern University Press, 1993), 91–104.

3. Michel Foucault, "The Discourse on Language," in *The Archaeology of Knowledge and The Discourse on Language,* trans. A. M. Sheridan Smith (New York: Pantheon Books, 1972), 230. See also François Zourabichvili, *Deleuze: Une philosophie de l'événement* (Paris: Presses Universitaires de France, 1994). A deconstructive thought of the event — typically in the singular — aims to tackle the practical, ideological, and political, for example, in Reiner Schürmann, *Heidegger on Being and Acting: From Principles to Anarchy,* trans. Christine-Marie Gros (Bloomington: Indiana University Press, 1990); Paul de Man, *Aesthetic Ideology,* ed. and intro. Andrzej Warminski (Minneapolis: University of Minnesota Press, 1996); and Jacques Derrida, *Spectres of Marx: The State of the Debt, the Work of Mourning, and the New International,* trans. Peggy Kamuf (London: Routledge, 1994). However radical or anarchical, though, their perspective seems in principle alien to the historical inscription of the event in a specific situation — which is precisely what makes their radicality so appealing but ultimately unproductive. This contrasts sharply, I believe, with the elaboration of a situational concept of events — in the plural — by a political thinker such as Alain Badiou in *Peut-on penser la politique?* (Paris: Seuil, 1985) and, especially, *L'être et l'événement* (Paris: Seuil, 1988). For a detailed comparison of Deleuze and Badiou, see the latter's *Deleuze: "La clameur de l'être"* (Paris: Hachette, 1997). A similar tension earlier seems to lie at the basis of the reciprocal violence of misunderstanding between Derrida and Foucault. For conversations that helped me clarify this distinction within the philosophy of the event, which will be taken up elsewhere in greater detail, I am grateful to Raúl Cerdeiras, editor of the Argentine journal *Acontecimiento: Revista para pensar la política.*

4. Deleuze and Guattari, *What Is Philosophy?* 32–33, 101. A textual approach almost automatically leads into territoriality as soon as the question of reference is once more brought to the fore. This occurs in J. Hillis Miller, *Topographies* (Stanford, Calif.: Stanford University Press, 1995). See also Nicholas Alfrey and Stephen Daniels, eds., *Mapping the Landscape: Essays on Art and Cartography* (Nottingham: University Art Gallery — Castle Museum, 1990); and Geoff King, *The Mapping of Reality: The Exploration of Cultural Cartographies* (Basingstoke, England: Macmillan, 1995).

5. Compare Rosalind E. Krauss, "Grids," in *The Originality of the Avant-garde and Other Modernist Myths* (Cambridge, Mass.: MIT Press, 1994), 17. My working hypothesis is greatly indebted to Fredric Jameson's review-article, "On 'Cultural Studies,'" *Social Text* 34 (1993): 17–53. In a marvelous book, *L'oeil cartographique de l'art* (Paris: Galilée, 1996), Christine Buci-Glucksmann describes the cartographic turn in art from a perspective variously informed by Deleuze and Guattari, Krauss, and Badiou.

6. Christian Jacob, *L'empire des cartes: Approche théorique de la cartographie à travers l'histoire* (Paris: Albin Michel, 1992), 21, 19.

7. Gilles Deleuze, *Foucault,* trans. Seán Hand, introd. Paul Bové (Minneapolis: University of Minnesota Press, 1988). See also Guattari's remarks about the "analytic cartography" of Foucault in his conference "Microphysique des pouvoirs et micropolitique des désirs," in *Les années d'hiver 1980–1985* (Paris: Bernard Barrault, 1986), 207–22; now in *The Guattari Reader,* ed. Gary Genosko (Cambridge: Blackwell, 1996), 172–81.

8. Leon Trotsky, *Problems of Everyday Life: Creating the Foundations for a New Society in Revolutionary Russia* (New York: Pathfinder, 1973), 123, 152.

9. Guy Debord, "Theory of the Dérive" and "Introduction to a Critique of Urban Geography," in *Situationist International Anthology*, ed. and trans. Ken Knabb (Berkeley: Bureau of Public Secrets, 1989), 53, 5–8. Compare Debord's discussion "Environmental Planning," in *The Society of the Spectacle*, trans. Donald Nicholson-Smith (New York: Zone Books, 1994), 119–27. For a concise analysis, see Thomas F. McDonough, "Situationist Space," *October* 67 (1994): 59–77.

10. See "Théorie des moments et construction des situations," *Internationale Situationniste* 4 (1960): 11 (unsigned article). Compare Henri Lefebvre's view of moments, in *La somme et le reste* (Paris: La Nef, 1959). Few critics observe how, even in his later work *The Production of Space*, trans. Donald Nicholson-Smith (Cambridge: Blackwell, 1991), Lefebvre lapses into a conventional prejudice against alienated space in favor of labor-time. About real knowledge of the production of space, he writes: "Such a knowledge, in contrast to the dissection, interpretations and representations of a would-be science of space, may be expected to rediscover *time* (and in the first place the time of production) in and through space," whereas today under capitalism, "[t]he primacy of the economic and above all of the political implies the supremacy of space over time" (91, 95; cf. 278). In many ways, these kinds of assertions — not to mention the unforgivingly negative take on language and vision — simply throw us back to square one.

11. Ernst Bloch, *Erbschaft dieser Zeit* (Frankfurt: Suhrkamp, 1962), 322, quoted in Johannes Fabian, *Time and the Other: How Anthropology Makes Its Object* (New York: Columbia University Press, 1983), 37; and Max Horkheimer and Theodor Adorno, *Dialectic of Enlightenment*, trans. John Cumming (New York: Continuum, 1989), 180.

12. Ernesto Laclau, *New Reflections on the Revolution of Our Time* (London: Verso, 1990), 68. For an impeccable criticism of this thesis, see Doreen Massey, "Politics and Space/Time," in *Place and the Politics of Identity*, ed. Michael Keith and Steve Pile (New York: Routledge, 1993), 141–61.

13. Edward W. Soja, *Postmodern Geographies: The Reassertion of Space in Critical Social Theory* (London: Verso, 1989), 75; idem, *Thirdspace: Journeys to Los Angeles and Other Real-and-Imagined Places* (Cambridge: Blackwell, 1996).

14. Fredric Jameson, "Cognitive Mapping," in *Marxism and the Interpretation of Culture,* ed. Cary Nelson and Lawrence Grossberg (Urbana: University of Illinois Press, 1984), 347–60; and Kevin Lynch, *The Image of the City* (Cambridge, Mass.: MIT Press, 1960).

15. Georg Lukács, *The Theory of the Novel: A Historico-philosophical Essay on the Forms of Great Epic Literature*, trans. Anna Bostock (Cambridge, Mass.: MIT Press, 1994), 29–31. For Jameson's ongoing dialogue with Lukács from a cartographic point of view, see among other texts "Reflections in Conclusion," in *Aesthetics and Politics* (London: Verso, 1980), 212; and idem, *Theory of Culture: Lectures at Rikkyo* (Tokyo: Rikkyo University, 1994), 58–72.

16. Colin MacCabe, preface to Fredric Jameson, *The Geopolitical Aesthetic: Cinema and Space in the World System* (Bloomington: Indiana University Press — British Film Institute, 1992), xv. Compare Jameson, *The Prison-house of Language: A Critical Account of Structuralism and Russian Formalism* (Princeton, N.J.: Princeton University Press, 1972), 134, 216; and idem, *Postmodernism, or, The Cultural Logic of Late Capitalism* (London: Verso, 1991), 1–54, 270, 373, 399–418. Guattari for his part speaks of "transcoding" in reference to the paintings of Gérard Fromanger, in *Les années d'hiver*, 252.

17. Félix Guattari in *Pratique de l'institutionnel et politique*, ed. Jacques Pain (Vigneux: Matrice, 1985), 54–55; published in English under the title "Institutional Practice and Politics," trans. Lang Baker, in *The Guattari Reader*, 124–25 (trans. modified above all to render *réagencer* as "to reenact" rather than "to reassemble"; see below for comments).

18. Félix Guattari, *The Three Ecologies*, trans. Chris Turner, *New Formations* 8 (1989): 138; and *Les années d'hiver*, 168. About misguided articulations of the human and the social sciences, see Guattari's early essay, "Réflexions pour des philosophes à propos de la psychothérapie institutionnelle," in *Psychanalyse et transversalité: Essais d'analyse institutionnelle*, preface Gilles Deleuze (Paris: François Maspero, 1972), 86–97. With regard to Marxism and Freudianism, see "La fin des fétichismes," in *La révolution moléculaire* (Fontenay-sous-Bois: Recherches, 1977), 17–28; English trans.: *Molecular Revolution*, trans. Janis Forman (New York: Penguin, 1984), 253–61. Several remarks about an intensive logic of the included middle as opposed to classical and dialectical reason can be found in *Les années d'hiver*, 219; *The Three Ecologies*, 135–37, 140–41; *Cartographies schizoanalytiques* (Paris: Seuil, 1989), 12–13, 51–52. See also *Chaosmosis*, trans. Paul Bains and Julian Pefanis (Bloomington: Indiana University Press, 1995), 28, 50–52, 65, 92–93.

19. Deleuze, *Foucault*, 9–10. For Louis Althusser's definition of ideology, see *Lenin and Philosophy and Other Essays*, trans. Ben Brewster (New York: Monthly Review Press, 1971), 162. For his theory of structural causality, see *Reading Capital*, trans. Ben Brewster (London: Verso, 1979), 182–93. Guattari himself staunchly rejects Althusser's exclusionary ideal of theoretical scientificity (*Molecular Revolution*, 25, 33, 176), but he does seem to adopt the notion of ideological state apparatuses, which he labels "collective equipments" (*équipements collectifs*) in opposition to "collective assemblages" (*agencements collectifs*).

20. Deleuze, *Foucault*, 22 (compare 5, 24, 39, 91, 94, 115, 144n. 28).

21. Foucault, "The Discourse on Language," 230. Compare with Deleuze's reference to Althusser in *Foucault*, 136n. 32. For Guattari's distinction between machines, mechanisms, and structures, see "Machine et structure," in *Psychanalyse et transversalité*, 240–48; *Chaosmosis*, 37–38, 48, 58, 74–75, 93, 108.

22. Althusser, "Le courant souterrain du matérialisme de la rencontre (1982)," in *Écrits philosophiques et politiques*, vol. 1, ed. François Matheron (Paris: Stock/IMEC, 1994), 539–76. For the use of the concept of transversality, see Althusser, "Notes sur la philosophie (1967–68)," in ibid., vol. 2, pp. 323–24. Together with Heidegger's thinking, Althusser's materialism of the aleatory encounter should be put at the center of any genealogy of the philosophy of the event. I thank Geoff Waite for bringing this to my attention.

23. Guattari, "Institutional Practice and Politics," 121 (trans. modified).

24. Guattari, *Les années d'hiver*, 134–35.

25. Guattari, *Chaosmosis*, 9.

26. Guattari, *L'inconscient machinique*, 177, 190.

27. Mark D. Seem, "Interview/Félix Guattari," *Diacritics* 4, no. 3 (1974): 38. For Guattari's early semiotics, see especially "Echafaudages sémiotiques," in *La révolution moléculaire*, 239–84, most of which is translated in "The Role of the Signifier in the Institution," "Towards a Micropolitics of Desire," and "Towards a New Vocabulary," in *Molecular Revolution*, 73–107, 120–72. In continuation, see "Sortir de la langue"

and "Agencements d'énonciation" as well as "La traversée moléculaire des signes," in *L'inconscient machinique*, 21–73, 205–35. In *A Thousand Plateaus*, trans. Brian Massumi (Minneapolis: University of Minnesota Press, 1987), see "The Geology of Morals," "Postulates of Linguistics," and "On Several Regimes of Signs," 39–148. For an analysis, compare Dorothea Olkowski, "Semiotics and Gilles Deleuze," in *The Semiotic Web 1990*, ed. Thomas A. Sebeok, Jean Umiker-Sebeok, and Evan Young (Berlin: Mouton de Gruyter, 1991), 285–305; Therese Grisham, "Linguistics as an Indiscipline: Deleuze and Guattari's Pragmatics," *SubStance* 20 (1991): 36–54; and John Johnston, "Theoretical Invention and the Contingency of Critique: The Examples of Postmodern Semiotics," in *Signs of Change*, 49–68. With regard to cartography, specifically, see Charles J. Stivale, "The Literary Element in *Mille Plateaux*: The New Cartography of Deleuze and Guattari," *SubStance* 44–45 (1984): 20–34.

28. Jean Oury, in *Pratique de l'institutionnel et politique*, 42.

29. Félix Guattari and Antonio Negri, *Les nouveaux espaces de liberté* (Paris: Dominique Bédou, 1985), 85, 94–95; English trans.: *Communists like Us: New Spaces of Liberty, New Lines of Alliance*, trans. Michael Ryan, with a postscript by Antonio Negri, trans. Jared Becker (New York: Semiotext[e], 1990), 131, 147.

30. Guattari, *Cartographies schizoanalytiques*, 51.

31. Guattari, *Chaosmosis*, 133

32. Ibid., 135.

33. Guattari, "Transversalité," in *Psychanalyse et transversalité*, 72–85; *Molecular Revolution*, 11–23. For a remarkable discussion of the philosophical background and possible implications of Guattari's concept in answer to the impasses of modernity and postmodernity, see Calvin O. Schrag, "Transversal Rationality," in *The Question of Hermeneutics*, ed. Timothy J. Stapleton (Dordrecht: Kluwer, 1994), 61–78.

34. Guattari, *Chaosmosis*, 60; *The Three Ecologies*, 135.

35. Guattari, *L'inconscient machinique*, 162 and 231; *Chaosmosis*, 25, 28, 105, 115–17. Compare with Deleuze and Guattari's constructivism in *What Is Philosophy?* 7, 35–36, 81. Rather than to theological doctrines, does this perhaps link Guattari's work to the historical avant-garde movement of *creacionismo* initiated by the Chilean poet Vicente Huidobro, whose credo was: "You have to create" ("Why do you sing the rose, oh Poets! / Make it flower in the poem")?

36. Guattari, *Psychanalyse et transversalité*, 79 and 85; *Molecular Revolution*, 17 and 23 (trans. modified); *Chaosmosis*, 116. A group analyzer rarely coincides with a personal expert or a specific group but rather requires a collective agency of enunciation: "Only the network of nuclei of partial enunciation — comprising groups, meetings, workshops, responsibilities, spontaneous constellations and individual initiatives — could arguably hold the title of institutional analyzer" (*Chaosmosis*, 71).

37. Guattari, *Psychanalyse et transversalité*, 80; *Molecular Revolution*, 18 (trans. modified).

38. Guattari, *La révolution moléculaire*, 23; *Molecular Revolution*, 257 (trans. modified). See also Guattari's later statement in *Chaosmosis*: "Schizo chaosmosis is a means for the apperception of abstract machines which work transversally to heterogeneous strata" (82–83).

39. Guattari, *Les trois écologies* (Paris: Galilée, 1989), 18 (not translated in the abridged English version). Regarding the breakdown of older sociological class op-

positions and the emergence of mixed entities making a cartography of the social field increasingly difficult, see *Les années d'hiver*, 158.

40. Guattari, *Les années d'hiver*, 66–67. In *Chaosmosis*, a case in point is once more the French ecological movement: "In truth their problem today is not how to keep themselves at an equal distance from the left and the right, but how to contribute to the reinvention of progressivist polarity, how to rebuild politics on different bases, how to rearticulate transversally the public and the private, the environmental and the mental" (128).

41. Guattari, *Les années d'hiver*, 292.

42. Guattari, *Cartographies schizoanalytiques*, 67–92.

43. Guattari, *La révolution moléculaire*, 312; *Molecular Revolution*, 172 (trans. modified).

44. Guattari, *Les années d'hiver*, 102.

45. Guattari, *Chaosmosis*, 18.

46. Guattari, *L'inconscient machinique*, 190.

47. Guattari, *Les trois écologies*, 27–28; *The Three Ecologies*, 132 (trans. modified).

48. Gilles Deleuze, "What Children Say," in *Essays Critical and Clinical*, trans. Daniel W. Smith and Michael A. Greco (Minneapolis: University of Minnesota Press, 1997), 63.

49. Guattari, *Psychanalyse et transversalité*, 73–74; *Molecular Revolution*, 11, 13 (trans. modified).

50. Guattari, *Cartographies schizoanalytiques*, 75.

51. Guattari, *La révolution moléculaire*, 310; *Molecular Revolution*, 170; *Les années d'hiver*, 290. For Peirce, diagrams constitute one of three types of icons, that is, relational hypo-icons, the other two being images and metaphors. See "Logic as Semiotic: The Theory of Signs," in *Philosophical Writings of Peirce*, ed. Justus Buchler (New York: Dover, 1955), 104–7. Guattari, on the contrary, files images and diagrams separately under the respective headings of "symbolic" and "a-signifying" semiotics. Toward the end of his life, interestingly enough, Peirce also developed a keen sense for "diagrammatic" modes of thinking, to the point of considering the so-called existential graphs the masterpiece of his life. See Don D. Roberts, *The Existential Graphs of Charles S. Peirce* (The Hague: Mouton, 1973).

52. Deleuze and Guattari, *Anti-Oedipus: Capitalism and Schizophrenia*, trans. Robert Hurley, Mark Seem, and Helen R. Lane (Minneapolis: University of Minnesota Press, 1983), 242–43.

53. Louis Hjelmslev, *Prolegomena to a Theory of Language*, trans. Francis J. Whitfield (Madison: University of Wisconsin Press, 1969), 49–60; Ferdinand de Saussure, *Cours de linguistique générale*, ed. Charles Bally and Albert Sechehaye (Paris: Payot, 1962), 156–57.

54. Hjelmslev, *Prolegomena*, 57.

55. Jacques Lacan, *Ecrits* (Paris: Seuil, 1966), 819. See Guattari, *La révolution moléculaire*, 282; *Molecular Revolution*, 76; *Chaosmosis*, 45. For comments regarding Lacan's theory of the subject, I have benefited from Ph. Van Haute, *Psychanalyse en filosofie: Het imaginaire en het symbolische in het werk van Jacques Lacan* (Louvain: Peeters, 1990), 103–22; and Alain Badiou, *Théorie du sujet* (Paris: Seuil, 1985).

56. Guattari, *Chaosmosis*, 58–76, esp. 72–76. In French, the reader can consult

Cartographies schizoanalytiques for analyses of Balthus, Jean Genet, Stanislaw Ignacy Witkiewicz, Keiichi Tahara, and one of Guattari's own dreams.

57. Guattari, *Chaosmosis,* 18, 131.

58. Ibid., 24.

59. Ibid., 106, 112.

60. Francisco J. Varela, *Cognitive Science: A Cartography of Current Ideas* (1988); I have consulted the French translation, *Invitation aux sciences cognitives,* trans. Pierre Lavoie (Paris: Seuil, 1996), 111. See also Varela, Evan Thompson, and Eleanor Rosch, *The Embodied Mind: Cognitive Science and Human Experience* (Cambridge, Mass.: MIT Press, 1991). Varela traces the genealogy of this doctrine by invoking the criticisms of representational thinking in the work of philosophers such as Heidegger, Gadamer, Merleau-Ponty, and Foucault. His term of enaction translates the German *hervor-bringen,* in French *faire-émerger,* while retaining the conception of truth as aletheia. Varela's threefold history of cognitive science (cognitivism, connectionism, enaction) presents interesting parallels with the path followed by French theory and philosophy (structuralism, poststructuralism, and what appears to be a new pragmatism or constructivism such as Deleuze and Guattari's). Jean-Claude Milner points out the need to study these family resemblances in his review-article of an earlier edition of Varela's *Invitation,* in *Annuaire philosophique 1988–1989* (Paris: Seuil, 1989), 199–210.

61. Guattari, *Cartographies schizoanalytiques,* 51n. 1. With reference to the common example of Jorge Luis Borges, I have discussed this idea in relation to Jean Baudrillard's theory of simulation and Umberto Eco's view of abduction, in "A Misreading of Maps," 132–38.

62. Guattari, *Chaosmosis,* 33; and "Institutional Practice and Politics," 74.

63. Guattari, *Chaosmosis,* 30. In the same book, Guattari later writes: "Perhaps it is necessary to straddle these two perspectives: [the real] was already there as an open virtual reference, and it arises correlatively as a production sui generis of a singular event" (78).

64. Guattari, *Les années d'hiver,* 276–77.

65. Michel de Certeau, *La possession de Loudun* (Paris: Gallimard-Julliard, 1990), 3. For a brilliant discussion of de Certeau's work, see Koenraad Geldof, *Analytiques du sens: Essais sur la sociologie de la culture* (Louvain: Peeters, 1996), 128–64.

66. Deleuze, *Essays Critical and Clinical,* 61. In "Percept and Concept," William James writes: "Concepts not only guide us over the map of life, but we *revalue* life by their use"; "They steer us practically every day, and provide an immense map of relations among elements of things, which, though not now, yet on some possible future occasion, may help to steer us practically" (in *The Writings of William James: A Comprehensive Edition,* ed. John McDermott [Chicago: University of Chicago Press, 1977], 234). For a further discussion of this pragmatist view, see my *After Borges: Literary Criticism and Critical Theory* (Ann Arbor, Mich.: UMI, 1995), 272–395.

67. Guattari, *Chaosmosis,* 22, 25 (trans. modified).

68. Tom Conley, *The Self-Made Map: Cartographic Writing in Early Modern France* (Minneapolis: University of Minnesota Press, 1996), 3.

69. Guattari, *The Three Ecologies,* 133.

Guattari's Schizoanalytic Semiotics

Mixing Hjelmslev and Peirce

Gary Genosko

The glossematic theory developed by Louis Hjelmslev and H. J. Uldall during the 1930s as members of the so-called linguistic school of Copenhagen, and later elaborated by them separately in the 1940s, has the reputation of being theoretically abstruse and Byzantine in its complexity.[1] Linguists are, however, prepared to admit both that Hjelmslev was "without pity for his readers" and that reading him is "as arduous as it is rewarding." Bertha Siertsema's effort to explain rather than to build upon glossematics, albeit in a manner with which Hjelmslev would not have always concurred, and to propose changes to his definition-riddled theory that would straighten out inconsistencies arising over the course of its development and bring it into line with current linguistic coinage has led at least one critic to comment with some irony on her work: "[S]o well has she carried out her task that one may fear lest her success in rendering the terminology more easily intelligible might contribute to its wider spreading."[2] The "no pain, no gain" response to Hjelmslev must ultimately reckon with the agonies of success. This is, I believe, no less true of Félix Guattari's uses of Hjelmslevian and Peircean concepts in the description and application of a mixed semiotics. In spite of its reputation, Guattari has made glossematics serve the pragmatic ends of schizoanalysis. At the heart of this essay is the question of how an arid algebra of language may serve a pragmatics of the unconscious and take a place in Guattari's call to radically recast social practices.

At the time of Hjelmslev's death in 1965, his writings were well known to French linguists and semioticians through the pioneering study in 1946 of André Martinet on Hjelmslev's seminal *Prolegomena to a Theory of Language*,[3] which was then available only in Danish. In addition to the influential work of Martinet one may add the writings of Nicolas Ruwet, oft-quoted by French readers of Hjelmslev;[4] and it was through the initiative of a group of linguists centered around A. J. Greimas that Hjelmslev's *Le langage* appeared in France a year after the Danish master's death in 1965 (two years later, the French translation of the *Prolégomènes* appeared).[5]

It was, however, Roland Barthes who popularized Hjelmslevian terminology by developing a connotative semiotic whose staggered systems were modeled on Hjelmslev's distinction between connotation and metasemiotic (metalanguage); Expression-Relation-Content described the relation of the former semiotic of the expression plane with the latter metasemiotic of the content plane. Barthes's trademark analysis of stacked and staggered systems was introduced in its simplest form during the 1950s in *Mythologies* and developed in the 1960s through the seminal essay "Eléments de sémiologie" and his study of the fashion system, *Système de la mode*.[6] This brand of structuralism was caught in the critical antistructuralist sweep conducted in the early 1970s by Jean Baudrillard among other thinkers for whom signifying relations were homologous with repressive and reductive social structures. What made Baudrillard's work of the period unusual was that he fully elaborated homologies and structural correspondences in a way that enabled him to collapse them from the inside on the basis of his key concept of symbolic exchange.[7]

In a milieu characterized by a variety of critical engagements with and creative departures from structuralism and semiology, Deleuze and Guattari's *Anti-Oedipus* found a place in the widespread critique of the signifier and the prevailing anti-Saussureanism of the period but with one important exception. Unlike Baudrillard, for instance, who saw in the linguistic theories of Hjelmslev and Barthes further examples of the ideology of signification, Deleuze and Guattari combined a critique of a linguistics of the signifier with praise for Hjelmslev: "We believe that, from all points of view and despite certain appearances, Hjelmslev's linguistics stands in profound opposition to the Saussurean and post-Saussurean undertaking."[8] Neither Deleuze nor Guattari followed Barthes's translinguistic approach to semiology.[9] To do so would have brought them into step with the practices of specialists who exercise control over diverse signifying phenomena by making them dependent upon language. To claim, for instance, that translinguistics is imperialistic is to recognize that signification is a power relation, one of whose effects has been the colonization of all signifying phenomena. What is most disturbing in the tag of "linguistic imperialism" is that Hjelmslev has long been recognized as one of its agents, even though his sense of language is not, strictly speaking, reducible to actual languages. While linguistics ordinarily concerns particular languages, Hjelmslev's algebra aims to calculate the general system of language in relation to which particular languages would reveal their characteristics. But the calculation of theoretically possible formal relations at the level of the general system includes nonmaterialized elements, that is, elements not realized in any existing languages. The glossematist is not, then, a linguist proper. And this suits Guattari well as he did not find in linguistics principles directly applicable to his projects.

Although it is commonly understood that Hjelmslev's debts to Saussure were enormous, the position taken by Deleuze and Guattari on their relationship may be arrived at by seizing on Hjelmslev's statement that "glossematic theory must not be confused with Saussurean theory."[10] The specific object of Hjelmslevian structural linguistics is *la langue* — an essentially autonomous entity consisting of internal dependencies among categories. Glossematics studies neither *le langage* nor *la parole,* as Saussure employed them. Hjelmslev's purely structural-logistical type of linguistic research, which conceives of *la* langue as form independent of substance, takes off from the final sentence of Saussure's *Cours de linguistique générale:* "[T]he true and unique object of linguistics is language [*la langue*] studied in itself and for itself."[11] Hjelmslev's immanent linguistics cannot be counted among any of the post-Saussurean projects such as that of the Prague school in which *la langue* is not independent but, rather, dependent upon usage and *la parole;* nor does glossematics adhere to the letter of Saussurean linguistics as it is read by Saussure's Genevan interpreters. While Hjelmslev generously admitted that the *Cours* could be read in different ways owing to certain ambiguities in the text, glossematics would nevertheless pursue the ideal of studying *la* langue "in itself and for itself." Moreover, Hjelmslev's divergence from Saussure may be explained in large measure by his, as one reviewer of the *Prolegomena* put it, "one-sided interpretation of the Saussurean concept of *la langue*" as form and not substance, emphasizing Saussure's theory of value.[12] Where does this leave substance? It is Guattari's answer to this question that interests me.

The work of Hjelmslev is for Deleuze and Guattari "profoundly opposed" to Saussurean and post Saussurean "isms" inasmuch as it takes the high road of form by studying *la* langue — *la langue* is a manifestation of a typological class to which it belongs, and the type is a manifestation of and thus subordinate to the class of classes, *la* langue or species-language.[13] Deleuze and Guattari do not complain that Hjelmslev's theory is too abstract. For its high level of abstraction is precisely one of its virtues, and they rejoice in the irreducibility of the planes of expression and content to signifier and signified. Hjelmslev was not a "signifier enthusiast"; nor did his definitions of the planes require their manifestation in psychological substances, as Saussure indicated.

Deleuze and Guattari think that Hjelmslev's theory "is the only linguistics adapted to the nature of *both* the capitalist *and* the schizophrenic flows: until now, the only modern (and not archaic) theory of language."[14] This kind of linguistics theorizes language as an inclusive and intensive continuum, whose variations conform neither to linguistic constants nor to variables but are open to continuous and hitherto unrealized conjunctions.

Glossematics may be brought into the schizoanalytic fold because it offers a rarely permitted (grammatically, that is) freedom to connect and combine phonemes into possible morphemes; to pursue, in other words, unusual if not unnatural connective syntheses, generalizable in structural terms as unrestricted and unpoliced passages, meetings, and alliances at all levels and places. Glossematics starts to "schizz" in the *Prolegomena* as Hjelmslev "feel[s] the desire to invert the sign-orientation" of traditional linguistics.[15] For Hjelmslev, a sign is a two-sided entity whose expression and content planes are understood as functives that contract their sign-function. These functives are present simultaneously since they are mutually presupposing. Glossematics becomes modern at the moment when Hjelmslev, reflecting on the fact that a sign is a sign of something, maintains that this entity can no longer be conceived of as only a sign of content-substance (a content-substance or the conception of a thing is ordered to and arranged under a content-form by the sign). A sign is equally a sign of an expression-substance (the sounds subsumed by an expression-form of phonemes). Expression and content and form and substance are the double dichotomies of Hjelmslevian signification. Hjelmslev attempts to destroy the hierarchy and directionality of signification that was hitherto based upon the definition of the sign as that of an expression-substance for a content-substance by carrying to its radical end the mutual solidarity and equality of linguistic expression and content. It should be possible, Hjelmslev believed, to devise a grammatical method for the study of linguistic expression by "start[ing] from the content and proceed[ing] from the content to the expression."[16] Against Hjelmslev, Siertsema and others have argued that it is only possible to analyze content by proceeding from linguistic expression.[17] This argument has provoked charges of idealism against Hjelmslev because the inversion implies that an analysis might begin with a concept (content-substance) ordered to its form by the sign in a way which forgoes words or the means to identify the content in question without first expressing it in some manner.

Glossematics may be "schizo," but was Hjelmslev schizophrenic? That is, did Hjelmslev not only think like a schizoanalyst and theorize the schizo-process in order to free the flows of language but also suffer from something called schizophrenia? Was he another Antonin Artaud, Vincent Van Gogh, Mary Barnes — a Judge Schreber whose breakthroughs enlightened us all? Deleuze and Guattari do not explicitly answer these questions, although they welcome Hjelmslev to this cadre. On the floors of conferences, in obituaries, in diagnostic speculations, Hjelmslev's "depression," his "long and tragic illness," is made reference to not as breakthroughs but as breakdowns. For all the care Deleuze and Guattari take in recognizing the dangers of turning clinical issues into metaphors, and to the extent that Guattari bases his extrapolations on decades of clinical experience, they have said nothing about his "case."

Although Hjelmslev may have pursued a rarefied vision of linguistic form, this venture does not entail for Deleuze and Guattari an "overdetermination of structuralism." They clearly reject Ruwet's critique of the combinatory freedom permitted by Hjelmslev's generative grammar in order to recoup Lewis Carroll's "Jabberwocky" and James Joyce's *Finnegan's Wake* — the two texts that Ruwet uses as examples of a "type of creativity [with] only extremely distant connections with the creativity which operates in the ordinary use of language."[18] Joyce's phonemes can be monstrous, exploiting phonologically grammatical possibilities (and otherwise!) and raising the stakes of semantic content. Deleuze and Guattari refigure Ruwet's appeal to the proximity of ordinary language and rule-based creativity, but not in order to uncritically valorize an unbounded creativity well beyond the demands of a grammatical model to account for competence and the subtleties of degrees of acceptable usage in which, after all, they, too, communicate; to be sure, the concept of linguistic competence is not one that Deleuze and Guattari hold in high esteem. The examples they cite (Carroll, Joyce, e.e. cummings) are not marginal literary figures, and their choices reveal that a-grammaticality is not produced by and reducible to correct grammar. In fact, for Deleuze and Guattari it is precisely the opposite since a-grammatical writing forces language to face its limitations.

Although Deleuze and Guattari are at odds with Ruwet on several points, they embrace his observation that the order of the elements is not relevant in glossematic syntax. This is one of the reasons why Hjelmslev's linguistics is "profoundly opposed" to Saussureanism: "[T]he order of the elements is secondary in relation to the axiomatic of flows and figures."[19] Ruwet points out that Hjelmslev has a set syntax rather than a concatenation or string syntax. The order of elements in the set is not relevant at the level of content-form (what would correspond in transformative grammar to deep structure) and contains less information than the string.[20] What is axiomatic for Deleuze and Guattari and Hjelmslev is that a set is a more productive flow-machine than a string. The creative aspects of language are at the outset marginalized and trapped by the dominant grammatical and syntactical machines, as Guattari has argued in *La révolution moléculaire,* yet there are experimenters boring through the walls of dominant encodings.[21]

Guattari's brand of antistructuralism hinges on a definition of signification that is itself based upon Hjelmslev's rethinking of *la barre saussurienne* between the signifier and the signified as a semiological function rather than an association. Saussure's definition allowed structuralists to separate the signifier from the signified (that is, this is how *la barre lacanienne* works) in the name of the signifier (that is, a postmodern metonymic slide and all other reductions of content to formal signifying chains). Guattari adopted Hjelmslev's position on the mutually presupposing solidarity of expression and content in order to ensure that neither term would become as a simple matter of course independent of or more dependent on the other. This was a prophylaxis against signifier fetishism. Guattari interrogated the aforementioned solidarity so as "to search for the points of articulation, the points of micropolitical antagonism at all levels."[22]

Guattari defines signification as an encounter between diverse semiotic systems of formalization (a-signifying and signifying) on the planes of expression and content imposed by relations of power. The encounters between formalizations of expression and content require that the semiological function is read micropolitically because the mutual presupposition of the planes exhibits a variety of shifting power relations. Guattari attempts to uncover the social and political determinations of signifying phenomena through the use of modified versions of Hjelmslevian categories.

How does a schizoanalyst study modes of semiotization without being contaminated by the apolitical and largely asocial categories of linguistics and semiology? The answer to this question, Guattari claims,[23] is either to smash or dismantle their categories through a detour by way of Hjelmslev. I want to emphasize two elements of this detour as they pertain to the semiotization of matter. The schizoanalyst takes great interest in the formation of matter — that is, in nonsemiotically formed and semiotically formed matter. First, a few words on Hjelmslev are in order.

For Hjelmslev, there is an unformed thought-mass common to all languages called purport (matter). Unformed purport is formed differently in English ("I do not know") and in French ("Je ne sais pas"), as well as in other languages. Purport is like sand, Hjelmslev suggests, formed in different ways in different molds (languages).[24] Purport is formed into substance. In fact, Hjelmslev writes that "it has no possible existence except through being substance for one form or another." Content-purport is ordered by a specific form into content-substance. The form is in an arbitrary relation to the purport. In the same way, expression-purport is ordered by a specific expression-form into an expression-substance.

Consider the following representation proposed by Jürgen Trabant:[25]

$$EP \rightarrow ES \rightarrow EF \leftrightarrow CF \leftarrow CS \leftarrow CP$$

The unilateral arrows on both the expression and content sides represent the formation of purport into substance. The bidirectional arrows in the center between expression-form and content-form show that the sign-function is dematerialized into pure form. Hjelmslev designates the two functives that contract the sign-function as content-form and expression-form, by virtue of which exist content-substance and expression-substance. The form, Hjelmslev remarks in one of his most famous examples — which Guattari also quotes — is "projected on to the purport, just as an open net casts its shadow down on an undivided surface."[26] Form is as abstract as a shadow; it is not the net but its shadow.

Purport is formed in different ways in different languages. There is for Hjelmslev no universal formation, although he considers the formation of purport to be a universal principle. Purport itself cannot be known except through its formation. In other words, linguistics doesn't analyze purport: it studies form; nonlinguistic sciences such as physics study purport. The specific task of linguistics is the study of form in the service of a science of expression and content taken on "an internal and functional basis."[27] What Hjelmslev has in mind is an algebra of language whose terms have no natural designations. In addition, the analysis does not depend on individual natural languages, even if these are included in its general calculus. What matters for Hjelmslev is whether structural types are "manifestable in any substance." "Substance," Hjelmslev writes, "is thus not a necessary presupposition for linguistic form, but linguistic form is a necessary presupposition for substance."[28] Linguistic form is a constant that is manifested, and substance is a variable that is manifesting.

With this in mind, I will turn to Guattari's specific interventions. In any Hjelmslevian analysis, one must consider the formation of matter into substance (form-matter-substance) on the planes of expression and content. There are, then, five intersecting criteria or strata. But Guattari's approach to three of these criteria needs to noted. Guattari makes two claims about form. First, Hjelmslev did not consider it alone. While this is technically accurate, one needs to recall that substance is not a necessary presupposition of form. Beyond this fine point of interpretation, there is a larger issue at stake. Guattari detours through Hjelmslevian form because he wants to abandon, with reference to Hjelmslev's distinction between system and process, any consideration of autonomous forms. Forms in his estimation do not exist unless they are put into action. The point Guattari makes concerning system and process — that it would be a mistake to autonomize the process — refers to Hjelmslev's distinction between system (language) and process (text) that contracts their function, even though Guattari is prepared to overlook the notion that the process cannot exist without the system and the system is "not unimaginable without a process," as Hjelmslev put it,[29] for the reason that there may be a text as yet unrealized. For Guattari, form is considered in terms of an abstract machine that brings about meaning and meaning-making formations with matter: form semioticizes matter. Substance, which Guattari treats as a couple substance/form, is what results when becomings of abstract machines are actualized or fluxes harnessed. Against the grain of Hjelmslev, matter is for Guattari considered independently from its formation as a substance and in terms of unformed, unorganized material intensities. With Hjelmslev, Guattari notes that his French translators were wise to identify *matière* and *sens*, as in *matière-sens*, for the Danish *Mening* (purport).

Guattari further explains the detour through Hjelmslev as a way of: (1) escaping the tyranny of the signifier-signified binarism; (2) eluding the abstraction of the signified; (3) breaking the negative, differential identity of the sign defined against other signs ad infinitum; and (4) challenging signifier despotism and fetishism. Guattari develops a tripartite typology of modes of semiotization through an analysis of the intersection of the five criteria (strata). The first are a-semiotic encodings. These include "genetic encoding or any type of so-called natural encoding that functions independently of the constitution of a semiotic substance. These modes of encoding formalize the field of material intensities without recourse to an autonomous and translatable 'écriture.' "[30] A-semiotic encodings are in an external relation (outside the expression-content planes) to the intersecting criteria, engaging form and matter but not substance. There is no semiotic substance at issue. Here, then, Guattari employs Hjelmslevian concepts to create a new category of encoding: if semiotically formed matter is substance, then a-semiotic encodings are nonsemiotically formed matter. Guattari's statement that "there is no genetic writing" implies that "natural" a-semiotic encodings cannot be totalized or territorialized on a specific semiotic substance or stratum. They are, after all, a-semiotic: "There is no differentiation and autonomization between one biological stratum, the object of encoding, and an informational stratum."[31] Without a semiotic substance, such encodings cannot be directly translated into another system. This does not prevent, it is important to add, biologists from transposing a-semiotic encodings into graphic semiotic or signifying substances. This is a form of semiotic capture, organization, or, even better, as Guattari notes, discipline. Connective syntheses are disciplined by reterritorializing disjunctive syntheses. Strictly speaking, the connective syntheses generated by natural encodings are outside of representation.

Second, consider signifying semiologies. These concern sign-systems with semiotically formed substances on the expression and content planes. Guattari distinguishes between symbolic semiologies and semiologies of signification. The former involves several semiotic substances whose quasi-autonomy is retained because they cannot be completely translated into a single substance (Guattari refers to what are known as simpler, perhaps even cruder, nonlinguistic semiotic systems, whose very crudity allows them to retain a certain degree of independence from universalizing encodings); these remain decentered, as it were. Guattari has turned the semiotic tables around by reversing the standard claim that nonlinguistic systems are translatable into linguistic systems but that linguistic systems are not fully translatable into nonlinguistic systems. Symbolic semiologies have numerous strata, none of which can constantly overcode the others. The substances or strata of semiologies of signification are centered on a single substance that dominates and overcodes all of them (commonly, this is linguistic substance and the totalitarian signifier). Guattari has moved, then, within the second mode of semiotization, from semiologies with multiple to only two strata (which are really only one in the case of the semio-linguistic machine showing two faces and producing conjunctive syntheses). Connective syntheses are reterritorialized in the double articulation of expression and content, that is, by the disjunctive syntheses that capture them, but themselves remain capable of reconnection. The productivity of the connective syntheses is divided between and distributed among two planes in signifying semiologies (which have distorted the Hjelmslevian planes in the image of the linguistic sign) under the referential function of the sign: a denoted real and a representational image.

The sign, Guattari specifies,[32] is cut off from the real because it must pass through the mental world of representations. To be cut off from material intensities is to be trapped in a "signifying ghetto" lorded over by a despotic signifier whose goal is to "treat everything that appears in order to represent it through a process of repetition which refers only to itself."[33] Signification echoes to infinity because it is supremely redundant. The subjectivity produced in the world of signification is a shut-in, a semiological shipwreck. Enunciative polyvocity is crushed by being split between a subject of enunciation and the subject of the statement: "The subject of the statement has become the respondent of the subject of enunciation by the effect of a sort of reductive echolalia."[34] This splitting effectively accomplishes the individuation, personalization, and gender specification of the subject of the statement bound to *je-tu-il-elle*. Polyvocity becomes bi(uni)vocity. In all of this, Guattari's goal remains the discovery of "the residual traces, the transversal flights of a collective assemblage of enunciation which constitutes the real productive insistence of all semiotic machinism."[35] In order to reach this schizoanalytic goal, Guattari requires a third category.

The third category is that of a-signifying semiotics. There is a circular connection, skirting around signifying semiologies, between form and matter but without leaving — unlike a-semiotic encodings — the expression and content planes. It is this circularity that allows a-signifying semiotics to remain independent of, and in a nonhierarchical relation with, signifying semiologies and language. Guattari specifies that a-signifying semiotics retain, however, a partial use for signifying semiologies. The polysemiotic connections established between the abstract machines (form) and material intensities escape, then, the overcoding functions of signifying semiological systems. But they are neither completely deterritorialized nor reterritorialized. Consider an example from linguistics such as idioms. Idioms jump over denotation and form assemblages by grouping existing words together, giving them new connotations. Idioms even focus on what are called "prone words" (such as, in English, "take" and "get") and hijack them. The a-signifying semiotic potential of idiom formation is constantly threatened by paranoiac recodings of signifying semiologies (respectable academic grammar) that want to reduce them to a single proper, formal, substance. A-signifying semiotics leave behind significative redundancies for the production of nonredundant, even improbable, and original conjunctions of signs and material fluxes. Such conjunctions between semiotic and real material machines, which create a-signifying collective assemblages, do not imply that the semiotic machines are less real than the material machines, nor that the material machines are less semiotic. On the contrary, they share these attributes. The conjunctions between signs and fluxes, between abstract machines and material intensities, between form and matter, are all unmediated by representation; they are, in other words, in constant and direct contact. There is no need for recourse to representative structures. Guattari describes the shift from signifying semiologies to a-signifying semiotics in terms of the de-localization, de-privatization, an-oedipalization of the individuated subject of enunciation to a collective assemblage of enunciation. He correlates the individual with signification and the collective with machinic assemblage, adding that the signifier plus the signified and form plus substance equals signification (individuation of phantasms belonging to subjugated groups) and that collective assemblages of enunciation consisting of conjunctions of abstract machines and material fluxes belong to the phantasms of subject groups. Guattari then enumerates dialectically negative and positive attributes of the individual-collective relation: signification involves self-reference and thus the rupture of machinic conjunctions, whereas collective assemblages give up comprehension, being in some instance without signification for anyone, for the sake of creating meaning directly from the fluxes.[36] Signification thus has no machinic meaning because of the absence of conjunctions with the real fluxes.

The collective assemblages composed by creative machinic connections of semiotic and material fluxes cannot be individuated, having left the field of representation. A-signifying semiotic machines free desiring-production, the singularities of desire, from the signifiers of national, familial, personal, racial, humanist, and transcendent values (including the semiotic myth of a return to nature, to the presignifying world of a-semiotic encodings); in short, desiring-production is freed from all "territorializing alienations" and set coordinates.[37] But this freedom must not be exaggerated. Signifying semiologies are only tools to be employed in semiotics of schizoanalytic practice in and outside of the psychiatric institution. Assemblages are not, then, groups composed of individuals. Schizoanalytic mixed-semiotics has the task of "furthering the formation of relatively autonomous and untranslatable semiotic substances, by accommodating the sense and non-sense of desire as they are, by not attempting to adapt the modes of subjectification to signification and to dominant social laws. Its objective is not at all to recuperate facts and acts that are outside the norm; on the contrary, it is to make a place for the singularity traits of subjects who, for one reason or another, escape the common law."[38] For Guattari, this is the task of a genuine analytic practice. One of the important elements of this practice concerns the recognition that the subject in contact with desiring-machines in a-signifying semiotics oscillates between re-territorializations on signification and deterritorializations into new machinic conjunctions. This oscillation helps to explain why signifying semiologies still have a role to play. Guattari's semiotics is always, it needs to be emphasized, mixed. Further, on this point Guattari writes: "[I]n schizoanalysis free rein will be given to oedipalizing representations and paranoid-fascist fantasms in order to better plot the effects of their blockage of the fluxes, and to relaunch the process in a sort of machinic forward flight."[39] Indeed, one of the trademarks of Guattari's schizoanalysis is his focus on subjective redundancies (refrains, black holes, and so on).[40]

These technical details should not obscure the more general issue of whether or not the detour solves more problems for schizoanalysis than it creates. By the time Guattari published *L'inconscient machinique* in 1979, his reasons for turning to Hjelmslev had become more explicit. Guattari's opening salvos are directed against linguistic imperialists because they attempt to annex both semiotics and pragmatics and use structural analysis to depoliticize their domains of inquiry; these salvos lead at once to the choice of Hjelmslev as an alternative while running against the grain of glossematics. For if there is no language in itself (unified and autonomous), and if, on the contrary, language "always remains open to other modes of semioticization," as Guattari thinks,[41] then Hjelmslev's efforts to establish the truth of Saussure's linguistics must be counterbalanced (to say the least) in some manner. Guattari detours since he does not continue the Hjelmslevian project; instead, he takes up certain categories because they "appear to be the only ones resulting from a truly rigorous examination of the whole of the semiotic problematic, by drawing out, in particular, all of the consequences of calling into question the status of content and expression."[42] Guattari had, however, two regrets about glossematics: (1) "le bi-face hjelmslevien" of expression and content coincided with other "binarist reductions"; (2) Hjelmslev seemed to willingly participate in the sovereign overcoding of language when he wrote "in practice, a language is a semiotic into which all other semiotics may be translated,"[43] thus leaving ample room for the Barthesean reversal of Saussure's statement concerning the place of linguistics in semiology. Guattari wanted nothing to do with this dogma cherished by linguists.

Guattari's attention to the semiotic formation of substances on the planes of expression and content is nevertheless modeled on Hjelmslev's interpretation of the formation of linguistically unformed matter into substance. A language casts a shadow like a net over the amorphous thought-mass of purport and lays down boundaries in this sand; purport is continually reworked in different ways by different languages. The French word *car* (for, because) and the English word *car* (automobile) have the same expression-purport but different content-purport; the French *dix* (10) and the English *ten* (10) have the same content-purport but a different expression-purport. Guattari makes light of Hjelmslev's metaphors of the "net" and of "sand" by arguing that there are not, on the one side, "little building blocks of semiological construction and, on the other side, the amorphous mass of possibility."[44] For Guattari, the Hjelmslevian sand is already "as differentiated as the most material of matters." Anyone who has been to a beach would recognize this under foot.

There are, then, several species of signs and semiotic connections involved in the formation of matter and the conjugations of unformed material fluxes, and many of these are borrowed from the work of Charles Sanders Peirce. Although some semionauts hold that semiology lifted off under Hjelmslev from the Saussurean launching pad, it is Peirce, as Deleuze and Guattari write, who "is the true inventor of semiotics. That is why we can borrow his terms, even while changing their connotations." Deleuze and Guattari regret that Peircean icons, indexes, and symbols "are based on signifier-signified relations (contiguity for the index, similitude for the icon, conventional rule for the symbol); this leads him to make the 'diagram' a special case of the icon (the icon of relation)."[45] In order to liberate the diagram from the supposed yoke of the Saussureanism that infects icons, for example, Guattari in particular has developed the semiotic category of diagrammatism through the division of icon and diagrams along the lines of signifying semiotics and a-signifying semiotics, the latter involving signs that are more deterritorialized than icons.

Diagrammatic machines of signs elude the territorializing systems of symbolic and signifying semiologies by displaying a kind of reserve in relation to their referents, forgoing polysemy and eschewing lateral signifying effects. Although they have meaning for me, most of my scribbles concerning this notion did not make their way into this essay because they could not be translated into a communicable semiology. Still, such scribbles function independently "of the fact that they signify or fail to signify something for someone," which is only to say that they do not behave like well-formed signs in a universal system of signification and fail to pass smoothly through the simulacral dialogism of ideal models of communication.[46]

For Peirce, diagrammatic reasoning is iconic: "A Diagram is mainly an Icon, and an icon of intelligible relations in the constitution of its Object."[47] In Guattari's terminology, a diagram connects deterritorialized material fluxes without the authority of a signifying semiology. Returning to Peirce, a diagram is mainly but not exclusively an icon. It incorporates certain habits involved in the creation of graphic abstractions (in geometry and syllogistics); it also has the indexical feature of pointing "There!"[48] without, however, describing or providing any insight into its object. Since a diagram displays in itself the formal features of its object, it may be said to take the place of its object: "[T]he distinction of the real and the copy disappears, and it is for the moment a pure dream."[49] This simulation defies, Guattari specifies, the territorializing effects of representation and denotation. In Peirce's work, too, diagrams can be deterritorializing because they are iconic — icons do not lead one away from themselves to their objects; rather, they exhibit their object's characteristics in themselves. Icons can be indifferent to the demands of dominant semiotic formalizations. While a Peircean could rightly claim that Deleuze and Guattari have engaged in acts of interpretive violence by playing favorites with iconic phenomena, their approach to Peirce is, I think, uncannily Peircean. It needs to be recalled that Deleuze and Guattari feel no compulsion to honor the concepts that they borrow from their semiotic masters.

In their reading of this American master, Deleuze and Guattari adopt a Peircean attitude toward Peirce. They read him against himself by extending interpretation beyond his conventional definitions. This is precisely the approach Guattari adopted in his use of Hjelmslevian categories, and it is what Peirce called critical-philosophical thinking since it requires that one observe an author's line of thought, from which one then extrapolates imaginatively. Take, for example, Deleuze and Guattari's phrase: "Look at mathematics: it's not a science, it's a monster slang, it's nomadic."[50] This glance at mathematics is Peircean. An active mathematical mind is, according to Peirce, necessary for interpreting signs. The ability of mathematics to travel is part of its dynamic character. Peirce held that mathematical practice or what he called theorematic reasoning bears little relation to the semimechanical deductive inferences and demonstrations of logical calculus. A monster slang is not limited to a class or profession or generation. It is a playful practice involving active and creative experimentation. In his discussion of theorematic reasoning,[51] Peirce wrote: "It is necessary that something be DONE." An a-signifying abstract machine is diagrammatic. So too is theorematic reasoning. What was a necessary question for Lenin and Jerry Rubin was a question of necessity for Peirce. Points are made and stretched. Hypotheses are advanced. Algebraic relations pour forth. Pins are stuck in maps. Pages are covered in scribbles. Living mathematical thought involves the construction of diagrams and experiments with points, surfaces, lines, and so on. Deleuze and Guattari's diagram is also constructive. It conjugates physically and semiotically unformed matter; in Hjelmslev's linguistics, functives contract (draw together) their function. A diagram is a pure matter-function machine joining together and changing the shape of semiochips — edges, points, particles, degrees of intensity, and so on. In short, the diagram facilitates connections between the most deterritorialized particles of expression and content. Diagrams are irreducible to icons, Guattari contends, because icons remain encysted in preestablished semiotic coordinates.[52] Guattari adds that semiotically formed substances may be diagrammaticized by being emptied as if pieces of them were flung centrifugally along certain vectors toward new spaces to which they cling.

Let's revisit Hjelmslev's metaphor of the net. Hjelmslevian purport is like sand that can be put into different molds (that is, the formal molds of different languages). In the formation of purport into a content-substance and expression-substance by content-form and expression-form, form lays down lines like a net casting its shadow onto an "undivided surface." For Guattari, this sand is already differentiated and in some ways formed, but not as a linguistic substance or even as semiotic substance. Is this net a diagram? The idea of this net throwing its shadow and "netting" purport is antithetical to certain aspects of Guattari's polysemiotic typology; the idea suggests that diagrammatic, a-signifying semiotic productions of meaning have not escaped the signifying machines of semiological authority. A-signifying semiotics establishes connections between material fluxes that have not been semiotically formed as substances, but these connections mix with signifying semiological substances, even of the most despotic types driven by signifier fetishism and the demands of structural isomorphism. The net is a signifying semiology driven by the linguistic domination of purport, but it is also full of a-signifying holes irreducible to the ties that bind it.

My own "prolegomenon" to an understanding of how Guattari does things with Hjelmslev in the end required a brief investigation of the semiotic of Peirce since Guattari enlivened the form-substance relation with the sign particles of a diagrammatic function borrowed and adapted from him. It would be necessary to examine in detail the schizoanalytic cartographies of Guattari (by which I mean literally his map- and diagram-making) in order to trace the subtleties of his brand of political polysemiotics.

Hjelmslev puts the linguist on guard against substance and warns of the extralinguistic seductions of purport. Guattari puts the glossematician on guard against formed substances. Hjelmslev's sand became substance for new linguistic forms, to which substance was inferior and upon which it depended. But Guattari thought that this kind of study of substance occluded the mapping of purport (unformed matter) about which linguistics, Hjelmslev believed, would not concern itself and, even if it did, could only come to know purport to the extent that it was formed. Guattari deviates from Hjelmslev on this point by deviating from Peirce and opening up the categories of a-semiotic encodings and a-signifying semiotics. It was clearly not a deviation from Deleuze and Guattari for Brian Massumi to begin his *User's Guide* with an analysis of a complex substance (woodworker-tools-wood) in order to develop the interrelations at play in its formation and to identify, among other things, its Hjelmslevian components. I have taken a different approach to a similar goal by reading Deleuze and Guattari (primarily the latter) through the problems inherent in glossematics. This is not so much a deviation as a study of how, programmatically at least, the vicissitudes of glossematics can serve schizoanalysis.

Notes

1. See Giulio C. Lepschy, "European Structuralism: Post-Saussurean Schools," in *Current Trends in Linguistics,* vol. 13, ed. T. A. Sebeok (The Hague: Mouton, 1975), 189; and idem, *La linguistique structurale,* trans. Louis-Jean Calvet (Paris: Payot, 1968), 81–98; see also Umberto Eco, *A Theory of Semiotics* (Bloomington: Indiana University Press, 1976), 54, and idem, "The Influence of Roman Jakobson on the Development of Semiotics," in *Classics of Semiotics,* ed. Martin Krampen, Klaus Oehler, Roland Posner, T. A. Sebeok, and Thure von Uexküll (New York: Plenum Press, 1981), 111.

2. Bertha Siertsema, *A Study Of Glossematics: Critical Survey of Its Fundamental Concepts*, 2d ed. (The Hague: Martinus Nijhoff, 1965 [1955]). See also the review of Siertsema by W. Haas, "Concerning Glossematics," *Archivum Linguisticum* 8, no. 2 (1956): 105.

3. André Martinet, "Au sujet des fondements de la théorie linguistique de Louis Hjelmslev," *Bulletin de la Société de Linguistique de Paris* 42 (1942–45): 19–43; for a later but no less influential paper, see idem, "La double articulation linguistique," in *Recherches structurales 1949: Interventions dans le débat glossématique: Publiée à l'occasion du cinquantenaire de M. L. Hjelmslev* (Copenhagen: Nordisk sprog-og kulturforlag, 1970); Louis Hjelmslev, *Prolegomena to a Theory of Language*, trans. Francis J. Whitfield (Madison: University of Wisconsin Press, 1969 [1961]) (original: *Omkring Sprogteoriens Grundlaeggelse*, 1943).

4. Nicolas Ruwet, *An Introduction to Generative Grammar*, trans. Norval S. H. Smith (Amsterdam: North-Holland Publishing, 1973); idem, "La linguistique générale aujourd'hui," *Archives européennes de sociologie* 5 (1964): 277–310.

5. Louis Hjelmslev, *Le langage*, preface by A. J. Greimas (Paris: Minuit, 1966) (original: 1963); idem, *Prolégomènes à une théorie du langage* (Paris: Minuit, 1968) (English translation: *Language: An Introduction*, trans. Francis J. Whitfield [Madison: University of Wisconsin Press, 1970]); see the review by Nicole Gueunier for a general contextualization of the impact of the *Prolégomènes*, "Expression et contenu," *La quinzaine littéraire* 71 (16–30 April 1969): 24.

6. See especially Roland Barthes, "Eléments de sémiologie," *Communications* 4 (1964): 1–27 (English translation: *Elements of Semiology*, trans. Annette Lavers and Colin Smith [New York: Hill and Wang, 1968]). Barthes popularized what was already "in a sense" a popularization of glossematics (the *Prolegomena*), according to Francis Whitfield in the "editor's introduction" to Louis Hjelmslev, *Résumé of a Theory of Language* (Madison: University of Wisconsin Press, 1975).

7. Jean Baudrillard, *For a Critique of the Political Economy of the Sign*, trans. Charles Levin (St. Louis: Telos, 1981), 162ff. (original: 1972); see also my *Baudrillard and Signs* (London: Routledge, 1994), 1–27.

8. Gilles Deleuze and Félix Guattari, *Anti-Oedipus: Capitalism and Schizophrenia*, trans. Robert Hurley, Mark Seem, and Helen R. Lane (New York: Viking Press, 1977), 242 (original: 1972).

9. For a further clarification of this point see Brian Massumi, *A User's Guide to Capitalism and Schizophrenia: Deviations from Deleuze and Guattari* (Cambridge, Mass.: MIT Press, 1992), 154–55n. 45.

10. Louis Hjelmslev, "L'analyse structurale de langage," in *Essais linguistiques* (Paris: Minuit, 1971), 39.

11. Ferdinand de Saussure, *Course in General Linguistics*, trans. Wade Baskin (New York: McGraw-Hill, 1966), 232 (ms. 1906–11).

12. Paul L. Garvin, "Review of *Prolegomena to a Theory of Language*," *Language* 30, no. 1 (1954): 90.

13. Hjelmslev, "Linguistique structurale," in *Essais*, 31–32.

14. Deleuze and Guattari, *Anti-Oedipus*, 243, with slight changes from the English translation in accordance with the original text, *L'anti-oedipe*, new expanded edition (Paris: Minuit, 1975 [1972]), 288–89. See also Deleuze and Guattari, *A Thousand*

Plateaus, trans. Brian Massumi (Minneapolis: University of Minnesota Press, 1987 [1980]), 66ff. and 98ff.

15. Hjelmslev, *Prolegomena,* 57.
16. Ibid., 75.
17. Siertsema, *Study,* 61–63.
18. Ruwet, *Introduction,* 30.
19. Deleuze and Guattari, *Anti-Oedipus,* 242–43 and note.
20. Ruwet, *Introduction,* 293–94.
21. Félix Guattari, *La révolution moléculaire* (Fontenay-sous-Bois: Recherches, 1977), 307ff.
22. Ibid., 242.
23. Guattari, *L'inconscient machinique* (Fontenay-sous-Bois: Recherches, 1979), 39ff (English translation: "Semiological Subjection, Semiotic Enslavement," trans. Peter Trnka, in *The Guattari Reader* [Oxford: Blackwell, 1996], 145ff.).
24. Hjelmslev, *Prolegomena,* 52.
25. Jürgen Trabant, "Louis Hjelmslev: Glossematics as General Semiotics," trans. Ian Boyd Whyte, in *Classics of Semiotics,* ed. Martin Krampen et al. (New York: Plenum Press, 1981), 94.
26. Hjelmslev, *Prolegomena,* 57; Guattari, *Révolution moléculaire,* 278.
27. Hjelmslev, *Prolegomena,* 79.
28. Ibid., 106.
29. Ibid., 39.
30. Guattari, *Révolution moléculaire,* 279; see also idem, "The Place of the Signifier in the Institution," trans. Gary Genosko, in *The Guattari Reader,* 149.
31. Guattari, *Révolution moléculaire,* 253.
32. Ibid., 255.
33. Ibid., 256.
34. Ibid.
35. Ibid., 256–57.
36. Ibid., 260.
37. Ibid., 263.
38. Ibid., 284; see also idem, "The Place of the Signifier," 153.
39. Guattari, *Révolution moléculaire,* 269.
40. Massumi, *User's Guide,* 151n. 33.
41. Guattari, *L'inconscient machinique,* 25.
42. Ibid., 40; Guattari, "Semiological Subject," 145.
43. Hjelmslev, *Prolegomena,* 109.
44. Guattari, *L'inconscient machinique,* 205.
45. Deleuze and Guattari, *A Thousand Plateaus,* 531n. 41.
46. Guattari, *Révolution moléculaire,* 310–11.
47. Charles Sanders Peirce, *The Collected Papers,* ed. Charles Hartshorne and Paul Weiss (Cambridge, Mass.: Harvard University Press, 1935–1966), 4.531.
48. Ibid., 3.361.
49. Ibid., 3.362.
50. Deleuze and Guattari, *A Thousand Plateaus,* 24.
51. Peirce, *Collected Papers,* 4.233.
52. Ibid., 141ff.; Guattari, *L'inconscient machinique,* 224.

Becoming a Body without Organs

The Masochistic Quest of Jean-Jacques Rousseau

Bryan Reynolds

Jean-Jacques Rousseau sweated, urinated, defecated, and ejaculated. He produced and reproduced. Like all human beings, according to the "schizoanalytic" theory of Gilles Deleuze and Félix Guattari, Rousseau was a desiring-machine; he was desiring-production, desiring because of desire's natural desire to produce desire. For Deleuze and Guattari, desire is both the subject and object of desire; it is not about acquisition or lack but rather about production and a process of desiring-production; it cannot be defined as the lack of a real object. This is not to assert that one cannot feel the lack of a real object and therefore direct one's desire toward that real object, but that one does not desire simply as a result of feeling the lack of a real object — or anything else. To comprehend desire as only lack is to disregard "the intrinsic power of desire to create its own object — if only in an unreal, hallucinatory, or delirious form — or from representing this causality as stemming from within desire itself."[1]

For the myth of desire-as-lack to achieve axiomatic status, the material world would have to lack at least one real object, a paradoxically missing yet known object that desire experiences as lack. This out-of-this-world object would have to account for the desire and production of things not modeled on things already existent in this world. It would have to account for such phenomena as innovation, invention, and science fiction. But inasmuch as the probability of an imagined and existent out-of-this-world reality is an overwhelming impossibility, so is the desire-as-lack formulation. Deleuze and Guattari point out that if we were to accept the notion of desire as the lack of the real object and that its existence as a real entity thus depends upon an essence of lack (as explained by psychoanalysis), desire would still have to produce, at some point, a fantasized or symbolic object that functions as a double of reality. Hence, it is illogical to insist that feelings of lack or an imaginary object are requisite to the inspiration, conception, and actuality of desire.

Deleuze and Guattari maintain that desire is only a machine producing the desire for production, a condition perpetuated by additional desiring-machines as the by-products of the desire for production. This process of desiring-production necessitates a chain of desiring-machines that is continuous and generative. Rousseau was a desiring-machine, and he was comprised of various desiring-machines connected to other desiring-machines, both inside and outside of his own body:

> [O]ne machine is always coupled with another.... [T]here is always a flow-producing machine, and another machine connected to it that interrupts or draws off part of this flow (the breast — the mouth). And because the first machine is in turn connected to another whose flow it interrupts or partially drains off, the binary series is linear in every direction.[2]

Desiring-machines never constitute a whole, but rather each is a component of a universal continuum of ceaseless production and consumption. In other words, desire is an innate psychic force that is always already compelled to create/produce. This force in effect produces stimuli, real (progeny, dry goods, businesses) or unreal (fictions, dreams, hallucinations), which in turn stimulate its congenital yearning to create (desiring-production), causing it to create more stimuli, and so on. Desire is a desiring-machine that manufactures, in every way possible and with any available materials, the desire to produce. As parts of a psychic mechanism, desiring-machines are not merely thought-machines or dream-machines. They are machines that work to elevate, ultimately, the intensity of desiring-production. Unless there is repression, desiring-machines have no fixed object of desire other than desiring-production. If there is repression, which is almost always the case, the desiring-machines become disorganized and wayward; they desire not only desiring-production but also other usually exterior and real objects, and their subjects are other desiring-machines connected to the repressed desiring-machines. Desiring-machines subsequently produce a reality of desiring-production that parallels the vast social production that is itself a collective result of the similar desiring-machines of numerous individuals.

For Deleuze and Guattari, need is derived from desiring-machines. It is the counterproduct within the real that is manufactured by desire, and lack is a countereffect of desiring-production within this real that is natural and socially constructed. Desiring-machines create voids that they need to fill. Ergo they search for the materials that their bodies and minds, the communal products of other bodies, have determined to be lacking. Lack is never primary to production because production is never organized on the basis of a preexisting need or lack. Both need and lack develop and operate in the social realm of the real created by desiring-machines. As a counterproduct of the pressures of antiproductivity, lack is founded, designed, and instituted by the business of social production: "This involves deliberately organizing wants and needs (*manque*) amid an abundance of production; making all fall victim to the great fear of not having one's needs satisfied; and making the object dependent upon a real production that is supposedly exterior to desire (the demands of rationality), while at the same time the production of desire is categorized as fantasy and nothing but fantasy."[3] Deleuze and Guattari claim that psychoanalysis stifles and besmirches the favorable processes of desiring-production and social production by speciously shunting them into a conception of unconscious representation that associates, reduces, and comprehends everything (the productive unconscious, desiring-machines, desiring-production) as an expression of the unconscious. "The unconscious ceases to be what it is — a factory, a workshop — to become a theater, a scene and its staging"; it becomes a theatrical representation of the oedipal familial romance, and "the psychoanalyst becomes a director for a private theater, rather than the engineer or mechanic who sets up units of production, and grapples with collective agents of production and antiproduction."[4] This idea of the unconscious marks from the beginning psychoanalysis's own bankruptcy or abnegation: an unconscious (or preconscious) that no longer produces but is content to believe. It believes in its own theatricality; it believes in desire-as-lack; it believes in Oedipus, in castration, in the law. In short, it can be brainwashed to believe in just about anything. Once the unconscious has been forced to bow down to psychoanalysis, it is easy for the conscious individual to be deluded and controlled. This person is now forever vulnerable to the uncertainty, guilt, shame, and anxiety instituted by oedipalization.[5]

Deleuze and Guattari's theory of the productive unconscious attempts to explain irregularities and unconventionalities in human thought and behavior in relation to the antiproductivity with which they are commonly associated. The oedipal paradigm is displaced by a paradigm of constant struggle between the desire for the intensity of desiring-production and the desire for the plane of consistency proper to desire on which desire is immanent and pure intensities flow free from the impulse to produce. Existing alongside the connective syntheses achieved by the desiring-machines are the disjunctive syntheses achieved on this plane. Deleuze and Guattari call these disjunctive syntheses "the body without organs (BwO)." The desiring-machines and the BwO coexist as two separate yet interrelated constituents of the psychic process of repulsion and attraction, antiproduction and production, deterritorialization and reterritorialization, that extends beyond the individual and into the social world. Freud has a somewhat similar theory known as the "pleasure principle," in which the "mental apparatus endeavors to keep the quantity of excitation present in it as low as possible or at least to keep it constant" in an effort to attenuate or avoid "unpleasurable tension."[6] The main difference between Deleuze and Guattari's and Freud's theories lies in the greater degree to which the BwO theory is seen as critical to the interpretation of all psychic phenomena. The BwO theory maintains that there is an ideal to which all human beings continually aspire, whether consciously or not. This ideal is the psychic state in which we experience ourselves as nothing other than a deterritorialized, antiproductive, and uninterrupted continuum of excitant desire. In this state, the desiring-machines no longer desire the intensity of desiring-production: there is no production; there is only the electric fervor of desire. Simply put, all human beings wish to become a body without organs: no brain, no ears, no eyes, no stomach, no heart, no lungs, no kidneys, no clitoris, no penis, and so on. "The BwO is what remains when you take everything away."[7]

The totalized BwO, according to Deleuze and Guattari, possesses neither awareness of needs or lacks nor burdensome organs. To possess organs is, by nature of their accessibility, to attract persistent harassment from desiring-production. In the words of Antonin Artaud, "When you will have made him a body without organs, then you will have delivered him from all his automatic reactions and restored him to his true freedom."[8] The human-being/desiring-machines is a battlefield. The psychic mechanisms of desiring-production strive to cross over, break into, and utilize the always already desiring to be static BwO. In no way a docile body, the BwO repels and represses the desiring-machines since it experiences them as enemies of its ecstatic, antiproductive existence. According to Artaud,

> The body is the body
> it is all by itself
> and has no need of organs
> the body is never an organism
> organisms are the enemies of the body.[9]

However, the repulsion and repression of desiring-machines by the BwO is not enough to prevent desiring-production. The conflict between the desiring-machines and the BwO is an inherently never-ending one. As mentioned above, the BwO's repression of the desiring-machines encourages desiring-production as attention is deflected away from the BwO; this causes the designation of external objects of desire and creates the desire to produce these objects. Pursuit of these objects by the desiring-machines serves to defer a complete takeover of the BwO. Yet the BwO also limits its own potentiality of ever fully inhabiting the deterritorialized ideal. The strenuousness of the endless tussle between the desiring-machines and the BwO causes the BwO to respond paranoically to a counterinside or counteroutside in the form of a persecuting organ or some exterior agent of persecution. Ultimately, both the BwO and the desiring-machines locate something external on which to demonstrate their redirected desires, misdirected retaliations, and persistent frustrations. The outside, outer-body world becomes the virtual battlefield and recording surface for the internal struggle.

Hence, there is no certain or easy way to become a BwO. In fact, Deleuze and Guattari claim that "you never reach the Body without Organs, you can't reach it, you are forever attaining it, it is a limit.... But you're already on it, scurrying like a vermin, groping like a blind person, or running like a lunatic: desert traveller and nomad of the steppes."[10] Nevertheless, according to Deleuze and Guattari's schizoanalytic theory, at least five types of bodies can come close to realizing the BwO, even though their proximity to it can be encumbering, expensive, and perhaps fatal: (1) the hypochondriac body, which disorganizes and eventually destroys its own organs through neglect and drug-abuse; (2) the paranoid body, which though delightfully preoccupied, must always be under attack; (3) the schizophrenic body, waging its own personal war against the organs, at the cost of catatonia; (4) the drugged body, which is depressingly ephemeral and afflicted sporadically by withdrawal; and (5) the masochist body, which usually suffers unforeseen and frequently destabilizing side effects and almost always requires the assistance of a sadist.

For the purpose of this "schizoanalysis," as coined by Deleuze and Guattari, I will examine the masochistic, hypochondriac, and paranoiac Jean-Jacques Rousseau. Intelligibly revealing Rousseau's struggle to make himself a BwO, and not yet muddled by the ideology of psychoanalysis and capitalism, the exemplary self-conscious, autobiographical writings of Rousseau seem to invite a schizoanalytic investigation. This essay is therefore an attempt to present a schizoanalytic literary-critical model from which we can better understand both the theory of the body without organs as well as the rich experiences of Jean-Jacques Rousseau.

The joy of steady pain was discovered by Rousseau at the youthful age of eight. Deleuze and Guattari explain that this type of joy is fundamentally different from pleasure. They point out that it is commonly and erroneously asserted that the masochist, like everybody else, quests for pleasure, but can only attain it via pain and fantasized humiliations, which function to alleviate or deflect deep anxiety. Instead, Deleuze and Guattari maintain that

> the masochist's suffering is the price he must pay, not to achieve pleasure, but to untie the pseudobond between desire and pleasure as an extrinsic measure. Pleasure is in no way something that can be attained only by a detour through suffering; it is something that must be delayed as long as possible because it interrupts the continuous process of positive desire. There is, in fact, a joy that is immanent to desire as though desire were filled by itself and its contemplations, a joy that implies no lack or impossibility and is not measured by pleasure since it is what distributes intensities of pleasure and prevents them from being suffused by anxiety, shame, and guilt. In short, a masochist uses suffering as a way of constituting a body without organs and bringing forth a plane of consistency of desire.[11]

Rousseau's description of his earliest encounter with pain, punitively inflicted upon him by his surrogate mother, Mlle Lambercier, illustrates Deleuze and Guattari's idea of the necessary postponement of pleasure.[12] It shows how pleasure-postponement operates on both individual and social levels as a means of control and a way of approaching the BwO. Unlike Freud's "reality principle," which "does not abandon the intention of ultimately attaining pleasure, but it nevertheless demands and carries into effect the postponement of satisfaction, the abandonment of a number of possibilities of gaining satisfaction and the temporary toleration of unpleasure as a step on the long indirect road to pleasure,"[13] Deleuze and Guattari's understanding of pleasure-postponement is not really about "toleration" or "unpleasure" or "postponement of satisfaction." For the most part, it is about precisely the opposite. By postponing pleasure, say Deleuze and Guattari, the joy of constant desire is strongly intensified, and it is from this intensity of joyful desire, and not from the vitality of pleasure, that a profound satisfaction is derived.

Rousseau recalls that Mlle Lambercier initially "confined herself to threats, and the threat of a punishment entirely unknown to me frightened me sufficiently" (25). But what does Rousseau mean by "frightened me sufficiently"? Inasmuch as the terrorizing threats of a mysterious castigation did not prevent Rousseau from pursuing and eventually receiving this castigation, it is difficult to determine in what way he was sufficiently frightened or why he relates the circumstances in a positive tone. Rousseau's affirmative reading of the situation is further revealed when he declares that he "earned," rather than, say, "received" or "suffered," the chastisements that were finally inflicted upon him. Rousseau seems to have found Mlle Lambercier's threats sufficient because he actually enjoyed the terror effected and perpetuated by them. After all, it was this original experience with the intensity of this terror that induced him to seek, consciously or not, the unknown punishment. It is not surprising, then, that Rousseau says, "when in the end I was beaten I found the experience less dreadful in fact than in anticipation; and the very strange thing was that this punishment increased my affection for the inflicter" (25). Rousseau's comprehension of his "anticipation" is comparable to Deleuze and Guattari's notion of the joy that is immanent to desire. That is, when "in anticipation," Rousseau was in the impassioned and uninterrupted state of desiring-alleviation from the terror, which, in his case, required the realization of the feared punishment. Yet, like pleasure, the punishment had to be delayed as long as possible since it would interrupt the continuous process of positive desire necessitated by the duration and intensity of the terror, unless, of course, the punishment itself was to be administered continuously. In this case, the joyful process of positive desire, the desire for alleviation from the punishment, would be ceaseless.

Whereas, as Rousseau acknowledges, there might have been "some degree of precocious sexuality" in his increased affection for the inflicter (25), Deleuze and Guattari would assert that it was primarily the joyful effects of the beating that caused Rousseau to contemplate deliberately earning more beatings. Nevertheless, Rousseau did not intentionally earn more beatings: "It required all the strength of my devotion and all my natural gentleness to prevent me from deliberately earning another beating; I had discovered in the shame and pain of the punishment an admixture of sensuality which had left me rather eager than otherwise for a repetition by the same hand" (25). However unconsciously, Rousseau behaved in such a way as to keep himself on the verge of being punished; he lingered on the very brink of punishment, and he did this to sustain the fervor of positive desire brought about by the terror and anticipation that such circumstances forced him to endure. However consciously, Rousseau avoided the blatantly masochistic joy of his population by intensities of what Deleuze and Guattari call "pain-waves."[14] He declares, "[I]f I refrained from earning a fresh punishment, it was only out of fear of annoying Mlle Lambercier" (26). Although Rousseau opted for the more socially acceptable joy that is immanent to the process of positive desire connected to his "fear of annoying Mlle Lambercier," which is probably less intense than the joy connected to the corporeal punishment, he did not allow his masochistic quest for the supreme intensity of BwO status to be tempered or led astray so easily, at least not during this callow and eager stage of his life.

After putting it off presumably as long as possible, to reap fully the benefits of the socially imposed terror (anxiety, shame, and guilt) that was associated with his conventionally aberrant and "strange taste" for pain-waves (27–28), Rousseau acquired another punishment: "[T]he next occasion, which I postponed, although not through fear [of the punishment], occurred through no fault of mine — that is to say I did not act deliberately" (26). Aware that this beating would probably be his last because he would not respond to it as Mlle Lambercier would expect, since "Mlle Lambercier had no doubt detected signs that this punishment was not having the desired effect" (26), for he enjoyed the beatings, therefore giving her no reason to persist with this kind of punishment, Rousseau chose to remain in the state of desiring-pain-waves ("I did not act deliberately"). In other words, because it was likely that Mlle Lambercier would discover that he enjoyed the beatings and thus cease to administer them, Rousseau avoided the beatings in order to prolong his painful craving for them; that is, he wanted to prolong the intense state of desiring-pain-waves caused by his desperate longing for the beatings. The intensity of this painful craving was potentially longer lasting, more economically painful, than the pain-intensities of any final beating. Insofar as the longevity of this desiring-condition would probably prove more rewarding than either the state of desiring-alleviation from the fear of punishment or the short-lived intensity of the punishment, the state of desiring-pain-waves (the painful craving) is most practical for the masochist striving to become a BwO. Rousseau admits of the situation without recognizing the full implications of his confession: "But I may say that I took advantage of it with an easy conscience" (26).

Rousseau interpreted what, according to the theories of Deleuze and Guattari, was really a common and perfectly natural manifestation of the reaction of his desiring-machines to their repression as an unfortunate and formative incident in the development of his psychology, one with which he would forever have to cope: "Who could have supposed that this childish punishment, received at the age of eight at the hands of a woman of thirty, would determine my tastes and desires, my passions, my very self for the rest of my life, and in a sense diametrically opposed to the one in which they should normally have developed" (26). Freud seems to concur with Rousseau's interpretation:

> Ever since Jean-Jacques Rousseau's *Confessions*, it has been well-known to all educationalists that the painful stimulation of the skin of the buttocks is one of the erotogenic zones of the *passive* instinct of cruelty (masochism). The conclusion has rightly been drawn by them that corporal punishment, which is usually applied to this part of the body, should not be inflicted upon any children whose libido is liable to be forced into collateral channels by the later demands of cultural education.[15]

If the interpretations of Rousseau and Freud are compatible with popular conceptions of sexual normality and psychological development, and I think they are, are we to passively accept their accuracy? Maybe we are ready to do so because such an act of acceptance is in conjunction with what we have been taught or because the common, passive, and masochistic acceptance of these traditionally informed perceptions contributes to the psychosexual frustration we all already (unconsciously) enjoy. Was, as Deleuze and Guattari might argue, Rousseau's experience merely the result of an instinctive yet culturally repressed desire for pain-waves? If Freud is correct in claiming that the purportedly detrimental potentialities of corporal punishment were well known to educationalists, then why does corporeal punishment remain a principal form of punishment for them?

On the conscious level, nevertheless, Rousseau's experience does seem unfortunate for three major reasons: (1) the known and unknown ways in which it made his life more difficult at the time; (2) the various negative effects it may have had on him (such as contributing to his dread of women or by teaching him that violence is an appropriate tool for teaching children); and (3) because it acquainted him with a natural but socially unacceptable form of deriving pleasure, one that he was never again able to relish and thus ostensibly tormented him psychologically throughout his lifetime. As the product of a culture fashioned inadvertently to prevent the realization of any BwO, Rousseau could not help from misunderstanding his congenital inclination toward making himself one; he perceived himself as peculiarly adulterated by his newfangled masochism: "My morals might well have been impaired by these strange tastes, which persisted with a depraved and insane intensity" (26). What is curious, however, is that he was aware of the "insane intensity" of his desiring-condition, his apparent schizophrenia or schizo-thymia, which exposes itself more and more as his hypochondria and general paranoia increasingly overshadow his narrative. The blank pages on which Rousseau wrote his story were clearly the recording surfaces, the products of his desiring-production, the discursive representation of an intuitive intellect investigating retrospectively his own displaced struggle to totalize his BwO.

When one is having difficulties performing or when one is not producing the prescribed quota for production, there must be something wrong. If the problem is not obvious, it must be invented. A problem must be produced from within, or one must be produced from without. In any case, something or someone else is inevitably to blame. Call the police! Bring in the psychoanalysts! Let's begin the oedipalization process! Who done it — mommy, daddy, or me? Psychoanalysis informs us: if you do not internalize the Oedipus myth so as to better rediscover it on the outside, in social authority, where it will be made to proliferate and be passed on to future generations, if you do not follow the demarcated configuration of differentiation — daddy(the law)-mommy-me — and the exclusive alternatives that delineate it, and thereby "resolve" Oedipus, then you will be marginalized and bewildered in the neurotic darkness of the imaginary identifications of the undifferentiated.[16] The oedipal theory is designed to weed the bad eggs from the good; it must separate the "abnormal" and cryptic people from the "normal" and readily categorized. But it is just a theory, a now very powerful and suspiciously all-encompassing phallocentric theory founded primarily on conjecture and a false model (Sophocles' Laius tried to kill Oedipus first, not the other way around).[17]

To avoid such neurotic categorization, Deleuze and Guattari argue that when attempting to construct a genealogy of one's psychology we must refrain from relying on Freud's oedipal paradigm. We must follow Artaud:

> I don't believe in father
> in mother,
> got no
> papamummy[18]

Indeed, according to Deleuze and Guattari, we must not attempt to construct a genealogy of one's psychology in the language of psychoanalysis at all. We must not attempt, like psychoanalysis, to "understand BwO phenomena as regressions, progressions, phantasies, in terms of an *image* of the body.... [Psychoanalysis] only grasps the flipside of the BwO and immediately substitutes family photos, childhood memories, and part-objects for a worldwide intensity map."[19] This does not mean that we should not analyze what appear to have been formative events in the development of an individual's psychology but that we must examine those events with respect to the underlying conflict between the BwO and the desiring-machines. There is no psychological chronology or narrative, but only arbitrary stratification and a road map rife with potholes and roadblocks. Simply put, Deleuze and Guattari assert that we must consider all psychological phenomena in relation to the egg:

> We treat the BwO as the full egg before the extension of the organism and the organization of the organs, before the formation of the strata; as the intense egg defined by axes and vectors, gradients and thresholds, by dynamic tendencies involving energy transformation and kinematic movements involving group displacement, by migrations: all independent of *accessory forms* because the organs appear and function here only as pure intensities.[20]

The egg, as principal of production, is the milieu of pure intensity and zero intensity. The BwO is the egg. The BwO does not exist before the organism; "it is adjacent to it and is continually in the process of constructing itself."[21]

"My heart pounded with joy on the road," exclaims Rousseau of his 1737 journey back to his beloved Mme de Warens (known to him as "Mamma") (234). This summer, Rousseau says, was one of the happiest periods of his life. Again, as with his recollection of the beatings, it is peculiar and paradoxical that Rousseau has such a positive memory of what was really a very difficult period for him. This summer marked the culmination of Rousseau's hypochondria: his exaggerated anxiety over his bodily health and the various psychosomatic manifestations of this anxiety. In conjunction with his hypochondria, either as sources or as symptoms, Rousseau's capacity for satisfying his own quota for self-productivity and his standard for self-reliance were at an all-time low:

> Meanwhile my health was far from recovering; on the contrary I was visibly wasting away. I was deathly pale and as thin as a skeleton; the throbbing in my arteries was terrible, and my heart palpitations more frequent. I was continually short of breath, and finally I became so weak that I found it difficult to move....I could not lift a small weight, and was reduced to an inactivity most painful to a man as restless as I am. No doubt their was a great deal of *vapours* mixed up in all this. The *vapours*, being the malady of happy people, was therefore mine....When I might have been enjoying the delights of life, my decaying physique prevented me, though no one could make out the true seat or cause of the disease. (235)

Rousseau apparently came closest to totalizing his BwO at this time more than at any other point during his life. The intensities of pain-waves, zero productivity, and desiring-production expressed in this passage are emphatic and revealing. Rousseau was practically immobilized by his maladies, all of which were symptoms allegedly caused by an unknown disease. Compelled to research the possible origins of his ailments, and after much investigation, Rousseau deduced: "Since I found in every disease some symptoms of my own, I believed I had them all" (235). Rousseau had unconsciously launched a full-scale, pro-BwO attack against his organs.

Somewhat aware of his hypochondriacal anxiety and the deep relationship between this anxiety and his inner masochistic drive for desiring-pain-waves, Rousseau refers paranoically to the mysterious *"vapours"* (an eighteenth-century word meaning hypochondria or hysteria) "mixed up in all this." He even makes the meaningful connection, albeit probably a slip of the pen (as Freud would put it), between the necessity for physical fitness and his body as an effective surface for recording the contention between his desiring-machines and BwO. He does these things without questioning the rationale behind his suffering; he simply presupposes that he must suffer, and he seems to take pride in this idea: "[D]espite my declining years and very real and serious maladies, my body seems to have regained its strength, the better to feel my suffering.... [R]acked by pains of every description, I feel more strength and life in me with which to suffer than I had for enjoyment when I was in the flower of my youth" (235). For Rousseau, suffering was an ambiguous and unavoidable reality, or was it?

Of course, Rousseau's desiring-machines' continual desire for desiring-production and the never-ending effort of his BwO to repress their desire and deterritorialize itself were unidentified and thus incomprehensible to Rousseau. However, the overall effects of the conflicts were not entirely removed from his conscious regulation. Evidently, his suffering could be lessened or averted, and this happened when his desiring-production subverted its repression by the BwO and was realized and encoded externally, like his pain-waves, on some object (such as his own body), in a creation of his (such as his writings) and/or by impregnating the complexities of a social situation. Freud observes that "hypochondria, like organic disease, manifests itself in distressing and painful bodily sensations, and it has the same effect as organic disease on the distribution of the libido. The hypochondriac withdraws both interest and libido — the latter specially markedly — from the objects of the external world and concentrates both of them upon the organ that is engaging his attention."[22] Accordingly, Rousseau's hypochondriac affliction and antiproductivity were diminished as his libidinal energy was augmented. For instance, when Mme de Larnage took an interest in him, Rousseau declares: "So she undertook my conquest, and it was good-bye to poor Jean-Jacques, or rather to his fever, his *vapours,* and his polypus. It was good-bye to everything when in her company, except certain palpitations which remained and of which she did not wish to cure me" (237). Rousseau's desiring-production temporarily eclipsed or blocked the progress made by his BwO.

"It was clear," admits Rousseau, "that my doctors, who had discovered nothing about my illness, regarded me as a hypochondriac" (245). Freud, like Rousseau's doctors, would have also considered him someone suffering from the "phenomena of hypochondria."[23] Freud treats hypochondria as a slippery and obscure disorder, one that he could not easily explain or distinguish. In contrast, Deleuze and Guattari offer a sensible explanation for hypochondria as a probable consequence of the BwO tussle: plagued by the nervous and often painful intensities of imaginary diseases, the hypochondriac body is one of the body-types capable of coming close to realizing the BwO; hypochondria is a common manifestation of any body desperately seeking BwO status. Therefore the schizoanalyst would not consider Rousseau's hypochondria a mental disorder per se; Rousseau would not be perceived or treated as strange, abnormal, or enigmatic. Thus, under the influence of schizoanalytic theory, it is unlikely that Rousseau would have internalized the pejorative implications of these sentiments; it is less likely that his contemplation of the illness would have resulted in a negative self-concept.

Rousseau's encounter with the prostitute Giulietta is a conspicuous external, social manifestation of his internal predicament. Rousseau states that his rendezvous with Giulietta was the "one incident in my life which plainly reveals my character" and that it will provide his readers with "complete knowledge of Jean-Jacques Rousseau" (300). For him to recount this incident and accomplish "the purpose of my book" (300), which is, says Rousseau, "to reveal my inner thoughts exactly in all situations of my life" and give "a history of my soul" (262), Rousseau maintains that he "shall" possess the necessary "strength to despise the false modesty which might prevent my fulfilling it" (300). Once more, in his introduction to the incident, we are confronted with Rousseau's pleasure-postponement: the repressive forces of his BwO emerge in what he terms his "false modesty," that idiosyncrasy that still "might prevent" the pleasurable fulfillment of his self-proclaimed "purpose." This "purpose," according to Deleuze and Guattari, could have been predominantly inspired by (1) Rousseau's desiring-production; (2) the symptomatic paranoia of his BwO (the desire to rationalize publicly the nature of his character and thus defend himself and his BwO against their imaginary "enemies" — as Rousseau himself frequently calls them);[24] and/or (3) the desiring-recording inadvertently inaugurated by the fierceness of the war between Rousseau's BwO and desiring-machines. Whether Rousseau's "false modesty" was victorious in impeding or distorting his account of his meeting with Giulietta, even partially so, is something that we can never know for certain. As schizoanalytical material, however, the "two or three pages" (300) that Rousseau does proffer on the topic are very informative.

"Never was such sweet pleasure offered to mortal heart and senses," says Rousseau regretfully of his brief relationship with Giulietta: "Alas, had I only known how to enjoy it fully and completely for a single second....I dulled all its delights. I killed them as if on purpose" (300). But why did Rousseau kill its delights "as if on purpose"? And if he did not do it on purpose, then how and why might he have done it? Rousseau himself divulges that he "has always had a disgust for prostitutes" (296). Yet if he truly had such a "disgust for prostitutes," why did he visit them? According to a Freudian interpretation, Rousseau's meetings with prostitutes could plausibly be explained as stemming from a common male precondition for loving. At an early age, claims Freud, the boy child "tells himself with cynical logic that the difference between his mother and a whore is not after all so very great, since basically they do the same thing": they welcome the penis; they copulate.[25] Inasmuch as the boy child combines traditionally antithetical stereotypes, and since conscious binary oppositions such as this Madonna/whore dichotomy often exist in the unconscious as a unity, Freud asserts that the prostitute is a likely "object-choice" for a man because she functions as a replacement for his now-repressed childhood object of sexual desire: his mother.[26] While for Freud, of course, this explanation is directly related to his theory of the Oedipus complex, Deleuze and Guattari would understand Rousseau's motivation to visit prostitutes as predominantly masochistic, as a psychological procedure for the realization of his suppressed masochism; his "disgust" would be considered a phobia, an aspect of his paranoia or hypochondria: his deep craving for anxiety-intensities.

When speaking of an earlier rendezvous with a different prostitute, Rousseau confesses: "I was so strangely stupid as to give in to her scruple," and after the sexual interaction, "so certain that I had caught the pox that the first thing I did on my return was to send for the surgeon and ask for some medicines" (297). Not surprisingly, the medicines were apparently ineffective: "Nothing can equal the uneasiness I felt for a whole three weeks," says Rousseau, "without any real discomfort or any obvious symptom to justify it" (297). Rousseau's intense dread of disease, his view of prostitutes as insidious transmitters of disease, and the subsequent anxiety he experienced after being with prostitutes all seem to indicate that his engagements with them were certainly masochistic. For the unconscious or preconscious Rousseau, the prostitutes constituted the female torturers or sadists for whom he had longed since childhood. His voluntary and repeated meetings with them caused him to suffer from a variety of invented ailments, as well as from guilt and shame, all of which successfully tormented him for a long time, maybe for the rest of his life.

Rousseau was so overcome by the "value" of Giulietta's "charms and caresses" that, "fearing to lose the fruit prematurely," he "tried to make haste and pluck it" (300). Nevertheless, his venture was thwarted: "Suddenly," recalls Rousseau, "I felt a deathly cold flow through my veins; my legs trembled; I sat down on the point of fainting, and wept like a child" (300). What happened to poor Jean-Jacques? "It is true," acknowledges Freud, "that psychoanalysis puts forward absence of sexual satisfaction as the cause of nervous disorders."[27] Central to this premise, and rather analogous to the nervous characteristics commonly stimulated by the contention between the desiring-machines and the BwO, is Freud's claim that "nervous symptoms arise from a conflict between two forces — on the one hand, the libido (which has as a rule become excessive), and on the other, a rejection of sexuality, or a repression which is over-severe."[28] In comparison to schizoanalytic theory, the "libido" of psychoanalysis functions similarly to desiring-production, and psychoanalysis's ideas of "rejection of sexuality" and "repression" could easily be seen as antiproductive symptoms and integral aspects of the BwO struggle. When psychoanalysis and schizoanalysis are applied, however, these parallels in their structures yield very different conclusions.

For psychoanalysis, on the one hand, Rousseau's temporary breakdown and later scrutiny of Giulietta's body are primarily results of his nervous disorders: they are unconsciously motivated denunciations of Giulietta as a mother-replacement/love-object and thus as an acceptable commodity fetish; and, if Rousseau was suffering from a prolonged castration complex, they could represent his fear of castration by the terrifying and devouring female genitalia. Accordingly, Rousseau's scrutiny necessarily discovers on Giulietta's body the "secret flaw" (301) that confirms for him biologically that she is a being of inferior and unworthy status, "some kind of monster, rejected by Nature, men and love" (301).

Schizoanalysis, on the other hand, might perceive Rousseau's breakdown as an obvious external manifestation of his BwO's success in ephemerally vanquishing his conscious intention to mollify with sexual activity the consciously felt pressures of his desiring-production. Or the breakdown itself could indicate that it was masochistic enough simply for Rousseau to have visited Giulietta (a prostitute) without ever needing to consummate the endeavor. In the long run, Rousseau's obstruction of the presumed purpose of the meeting (copulation/orgasm) may have been even more masochistically rewarding for him than he unconsciously anticipated. Unable to "repair my mistakes" during the next scheduled appointment because Giulietta did not show, Rousseau laments, "[M]y insane regret has never left me" (302). Rousseau's hypochondria and paranoia are explicitly illustrated in his representation of the encounter. Again a prostitute has become for him an infectious threat ("it did not so much as occur to me that the pox might have something to do with it" — her "secret flaw" [301]) and the administer of pain-waves, and now also the external object on which to project his internal conflict: on her breast he "perceived that she had a malformed nipple" (301).

In addition to the differences already highlighted, there are some general differences between psychoanalytic and schizoanalytic theory that are apparent even within the confines of this application. Whereas psychoanalysis presupposes and privileges the libido as the biological origin and principal catalyst

in the development of human psychology, schizoanalysis understands libidinal energy as only one of several primary side effects brought about by the
interaction of two profound psychic processes (the desiring-machines and the
BwO) that contribute capriciously and in a variety of ways to psychological
formation. The libido is neither determined centrally nor centrally located by
schizoanalysis but seen as forever suffusing different assemblages of machines
within which we are caught up at different times; Rousseau was caught up in
an assemblage with Giulietta. Libidinal assemblages invest and are invested by
the social field, with all the machineries they bring into play, all the multiple
love-subjects and love-objects. Any libidinal investment is necessarily a collective statement, since in any social field "there are no individual statements,
only statement-producing mechanic assemblages."[29] For Freud, "the libido
must be desexualized and sublimated in order to invest society and its flows,"
but for Deleuze and Guattari, "it is love, desire, and their flows that manifest the directly social character of the nonsublimated libido and its sexual
investments."[30] Every assemblage is fundamentally libidinal and unconsciously
motivated, and every libido or unconscious is fundamentally associated with
certain assemblages. Nothing exists independently. Everything is plugged in
everywhere.

   Psychoanalysis is a sociopolitical apparatus with an ideological investment
in the distribution of power within the social field. Striving both to represent the interests of the dominant classes and distinguish itself from all
assemblages, it imagines and presents itself as the master decoder and inter-
polator of psychological meaning. To accomplish this, psychoanalysis "subjects
the unconscious to arborescent structures, hierarchical graphs, recapitulatory
memories, central organs, the phallus, the phallus-tree — not only in its
theory but also in its practice of calculation and treatment" and "bases its
own dictatorial power on a dictatorial conception of the unconscious."[31] The
psychoanalyst conveniently explains the unconscious in such a way that all
psychological phenomena can be understood according to a phallocentric for-
mula, a patriarchal, heterosexist credo: in the final analysis, psychological
whole(some)ness is an ideal only attainable for heterosexual men. The psychoanalyst does what it takes to perpetuate the order of things, simultaneously
using and reinforcing the privileged position of psychoanalysis within that
order: this entails molding the patient's unconscious to the predetermined
model, neuroticizing the thought-patterns of the patient if necessary, subju-
gating the patient through a diagnostic process of classification. To be sure,
psychoanalysis is a despotic theory: "[T]here is always a general, always a
leader (General Freud)."[32] But since psychoanalysis depends on and is cir-
cumscribed by this hermeneutic and authoritative arrangement, one that is
reductive and absolute, it is necessarily limited in maneuverability and scope.

   Like psychoanalysis, schizoanalysis is also a sociopolitical apparatus with
an ideological investment in the distribution of power within the social field.

However, schizoanalysis strives to complicate, redefine, and equilibrate the existing order of things rather than consolidate it. To accomplish this, schizoanalysis reformulates the unconscious of psychoanalysis and transforms it into an a-centered system, a machinic network, that cannot be reduced or interpreted according to a tree model. Schizoanalysis's unconscious is in no way an obstacle, a key, or a mysterious thing that must be revealed, reckoned with, and adopted: "[T]he unconscious no longer designates the hidden principle of the transcendent plane of organization, but the process of the immanent plane of consistency as it appears on itself in the course of its construction. For the unconscious must be constructed, not rediscovered. There is no longer a conscious-unconscious dualism machine, because the unconscious is, or rather is produced, there where consciousness goes, carried by the plane."[33] Schizoanalysis comprehends the unconscious not as a symbolic structure but as an informative process always already particular, arbitrary, and produced (with new statements, different desires) within a totality of historical determinations within which the related conscious operates.

"The task of schizoanalysis," as Deleuze and Guattari emphasize, "therefore is to reach the investments of unconscious desire of the social field, insofar as they are differentiated from the preconscious investments of interest, and insofar as they are not merely capable of counteracting them, but also of coexisting with them in opposite modes."[34] Instead of attempting, like psychoanalysis, to appropriate and solidify egos under the auspices of a certain idea and hierarchical scale of normality, schizoanalysis takes apart egos and their presuppositions; it liberates the prepersonal psychological singularities that they contain and repress; it mobilizes the ideational flows they would be capable of transmitting, receiving, or intercepting; it establishes further and more sharply the ambiguities, slippages, and fractures well beneath conditions of identity; it assembles the desiring-machines that countersect everyone and group everyone with others.[35] In effect, schizoanalysis posits an understanding of difference that is dependent on neither negation nor opposition but on the positive recognition of intersections; mutual, parallel, and disjunctive flows and desires; and assemblage-statements — the infinite network to which we are all connected. Schizoanalysis acknowledges, encourages, and accepts difference as an affirmative movement and actuality: it seeks only a community of positive differences.

Notes

My thanks to Leo Damrosch, Kim Savelson, and James Intriligator for their many helpful suggestions throughout the writing of this essay.

1. Gilles Deleuze and Félix Guattari, *Anti-Oedipus: Capitalism and Schizophrenia*, trans. Robert Hurley, Mark Seem, and Helen R. Lane (Minneapolis: University of Minnesota Press, 1983), 25.

2. Ibid., 5.

3. Ibid., 28.

4. Ibid., 55.

5. See ibid., 296–322.

6. Sigmund Freud, "Beyond the Pleasure Principle," in *The Freud Reader*, ed. Peter Gay (New York: Norton, 1989), 595.

7. Gilles Deleuze and Félix Guattari, *A Thousand Plateaus: Capitalism and Schizophrenia*, trans. Brian Massumi (Minneapolis: University of Minnesota Press, 1987), 151.

8. Antonin Artaud, *Selected Writings*, ed. and intro. Susan Sontag (Berkeley: University of California Press, 1976), 571.

9. Artaud cited in Deleuze and Guattari, *Anti-Oedipus*, 9.

10. Deleuze and Guattari, *A Thousand Plateaus*, 150.

11. Ibid., 155. See Gilles Deleuze, *Coldness and Cruelty*, published with Leopold von Sacher-Masoch's *Venus in Furs* (New York: Zone Books, 1991), for a discussion of masochism's relationship to sadism and the law and of the relationship between psychoanalysis and the state. Central to this discussion is Deleuze's assertion that "a close examination of masochistic fantasies or rites reveals that while they bring into play the very strictest application of the law, the result in every case is the opposite of what might be expected (thus whipping, far from punishing or preventing an erection, provokes and ensures it). It is a demonstration of the law's absurdity. The masochist regards the law as a punitive process and therefore begins by having the punishment inflicted upon himself; once he has undergone the punishment, he feels that he is allowed or indeed commanded to experience the pleasure that the law was supposed to forbid" (88). For Deleuze, masochism becomes a process of subverting and mocking the law; masochism locates the masochist beyond the law.

12. In *The Confessions*, Rousseau does inform us that he did, at some earlier point in his life, "receive blows intended" for his brother, but does not mention any pain related to this incident (*The Confessions*, trans. and intro. J. M. Cohen [London: Penguin, 1953], 21). I am not including the original French since the English translation in no way problematizes my reading. All subsequent references to *The Confessions* will be included parenthetically in the text.

13. Sigmund Freud, "Beyond the Pleasure Principle," 596.

14. Deleuze and Guattari, *A Thousand Plateaus*, 152.

15. Sigmund Freud, "Three Essays on the Theory of Sexuality," in *The Freud Reader*, 270.

16. Deleuze and Guattari, *Anti-Oedipus*, 78–79.

17. Psychoanalysis does not account for the fact that in Sophocles' *Oedipus the King*, the literary model from which Freud derived the name "Oedipus" for his fundamental complex/theory, Oedipus killed his father (Laius) only after Laius attempted to kill him: Oedipus killed his father in self-defense (see lines 885–98). Freud does indicate that a father might be jealous of his son's close relationship with the mother, but, according to Freud, this jealousy does not necessarily imply that the father wants the son removed from the picture; nor does it occur at any regular period in the oedipal process.

18. Antonin Artaud, *Artaud Anthology*, trans. F. Teri Wehn and Jack Hirschman (San Francisco: City Lights, 1965), 247.

19. Deleuze and Guattari, *A Thousand Plateaus*, 165.
20. Ibid., 153.
21. Ibid., 164.
22. Sigmund Freud, "On Narcissism: An Introduction," in *The Freud Reader*, 551.
23. Ibid., 552.
24. See, for example, Rousseau, *Confessions*, 590.
25. Sigmund Freud, "A Special Type of Choice of Object Made by Men," in *The Freud Reader*, 391–92.
26. Ibid., 389–91.
27. Sigmund Freud, "'Wild' Psycho-analysis," in *The Freud Reader*, 353.
28. Ibid.
29. Deleuze and Guattari, *A Thousand Plateaus*, 36.
30. Deleuze and Guattari, *Anti-Oedipus*, 353.
31. Deleuze and Guattari, *A Thousand Plateaus*, 17.
32. Ibid., 18.
33. Ibid., 284.
34. Deleuze and Guattari, *Anti-Oedipus*, 350.
35. Ibid., 362.

5

Philosophy and Ethics

Quantum Ontology
A Virtual Mechanics of Becoming
Timothy S. Murphy

"Ontology" and "metaphysics" have become dirty words in philosophy, as they have in physics. This is not a recent development; in the preface to the first edition of the *Critique of Pure Reason*, Kant notes the disrepute into which "higher physics" had fallen in his day and promises to rescue it, but in so doing he displaces the "science of being" in the direction of "phenomena" — that is, being is displaced into its representation for consciousness. Hegel, the next man in the relay, formalizes the displacement by raising phenomena to the level of "science" and subsuming all being within a phenomenology of mind or spirit. From this "science" arise most of the dominant forms of Continental philosophy and its competitors: Husserlian and Heideggerian phenomenology, Freudian and Lacanian psychoanalysis, structural anthropology and sociology, even some forms of Marxism. They are all marked by the refusal of ontology and the critique of metaphysics inaugurated by the Kantian displacement of being into its representation for consciousness. It is no coincidence that Kant, the historical point of displacement, is the first and last philosopher in this phenomenological line to act as a consistent point of reference for the physical sciences. But the philosophy of science eventually manifests the representational mediation that it has repressed. Philosophies of science share what Werner Heisenberg calls "realism": "We 'objectivate' a statement if we claim that its content does not depend on the conditions under which it can be verified."[1] For Heisenberg, there are three types of realism: practical, in which we assume that *most* of our experience consists of statements that can be objectivated; dogmatic, in which we assume that *all* of our experience consists of such statements; and metaphysical, in which we make the additional, unverifiable assumption that "the things [about which we make statements] really exist."[2] Materialist ontology is metaphysical, and classical Newtonian mechanics is dogmatic, while quantum physics, for Heisenberg, requires a practical-realist point of view in that its results cannot be separated from the devices that measure them and the statistical formalism that expresses them.

In the Copenhagen interpretation of quantum physics, buttressed by Heisenberg's own indeterminacy principle,[3] the statistical structure of the equations makes it meaningless to ask what happens to a particle or field between observations; therefore it is meaningless to claim that the particle or field exists when it is not being observed. All that *is*, all that has meaning, is the mathematical expression of probabilities. In this way, the Kantian phenomenal displacement is ultimately repeated by physics, but as an objective phenomenality, depending on technical measuring instruments, rather than a subjective phenomenology, relying on self-consciousness. "Things" can be known only through the formalism of representational mediation, which means that only the mediation itself can be known in any way.

Yet there are physics other than phenomenality, and philosophies other than phenomenology. Gilles Deleuze's philosophy is one of the latter, so he makes no attempt to suspend metaphysical realism, that is, ontological speculation. As the principles of Deleuze's ontology have come to light, it has become clear that it does not fit into the dominant phenomenological line of descent of Western philosophy. This lack of connection with the dominant strains of thought in the human sciences has slowed and distorted the reception of Deleuze's ontology in anglophone circles; his work appears as an odd mixture of precision, reduction, and omission to critics schooled in derivations of phenomenology. This is because his problems, the encounters with the unthought that give his thought its impetus, are not the problems of phenomenology, and in order to understand his work, "the conditions under which the problem acquires a maximum of comprehension and extension must be determined, conditions capable of communicating to a given case of solution the ideal continuity appropriate to it."[4] In order to follow Deleuze's lines of flight, one must move onto the terrain that his work has defined and engage with the tradition that he has created for himself, a tradition that intersects phenomenology at only a few points. Rather, Deleuze's work finds its antecedents in materialist and rationalist philosophy, primarily Spinoza and Nietzsche. On the contemporary scene, his work resonates not so much with the human sciences as with the physical sciences. Manuel De Landa has shown the important connections that link Deleuze to recent work in cybernetics and information theory, while Brian Massumi has demonstrated the lines of flight that link Deleuze's work to the biochemical and thermodynamic work of Ilya Prigogine, one of the primary theorists of complex dissipative systems or "chaos";[5] Prigogine has named Deleuze one of the contemporary thinkers in whom he has "found inspiration" for his work on self-organizing complex systems, such as living organisms.[6] If this "extension of the conditions of the problem" is necessary to reveal the full scope of Deleuze's work, then the most important task that remains in this area is to link Deleuze's thought to contemporary work in physics.

Among the physical sciences, physics is the most abstract discourse that

claims material reference for its statements, even though the Copenhagen interpretation of quantum physics has restored the hegemony of representational
mediation and post-Kantian phenomenality that physics had long ignored.
That hegemony has been challenged in much the same way that Deleuze has
implicitly challenged phenomenology. A number of contemporary physicists,
including Roger Penrose, J. S. Bell, and David Bohm, have attempted to formulate a consistent and useful method of treating quantum mechanical events
as actual occurrences rather than as probabilities that fulfill formal equations
(and nothing else); chief among these was the late David Bohm, who made
a concerted effort to formulate not only a new method of treating quantum
equations but also a realist ontological framework into which to contextualize
the mathematics. His attempt to go beyond Bohr's principle of wave-particle
complementarity to found new models for thought in physics finds its relay
in Deleuze's attempt to create new images for philosophical thought; an articulation of the two produces an ontological mechanics, not of static being
but dynamic becoming.

   That such new images and models are necessary may not be admitted, and
the suggestion that they could be constructed in the precritical tradition of
metaphysics will almost certainly meet great skepticism. The first argument
that will no doubt be raised against this return to ontology is the self-evident
one of its necessary textual articulation: an ontology that purports to explain
the material world is a representational structure, expressed in logical arguments contained in books and seminars. These books and seminars would
be constantly susceptible to the disseminative power of their own rhetoric,
and that rhetoric would be the only materiality with which the theory could
deal. Positivist or pragmatist philosophies of physics would express this criticism in the language of mathematical formalism and thought-pictures, but
the logic is the same. Neither Bohm nor Deleuze accepts the epistemologi-
cal assumptions that underlie such criticism. Neither science nor philosophy,
in their view, is concerned with knowledge or truth as the representation of
an extrarepresentational reality or the accumulation of absolute referential information. Theory does not take on a representational function, but rather
an active, practical one: it is a "box of tools" having "nothing to do with the
signifier."[7] Every theory, then, is a "mechanics" in that it is such a toolbox,
filled not with instruments teleologically designed for given functions but with
bizarre instruments that make possible unprecedented functions. Theoretical
tools must unsettle and disturb those who would use them in order to bring
new objects and events within range of thought. If they cannot do so, the
theory must be altered or abandoned in favor of different tools.

   For Bohm, "it is the fate of all theories eventually to be falsified[;] they
are relative truths, adequate in certain domains. . . . But if this is the case then
the accumulation of knowledge cannot be regarded as the *essential* purpose of
scientific research, simply because the validity of all knowledge is relative to

something that is not in the knowledge itself."[8] Validity is a function of use, of efficacy in extending the field of the problem (rather than in the pragmatic or utilitarian sense, which accepts preestablished ends). Realist science is instead an extension of active human perception, not a storehouse of truth, and in this way the theories that are constructed and proposed in science are no different from the mechanical apparatuses that allow scientists to "perceive" sensations that are beyond the range of their organic senses. Theories for Bohm "are now science's major link with reality. Theories determine not only the design of scientific instruments but also the kinds of questions that are posed in the experiments themselves. . . . Perception in modern science, particularly in physics, takes place essentially through the mind."[9] We must be careful not to reintroduce the phenomenal subject here, however; perception as Bohm conceives it does not require a subject. Plants and animals perceive, in that they cause and respond materially to changes in their environments, but they do so without subjectivity (at least in the normative phenomenological sense); so too do micro-organisms, as well as inorganic structures like crystals. Machines perceive in this way. The mind, Deleuze notes, is not a space of subjective representation but a sensorimotor interval, a gap that allows difference to intervene between stimulus and response.[10] The mind is the interval of freedom and creativity, but it is not fundamentally human or limited to humans; perception is an aspect of the "machinic phylum" that cuts across the organic/inorganic and subject/object antinomies.

A scientific theory is a box of tools, to be used in conjunction with machines in order to intervene in a physical system, so that its behavior can be assessed. A metaphysical or ontological theory is a box of tools also, provided that its metaphysical aspects lead to new experimental arrangements that produce definite, differentiable effects. This is what Deleuze insists marks the new relationship between theory and practice inaugurated by the critique of the phenomenological subject: "Practice is a set of relays from one theoretical point to another, and theory is a relay from one practice to another."[11] Theories are always local and nonrepresentational forms of action and must escape their constitutive impasses by moving through other, practical forms of action. Thus both are essentially social. Theory functions as an intensifying fantasy that can "invest all of an existing social field, including the latter's most repressive forms," or "launch a counterinvestment whereby revolutionary desire is plugged into the existing social field as a source of energy."[12] A theory produces certain actions, which produce certain effects and reactions that extend the theory or alter it; a realist ontology does not describe or double the world except as a residual effect of directing, damping, or amplifying an action in the world.

The ontologies in question, Bohm's and Deleuze's, arise in different disciplines and extend themselves through different contexts, but they share a surprisingly large amount of terminology, logic, and operational structure, beginning with a common point of departure. This point of departure is a very singular dissatisfaction, a "problem," with the conceptual structure and operations of phenomenal thought. For Bohm, this dissatisfaction takes the form of a critique of the intuitive models of contemporary physics, the wave model and the particle model, as well as the principles that demonstrate them to be unsurpassable (Bohr's complementarity, Heisenberg's indeterminacy principle, and von Neumann's proof of them). Matter and energy, which are interchangeable according to Einstein's equation $E=mc^2$, behave in different ways depending on the ways in which they are observed; sometimes they appear as waves moving through fields of force, and sometimes they appear as discrete particles interacting with one another. Both forms of behavior cannot be observed at the same time, because the two forms of behavior require different apparatuses to measure them; nevertheless, both must be taken into account in order to explain and predict the overall "properties" of matter and energy. Matter has wave-like properties, while fields of waves have particle-like ones.

This ambiguity in the nature of the "object" of quantum mechanics confused many physicists, and Bohr proposed the complementarity principle to avoid this. In essence, complementarity suggests that the attribution of existence in any form, wave or particle or something else, to quantum objects is a metaphysical gesture that has no measurable effects, since the object only exhibits properties when it interacts with the experimental apparatus, at which point the object and the apparatus form an unanalyzable whole. "Event" would thus be a better term than "object." All that the physicist should do is juxtapose the wave and particle models to obtain as precise a statistical picture of the measured event as possible. Bohr suggested that "the description of the experimental arrangement and the recording of observations . . . be given in plain language, suitably refined by the usual physical terminology" and *no language at all be used to refer to the quantum event* because "plain language," with its analytical form and causal ordering of events and times, cannot adequately deal with the wholeness and indeterminism of quantum events. Their mode of existence can only be described analogically by probability. The proposal of other models is ruled out a priori: "[A]ll departures from common language and ordinary logic are entirely avoided by reserving the word 'phenomenon' solely for reference to unambiguously communicable information."[13] The only alternatives for physical thought are the historically given language and concepts of classical mechanics, wave and particle, or no concepts whatsoever; these limits to analysis and inquiry are phenomenal, in that they are imposed on thought arbitrarily, on the basis of the *possibility of representation* of that thought at one moment in history. Heisenberg seconded this Copenhagen interpretation through his indeterminacy principle. To the antinomian symmetries of the wave/particle models and event/observer languages, he added the symmetry of position and momentum: at a certain level of scale, one of the two can be measured precisely only at the expense of increasing imprecision in the measurement of the other.[14] The mathematician Johann von Neumann then produced a proof that purported to demonstrate that, in essence, the Copenhagen interpretation could not be superseded by the addition of levels of activity below the Heisenberg indeterminacy limit, which amounts to a demonstration that the assumption of a physical reality below that limit could only be a useless gesture, a "metaphysical" one in the derogatory sense. The subtle veneer of formal mathematical representation is all that remains of the physical world below this threshold.

Bohm's response to this foreclosure of the event in favor of its representation in the phenomenon is characteristically nondialectical: he questions the adequacy of the existing representational models, particularly the principle that no alternative could be constructed. Using the wave model to correct the inadequacies of the particle model and the particle model to correct the wave model seems imprecise, reductive, and static. Could there not be a theory that could account for the statistical accuracy of quantum calculation and yet offer new experimental opportunities? The theory Bohm proposed has been called variously a "hidden variable" interpretation, in that it postulates the existence of subquantum factors that affect events (the sort that von Neumann had ruled out), and a "pilot wave" model of quantum events, in that it requires the assumption of an infinitesimal wave pattern that simultaneously links all aspects of an extended field of forces. The immediate importance of this proposal, from the point of view of experimental physics and materialist ontology, is double: it allows the physicist to "describe the *experimental results themselves* (and, more generally, the experimental conditions as well) in terms of a new language form that is neither 'classical' nor 'quantum,' "[15] and it eliminates the "need for a vague division of the world into 'system' on the one hand and 'apparatus' or 'observer' on the other"[16] by positing the reality of the system under consideration *independent* of observation.

Bohm adduces strong logical arguments in favor of his "hidden variable" interpretation and against the Copenhagen interpretation, particularly against von Neumann's purported "proof." Bohm points out that, like all mathematical proofs, von Neumann's is based on a number of theorems that are themselves based on the "assumption . . . that certain features associated with the current formulation of the theory are absolute and final, in the sense that they will never be contradicted in future theories and will never be discovered to be approximations."[17] Bohm's own method treats theorems as tools, to be systematically varied in order to discover new forms of intervention, to extend the range of perception and define new problems for research. The mathematical formalism must be explained, contextualized, and not simply reified. In the same way, Deleuze will characterize his own work as "problematic" and explicitly criticize the "theorematic conception of geometry" as follows: he defines the "problem by means of the events which come to affect a logical subject matter (sections, ablations, adjunctions, etc.), whereas the theorem deals with the properties which are deduced from an essence."[18] Theorems are static and dogmatic, while problems are dynamic and flexible.

Deleuze begins with guiding principles similar to Bohm's in his attempt to evade the symmetry of the mind/matter split and the phenomenological "resolution" or "suspension" that has traditionally rendered it interminable. The first principle is a critique of the dialectic drawn from Bergson. Like Bohm's criticism of complementarity, it questions the adequacy of antinomian concepts in attaining the specificity of concrete singularity: "[O]f what use is a dialectic that believes itself to be reunited with the real when it compensates for the inadequacy of a concept that is too broad or too general by invoking the opposite concept, which is no less broad and general?"[19] Abstract and general ideas, like mathematical theorems, do not explain anything, but rather must be explained; a more precise approach must be created. Along with this, Deleuze articulates a critique of the phenomenological method much like Bohm's objection to the phenomenalist imprecision in Bohr's holistic model of quantum events, but derived from Nietzsche and Sartre:

> The error of all efforts to determine the transcendental as consciousness is that they think of the transcendental in the image of, and in the resemblance to, that which it is supposed to ground. In this case, either we give ourselves ready-made, in the "originary" sense presumed to belong to the constitutive consciousness, whatever we were trying to generate through a transcendental method, or, in agreement with Kant, we give up genesis and constitution and limit ourselves to a simple transcendental conditioning.[20]

In other words, Deleuze attempts to avoid placing the human subject at the beginning or center of his investigations. To assume the subject as transcendentally given is to assume what you would explain; to transfer a conditioned empirical figure onto the transcendental conditions that render it actual is to invert their true relation. This is not to suggest that the subject is not a problem; on the contrary, an account of the constitution of the subject will be one of the minimal criteria for a more adequate theory. The subject will be constituted, but as one of many possible effects that can arise from the principles of Deleuze's ontology. The subject's representational structure must be explained, as the formalism of quantum mathematics must be explained; neither can be raised to the level of a priori principle.

If one does not begin thinking with the fact of the thinking subject, as Descartes and Kant (and their followers) did, with what does one begin? One cannot pretend to begin at something that would be an origin or at some regulative idea that would be an end or a telos. The phenomenal tradition is correct in its assumption that one must begin where and when one is, in a moment that is not present because it is continually divided against itself; the tradition goes wrong, Bohm and Deleuze argue, when it assumes that this moment is necessarily represented by and to a mediate consciousness. The problem of the transcendental subject is a false problem, a badly analyzed composite. Rather, the moment is a moment because it is asymmetrically divided and moving, because it becomes without being, certainly without being the synthesis of the dialectic being/nonbeing. The division and the movement are the faces of time, the true problem: "The future is not yet. The present *is,* but it cannot be specified in words or in thoughts, without its slipping into the past. When a future moment comes, a similar situation will prevail. Therefore, from the past of the present we may be able to predict, at most, the past of the future. The actual immediate present is always the unknown."[21] But this description of time remains phenomenal, and its constitutive division must be extended to provide a direction for intervention. We must investigate the paradoxes of pure becoming.

To do so, Deleuze identifies three syntheses of time that coexist. The first is the passive synthesis of the living present that contracts all of the past and the future, allowing time to pass unidirectionally; from this perspective, the past and future are modalities always contained in the conditioned present, which alone exists. The second is the active synthesis of the pure past, the memory that represents the old past and the current representation of that past; the pure past is the past that is a priori, that was never present and is necessary to found the past as memory. Deleuze's second synthesis relies on Bergson's intensive theory of memory, which asks us to treat the past as a virtual space into which we project ourselves in order to find the appropriate level of the past that we seek. This is a complex operation, since each level of the past contains the whole of the past, in virtual coexistence but at different degrees of dilation and intensity.[22] Similarly, Bohm's model proposes that

> each moment of time is a projection...[that] must contain further projections of earlier moments, which constitute a kind of nested sequence of enfolded images of the past. These may take the form of memories. More generally, however, they may be the enfolded "reverberations" of earlier moments within the moment in question.... Such projection is still to be thought of primarily as a kind of creativity, but here we are discussing *the creation of a moment that is related to its past in a definite way.* ... Of course, all these projections into any given moment will have the past of the entire universe as their potential content, which is thus enfolded into the moment in question.[23]

The moments of the past, for both Deleuze and Bohm, are like Leibniz's monads or Borges's aleph, reflecting obscurely the entire universe of which they are parts. They constitute an intensive subspace or prespace that determines, in part, the structure of time itself.

The third synthesis is the static synthesis of the pure and empty form of time that, according to Deleuze, displaces the relation between the others to create the future; like the pure past, it is a conditioning, rather than a conditioned, time, but one capable of breaking the repetitive symmetry between living present and pure past.[24] How would such a "pure and empty form of time" create the future? How does it relate to space, to the extended events it would measure and relate? Bohm has proposed, on the basis of contemporary field theory, a model of space-time as a set of dynamic fields of force. This would be the first level of his "implicate order": "When these fields are treated quantum-mechanically, we find that even in what is called a vacuum there are 'zero-point' fluctuations, giving 'empty space' an energy that is immensely beyond that contained in what is recognized as matter.... [M]atter may then be compared to a set of small waves on the immense 'ocean' of the vacuum state."[25] "Empty" space is not empty but rather is constituted of different forms of energy that produce matter as one of their residual effects. Similarly, Deleuze has postulated that the universe is "chaos," enfolding in each point infinite speed and energy: "It is not even sufficient to say that intense and moving particles pass through holes; a hole is just as much a particle as what passes through it. Physicists say that holes are not the absence of particles but particles traveling faster than the speed of light."[26] Bohm explains that this vacuum state has no classically meaningful notion of time because its "'state-function' (which represents the whole of space and time) oscillates uniformly at a frequency so high that it is utterly beyond any known physical interpretation," so "[a]ll the physically significant properties of these states are then completely independent of this 'zero-point' oscillation." This means that if time is an abstraction from an ordered sequence of events, "we would be justified in saying that the vacuum state is, in a certain sense, 'timeless'"[27] because its oscillation renders all our notions of succession and simultaneity useless.

To read this "timelessness" as "eternity" would be to give "the pure and empty form of time" a sense, but this sense would be a bad analysis of the composite. The term "timelessness" refers to a reality "'beyond time' at least as time is now known, measured, and experienced."[28] For Bohm, the rapid, energetic "zero-point" fluctuations mean that the small-scale structure of space-time, the vacuum state, can give rise to phenomena like particles and fields, which appear to be discrete and separable but which are really only relatively stable structures that can be abstracted from their contexts for experimental purposes. These stable structures are Deleuze's problems, which must be extended as far as possible to determine their limits, their uses. The traditional notion of time is just such a stable structure, just such a problem, but one that is fixed only within the limited contexts of absolute classical temporality and convertible relativistic temporality.

Bohm defines this stability of the problem in a very Deleuzian way, in terms of difference. He claims that "information is a difference that makes a difference.... A little reflection will show that our ability to abstract a limited context out of a universe of immense size... arises in a very simple way[:]... the differences in the essentially infinite context that has been left out make no significant difference in the context that has been selected for investigation."[29] When the differences in infinite context begin to make a difference in the limited context, it is necessary to change the context and hence the problem. The state-function oscillations of the vacuum state begin to make a difference in the traditional context of time at the level of the quantum interactions of particles and fields: these oscillations may affect the movements of the constituent parts of things, but at present the oscillations can only be treated statistically. Under the Copenhagen interpretation, these oscillations have no experimental use value; they are merely "metaphysical" and have no effect on the equations. But in Bohm's theory, they suggest that other structures of time may be implicit in normal space-time.

If we extend the traditional idea of time, we reach its limit in the state-function oscillations, and we must displace the problem to find a new way to proceed. There is no reason to privilege a frame of reference, an ultimate level of reality that would determine all the lower ones; on the contrary, the process of space-time production seems to move in both directions, from smaller contexts out into relatively larger orders and back from the larger context into the smaller levels of implication. The "time" of the vacuum state requires an extension of the original problem of time to allow it to function in the different context. Deleuze's third synthesis is such an extension; he suggests that every stable context-structure "has a purely logical, ideal or dialectical time. However, this virtual time itself determines a time of differenciation, or rather rhythms or different times of actualization which correspond to the relations and singularities of the structure and, for their part, measure the passage from virtual to actual."[30] Within each structure there are multiple times, subsisting in a virtual state, waiting to be actualized through the movement of the structure. The unimaginable time of the zero-point oscillations "opens the way for a new kind of time, which has primarily to do with the vacuum state.... A new system of time will have been introduced that is both very fast and very slow compared with ordinary physical times."[31] In this sense, the vacuum state would be an enfolded virtual generator of times (and spaces) yet unknown and unmeasured. Bohm's ideas would thus seem to provide much-needed specification to Deleuze's rather abstract "virtual times" and would lay the foundation for a mechanics of the generation of space-times and for what we might call, provisionally, a taxonomy of them. The present state of experimental technology prevents these hypotheses, these virtual times, from being directly testable; however, some problem-solving techniques in physics, particularly the interaction diagrams and "sum over histories" method introduced by Richard Feynman,[32] suggest that a multiple form of time is already a useful tool.

Once we have a useful transformative theory of extension and duration, space and time, to orient our interventions, we can begin to postulate logics that could account for the manifestations of matter and energy that "become" at the scale of particles, of the subject and other levels of scale. Deleuze proposes his logic in the traditional languages of ontology, mathematics, and the physical sciences, derived not only from his early work on Bergson but also, more significantly, from his studies of Spinoza's and Leibniz's anti-Cartesian rationalism, studies that analyze logics of folding — *complicatio, explicatio,* and *implicatio.* Bohm too presents his "implicate order" in a mélange of discursive registers, juxtaposing quantum field theory with analogies from Freud; his vocabulary is derived from his etymological reflections on the same term, folding, in relation to Bohr's holistic model of quantum events. Both treat the universe as origami. This common choice of terminology, which is surprising in light of the distinct intellectual itineraries followed by its expositors and the apparent lack of familiarity of each with the other's work, prefigures the form that these ontologies will take. The first problem addressed in the terminology is the issue of generality, the subsumption of individual events under general categories. Deleuze chooses the term "singularity" to specify that the events are not strictly subsumable under general categories. The object subsumed under a general category is a "particular," whose dialectic operates through the paradox known as the hermeneutic circle. This does not mean that Deleuze refuses all "categorization," for want of a better term. Instead of generalization, he offers a displaced use of the concept. For Deleuze, the concept does not abstract the common properties of things subsumed beneath it, but rather "the concept itself has become the thing. It is a universal thing, if you like, since objects sketch it out like so many degrees, but a concretion, not a genre or a generality."[33] In *Difference and Repetition,* he renames this displaced notion of the concept "Idea." Bohm echoes this when he insists that "the general is now seen to be present *concretely,* as the activity of the generative principle within the generative order."[34]

Recall that the basic unit or quantum of quantum mechanics *and* philosophy is no longer the particle or the subject but the singularity, the differential event, which Bohm calls "moment"[35] and Deleuze calls "haecceity."[36] These are the "categorical" forms of individuation. The "moment" and the "haecceity" are concrete, metaphysically real, but this does not mean that they have been "realized" on the basis of some broader idealist structure that might be called "possibility." For Bohm and Deleuze, the antithesis of possibility and reality must also be displaced, into the couple virtuality/actuality (Bohm, on the basis of precedent uses in physics, prefers the term "potentiality" to "virtuality," but his use of the term is the same as Deleuze's use of "virtuality"). Deleuze explains:

> The possible is opposed to the real; the process undergone by the possible is therefore a "realization." By contrast, the virtual is not opposed to the real; it possesses a full reality by itself. The process it undergoes is that of actualization. [In realization,] [d]ifference can no longer be anything but the negative determined by the concept: either the limitation imposed by possibles . . . in order to be realized, or the opposition of the possible to the reality of the real. The virtual, by contrast, is the characteristic state of Ideas; it is on the basis of its reality

that existence is produced, in accordance with a time and a space immanent in the Idea.[37]

Hecceities and moments are virtual events in this sense, that they themselves do not so much exist as *insist* or *subsist* in an enfolded form of space-time that is real despite its apparent ideality or abstraction: "The reality of the virtual is structure,"[38] the context-structure defined above in terms of significant difference, which we have been discussing as the extended space-time of the problem. Hecceities and moments are also virtual *in sense;* the French word *sens,* signifying "sense," "direction," or "meaning," is one of Deleuze's terms for the abstract plane of consistency on which is constituted the reality of the virtual. Bohm also prefers to deal with forces that are potential yet real, and his model of the quantum world relies on the postulate of the "quantum potential" or "pilot wave" that, like the magnetic potential, has very real effects separate from the classically real fields that measure the rates of change of the potential in classical electrodynamics.[39]

But the difference between the duality possible/real and the duality virtual/actual does not end with the postulate of complete reality. If the "realization of the possible" is a process of limitation, it is also a process of similarity that "refers to the form of identity in the concept." It is thus a static, deterministic process. The "actualization of the virtual," in contrast, "always takes place by difference, divergence or differenciation....Actual terms never resemble the singularities they incarnate. In this sense, actualization or differenciation is always a genuine creation"[40] rather than a predetermined procedure. Bohm as well recognizes this disjunction between the virtual/potential and the actual when he explains that the "projection [of explicate orders from implicate ones] can be described as creative, rather than mechanical, for by creativity one means just the inception of new content, which unfolds into a sequence of moments that is not completely derivable from what came earlier in this sequence or set of such sequences."[41] Thus the singularities that form energy and matter, including the subject and its variants, are produced in the same way that our previous discussion showed times and spaces to be produced. Henceforth it will be more precise to speak of Deleuze's and Bohm's positions as "metaphysical actuality" rather than "realism."

Deleuze models the virtual or conceptual assemblage of these unsubsumable singularities in terms of a logic of series but ultimately arrives at a logic of folding. In *The Logic of Sense,* he gives three conditions for the creation of a structure, applying them to what we have been calling "context-structures," which amount to a virtual mechanics of becoming:

1. "There must be at least two heterogeneous series . . . (a single series never suffices to form a structure)." (Heterogeneous series are disjunct, until they are traversed by the paradoxical element that conjoins and explicates them.)

2. "Each of these series is constituted by terms which exist only through the relations they maintain with one another. To these relations, or rather to the values of these relations, there correspond very particular events, that is, *singularities* which are assignable within the structure." (The formation of series is a process of connection, enfolding, or *implication*.)

3. "The two heterogeneous series converge toward a paradoxical element, which is their 'differentiator.' This is the principle of the emission of singularities" (which is the moment of conjunction, unfolding, or *explication*).[42]

These field-series produce, through their convergence, the singular events that constitute, at a larger level of scale, the objects of materialist ontology. The convergence and resultant events form a "world," a context-structure that is "metastable, endowed with a potential energy wherein the differences between series are distributed."[43] The structures emit or explicate differences, singular events, according to the singular form of their convergence. Other "worlds" begin where these series diverge to form other singularities, other context-structures, at other levels of scale and in relation to other series.

Bohm's "generative" or "implicate order," as its name implies, enfolds within itself a variety of context-structures that also explicate themselves at different levels of scale. His simplest analogy for this process is the holographic image, which is created by recording on a suitable glass plate the reflections of a laser off a three-dimensional object; the image can be reconstructed from the glass plate just as a photograph can be re-created from a film negative, but the holographic plate differs from film in that it encodes the entire three-dimensional image onto every part of the plate. If you break up a holographic plate, you can reconstruct a complete three-dimensional image from all of the separate pieces, though the parts will produce slightly different images (again, in the manner of Leibniz's monads).[44] To apply this idea to the universe, one must imagine each point, like each moment in time, to condense within itself the entire shifting structure of that universe, viewed from different perspectives; in fact, the same operation of implication/explication applies to both time and space. Bohm labels this differential omnipresence the "holomovement," since its one consistent characteristic is transformation or becoming.

But exactly how, beyond the analogy, does this constant enfolding and unfolding take place? If we recall that every point in the holomovement, even empty space, contains "zero-point" field fluctuations with tremendous energy, we can begin to work out the logic. According to Bohm's theory, a field model is more versatile than a particle one in describing the folding process, because Bohm's novel solutions to the quantum equations deprive particles of movement. The fluctuations of empty space contain an infinite number of immanent orders or fields that interact with one another; in Deleuze's terminology, Bohm's fields are series of intensities, forces that are differential and exist only as relations: *"Quantity itself is therefore inseparable from difference*

in quantity. Difference in quantity is the essence of force and of the relation of force to force."[45] In interacting at the subquantum level, the fields
produce effects at the larger level of scale that our measuring instruments
(and ultimately our subjective structures) occupy; in other words, the fields
emit singularities. These singular large-scale effects, which are relatively stable energetic structures in themselves, propagate along the force gradients of
the various interacting fields and produce yet more larger-scale effects as they
unfold out of the nested orders that produce them. Thus, a particle like an
electron would be a stable structure of the interaction of fields, a singularity
that propagates along a differential force gradient; this energy structure would
behave, in the large-scale frame of reference, like a material particle, but it
would have no continuous material existence. Rather, it would be made and
unmade at every instant, below the threshold of measurability.[46]

The constant making and unmaking of the "particle" along the wave front
deprives it of traditional being or essence, and it also cleaves the causal relation between material particles. Interactions between such particles can no
longer take the form of physical collisions that transfer energy but must be
understood as varieties of virtual co-creation that explicate many simultaneous
field-orders. Causality is not a direct relation but is mediated by the totality
of the virtual field or plane of consistency.[47] In Deleuze's terms, "cause" and
"effect" belong to two disjunct series momentarily articulated or explicated by
the singularity, which itself exceeds both series; the event is creative to the
extent that it is an "effect" that cannot be fully determined by its "cause."[48]

This discontinuous "existence" (or "subsistence" or "insistence"), this continual becoming whose mechanics Bohm describes, accounts for the discontinuous nature of energy intervals observed in all quantum interactions: the
emission and absorption of energy do not happen continuously, at a smoothly
linear rate, but rather happen in discrete units that are never observed to decompose into smaller units. These discrete units are the "quanta" from which
"quantum" physics takes its name. One of their most peculiar properties, unprecedented in classical science, is their ability to move from one position
to another without passing through any of the points between; this is the
quantum "jump," which Bohm's theory explains well with the model described
above. The progressive unfolding and enfolding of the convergent fields provide contours of potential, a differential "wave" that Bohm calls the "quantum
potential" or "pilot wave," along which the singularity flickers into and out of
existence. Like Deleuze's *sens*, this potential or virtuality is a form of implicit,
a-signifying meaning that Bohm calls "active information,"[49] which, like the
attractors of chaos theory, directs the form of the entire field convergence
without being a directly measurable quantity itself. Active information, however, is not signification; Bohm insists that to speak of information, difference
that makes difference, in this sense is "not to say *that it has* a meaning, *but
it is* its meaning."[50] This plane of consistency is an-entropic in the sense

that its infinitesimal energy gives order to the much greater energies of the converging fields, and it does not diminish in intensity with distance. These features of the quantum potential account, in Bohm's model, for both the interference observed in the famous double-slit interference experiment (that shows the wave/particle duality of matter and energy) and the phenomenon of "nonlocality," the apparently instantaneous linkage of regions separated by distances that are large with respect to the speed of light (and thus that could not communicate unless signals could move faster than light). The potential registers the whole configuration of field-becomings and interactions and communicates this constantly shifting configuration to all of the constituent fields and singularities. These parts act to conserve forms of virtual and actual motion, as if they "know" the changing state of the whole system before they could physically be "informed" of its flux by waves or particles moving at the speed of light.[51] On these questions, as on so many others, the Copenhagen interpretation is necessarily silent.

The potential is both the process of implication/explication and the wholeness of the interacting fields; the two concepts are inseparable. In Bohm's model, no particle or individual field is indivisible or basic because all are just measurable manifestations of higher-dimensional resonances, unfoldings of the enfolded potentialities implicit in every point of space-time. In this sense the implicate order model resonates with the geometry of fractals, objects that occupy fractional numbers of dimensions (between one-dimensional lines and two-dimensional planes, or between two-dimensional planes and three-dimensional bodies, and so on).[52] Like fractals, the implicate order generates complex structures on the basis of very simple implicate conditions, which Deleuze would call transcendental conditions or Ideas. If the quantum principle of nonlocality, which links particles according to motion-conservation laws, is extended to the largest imaginable scale, then the universe itself would appear as a giant fractal with as many implicit dimensions as it has particle- or field-structures. Since these structures only "exist" discontinuously, the dimensionality of the universe would change discontinuously; different times and spaces, as we saw above, would explicate and implicate themselves. Also like fractals (and monads and the aleph), the implicate order repeats, in every individuated point of its infinite levels, the implicit structure of the whole, from different perspectives and on different scales. This "new notion of hierarchy in which the more general principle is immanent, that is, actively pervading and indwelling,"[53] requires that creativity move from the concept/Idea to the conditioned empirical object and also the other way; the conditioned is capable of producing new conditions; the explicate order can alter the implicate order in unpredictable ways. Bohm insists that the process is always moving in two directions at every moment, just as Deleuze recognizes that conjunction is always simultaneously disjunction, and vice versa.

The subject, finally, is a structure that supervenes only at a very high level of explication; it is what Deleuze, in *The Logic of Sense,* calls a "surface effect" of the interaction of series or fields. It is determined by the same transcendental conditions that determine all other structures, but the subject resembles its conditions no more than does any other structure. The subject's representational form is not privileged in any way, and therefore the transformation of this form does not lead to a crisis in thought; the death of God is old news. The subject is a complex fold in the infinite surface of times and spaces that, like origami, can be unfolded and refolded into different shapes. For Bohm too, consciousness and the unconscious are merely moments that enfold the whole, in the same way that a fractal like the Mandelbrot set repeats its largest-scale structure at every smaller level of scale, or the way the aleph in Borges's story contains the entire universe and another aleph, which contains the universe and another aleph, to infinity. As the first letter in the Hebrew alphabet, the aleph, like the fold, also represents "Man."

These conclusions return us to our point of departure, our proposition that conditioned forms must be understood in terms of transcendental virtual conditions that do not necessarily resemble the empirical forms they render actual, whether those forms are waves, particles, or subjects. These structures are problems at a higher level of scale and as such are relatively autonomous of the lower levels of implication; thus classical physics approximates the implicate order for massive objects like planets or pendulums, just as phenomenological methods can approximate serial syntheses for certain determined subjectivities. At the limits of these structures, however, autonomy breaks down and new operations become important, at both higher and lower levels of scale. Other theories must be constructed to intervene and produce effects once the traditional models reach their limits. These new effects are not completely determinable; the theories that produce them are a bit like Mallarmé's throws of the dice that will not abolish chance but rather affirm it, or like Nietzsche's transvaluation of all values. Creativity is again possible, and it is only through creation that we may escape the crises of the old forms of thought.

This essay is not an attempt to demonstrate the existence of an extra-representational actuality; it is rather an argument in favor of a return to ontological thought under the new image given it by Deleuze and Bohm. The true problem is not Is there a reality beyond representation? but rather How can a theory have effects? How can it literally *make* a difference? I do not wish to overstate the case for Bohm's theory, which remains a minority view in the physics community; but the small yet significant number of experimental successes attributable to Bohm's physical models, like the magnetic potential and quantum nonlocality, demonstrate that such a theory can make such a difference, can have material consequences that follow from its ontological speculations. These material successes, like those of Prigogine in thermodynamics, provide the relays that extend Deleuze's problematics to their maximum comprehension and actualize the virtual mechanics of becoming.

Notes

1. Werner Heisenberg, *Physics and Philosophy* (New York: Harper, 1958), 81–82.

2. Ibid., 83.

3. I follow David Bohm in referring to Heisenberg's principle as one of indeterminacy rather than one of uncertainty: "[I]t is not to be supposed that [physically observable variables] are just 'uncertain' to us, because we are not able to measure them with complete precision. Rather, one assumes that their very mode of being requires them to be indeterminate" (*Causality and Chance in Modern Physics* [London: Routledge and Kegan Paul, 1957], n. 85). See also the discussion in David Bohm and F. David Peat, *Science, Order, and Creativity* (New York: Bantam, 1987), 76–84.

4. Gilles Deleuze, *Difference and Repetition,* trans. Paul Patton (New York: Columbia University Press, 1994), 162.

5. Manuel De Landa, *War in the Age of Intelligent Machines* (New York: Zone, 1991); and Brian Massumi, *A User's Guide to Capitalism and Schizophrenia* (Cambridge, Mass.: MIT Press, 1992).

6. Ilya Prigogine and Isabelle Stengers, *La nouvelle alliance* (Paris: Gallimard, 1979), 291–93.

7. Gilles Deleuze and Michel Foucault, "Intellectuals and Power," in Foucault, *Language, Counter-memory, Practice,* ed. and trans. Donald Bouchard (Ithaca, N.Y.: Cornell University Press, 1977), 208.

8. David Bohm, *The Special Theory of Relativity* (1965; reprint, Redwood City, Calif.: Addison-Wesley, 1989), 227.

9. Bohm and Peat, *Science, Order, and Creativity,* 65–66.

10. Gilles Deleuze, *Bergsonism,* trans. Hugh Tomlinson and Barbara Habberjam (New York: Zone, 1988), 107–10.

11. Deleuze and Foucault, "Intellectuals and Power," 206.

12. Gilles Deleuze and Félix Guattari, *Anti-Oedipus,* trans. Robert Hurley, Mark Seem, and Helen Lane (New York: Viking, 1977), 30.

13. Niels Bohr, *The Philosophical Writings,* vol. 3 (1963; reprint, Woodbridge, Conn.: Ox Box Press, 1987), 3, 6.

14. See Heisenberg, *Physics and Philosophy,* chaps. 3 and 8.

15. David Bohm, "Bohr's View concerning the Quantum Theory," in *Quantum Theory and Beyond,* ed. Ted Bastin (Cambridge: Cambridge University Press, 1971), 40.

16. J. S. Bell, *Speakable and Unspeakable in Quantum Mechanics* (Cambridge: Cambridge University Press, 1987), 173.

17. Bohm, *Causality and Chance in Modern Physics,* 96.

18. Gilles Deleuze, *The Logic of Sense,* trans. Mark Lester with Charles Stivale (New York: Columbia University Press, 1990), 54.

19. Deleuze, *Bergsonism,* 44.

20. Deleuze, *Logic of Sense,* 105.

21. David Bohm, "Time, the Implicate Order and Pre-space," in *Physics and the Ultimate Significance of Time: Bohm, Prigogine, and Process Philosophy,* ed. David Ray Griffin (Albany: State University of New York Press, 1986), 182.

22. See Deleuze, *Bergsonism,* chap. 3.

23. Bohm, "Time, the Implicate Order and Pre-space," 189–91.

24. Deleuze, *Difference and Repetition,* 70–71, 79–80, 88–89.

25. Bohm, "Time, the Implicate Order and Pre-space," 187.

26. Deleuze and Guattari, *A Thousand Plateaus*, 32.

27. Bohm, "Time, the Implicate Order and Pre-space," 189.

28. Ibid.

29. Ibid., 180.

30. Deleuze, *Difference and Repetition*, 211.

31. Bohm, "Time, the Implicate Order and Pre-space," 197.

32. Feynman's diagrams graph the interactions of subatomic particles, but they also allow the solution of problems involving antiparticles if the antiparticles are treated as normal particles *moving backward in time;* see Gary Zukav, *The Dancing Wu Li Masters* (New York: Bantam, 1979), 214–22. The "sum over histories" method involves equations that integrate all of the possible alternate histories of the particles involved.

33. Gilles Deleuze, "La conception de la différence chez Bergson," *Les etudes bergsoniennes* 4 (1956): 98, my translation.

34. Bohm and Peat, *Science, Order, and Creativity*, 164.

35. David Bohm, *Wholeness and the Implicate Order* (New York: Routledge, 1980), 207.

36. Gilles Deleuze and Claire Parnet, *Dialogues*, trans. Hugh Tomlinson and Barbara Habberjam (New York: Columbia University Press), 92, 151n. 9.

37. Deleuze, *Difference and Repetition*, 211.

38. Ibid., 209.

39. See David Bohm and Yakir Aharonov, "Significance of Electromagnetic Potentials in the Quantum Theory," *Physical Review* 115 (1959): 485–91, on the real effects of magnetic potential. They proved that electrons moving through a metal circlet would produce interference with the potential of a magnetic field, even if they were physically isolated from the field itself. Thus the potential, which had been treated as a mathematical expedient in classical electrodynamics, must now be treated as real. I would like to thank Laurence S. Hordon for bringing this point to my attention.

40. Deleuze, *Difference and Repetition*, 211–12.

41. Bohm, *Wholeness and the Implicate Order*, 212.

42. Deleuze, *Logic of Sense*, 50–51.

43. Ibid., 103.

44. Bohm, *Wholeness and the Implicate Order*, 144–47.

45. Gilles Deleuze, *Nietzsche and Philosophy*, trans. Hugh Tomlinson (New York: Columbia University Press, 1983), 43.

46. Bohm, *Wholeness and the Implicate Order*, 152.

47. Ibid., 126–27.

48. Deleuze, *Logic of Sense*, 6–7.

49. Bohm and Peat, *Science, Order, and Creativity*, 93.

50. David Bohm and Renée Weber, "Meaning as Being in the Implicate Order Philosophy of David Bohm: A Conversation," in *Quantum Implications: Essays in Honour of David Bohm*, ed. Basil J. Hiley and F. David Peat (New York: Routledge and Kegan Paul, 1987), 438.

51. This is the crux of J. S. Bell's theorem: the behavior of quantum systems demands that the actuality of these systems can only be maintained (as Bohm wishes to do) if we give up the classical idea that all interactions take place over very short distances. This has been tested experimentally by Alain Aspect, who determined that

interactions can in fact take place over very large distances (though many physicists dispute the adequacy of his experimental arrangement). On Aspect, see Bell, *Speakable and Unspeakable in Quantum Mechanics*, 139–58, and Zukav, *Dancing Wu Li Masters*, 294–95.

52. Deleuze and Guattari, *A Thousand Plateaus*, 486–88.
53. Bohm and Peat, *Science, Order, and Creativity*, 164.

Madness and Repetition

The Absence of Work in Deleuze,
Foucault, and Jacques Martin

Eleanor Kaufman

These pages are dedicated to the memory of Jacques Martin, the friend who, in the most terrible ordeal alone discovered the road to Marx's philosophy — and guided me onto it.

This dedication, which prefaces Louis Althusser's *For Marx*,[1] appeared two years after the suicide of Jacques Martin in 1963. Jacques Martin, placed in the middle between Althusser and Foucault at the École Normale Supérieure — four years younger than Althusser and four years older than Foucault — appears to have been an enigmatic and exceedingly brilliant man, in Althusser's words, "a sad yet warm homosexual, even in the distance of his latent schizophrenia, an incomparable friend."[2] Aside from short prefaces to his translations from the German and a highly acclaimed thesis "Mémoire de DES" on the notion of the individual in Hegel, Jacques Martin produced no work and ceased to advance in the French educational system, often relying on money loaned to him by Althusser and Foucault for his very subsistence.[3] Preoccupied with the idea of madness, Martin was apparently the first to equate madness with the absence of work (*l'absence d'oeuvre*), an association that was taken up by both Althusser and Foucault.

Althusser makes frequent and poignant references to Martin in his autobiographical work *L'avenir dure longtemps* (The future lasts a long time).[4] This work is punctuated with the refrain "thanks to Jacques Martin..."[5] It is Martin to whom Althusser owes his coming to philosophy and, in particular, his coming to Marx. He writes, "[T]he only one who gave me an idea (and a true one) about philosophy was Martin. Thanks to him, I was able to have an overall strategic idea of the philosophical situation, and several absolutely essential theoretical landmarks for getting my *bearings* in it."[6] Althusser credits Martin with more than bringing him to philosophy — according to Althusser, it was Martin who taught him how to *think,* and to think otherwise:

His was the sharpest mind I ever encountered, implacable like a lawyer, meticulous like an addition, and endowed with a macabre sense of humor that all the priests couldn't stand. In any case, he taught me to think, and especially that one could think otherwise than what our teachers claimed. Without him, I would never have strung two ideas together.[7]

Foucault's references to Martin are much less explicit.[8] In fact, they are perhaps best characterized in a sense that is altogether impersonal — they refer to an "effect" of Martin. It is an effect that follows shortly upon Martin's suicide, an effect marked by a proliferation of work. In 1963, Foucault published *Raymond Roussel* and *Naissance de la clinique*,[9] and in 1964 a short essay entitled "La folie, l'absence d'oeuvre" (Madness, the absence of work).[10] In this piece, which appeared three years after the publication of *Folie et déraison: Histoire de la folie à l'âge classique*, Foucault rearticulates the history of madness in terms of a double silencing, or double language: "Since Freud, Western madness has become a nonlanguage because it has become a double language (a language that only exists in this speech, a speech that only says its language) — which is to say a matrix of language that, strictly speaking, says nothing. Fold of the spoken which is an absence of work."[11] In this fashion, madness is paradoxically and tautologically doubled or absent: it is only decipherable in terms of a given set of articulations, and these articulations can only signify madness. All the terms fold perfectly back against each other and net a resounding absence — and not just an absence, but *the absence of work*. This, then, marks the tautology from which work, poetic or otherwise, is logically impossible, since whatever is produced only refers back to an originary madness and that madness is the all-encompassing sign for anything that may arise from it. The very concept of "work" is thereby bound up in the logic of the vicious circle.

Yet, Foucault continues:

> Discovered as a language fallen silent in its self-superposition, madness neither displays nor narrates the birth of a work...; it denotes the empty form from where this work comes, that is, the place from where it never ceases to be absent, where one will never find it because it is never found there. There in this pale region, in this essential hiding place, the twin incompatibility of work and madness is revealed; it is the blind spot of each of their possibilities and of their mutual exclusion. But since Raymond Roussel, since Artaud, it is equally the place where language and literature approach each other.[12]

Here, Foucault would seem to isolate an exception to this vicious circle of madness and absence of work, an exception to be found in certain literary articulations of madness (or, certain works by what *were to have been* madmen). Much has been written of the relative importance of "literature" to Foucault, his attempts in the early writings to give it, as well as madness, a sort of essence, and his subsequent (though contestable) repudiation of this.[13] Such a line of inquiry, albeit illuminating, is not directly at issue here. It is not the

purpose of this project to locate and distill those sites where the utter futil-
ity of the creative effort — whether through madness, sterility, or what have
you — is captured poetically in the fullness of its absence,[14] but rather to look
at the apparatus of capture itself. That is, this is about finding not plenitude in
the expression of nothingness but nothingness in the plenitude of expression.

My aim, then, is to map out this nothingness, or this absence of work, in
what would paradoxically appear as a vast and consummately repetitive outpouring of work. Such an outpouring occurs in and around Foucault (and,
in what follows, in and around Deleuze-Foucault) in the guise of a relentless
doubling structure. This doubling takes form on many layers and levels, some
of which mercilessly overlap. Two years after *Folie et déraison: Histoire de la
folie à l'âge classique,* Foucault, as mentioned above, published two works, *Raymond Roussel*[15] and *Naissance de la clinique,* both of which explore the double
structure of visibility, how death and language work to make what is already
visible — yet hidden — doubly visible. In "Le mot de Dieu: 'Je suis mort'"
(The word of God: "I am dead"), Denis Hollier delineates the doubling effect
of these two works:

> It has not been noted to what extent *Roussel* and *Naissance de la clinique* are
> twin books. Each is organized around the same main argument: death as the
> key to reading. It was the post-suicidal publication of *Comment j'ai écrit certains
> de mes livres* that made Roussel's oeuvre readable: the posthumous text made
> the enormous lesion constituting the work's secret nervure appear. With the
> transformation that Bichat's anatomopathology makes perceptible to the medical
> gaze, *Naissance de la clinique* focuses on another kind of posthumous revelation:
> the lesions discovered on the cadaver thanks to autopsy retrospectively give away
> the code to the illness's symptoms.[16]

Not only is there a doubling structure between *Roussel* and *Naissance de
la clinique,* but *Roussel* and the later *L'archéologie du savoir*[17] have been seen
as double books. In "Vers la fiction" ("Toward fiction"), Raymond Bellour remarks on the parallel attention to "method" in these two books, describing the
book on Roussel as Foucault's "first book on method, a kind of first version
of *L'archéologie du savoir.*"[18] Deleuze echoes this when he says that "Foucault's
book on Roussel (1963) is already like the poetic and comic version of the
theory of statements that Foucault establishes in *The Archaeology* (1969)."[19]
And, to add content to form, the question of the double is *the* question of
Foucault's *Roussel* where, for example, he explores the fantastical disjunctions
between two sentences that double each other except for one letter.[20] In expli-
cating, among other works, Roussel's verse novel *La doublure* (The lining),[21]
Foucault's very language resonates with the trill of the double: "lining unlined,
there is no longer anything but a silence, a look, slow motion gestures that unfold in the empty space beneath the masks"; or, "tear that unlines the double
and immediately restores it to its marvelous unity"; or still, "it is a question of
the same figure of a language split in two, inside of which a visible scene, pro-

duced by this distance's single call, takes up its abode"; and, finally, "this gentle shadow that makes things visible from beneath their surface and their mask and allows one to speak about them, isn't this from their birth, the proximity of death, of death that unlines the world like the peeling of fruit?"[22]

This doubling that Foucault reads in Roussel is linked all at once to silence, to language, and to death. It is about the silence that is the mirror, or double, of language touched by death, the silence that is both the motor force and the product of an excess of writing that follows upon a death. It is a silence paradoxically made visible in its opposite, a ceaseless flow of language. And this is a language that both says *nothing* and *signals the unnamable.* As Foucault writes in the conclusion of "La folie, l'absence d'oeuvre," "[F]ar from the pathological, from the direction of language, there where enfoldings occur with still nothing said, an experience is being born where our thought is at stake; its imminence, already visible but absolutely empty, cannot yet be named."[23] This visible yet unnamable imminence is the madness of language that says nothing, language doubled or repeated to the point that it cannot but say nothing.

It is this structure of the unnamable as repetition, which is also the structure of the double, that haunts the ongoing conversation between Deleuze and Foucault. This is a conversation that started officially in 1962, the year of their meeting, and has continued, albeit fitfully, through and beyond Deleuze's *Foucault,*[24] published in 1986, two years after Foucault's death. This is a conversation marked by extraordinary encomium and uncanny repetition, one that defies biographical explanation or theoretical *mise-en-abîme.* That is, it is insufficient either to decipher it as a misplaced biographical indicator or to delineate the way in which the structure and nature of the exchange mirror exactly what is being talked about (how such an exchange, to borrow terms from Foucault and Deleuze, is itself a preeminent "event," "diagram," or process of "subjectivation"). Rather, it is with a view to mapping out the sublime impasse, or disjunction, in such an either-or logic that I proceed, for indeed both interpretations *work* and *do not work,* and this in every sense of the word, in every madness of trying to equate excessive work with absence of work.

As Deleuze was later to recount, when asked when and where he met Foucault, "one remembers a gesture or laughter more than dates." But then he adds, "I met him around 1962, when he was finishing the writing of *Raymond Roussel* and *Naissance de la clinique.*"[25] So it is the mark of writing, the already doubled structure of *Raymond Roussel* and *Naissance de la clinique,* that sets off the otherwise gestural language of the laugh, of the presence. It is this ever-overlapping yet nonrelational[26] doubling of the trace of the person with the beautifully transcendent evocations of impersonal thought that serve as the signposts of the ongoing conversation between Deleuze and Foucault.

That is, in the highly laudatory exchanges between Deleuze and Foucault, there is an odd co-presence of that which would indicate a perfectly hermetic philosophical system and that which would rather outlandishly disrupt it.

One such visibly perfect *mise-en-abîme* structure is that of the double itself. When asked why he published a book on Foucault just after his death, Deleuze evokes the importance of the double in Foucault:

> This is not a work of mourning, nonmourning calls for even more work. If my book could have been still something else, I would have appealed to a constant notion in Foucault, that of the double. Foucault is haunted by the double, including in the alterity peculiar to the double. I wanted to extract a double from Foucault, in the sense that he imparted to this word: repetition, lining, return of the same, imperceptible difference, unlining, and mortal fissure.[27]

In this fashion, Deleuze not only signals the obsession with doubling in Foucault but suggests that his own text will extract, if not be, the double of Foucault's. In fact, Deleuze's *Foucault* — which represents a compilation of pieces published on Foucault during his lifetime, pieces written after Foucault's death, and course lectures devoted to Foucault — might be hailed as a more concise, exhaustive, and thorough doubling of Foucault than Foucault himself. As James Miller puts it, "[I]f any French thinker of his generation grasped the implications of Foucault's singular genius — including his unrelenting preoccupation with suicide and death — it was surely Gilles Deleuze."[28] Thus Deleuze, in mirroring or doubling Foucault, has perfectly repeated Foucault's preoccupation with the double.

Yet coexisting with this is a mysteriously personal and gestural evocation of the double in its specific relation to Foucault's death. In another 1986 interview, Deleuze responds as follows to Claire Parnet's question regarding the spirit in which the Foucault book was written: "I felt a genuine need to write this book. When someone whom one loves and admires dies, one sometimes has a need to make a sketch of him. Not to glorify him, even less to defend him, not for memory, but rather for drawing this ultimate resemblance that can only come from his death, and which makes one say 'that's he.' A mask, or what he himself called a double, a lining."[29] With this disarmingly candid remark, Deleuze seems resolutely outside the *mise-en-abîme* logic. In evoking the death of a loved one, and the eminently personified notion of announcing "that's he" (*c'est lui*), Deleuze conjures up a Foucault-as-presence, one that is entirely part of the "textual" Foucault who is haunted by the double yet also somehow beyond it. It is not at all that these two Foucaults, the impersonal and the personal, are mutually exclusive, but that they are slightly displaced, almost imperceptibly doubled. Such a displacement is illustrated by Giorgio Agamben's description of Eden and Gehenna in *The Coming Community:*

> According to the Talmud, two places are reserved for each person, one in Eden and the other in Gehenna. The just person, after being found innocent, receives

a place in Eden plus that of a neighbor who was damned. The unjust person, after being judged guilty, receives a place in hell plus that of a neighbor who was saved. Thus the Bible says of the just, "In their land they receive double," and of the unjust, "Destroy them with a double destruction." . . . In the topology of this Haggadah of the Talmud, the essential element is not so much the cartographic distinction between Eden and Gehenna, but rather the adjacent place that each person inevitably receives.[30]

The impersonal/personal displacement in Deleuze's evocations of Foucault could be thought along the lines of a doubling of place. Here it is as if two places have been reserved; because their place-markers must have a name, they are both called Foucault, and neither is exactly a misnomer, yet the one is by definition unnamable, while this one's adjacent neighbor, by doubling it and thereby exacting a title, betrays the unnamability with a proper name, Foucault.

Such a displacement is played out along other axes as well. Deleuze repeatedly emphasizes the impersonal aspects of style, how in a great writer style is a mode of existence and is not bound up with the personal:

Style, in a great writer, is always also a style of life, not at all something personal, but the invention of a possibility of life, of a mode of existence. It's funny how it is sometimes said that philosophers have no style, or that they write badly. This must be because they are not read. In France alone, Descartes, Malebranche, Maine de Biran, Bergson, even Auguste Comte with his Balzacian side, are stylists. But, Foucault also joins in this lineage; he is a great stylist. With him the concept takes on rhythmical value, or counterpoint, as in the curious dialogues with himself by which he ends some of his books. His syntax gathers reflections, sparklings of the visible, but also writhes like a lash, folds and unfolds, or cracks in time to the statements.[31]

It is remarkable how Deleuze's own style, his own "mode of existence," is, if anything, only heightened when he writes — or speaks — of Foucault. All that Deleuze so beautifully evokes in Foucault is certainly part and parcel of his own "oeuvre" as well, which is to say, of course, that neither oeuvre belongs properly to either of them. In this sense, too, the absence of work designates the work's improper belonging to a proper name. Moreover, the evocations of style and gesture are at once markers of the utterly personal, yet the form in which they are evoked signals something beyond the personal. This in turn resonates with Foucault's notion of "subjectivation," which Deleuze explicates as follows:

A process of subjectivation, that is, a production of a mode of existence, cannot be confused with a subject, unless it is to dismiss the latter from all interiority and even from all identity. Subjectivation does not even have anything to do with the "person": it is an individuation, individual or collective, that characterizes an event (an hour of the day, a river, a wind, a life . . .). It is an intensive mode and not a personal subject.[32]

In this fashion, Deleuze and Foucault are not so much individual writers and thinkers as they are a mode, or a configuration, or even a constellation. They are a multiplicity that encompasses, in every gesture or evocation, a vast network of domains that might be variously classified as the philosophical, the political, the personal. They are not one thinker or even one unit but rather an approach to thought — which is also a singularity — one that traverses a wide array of discourses. The concept of such a thought-configuration is nowhere better articulated, in fact enacted by being articulated, than in their corpus of mutually glorifying essays. Such a mode of encomium as conversation, neither critique nor original, might best be characterized as the replication or double of that which it describes: thought as pure event, thought as pure theater, thought as style and gesture.

Yet there is more. Let us return to another of Deleuze's evocations of Foucault, a subsequent interview that is virtually an exact repetition of the lines quoted above — but with a slight twist. Questioned again about subjectivation, Deleuze responds:

> Subjectivation is the production of modes of existence or styles of life.... Subjectivation as a process is an individuation.... There are individuations of the "subject" variety (this is you... this is me...), but there are also individuations of the event variety, without a subject: a wind, an atmosphere, an hour of the day, a battle. It is not certain that a life, or a work of art, is individuated like a subject, in fact to the contrary. Foucault himself — one did not grasp him exactly like a person. Even on insignificant occasions, when he entered a room, it was rather like a change of atmosphere, a kind of event, an electric or magnetic field, or what you will. This did not at all exclude gentleness or well-being, but it wasn't on the order of the person. It was an ensemble of intensities.[33]

Here, it is a question of Foucault "himself" (*lui-même*), yet Foucault-himself not as person but as intensity, not as subject but as process of subjectivation. In short, Foucault is not Foucault but rather the effect of Foucault. But does an effect really enter a room in an insignificant fashion? Is a presence that effects atmospheric changes not also indelibly linked to a sense of person-as-presence, even if it is only in the most instantaneous of gestures? In other words, how can Foucault-as-pure-effect, in entering a room, not at the very least evoke the longing for Foucault as just a person named Michel Foucault? Such a notion clearly runs counter to the intricate concept of subjectivation developed above and to its aura of impersonality. Yet it holds out the possibility of simultaneously thinking in opposition. It is not unlike the nonbeliever, irrevocably convinced of the absence or death of God, who can feel only a mischievous thrill in the thought that God might actually be up there watching. In this case, it is a matter of taking up a proffered temptation, that of picturing, in an overtly representational fashion, Foucault-the-man entering a room and Deleuze-the-man standing on the other side thinking, "Here has entered my friend Michel, just him and nothing more." Surely such a fantasy is philo-

sophically untenable and wildly untrue, *but* it is the brilliance of this exchange
to foreclose this possibility with a perfectly *mise-en-abîme* systematicity *and*
simultaneously to open it up, with every deftly dropped gestural trace, to open
up the unthinkable: maybe these are just two good friends saying very fine
things about each other. Indeed, such a double possibility of reading goes to
the very heart of the mode of philosophical encomium at issue here.

While my aim is to show how this mode — in its unique conjoining of
form and content — provides a new and more perspicacious lens from which
to view the work of the thinkers in question, there is a counterargument to
this position that always lurks in the background in the form of a continual challenge on the level of seriousness: Why should the writings of good
friends about each other be taken seriously in the first place? Can't this all be
explained as meaningless chatter between friends? It is important to acknowledge that the concept of "absence of work" at issue here begs the question of
insignificance or meaninglessness. And it is important that it does so, for this
underlying threat of insignificance is paradoxically what gives this delirious
mode of encomium its philosophical import. Because its seriousness is never
precisely legible, because its excessiveness is always defamiliarizing, because it
verges on the overpersonal — for all these reasons and more, such a form of
writing challenges us to pose questions that might otherwise not be asked:
What constitutes proper philosophical writing or proper critical writing? Is
a critical work's import only in its content, or, as in a literary domain, is it
also bound up with issues of form? If so, must the form and content come
together, or might a critical work indeed be nothing but form, and perhaps
nothing at all, and in this sense also be an absence of work?

If we take seriously the form of these personal evocations, then it is useful to consider the way that the gestural is central to this form. The gestural
moments in Deleuze's evocations of Foucault are too multiple and varied to
properly enumerate. Let it suffice to give a few examples. Deleuze is fond
of describing Foucault as a "seer." In *Foucault*, he writes: "Foucault delighted
in articulating statements, and in uncovering the statements of others, only
because he also had a passion for seeing: what defines *him in his own right*
is above all the voice, but also the eyes. *The eyes, the voice.* Foucault never
stopped being a seer, while at the same time marking philosophy with a new
style of statement, each of the two in a different step, in a double rhythm."[34]
The "double rhythm" that Deleuze suggests is, quite predictably by now, also
applicable to Deleuze's own text, which flows according to its proper double rhythm: the personal, visionary aspect of Foucault is at once absolutely
inextricable from Foucault the critical writer; indeed the very thinking of
the Foucauldian *énoncé*[35] is altogether bound up with the assemblages of vision and enunciation — the eyes, the voice — of the great visionary; and
yet, . . . What is one to make of the traces that would imply something also
beyond, something palpable only as the slightest yet weightiest of gestures

toward that which cannot be spoken, the "himself" (*lui-même*), the sentence-phrase "the eyes, the voice" (*les yeux, la voix*)? What wistful or hardened or trembling tones accompany such phrasings? Might it be the absent grain of the voice that marks the otherworldly double of an otherwise perfect *mise-en-abîme* apparatus?[36] It is hard to not be caught up in speculations of what these small phrasings might contain: the recent death of an estranged friend, an estrangement sparked by a political disagreement in 1977[37] after which Deleuze and Foucault never saw or spoke to each other again (though they did exchange letters about each other's work), Deleuze's retrospective comments on this and the pain it caused him.[38] It was an acute receptiveness to this realm of painful silence and the other forms of communication it occasions, their sublime beauty and frightful torments, that was in fact the unrelenting motivation for this framing of a topic.

In *Dialogues*, Deleuze conjures up Foucault when he explicates the encounter: "I can talk of Foucault, tell you that he has said this or that to me, set it out as I see it. This is nothing as long as I have not been able really to encounter this set of sounds hammered out, of decisive gestures, of ideas all made of tinder and fire, of deep attention and sudden closure, of laughter and smiles which one feels to be 'dangerous' at the very moment when one feels tenderness."[39] Here we have the gesture not only as it intersects the person of Foucault but also as it intersects philosophy. And this goes to the heart of the genre of the laudatory encounter as such. This form of encounter is in many ways a gestural one — while it is in one sense an encomium to the thought of another and an engagement with that thought, it is also a form of attentiveness to the gestural traces of the other ("the eyes, the voice") and an equally gestural engagement with them (an exchange of gesture for gesture). Finally, then, it is a way of doubling these two logics back onto each other, so that neither is clearly distinct.

To further explicate the gestural logic at work in the encounter between Deleuze and Foucault, we might turn to Walter Benjamin's emphasis on the *gestus* in his readings of Kafka and Brecht. In "Franz Kafka: On the Tenth Anniversary of His Death," Benjamin writes that "what Kafka could see least of all was the *gestus*. Each gesture is an event — one might even say, a drama — in itself.... Like El Greco, Kafka tears open the sky behind every gesture; but as with El Greco — who was patron saint of the Expressionists — the gesture remains the decisive thing, the center of the event."[40] In this fashion, Benjamin links Kafka to El Greco and the gesture to the event. What is striking here is the way in which the Benjaminian gesture, in its connection to the event, is neither precisely corporeal nor incorporeal, yet is also both at once. While the gesture is firmly linked to the body or to the person, its opening into the event is a delinking or depersonalizing that ushers in other realms ("tears open the sky behind every gesture"). In a strikingly similar fashion, Deleuze and Félix Guattari in *A Thousand Plateaus* link the event to "incorporeal transformations," in which "content" and "expression" intermingle in such a way as to at once remain distinct yet also become inextricably bound to the other.[41] Kafka, once again, provides an exemplary model for this type of assemblage: "No one is better than Kafka at differentiating the two axes of the assemblage and making them function together. On the one hand, the ship-machine, the hotel-machine, the circus-machine, the castle-machine, the court-machine, each with its own intermingled pieces, gears, processes, and bodies contained in one another or bursting out of containment.... On the other hand, the regime of signs or of enunciation: each regime with its incorporeal transformations, acts, death sentences and judgments, proceedings, 'law.'"[42] Both Benjamin and Deleuze and Guattari, each in their different ways, single out that way in which Kafka's world, like the gesture, functions at two levels, or along two axes. These levels might be likened to the physical entity or movement, on the one hand, and to the incorporeal intensity that the physical entity evokes, on the other hand. Deleuze and Guattari explicate this in a further passage when they write:

> We witness a transformation of substances and a dissolution of forms, a passage to the limit or flight from contours in favor of fluid forces, flows, air, light, and matter, such that a body or a word does not end at a precise point. We witness the incorporeal power of that intense matter, the material power of that language A matter more immediate, more fluid, and more ardent than bodies or words.... Gestures and things, voices and sounds, are caught up in the same "opera," swept away by the same shifting effects of stammering, vibrato, tremolo, and overspilling.[43]

By this analogy, the thoughts and gestures that circulate around Deleuze and Foucault form their own material force, one that is neither simply bodies nor simply words, but rather the product of the transformations that they inflict upon each other.

This provocative combination of gesture and event, of danger and tenderness, as it is unleashed suddenly by laughter or a smile, is, in its own right, poignantly striking. It is all the more so as an enunciation marked by a date — 1977 — the year in which Foucault and Deleuze ceased to see or to speak to each other. From this date on, such an ensemble of sounds and gestures, such a perceptual apparatus, no longer governed the conversation between Deleuze and Foucault. Rather, this conversation took new form in private comments and communications[44] and in the interviews, lectures, and essays that Deleuze devoted to Foucault. At issue, then, is how this new form continued or ceased to capture the gestic and event-laden quality that marked the more personal encounters. In the passage above, Foucault is indeed produced as an "event," not as a subject but instead as an ensemble of gestures and statements that surpasses the person of Foucault. Since it is never solely the person as such at issue, did the political falling-out between Deleuze and Foucault occasion a structural shifting of Deleuze-Foucault as event? Just as one might locate breaks and ruptures within Foucault's own oeuvre,[45] so too are there breaks and ruptures within the event that is the Deleuze-Foucault ensemble. One such rupture was their falling-out in 1977; another was Foucault's death in 1984. Neither rupture marks the cessation of their great conversation (as François Ewald so aptly describes in his presentation of their exchanges entitled "Foucault, Deleuze: Un dialogue fécond et ininterrompu" [Foucault, Deleuze: An abundant and uninterrupted dialogue]),[46] but they do mark important spatiotemporal reconfigurations.

Pronounced at the advent of such a reconfiguration, the juxtaposition of danger and tenderness, and of gesture and event, is also the prophetic future anterior of a subtle reassembling of Deleuze-Foucault. It is the already palpable nostalgia for what *will have been* an enchanted realm of speech and visibility, a realm that will henceforth exist under different economies of exchange and different modes of perception. And the subtlety lies precisely in this: that such ruptures necessitate, at the enunciative level, an acknowledgment of the new form of relation — one cannot act as if one is still speaking to someone when tangible communication has effectively ceased; one cannot regard someone or something else as not-dead when life has ceased or there has never been a living entity to begin with. To do otherwise would be considered madness. Yet sometimes it is altogether more appropriate to say that *nothing* has really changed, though such an articulation is strictly disallowed. The "danger," then, encompassed by the entity Foucault-Deleuze is not so much that the event of their coming together will be irretrievably lost but that it will soon have to be seen as lost or altered when in fact it never really was or is.

To repetitively summarize this argument, let me turn to a final Deleuzian evocation of Foucault:

> For those who met Foucault, what struck them were his eyes, his voice, and a straight stature between the two. The flashes and sparklings, the statements that tore themselves away from words, even Foucault's laughter was a statement. That there is a disjunction between the seen and the spoken, that the two are separated by a gap, an irreducible distance, signifies only this: the problem of knowledge (*connaissance*) (or rather of "knowledge" ["*savoir*"]) will not be resolved by appealing to a correspondence, nor to a likeness.[47]

Once again, the gestural traces of the eyes and the voice mark out the registers of this entity-beyond-a-mere-person that is Foucault. Separated by an irreducible difference — yet this time with the unprecedented figure of the "straight stature" in-between (What is one to make of this?) — the eyes and the voice are also the markers of the pure and irreconcilable difference between the impersonal Foucault and the virtually unspeakable personal one. With respect to this "personal" Foucault, it is interesting to note the prodigious industry of Foucault biographies.[48] In contrast to the overwhelming

surplus of details these biographies provide, the details that Deleuze prof-
fers — and they are generally the same gestural tracings (the eyes, the voice,
the laugh) repeated over and over again — seem paradoxically more revela-
tory. While the biographies say everything that can be said and then some,
Deleuze's quiet repetition of a few gestural details says even more by its vast
silences. While the biographies would present a Foucault laid bare, Deleuze
presents a Foucault who haunts. Just as Deleuze writes that "one thing haunts
Foucault — thought,"[49] so in turn does Foucault-as-thought haunt Deleuze.
The repetitive details thus unleashed are like a mantra of the haunted, a
mantra that enunciates far more than the precise words it repeats. Factually
speaking, these details present very little, but gesturally speaking they say more
than a torrent of words. The repetitive fixing upon select details or physical
aspects (the eyes, the voice) narrates a poignancy and intensity that are difficult to behold without flinching. They are a markers of a form of friendship
that contains within it its own forms of extremity, contradiction, and tragedy.

To return to the difference marking the *mise-en-abîme* structure of the impersonal Foucault and the gestural beyond of the personal one, it is useful to
cite Deleuze's *Différence et répétition* where he writes that "these two lines of
research spontaneously came together, because on every occasion *these concepts
of a pure difference and a complex repetition* seemed to connect and coalesce."[50]
There is, in this ceaseless repetition of slight difference, of slight displacement, which is Deleuze on Foucault, a haunting mantra that runs counter to
a notion of work as constructive expenditure or the work as a gradually produced and tangible corpus. Instead we are confronted with the gestural traces
of marked absence and marked repetition, the madness of the work's absence
in what would seem to be its incessant compilation.

It is with respect to Deleuze's *Différence et répétition* and *Logique du sens*[51]
that Foucault in his turn repeats and recasts the Deleuzian laudatory madness. In both "Ariane s'est pendue" (Ariadne hung herself) (Foucault's 1969
review of *Différence et répétition*)[52] and "Theatrum Philosophicum" (Foucault's
1970 review of *Différence et répétition* and *Logique du sens*),[53] Foucault extols
in magisterial tones the radical event that Deleuze has enacted in the realm of
thought. He writes in "Ariane s'est pendue" that "thought at the height of its
intensity will itself be difference and repetition: it will differentiate what representation tried to bring together; it will perform the indefinite repetition for
which obstinate metaphysics sought the origin."[54] As both philosopher of difference and repetition and producer of it in his own texts, Deleuze, according
to Foucault (which in turn echoes Deleuze), maps out thought as pure theater and with this performs a singular achievement. Foucault concludes that
"Deleuze's book is the marvelous theatre, always new, where those differences
that we are, those differences that we make, those differences among which

we wander, are playing. Of all the books that have been written for a long
while, this is the most singular, the most different, and that which best repeats the differences that intersect us and disperse us. Theatre of the now."[55]
In thus resuming the Deleuzian theater, Foucault speaks not as its critic but
as its even more audacious fellow player. In the even more effusively laudatory
"Theatrum Philosophicum," Foucault hails the singular thinker who has liber-
ated philosophy as theater, as event, and back again as thought: "[A] lightning
storm was produced which will, one day, be given the name of Deleuze: new
thought is possible; thought is again possible."[56] Such unabashedly extreme
encomium must be seen as itself the highest theatrical enactment of thought,
as in fact a new form of thinking. In this manner, the already familiar *mise-en-
abîme* structure takes a slightly different twist. Not only is Foucault enacting
precisely what he extols in Deleuze (and this in the very act of extolling
him), *but*, paradoxically, he is specifically *not* trying to produce new thought.
Foucault is neither offering up a critique of Deleuze nor striving to achieve
something original in his own right. As David Macey puts it, " 'Theatrum
Philosophicum' is a celebration rather than a critical review.... Foucault does
not expound or explain Deleuze's texts; he celebrates them by joining a dance
in which his partners include Leiris, de Sade, Bataille, Klossowski, and Lewis
Carroll's Alice."[57] In this regard, Foucault's mode might be likened to that
of biblical exegesis, in which the holy text is taken as a given and the commentary addressed to it neither works to amend it nor aspires to outshine it
but rather is compelled to magnify the divine illumination it already provides.
Somewhat ironically, then, the notion of *producing* thought is quite anathema
to Foucault's project; instead it is a question of reveling in a "Thought from
the Outside" that is beyond either production or reproduction. Such a logic is
still bound up with the *mise-en-abîme* structure, except that here it works in
perfect reverse; by *not* trying to enact what is theorized, by *not* attempting to
produce new thought, a new possibility of thinking otherwise, of thinking in
conversation, is opened up.

     And yet... there is surely something that remains. Again, it is an excess,
if not an outlandishness, of tone. The preeminent example is the often-cited
passage that begins "Theatrum Philosophicum": "I believe that these works
will continue to revolve about us in enigmatic resonance with those of Klossowski, another major and excessive sign, and perhaps one day, this century
will be known as Deleuzian."[58] The reference to Pierre Klossowski aside,[59]
this incomparably strong statement touches the same level of obscenity as
Deleuze's repetitive and understated evocation of the gesture. Like Deleuze's
quiet mantra of the haunted, the sheer flamboyance of Foucault's excessive ut-
terance also speaks an intensity that is perhaps too blinding to stare at straight
away. What blinds and immobilizes is the shame of not knowing exactly how
to read this yet also knowing that it exacts a reading. Deleuze himself registers such a shame when questioned directly about this statement. When asked

by Robert Maggiori to comment on Foucault's extraordinary pronouncement, Deleuze replies demurely — and diabolically:

> I don't know what Foucault meant. I never asked him. He had a diabolical sense of humor. Perhaps he meant this: that I was the most naive among the philosophers of our generation. We all use themes like multiplicity, difference, repetition. But I put forward almost crude concepts, while the others work with more mediations.... Perhaps it was this that Foucault meant: I wasn't the best, but the most naive, a sort of crude art, if you will; not the most profound, but the most innocent.[60]

The Deleuze-Foucault encounter is replete with what might be termed a playful yet very serious innocence, one that is joyfully timid in the knowledge that others may be watching.[61] Such a joyful timidity is captured in Deleuze's shyly comical footnote to "Theatrum Philosophicum." Just after the passage where Foucault talks affirmatively about the effects of drugs, Deleuze suddenly appears in the margin with the lines "What will people think of us?"[62] Such a statement is simultaneously an invitation for people to think about them — and possibly to think with them — and also a modest warning that such thought can be dangerous, that it is more easily dismissed than taken up, and if it is to be dismissed, then it is improper to stare it too long in the face, just as one is taught not to stare at those who are mad.

Writing from my small-town vantage point, I might add that just today we have reencountered another starer, one who has recently moved here, perhaps to join the ranks of this town's large delegation of "sub-sane" (as a local coffee shop ad puts it) in which we circulate timidly. This person's beady gaze from outside the fast-food establishment where we sit is terrifyingly relentless (perhaps we recognize something in it that mirrors our own mode of paranoid perception). The stare catches us in the exact reciprocation, the perfect doubling, of our own mode of existence. Yet to be looked at makes us timid, desirous of escape, ready to flee toward something outside this monstrous reciprocity. The unforgiving stare captures it all — the coexistence of a perfect doubling and a will to something beyond.

So, too, "What will people think...?" both assures that people will be thinking and asks them not to look. Will people think that Deleuze and Foucault are up to something unsavory or even just up to nothing? It is a possibility that must be taken quite seriously. Where exactly is the work, the "oeuvre," in all of this? Could one liken it to Borges or to Stanislaw Lem writing book reviews for works that do not exist? Certainly *Histoire de la folie, Différence et répétition,* and the myriad other writings of Foucault and Deleuze do exist, but they are also a dizzying camouflage for the absent work, the obscenely impersonal *and* personal set of gestures that remains apart from the work, only to be touched in lingering moments in an altogether different mode of exchange, one of delirious exegesis.

If Nietzsche signals the disappearance of God, Foucault the disappearance of the author, then perhaps Deleuze-Foucault hail the disappearance of the work (in which case, perhaps one day this century will be known as Deleuze-Foucauldian). By bringing the work both to the absolute state of *mise-en-abime* doubling and reciprocity *and* to something altogether apart from that, Foucault-Deleuze instantiate a nonchalant "one or the other, both and the same, either or both are OK" logic that is itself an *other* form of madness. Jacques Derrida writes in "La parole soufflée" of "the *other* madness, . . . the metaphysics which lives *within* difference, within metaphor and the work, and thus within alienation; and lives within them without conceiving them *as such,* beyond metaphysics. Madness is as much alienation as inalienation. It is the work or the absence of the work."[63]

It is a new form of exegetical madness that is all text and no text, the excessive laudatory commentary that produces the extraordinary effect of never having written anything. Let us return to Jacques Martin. He wrote something and then struggled and wrote nothing, and then what was written was lost, and then again what was not written was gained, gained for the very fact of its being irretrievably lost. Here the contours of the work, because they are not filled in, will always be there. When the work is emphatically missing, it is strangely all the more there. With Deleuze and Foucault, there is so much there that even the outline is lost, even what is missing can be eclipsed by the perfect *mise-en-abime* of what is not missing. In this excess of doubling and repetition that says nothing, or else too much, resides a new form of madness, beautifully inoperative (*désoeuvré*),[64] which leaves one never where one thinks but which shamefully catches one thinking.

In *The Infinite Conversation,* Maurice Blanchot explicates several "concepts escaping every conceptualization." Of *"worklessness,* the absence of (the) work [*le désoeuvrement*]," he writes:

> As Michel Foucault has reminded us in the strongest terms, the absence of work is used by current ideology to designate as "madness" what it rejects. But the absence of work, confined in the asylum, is also always walled up in the work. If the work is elaborated on the basis of the work's absence, it will not rest until it has reduced this absence to insignificance, or, what is worse, rendered it proper to the understanding of a new order or the harmony of a new accord.[65]

With Deleuze-Foucault, the absence of work is no longer strictly "walled up (*murée*)" in the work, for it has also become that new accord that is the absence of walls within the work, which is then no longer even work at all.

Yann Moulier Boutang formulates a sharp division between Jacques Martin, on the one hand, and Foucault and Althusser, on the other, when he writes, "[F]or these two superior souls, Michel Foucault and Louis Althusser — fragile at the time, each in a different fashion — Jacques Martin is the shadow of failure, the mirror of what they could have become. The mythical philosopher 'without work,' which both made into a symbol, and sometimes a screen — this is Jacques Martin."[66] Here, it is necessary to reverse Boutang's perspective and wonder if perhaps it was not Jacques Martin that these two "superior" souls were striving to become, each after its own fashion. Indeed, Martin's absence of work is both a symbol and a screen for a certain moment of French thought, one that Deleuze-Foucault, in all their repetitive laudatory madnesses, have captured as a new form — absence of work.

Notes

1. Louis Althusser, *For Marx*, trans. Ben Brewster (New York: Pantheon Books, 1969).

2. Louis Althusser, *L'avenir dure longtemps* (Paris: Stock, 1992), 152. This work was translated into English after the writing of this essay. For purposes of argument, I have opted to retain my translation, but I include page references to the official translation in brackets. See Louis Althusser, *The Future Lasts Forever: A Memoir*, ed. Olivier Corpet and Yann Moulier Boutang, trans. Richard Veasey (New York: The New Press, 1993), [133].

3. These details are taken from Yann Moulier Boutang, *Louis Althusser: Une biographie*, vol. 1, *La formation du mythe, 1918–1956* (Paris: Grasset, 1992), 258–59, 449–60.

4. Boutang writes that "One day, [Althusser] explained to us that Martin had destroyed all of his papers and that, moreover, he was '*u philosopher without work*,' an expression that Foucault and [Althusser] himself consecrated, and which probably comes from Jacques Martin himself" (*Louis Althusser*, 1:258).

I will also note here that I have chosen to translate *l'absence d'oeuvre* as "the absence of work." It could equally be translated as "the absence of *the* work," which might preclude confusion in English between two definitions: (1) work, as in a masterpiece (*oeuvre*) and (2) work, as in carrying out a task (which would be *travail* in French). Since *oeuvre*, at least in certain French locutions, can be translated by *travail*, it seems fitting that the definitional ambiguity, which is all the stronger in English, be retained.

5. Althusser, *L'avenir dure longtemps*. See, for example, 188 [166], 192 [170], 202 [179], 206–7 [183], 446 [NA].

6. Ibid., 446 [NA].

7. Ibid., 356–57 [323].

8. David Macey, in *The Lives of Michel Foucault* (New York: Pantheon Books, 1993), notes that "Foucault never spoke of Jacques Martin in print, but, like Althusser, he may have borrowed something from him. From 1961 onwards, he would define madness as 'l'absence d'oeuvre'" (26). Macey also cites Artaud as a source for this definition of madness (102).

9. Michel Foucault, *Raymond Roussel* (Paris: Gallimard, Collection Le Chemin, 1963) (English trans.: *Death and the Labyrinth: The World of Raymond Roussel*, trans. C. Ruas [New York: Doubleday, 1986; London: Athlone, 1987]); and idem, *Naissance de la clinique* (Paris: Presses Universitaires de France, 1963) (English trans.: *The Birth of the Clinic*, trans. A. Sheridan [London: Tavistock; New York: Pantheon, 1973]).

10. Michel Foucault, "La folie, l'absence d'oeuvre," *La table ronde* (*Situation de la*

psychiatrie) 196 (May 1964): 11–21. Reprinted in *Histoire de la folie à l'âge classique,* 2d ed. (Paris: Gallimard, 1972), appendix 1, 575–82.

11. Ibid., 580.

12. Ibid., 580–81.

13. See Raymond Bellour, "L'homme, les mots," *Magazine littéraire* 101 (June 1975): 20–23; Jean Roudaut, "Bibliothèque imaginaire," *Magazine littéraire* 207 (May 1984): 46–47; Denis Hollier, "Le mot de Dieu: 'Je suis mort,'" in *Michel Foucault philosophe, rencontre internationale* (Paris: Seuil, 1989), 150–65; Raymond Bellour, "Vers la fiction," in *Michel Foucault philosophe,* 172–81; Judith Revel, "Histoire d'une disparition: Foucault et la littérature," *Extrait du débat* 79 (March–April 1994): 82–90; Frédéric Gros, "Littérature et folie," *Magazine littéraire* 325 (October 1994): 46–48.

14. Such a mechanism, by which the ultimate work of literature would be that which expresses the failure of language to ever produce an ultimate work of literature, is definitively illustrated by Paul de Man, especially in his early writings between 1952 and 1960. See *Critical Writings 1953–1978,* ed. Lindsay Waters (Minneapolis: University of Minnesota Press, 1989). De Man is in many regards the "American" counterpart to the constellation of French intellectuals discussed here, though of course his preeminently European upbringing and education put his Americanness into strange relief.

15. The book on Roussel was inspired by Foucault's reading of Roussel's *Comment j'ai écrit certains de mes livres* (How I wrote some of my books) (Paris: Jean-Jacques Pauvert, 1963), which Roussel prepared shortly before his suicide in Palermo in 1933 and which was first published in 1935. The parallels between this work and Althusser's *L'avenir dure longtemps* are indeed striking. Both are situated around death, Roussel's book after the death of his mother and just before his suicide, Althusser's after the death of his wife Hélène Rytman and just before his own. There is, to be sure, a difference, on the one hand, between "natural" death and suicide and, on the other, hand, between murder and "natural" death, yet this sort of comparison would hope to question the very notion that these are hard and fast distinctions. It is interesting to note, in this regard, that Althusser sees a vision of Jacques Martin as he was found lying in his bed several days after his suicide just as Althusser completes the act of strangling his wife (*L'avenir dure longtemps,* 34–35 [16]).

16. Hollier, "Le mot de Dieu," 159. Hollier then extends the comparison by delineating the role of the mirror as the marker of that liminal space of life that death makes visible. It should also be noted that, when Roussel's mother died, he had a plane of glass fitted into the top of her coffin, an act that has been the subject of much speculation (see ibid., 157).

17. Michel Foucault, *L'archéologie du savoir* (Paris: Gallimard, 1969) (English trans.: *The Archaeology of Knowledge,* trans. A. Sheridan [London: Tavistock; New York: Pantheon, 1972]).

18. Bellour, "Vers la fiction," 175.

19. Gilles Deleuze, "Un portrait de Foucault," in *Pourparlers 1972–1990* (Paris: Minuit, 1990), 145. *Pourparlers* has also been translated into English since the writing of this essay. Once again, I am retaining my translation with the page numbers from the official translation in brackets. See Gilles Deleuze, *Negotiations 1972–1990,* trans. Martin Joughin (New York: Columbia University Press, 1995), [107].

20. Foucault explores Roussel's method of narratively linking two sentences that

differ only by one letter but have vastly disparate significations. The best known example of this in Roussel is the fantastic narrative in "Parmi les noirs" (which served as the basis for Roussel's *Nouvelles impressions d'Afrique* [Paris: Librairie Alphonse Lemerre, 1932]) that links the two sentences:

> Les lettres du blanc sur les bandes du vieux billard.
> Les lettres du blanc sur les bandes du vieux pillard.

See Foucault's "Les bandes du billard," in *Roussel,* 21–40. For a very helpful commentary on Foucault's analysis of Roussel, see Pierre Macherey, "Foucault lecteur de Roussel: La littérature comme philosophie," in *À quoi pense la littérature? Exercises de philosophie littéraire* (Paris: Presses Universitaires de France, 1990), 177–91.

21. Raymond Roussel, *La doublure* (Paris: Librairie Alphonse Lemerre, 1897). For an account of this work's composition, see Rayner Heppenstall's often-hilarious guide to Roussel, *Raymond Roussel* (London: Calder and Boyars, 1966), 2–3, 10–31. For a more scholarly treatment of Roussel, see Sjef Houppermans, *Raymond Roussel: Écriture et désir* (Paris: Librairie Jose Corti, 1985), particularly the final chapter, "Le sexte et les doubles" (317–64), where *La doublure* is taken as the ultimate key, a sort of mirror stage (363), to all of the doubles in Roussel's oeuvre. See also Michel Carrouges, *Les machines célibataires* (Paris: Arcanes, 1954), 60–92.

22. Foucault, *Raymond Roussel,* 151, 153, 155, 156.

23. Foucault, "La folie, l'absence d'oeuvre," 582.

24. Gilles Deleuze, *Foucault* (Paris: Minuit, 1986) (English trans.: *Foucault,* trans. Seán Hand [Minneapolis: University of Minnesota Press, 1988]).

25. Gilles Deleuze, "Fendre les choses, fendre les mots," in *Pourparlers,* 115.

26. The idea of the nonrelation is taken from Maurice Blanchot. See especially "The Relation of the Third Kind (Man without Horizon)," in *The Infinite Conversation,* trans. Susan Hanson (Minneapolis: University of Minnesota Press, 1993), 66–74. Blanchot also writes of "the outside, the absence of work" (33), and states that "to write is to produce the absence of the work" (424).

27. Deleuze, "Fendre les choses," 117 [83].

28. James Miller, *The Passion of Michel Foucault* (New York: Simon and Schuster, 1993), 194. The homophobic implications of Miller's argument have been highly criticized, as he suggests that essentially all of Foucault's life and work were a quest for the "limit-experience" (the "passion" of the title) and that the trajectory of Foucault's interest in suicide, his S/M experiences in San Francisco, and his eventual death from AIDS represents the crowning finale to a lifelong quest. For a critique of this position, see John Guillory, "The Americanization of Michel Foucault," *Lesbian and Gay Studies Newsletter* (July 1993).

29. Deleuze, "Un portrait de Foucault," 139 [102].

30. Giorgio Agamben, *The Coming Community,* trans. Michael Hardt (Minneapolis: University of Minnesota Press, 1993), 23.

31. Gilles Deleuze, "La vie comme oeuvre d'art," in *Pourparlers,* 138 [100–101].

32. Ibid., 135 [98–99].

33. Deleuze, "Un portrait de Foucault," 156 [115].

34. Deleuze, *Foucault,* 58, my italics (English trans., 50, translation modified). See also the interview "The Intellectual and Politics: Foucault and the Prison," *History of the Present* 2 (spring 1986): 1–2, 20–21, where Deleuze twice describes Foucault as a "seer."

35. As Deleuze explicates the *énoncé*, "things must be taken for visibilities to be extracted.... Likewise, words or sentences must be split for statements to be extracted. ... Foucault's great historical principle is: each historical formation says all it can say and sees all it can see" ("La vie comme oeuvre d'art," 132 [96]).

36. Here, I should make an observation on the grain of the voice, Deleuze's voice, accessible on the cassette recordings of his lecture course on Foucault, "Foucault: savoir, pouvoir, subjectivation," given at Paris VIII from 29 October 1985 to 7 January 1986. These recordings are available at the Centre Michel Foucault in the Bibliothèque du Saulchoir in Paris. Deleuze's lectures, which preceded his *Foucault*, present an incomparably clear and systematic overview of his thinking on Foucault and are strikingly punctuated with soft-spoken references to the beauty of Foucault's writings. For example, when making a page reference, he often uses turns of phrase such as "as Foucault says on a very beautiful page of ..." or "developed by Foucault in a masterly fashion..."

37. This disagreement arose around the much-publicized Croissant affair: the West German lawyer Klaus Croissant, one of the principal defense attorneys in the 1975 trial of the Baader-Meinhof Gang, had escaped to France when he was about to be sentenced in Germany for unlawful support of the defendants. As he faced extradition to Germany, a powerful group of French intellectuals and luminaries was organized on his behalf, and a petition was circulated. While both Foucault and Deleuze supported Croissant, Foucault's support was on legal grounds, and he did not sign the petition that expressed a more vehement condemnation of West Germany's totalitarianizing tendencies. The clash between Foucault's position and Deleuze's more extreme one seems to have been the principal ground for their falling-out. For more on this, see Didier Eribon, *Michel Foucault*, trans. Betsy Wing (Cambridge, Mass.: Harvard University Press, 1991), 258–62, and Macey, *Lives of Michel Foucault*, 392–97.

38. See Miller, *Passion of Michel Foucault*, 297–98. This text includes a letter from Deleuze to Miller in response to the question "What happened [between Deleuze and Foucault]?" Deleuze writes, "What kept me from calling him on the telephone? It is here that there arises a reason more profound and more essential than all the others. Rightly or wrongly, I believed that he desired a deeper solitude, for his thought.... I now think that I should have tried to see him again, but I did not think to try, out of respect. I suffer still for not having seen him again, all the more so because I do not believe that there was any apparent reason" (298). Deleuze expresses a similar sentiment in "Fendre les choses," where he responds, "I felt that he wanted to be alone, to go to that place where one could not follow him, aside from several intimates. I needed him far more than he needed me" (115 [83]). Here, the recently published text of Deleuze's last written communication to Foucault should be noted. It is primarily a series of detailed notes on *Surveillir et punir* and *La volonté de savoir*, many of which focus, interestingly enough, on the body. See "Désir et plaisir," *Magazine littéraire* 325 (October 1994): 57–65.

39. Gilles Deleuze, with Claire Parnet, *Dialogues* (Paris: Flammarion, 1977) (English trans.: *Dialogues*, trans. Hugh Tomlinson and Barbara Habberjam [New York: Columbia University Press, 1987], 11). In "Un portrait de Foucault," Claire Parnet questions Deleuze on this passage from *Dialogues* and asks if there is something "dangerous" in Foucault's thought. Deleuze responds, "Yes, because there is a violence about Foucault. He had an extreme controlled, dominated violence, which became

courage.... He was a man of passion, and he gave a very precise meaning to the word passion. His death cannot be thought except as a violent death, one that came to interrupt his work" (140 [103]). This study could be equally framed under a different rubric, violence of work, which in many ways doubles or mirrors absence of work.

40. Walter Benjamin, "Franz Kafka: On the Tenth Anniversary of His Death," in *Illuminations*, trans. Harry Zohn (New York: Schocken Books, 1968), 121.

41. Gilles Deleuze and Félix Guattari, *A Thousand Plateaus*, trans. Brian Massumi (Minneapolis: University of Minnesota Press, 1987), 86–87.

42. Ibid., 88.

43. Ibid., 109.

44. Eribon notes that, when Deleuze and Foucault had stopped seeing each other, "[Foucault] spoke of Deleuze to his friends, particularly to Paul Veyne. He often said that Deleuze was 'the only philosophical mind' in France. And one of his fondest desires, shortly before his death, was to be reconciled with Deleuze" (*Michel Foucault*, 262).

45. Such a break is generally placed between the so-called literary period (1962–1967) and the more "archaeological," "historical," or "political" one (sometime between *L'archéologie du savoir* in 1969 and *Surveillir et punir* in 1975). While such genealogies are indispensable, they can also unduly accentuate a logic of rupture that, while once again indispensable, can nonetheless serve to occlude an equally strong mechanism of repetition and continuity. For an interesting and very different exploration of this, see John Rajchman, *Michel Foucault: The Freedom of Philosophy* (New York: Columbia University Press, 1985), especially "The Ends of Modernism," 9–41.

46. François Ewald, "Foucault, Deleuze: Un dialogue fecond et ininterrompu," *Magazine littéraire* 257 (September 1988) (special issue on Deleuze): 48. This prefaces two short excerpts of their writings about each other, Foucault's introduction to Deleuze and Guattari's *Anti-Oedipe* (49–50) and Deleuze's "Foucault, philosophe du devenir" (51–52), which was expanded into "Qu'est-ce qu'un dispositif?" in *Michel Foucault philosophe*, 185–95.

47. Deleuze, "La vie comme oeuvre d'art," 132 [96].

48. Eribon, *Michel Foucault*; Macey, *Lives of Michel Foucault*; and Miller, *Passion of Michel Foucault*. One cannot help but wonder how much the scandalous potential of Foucault's homosexuality helped spawn the biographical urge. For Miller it avowedly did (375). For a response to Miller, see the more recent autobiography by David M. Halperin, *Saint Foucault: Towards a Gay Hagiography* (New York: Oxford University Press, 1995). For a fictionalized account of the end of Foucault's life, see Hervé Guibert, *To the Friend Who Did Not Save My Life*, trans. Linda Coverdale (New York: Atheneum, 1991).

49. Deleuze, *Foucault*, 116.

50. Gilles Deleuze, *Difference and Repetition*, trans. Paul Patton (New York: Columbia University Press, 1994), xx.

51. Gilles Deleuze, *Logique du sens* (Paris: Minuit, 1969) (English trans.: *The Logic of Sense*, trans. Mark Lester with Charles Stivale [New York: Columbia University Press, 1990]).

52. Michel Foucault, "Ariane s'est pendue," *Le nouvel observateur* 229 (31 March–6 April 1969): 36–37.

53. Michel Foucault, "Theatrum Philosophicum," in *Language, Counter-memory,*

Practice, trans. Donald F. Bouchard and Sherry Simon (Ithaca, N.Y.: Cornell University Press, 1977), 165–96.

54. Foucault, "Ariane s'est pendue," 37.

55. Ibid.

56. Foucault, "Theatrum Philosophicum," 196.

57. Macey, *Lives of Michel Foucault,* 253.

58. Foucault, "Theatrum Philosophicum," 165.

59. The centrality of Klossowski to this essay, and to Foucault's earlier writings, has not been given sufficient attention. Klossowski considered Foucault his greatest reader and bestowed on him the exclusive honor of reading the manuscript version of *Le Baphomet,* which he then dedicated to Foucault. Foucault's essay on *Le Baphomet,* "La prose d'Actéon," *Nouvelle revue française* 135 (1964): 444–49 (English trans.: "The Prose of Actaeon," introductory essay to the English version of *The Baphomet,* trans. Sophie Hawkes and Stephen Sartarelli [New York: Marsilio Publishers, 1992], xix–xxxviii), is similar in tone, if not in content, to "Theatrum Philosophicum" and engages in a parallel mode of high encomium.

60. Deleuze, "Fendre les choses," 122 [88–89].

61. See Jean Baudrillard, *Forget Foucault,* trans. Nicole Dufresne (New York: Semiotext[e], 1987), where he writes, in a not entirely laudatory tone, "[T]his collusion [of Deleuze's notion of 'desire' and Foucault's notion of 'power'] is too beautiful not to arouse suspicion, but it has in its behalf the quaint innocence of a betrothal. When power blends into desire and desire blends into power, let's forget them both" (19).

62. Foucault, "Theatrum Philosophicum," 191.

63. Jacques Derrida, "La parole soufflée," in *Writing and Difference,* trans. Alan Bass (Chicago: University of Chicago Press, 1978), 193. Also in this volume is Derrida's famous essay on Foucault's *Histoire de la folie,* "Cogito and the History of Madness," 31–63. Se also Foucault's response to Derrida in "Mon corps, ce papier, ce feu," printed as appendix 2 to the 1972 edition of *Histoire de la folie.* Interesting commentaries on this exchange include Edward Said, "The Problem of Textuality: Two Exemplary Positions," *Critical Inquiry* 4, no. 4 (summer 1978): 673–714, and Shoshana Felman, "Foucault/Derrida: The Madness of the Thinking/Speaking Subject," in *Writing and Madness,* trans. Martha Noel Evans and Shoshana Felman (Ithaca, N.Y.: Cornell University Press, 1985), 35–55. See also "Madness and the Literary: Toward the Question of the Book" (251–55), where Felman writes of madness as "a kind of *rhythm*..., a rhythm that is unpredictable, incalculable, unsayable, but that is nonetheless fundamentally narratable as the story of the slippage of a reading *between* the excessive fullness and the excessive emptiness of meaning" (254).

64. For all the complexities of the term *désoeuvré,* see Jean-Luc Nancy, *The Inoperative Community,* trans. Peter Connor (Minneapolis: University of Minnesota Press, 1991), as well as Maurice Blanchot, *The Unavowable Community,* trans. Pierre Joris (Barrytown, N.Y.: Station Hill Press, 1988). In *The Infinite Conversation,* Blanchot writes that " 'madness' is the absence of work, while the artist is one who is preeminently destined to a work — but also one whose concern for the work engages him in the experience of that which in advance always ruins the work and always draws it into the empty depths of worklessness, where nothing is ever made of being" (200).

65. Blanchot, *Infinite Conversation,* 420.

66. Boutang, *Louis Althusser,* 453.

The Place of Ethics
in Deleuze's Philosophy

Three Questions of Immanence

Daniel W. Smith

Michel Foucault, in his foreword to the first volume of *Capitalism and Schizophrenia* (and revealingly, with apologies to its authors), wrote that *"Anti-Oedipus* is a book of ethics, the first book of ethics to be written in France in quite a long time."[1] Foucault's comment was clearly meant to be provocative. It is true that France does not have a strong tradition of "moral philosophy"; the concerns of the discipline, it has been suggested, were largely taken up in France by the various human sciences such as psychology and sociology.[2] Yet *Anti-Oedipus* was itself a work known primarily as a critique of psychoanalysis, and it bore little resemblance to what usually passes, in academic circles, for moral philosophy. For Foucault to insist that it was a book of ethics was tantamount to forcing his readers, at the very least, to regard the notion of "ethics" in a new manner. At the time Foucault wrote his preface, in 1977, he was himself, we now know, in the process of recasting the entire *History of Sexuality* project around precisely this reformulation of "the ethical question."[3] What was the basis of this reconceptualization of ethics that Foucault recognized in Deleuze's philosophy and that he later explored, in his own manner, in his last works?

Deleuze nowhere explicitly attempts to put forward what could be called an "ethical theory" of his own. Yet he has always identified Spinoza and Nietzsche as his two primary philosophical precursors and wrote important monographs on each of them.[4] These two thinkers, in Deleuze's work, constitute a kind of "minor" tradition of ethical thought. What they have in common is an attempt to rethink ethics (and philosophy as a whole) from a purely *immanent* point of view. In several interviews given after the publication of *Foucault* in 1986, Deleuze attempted to characterize this immanent conception of ethics by offering his own version of the distinction between "ethics" and "morality," which has often been drawn to distinguish modes of reflection that place greater emphasis, respectively, on the good life (such as Stoicism) or on the moral law (such as Kantianism). He uses the term "morality" to define, in very general terms, any set of "constraining" rules, such as a moral code, that consists in judging actions and intentions by relating them to transcendent values ("this is good, that is evil"). What he calls "ethics" is, on the contrary, a set of "facilitative" (*facultative*) rules that evaluates what we do, say, and think according to the immanent mode of existence that it implies. One says or does this, thinks or feels that: *What mode of existence does it imply?* "We always have the beliefs, feelings, and thoughts we deserve," writes Deleuze, "given our way of being or our style of life."[5] Spinoza and Nietzsche argued, each in his own way, that there are things one cannot do or think except in the condition of being weak, base, or enslaved, unless one harbors a vengeance or *ressentiment* against life (Nietzsche) or unless one remains the slave of passive affections (Spinoza); and there are other things one cannot do or say except on the condition of being strong, noble, or free, unless one affirms life or attains active affections. Deleuze calls this the method of "dramatization": actions and propositions are interpreted as so many sets of symptoms that express or "dramatize" the mode of existence of the speaker. "What is the mode of existence of the person who utters a given proposition?" asks Nietzsche. What mode of existence is *needed* in order to be able to utter it? A pluralistic method of explanation by immanent modes of existence is in this way made to replace the recourse to transcendent values; an immanent ethical difference (noble/base) is substituted for the transcendent moral opposition (Good/Evil).

This immanent conception of an "ethics without morality," however, has not fared well in the history of philosophy. Few philosophers have been more maligned and ridiculed than Spinoza and Nietzsche. They were condemned by both their contemporaries and successors not only for being atheists but, even worse, for being "immoralists."[6] A potent danger was sensed to be lurking in the *Ethics* and the *Genealogy of Morals:* without transcendence, without universals, one will fall into the dark night of chaos, reduced to a pure "subjectivism" or "relativism." A philosophy of immanence, it is argued, far from resolving the question of justification, seems to shift the problem onto an unresolvable terrain. It seems unable to put forth normative criteria by which certain modes of existence can be judged as acceptable and others condemned as reprehensible and winds up espousing a kind of moral nihilism in which all "differences" are affirmed in their turn. Deleuze himself, in a late essay, states the problem in this way: "What disturbed us was that in renouncing judgment we had the impression of depriving ourselves of any means of assessing the differences between existing beings, between modes of existence, as if from now on everything were equally valid."[7] Nietzsche, for instance, famously criticized morality for having been derived from a reactive or base mode of existence. But by what "right," according to what criteria, is a noble or active mode of existence "better" or "worth more" than a base one? Put succinctly: How can one evaluate modes of existence using criteria that are immanent to the mode itself without thereby abandoning any basis for comparative evaluation?

It is this problem that lies at the heart of an ethics of immanence, and Deleuze's response to it is rigorous. A mode of existence can be evaluated, apart from transcendental or universal values, by the purely immanent criteria of its *power* or capacity (*puissance*), that is, by the manner in which it actively deploys its power by going to the limit of what it can do (or, on the contrary, by the manner in which it is cut off from its power to act and is reduced to impotence). Deleuze expresses this in various formulas throughout his work: modes of existence are evaluated "according to their tenor in 'possibilities,' in freedom, in creativity"[8] and by "the manner in which the existing being is filled with [*s'emplit de*] immanence";[9] the ethical task entails "an amplification, an intensification, an elevation of power, an increase in dimensions, a gain in distinction";[10] "there are never any criteria other than the tenor of existence, the intensification of life."[11] Modes of existence, in other words, must be evaluated according to the purely *intensive* criteria of power or, more precisely, by the manner by which they are able to possess or intensify their power. From afar, the meaning of this principle seems obscure and has at times been subject to naive caricatures (for instance, that it simply valorizes "powerful" modes of existence, "superhuman" individuals who capriciously exert their power and will upon others). What follows is an attempt to shed some light on that obscurity, first, by analyzing the complex formal relations an immanent conception of ethics maintains with Kantianism and, second, by elucidating, in summary fashion, some of the problems and positive tasks it poses, taking our cue primarily from Spinoza.

Somewhat surprisingly, Deleuze presents this immanent conception of ethics not, as one might perhaps expect, as a rejection of Kantianism but, on the contrary, as its *fulfillment*. Kant's genius, in Deleuze's interpretation, was precisely to have conceived of a purely *immanent* critique of reason, a critique that did not seek, within reason, errors that come from an external cause (the body, the senses, the passions) but illusions that arise from within reason itself through the illegitimate (transcendent) use of the syntheses of consciousness. Yet the post-Kantian philosophers, from Salomon Maimon to Hermann Cohen, argued that Kant himself was unable to fully realize this project of immanent critique because he lacked a method that would allow reason to be critiqued internally without giving it the task of being its own judge. Kant's project was a critique of reason by reason itself: reason is both the judge and the judged, the tribunal and the accused. He therefore saw critique as a force that should be brought to bear on all claims to knowledge and morality — but not on knowledge and morality themselves, which were considered to be the "natural interests" of reason and thus were never placed in question. What Kant condemned was simply those illegitimate employments (illusions) through which reason, in its natural state, confuses those interests and allows these domains to impinge on one another.

> Thus total critique turns into a politics of compromise: even before the battle the spheres of influence have already been shared out. Three ideals are distinguished: What can I know? What should I do? What can I hope for? Limits are drawn to each one, misuses and trespasses are denounced, but the uncritical character of each ideal remains at the heart of Kantianism like the worm in the fruit: true knowledge, true morality, and true religion. What Kant still calls — in his own terms — a fact: the fact of morality, the fact of knowledge.[12]

In his landmark book *Nietzsche and Philosophy*, Deleuze argues that it was Nietzsche who was finally able to fulfill the aims of the critical project precisely because he brought the critique to bear not merely on false claims to knowledge and morality but on truth itself, that is, on true morality and true knowledge. "We need a *critique* of moral values," writes Nietzsche in *The Genealogy of Morals*, "*the value of these values must first be called into question*." And again: "The will to truth requires a critique — let us thus define our own task — the value of truth must for once be experimentally *called into question*."[13] Nietzsche was not content to discover transcendental principles that would constitute the condition of possibility for the "facts" of reason (the "fact" of knowledge, the "fact" of morality); rather he was intent on discovering immanent principles that were truly genetic and productive, that would give an account of the *genesis* of knowledge and morality. What he called "genealogy" was a method that traced the origin of knowledge and morality to differential modes of existence that serve as their principle. As Deleuze writes

> The problem of critique is that of the value of values [knowledge, morality], of the evaluation from which their value arises, thus the problem of their *creation*. Evaluation is defined as the differential element of corresponding values, an element which is both critical and creative. Evaluations, in essence, are not values but ways of being, modes of existence of those who judge and evaluate, serving as principles for the values on the basis of which they judge.[14]

Deleuze's analysis of Kant's theory of the moral law is consequently worth examining in some detail here, since in effect it submits Kantianism itself to the critical reversal set in motion by Nietzsche. Deleuze suggests that, just as the *Critique of Pure Reason* effected a Copernican revolution by making the objects of knowledge revolve around the subject, so the *Critique of Practical Reason* effected an equally important revolution by making the Good revolve around the Law. He thereby inverted the relation that had prevailed since antiquity and seemed in a position to invert what Nietzsche called the ascetic ideal. But what actually takes place in the second *Critique*? In Plato, laws were a secondary or derived power, subordinate to the Good; if humans knew the Good, and how to conform to it, they would not need laws. From the point of view of *principles*, laws are only a "second resort," an imitation of the Good given to humans when the true politics is lacking. And from the point of view of *consequences,* the righteous person, in obeying the laws of his or her country, can nonetheless be said to be acting for the "Best," even though he or she retains the freedom to think of the Good and for the sake of the Good. Kant, in Deleuze's reading, effectively reversed this classical conception of the Law, as much from the point of view of the principles upon which the Law rests as the consequences it entails.[15]

1. From the point of view of principles, laws are no longer seen to find their foundation in a higher principle from which they would derive their authority. Instead, *the* Law is made into a first principle, a pure form of universality that has neither object nor content (since a content would imply a Good of which the Law would be the imitation...). It does not tell us what we must do; it does not present itself as a comparative or psychological universal ("Do unto others..."). Rather, it provides a subjective rule, a logical test, that we must obey no matter what our action: every action whose maxim can be *thought* without contradiction as universal, and whose motive has no other object than this maxim, will be a moral action or at least consistent with morality. Lying, for example, cannot be thought as a universal, because it at least implies people who believe the lie and who, in believing it, are not lying. In Kant, the Law becomes stripped of all content, its imperative being merely a categorical one. The Law does not tell us which *object* the will must pursue to be good but simply what *form* it must take to be moral. "It does not tell us what we must do, it simply tells us 'You must!' leaving us to deduce from it the Good, that is, the objects of this pure imperative."[16]

2. From the point of view of consequences, it is no longer possible to say that the righteous man obeys the Law for the sake of the Best. Since it is valid by virtue of its form alone and its content remains undetermined, the Law is not part of the domain of the understanding. The Law is not known and can never be known precisely because there is nothing in it to "know." We come across the Law only through its action, through a purely *practical* determination that is opposed to any speculative or theoretical proposition. The Law defines a realm of transgression where one breaks the Law *without ever knowing what it is.* It is this realm, Deleuze suggests, whose mechanisms were described with frightening detail by Kafka in *The Trial:* the Law acts and expresses itself through its sentence, and one can learn of this sentence only through its application in a punishment.[17] Consequently, the person who tries to obey the moral imperative of the Law no longer becomes or even feels righteous; on the contrary, the Law makes one feel guilty, necessarily guilty, guilty *in advance,* and the more strict one's obedience, the greater one's guilt. Freud, in his analysis of the superego, uncovered the secret of this paradox of conscience: if duty presupposes a renunciation of our interests and desires, the moral Law will inevitably exert itself all the more strongly and rigorously the deeper our renunciation. The Law thereby makes itself all the

more severe to the degree that we observe it with exactitude.[18] And even guilt and punishment will not give us a final knowledge of our faults: the Law remains in a state of indeterminacy equaled only by the extreme specificity of the punishment. *It never acquits us,* no more of our virtues than of our faults.

Deleuze, in short, defines the Kantian moral Law in terms of two paradoxical poles: formal transcendence, from the point of view of principles; and a priori guilt, from the point of view of consequences. The modern critique of Kant's moral philosophy has tended to take as its point of departure these two poles. In his 1967 study entitled *Masochism,* for instance, in which this analysis of the Law first appeared, Deleuze argued that Sade and Masoch presented two "perverse" modes of existence that had as their aim the subversion of the moral Law: either by a new revolt that aims at a higher sovereign principle beyond the Law, an *ironic* principle that would no longer be the Good but rather the Idea of Evil or primary nature (Sade's institutional model of anarchy); or else by a *humorous* submission that eludes the imperative of the Law by turning punishment into a condition that makes possible the forbidden pleasure (Masoch's contractual model).[19] Deleuze's analyses in *Masochism,* in turn, can be read as an atheistic version of Kierkegaard's analysis of the "suspension of the ethical": Job contests the Law in an ironic manner, "refusing all second-hand explanations, dismissing the general in order to attain the most singular as a principle, as a universal"; whereas Abraham submits to the Law humoristically, "but in this submission he recovers the singularity of the only son that the Law has commanded him to sacrifice."[20] But these critiques, important as they are, only expose the paradoxes of the Kantian Law, its limits, pointing either to a "leap" beyond the Law into the religious or a "transgression" of the Law through perversion.

Nietzsche's method of dramatization, by contrast, provides an immanent critique, not of the paradoxes but of the very principles of the moral Law. *Who* is it that says, "You must!"? It is the priest, and the categorical imperative expressed the purely formal aspect of the will to judge. *Who* is it that is always already guilty? It is the slave, laden with a responsibility-guilt of which he can never acquit himself. When Nietzsche laid out the three primary psychological categories of the slave in the *Genealogy of Morals,* he also marked out the evolution of the triumph of "morality," the genealogical origins of the moral Law: *ressentiment* ("It's your fault...," moment of projective accusation and recrimination); the bad conscience ("It's my fault...," moment of introjection; fault is internalized, turned back against oneself; one becomes guilty); and finally the ascetic ideal (moment of sublimation, triumph of reactive forces; life is "judged" in the name of values superior to life). At the same time, he also showed how the slave found its necessary correlate in the priest ("I want to judge, I must judge..."), who gives this guilt form, who exploits it to establish his power, who invents a new form of power as a power of judgment.[21] Morality, in this sense, constitutes what Deleuze calls a "system of judgment."

Nietzsche famously identified the condition of judgment in "the consciousness of having a *debt* toward the divinity." It is the debtor-creditor relation,
he argued, that lies at the origin of the ethico-moral realm: promises were
given, commitments made to the future, and the "justice of the laws" existed
to make one responsible for one's debts, "to create a memory for the future."
The system of judgment appeared precisely when this debt was rendered *infinite* and therefore unpayable (Christianity): we were no longer indebted to
another party but to the divine, to whom we have an infinite debt of which
we can never acquit ourselves. "Debt becomes the relation of a debtor who
will never finish paying to a creditor who will never finish using up interest
on the debt."[22]

For Deleuze, the moral Law in Kant is *"the juridical form assumed by the
infinite debt."*[23] Rather than submitting this system of judgment to a true critique, Kant erected "a fantastic subjective tribunal" that placed both the priest
and the slave within the subject.[24] It is *the same person* who now becomes both
priest and believer, legislator and subject, judge and judged. In the name of
practical reason, "reason" itself is made to represent our slavery and subjection
as something superior that makes us reasonable beings. "The more you obey,
the more you will become master, for you will only be obeying pure reason, in
other words . . . yourself."[25] Nowhere is this strategy made clearer than in the
trajectory of the transcendent Ideas (Soul, World, God) in Kant's work. In
the first *Critique*, Kant had denounced any transcendent use of the syntheses
as illegitimate and illusory, relegating the Ideas to the "horizon" of the field
immanent to the subject. But one by one, they are each resurrected in the
second *Critique* and given a practical determination. "Freedom," as the "fact"
of morality, implies *the cosmological Idea of a suprasensible world*, independent
of any sensible condition; in turn, the abyss that separates the noumenal Law
and the phenomenal world requires the intermediary of an intelligible author
of sensible Nature or a "moral cause of the world" (*the theological Idea of a
supreme being*) and can only be bridged through the "postulate" of an infinite
progress. Acquittal can only be hoped for, not in the here and now, but from
the point of view of a progress that continues to infinity in an ever more exacting conformity to the Law. Since this path exceeds the limits of our life,
it requires *the psychological Idea of the immortality of the soul* (the debtor must
survive if the debt is to be infinite). This indefinite prolongation leads less to
a paradise above than a hell here below; it does not bestow immortality but
condemns us to a "slow death," leaving us no other juridical alternatives than
those proposed by Kafka: either an "apparent acquittal" or an "unlimited postponement." Or rather, Deleuze argues, it is not that judgment is deferred, put
off until tomorrow, repressed to infinity; on the contrary, it is this very act of
deferring, of carrying things to infinity, of making the debt infinite, that renders judgment possible. The condition of judgment is this relation between
existence and infinity in the order of time, and "the one who maintains him-

self in this relation is given the power to judge and to be judged." The moral Law is thus a system of judgment that "condemns us to a servitude without end and annuls any liberatory process."[26]

The distinction between transcendence and immanence is not an absolute one, however, for even the illusions of transcendence can serve "to recharge the plane of immanence with immanence itself."[27] The Christian tradition, for example, contains an important line of inspiration that can be traced from Pascal to Kierkegaard. What was at stake in Pascal's celebrated wager, as Deleuze interprets it, was not the existence or nonexistence of a transcendent God but rather the immanent modes of existence of those who must *choose* between his existence or nonexistence. A complex typology results: there are the *devout*, the guardians of order, for whom there is no question of choosing; the *skeptics*, who do not know how or are unable to choose; creatures of *evil*, whose initial choice places them in a situation where they can no longer repeat their choice, like Goethe's Mephistopheles; and finally, the person of *belief* or grace, the "knight of faith" who, conscious of choice, makes an "authentic" choice that is capable of being repeated in a steadfast spiritual determination.[28] Kierkegaard drew out the necessary consequences of this line of thought, showing that choice covers as great an area as thought itself. It is a question no longer of the existence of a transcendent God but of the immanent possibilities of those who "choose" to believe. Nonetheless, Pascal's "gambler" (he who throws the dice) and Kierkegaard's "knight of faith" (he who makes the leap) remain men of faith: though the existence of God is not put into play in the wager, it is the perspective presupposed by it, the standpoint according to which one wins or loses. One still seeks to encounter a transcendence within the heart of immanence. This is why Deleuze argues that the comparisons often made between Nietzsche, on the one hand, and Kierkegaard and Pascal (or Leon Chestov and Charles Péguy), on the other, are only valid up to a certain point. As Nietzsche wrote: " 'Without the Christian faith,' Pascal thought, 'you, no less than nature and history, will become for yourselves *un monstre et un chaos*': This prophecy we have fulfilled."[29]

For Deleuze, then, Nietzsche's "method of dramatization" entails both an inversion and a completion of Kant's critical project: it completes the project by finding a truly immanent principle of critique, but it also inverts Kant's philosophy by eliminating from it all vestiges of transcendence. Kant inaugurated the modern attempt to save transcendence by treating the plane of immanence as a field of consciousness: immanence was made immanent *to* a pure consciousness, a transcendental subject that actively synthesizes the field of experience. Much of Deleuze's career can therefore be seen as a profound critique not only of the Kantian Law but equally of the Kantian subject that serves as its foundation. His first book, *Empiricism and Subjectivity* (1953), already informed by a rigorously post-Kantian viewpoint, argued that the essential question of Hume's empiricism was not "How is experience given to a subject?" but rather "How is the subject constituted within the given?"[30] In *Difference and Repetition* (1968), the Humean response — that the subject (human nature) is a derivative of the principles of association — was transformed into a "transcendental empiricism": the subject no longer is a transcendental instance that actively synthesizes experience but is constituted *within* a plane of immanence by syntheses that are themselves passive.[31] But it will be Spinoza, even more than Nietzsche, who provides Deleuze with the resources to effect his "transmutation," grounding ethics in the notion of immanent "modes of existence" rather than in an appeal to a transcendental "subject." We can briefly sketch out the nature of an immanent ethics by posing three questions concerning modes of existence: How is a mode of existence determined? How are modes of existence to be evaluated? What are the conditions for the creation of new modes of existence? These questions are derived from the three moments of what Deleuze calls *the* ethical question in his analysis of Spinoza's *Ethics*, though we shall apply them here in a more general sense.[32] Together they serve to mark out, in a summary fashion, the problems and tasks posed by the "system of affects" that Deleuze would have replace the "system of judgment."

1. *How is a mode of existence determined?* Both Nietzsche and Spinoza take the *body* as their model for the analysis of modes of existence. "Essential: to start from the *body* and employ it as a guide."[33] In the *Ethics*, Spinoza defines the body primarily in terms of two fundamental axes. On the one hand, a body is defined, extensively or kinetically, by a complex set of relations under which a multiplicity of parts is subsumed, which affect each other to infinity. On the other hand, a body is also defined, intensively or dynamically, by a certain degree of power, that is, by a certain capacity to affect or be affected by other bodies. On the first axis, I have knowledge of my body solely through its "affections" (*affectio*), which indicate the state of my body at a given moment insofar as it is submitted to the action of another body: sometimes, for instance, the two affected relations will combine to form a new composite relation (as when I ingest food), and sometimes one body will decompose the other, destroying the cohesion of one of its constituent parts (as when poison breaks down the blood). On the second axis, I have knowledge of my body through the "affects" (*affectus*) of which it is capable, that is, through the manner in which my affections augment or diminish my power in time: I experience *joy* or pleasure when a body encounters mine and enters into composition with it, augmenting my power (food nourishes me); and *sadness* or pain when, on the contrary, another body threatens my coherence and diminishes my power (poison sickens me) — or, at the limit, destroys me. Joy and sadness are passages, becomings, risings and fallings of my power, which pass from one state to another and are in constant variation.

It is this conception of the body that forms the basis for Spinoza's classification of modes of existence. A mode cannot be classified by the abstract

notions of genus and species, as in Aristotelian biology (an arborescent schema
of classification), but must rather be classified by its capacity to affect and to
be affected, that is, by the affections of which it is "capable" (a rhizomatic
schema).[34] When we define humans as "featherless bipeds" or "rational animals," for instance, we rely on *nominal* definitions that simply select out
certain affects or traits at the expense of others. We arrive at a *real* definition
of a mode of existence only when we define it in terms of its *power* or capacity
to be affected — a capacity that is not a simply logical possibility but is necessarily actualized at every moment. For a given being, what is it affected by in
the infinite world? What leaves it unaffected? What does it react to positively
or negatively? What are its nutrients and poisons? How can it take other beings into its world? What affects threaten its cohesion, diminishing its power,
or even destroying it? *What can its body do?* We can know nothing about the
power of a mode until we know what its affects are, how its body can (or cannot) enter into composition with the affects of other bodies.[35] In this manner,
we can arrive at a classification of immanent "types" of modes of existence
that are more or less general. (From this viewpoint, there are more differences
between a racehorse and a workhorse, for instance, than between a workhorse
and an ox: a workhorse does not have the same capacity to be affected as a
racehorse but rather has affects in common with the ox.) Whereas the theological doctrine of infinite debt determined the relation of the immortal soul
with a system of judgments, Spinoza's ethics attempts to determine the finite
relations of an existing body with the forces that affect it.[36]

This then is the first feature of an immanent ethics: it replaces the notion
of the transcendental subject with immanent modes of existence that are determined by their degrees of power and relations of affectivity. In his later
works, Foucault suggested replacing the term "subject" with the term "subjectivation." Just as there is no "pure" Reason or rationality par excellence, he
argued, but a plurality of heterogeneous *processes of rationalization* (of the kind
analyzed by Alexandre Koyré, Gaston Bachelard, and Georges Canguilhem in
the field of epistemology; Max Weber in sociology; and François Châtelet
in philosophy), so there is no universal or transcendental subject that could
function as a basis for a universal ethics, but only variable and extraordinar-
ily diverse *processes of subjectivation.*[37] The first positive ethical task would be
to analyze the processes of subjectivation (passive syntheses) by which modes
of existence are determined. It was this task that Foucault set for himself
in the reformulated volumes of *The History of Sexuality* (in which sexuality
forms only one aspect of these processes), where he analyzed the historical
formations of subjectivation in the Greek, Roman, and Christian periods —
modes of existence that could be said to have been summarily codified in the
formulas, "Know yourself!" (Greek), "Master yourself!" (Roman), and "Deny
yourself!" (Christian).[38]

This task is inevitably tied to the analysis of social formations, or what

Deleuze terms an "assemblage" (*agencement*), and Foucault, an "apparatus" (*dispositif*). Ethics is necessarily linked to political economy. But political philosophy is not necessarily tied to the political form of the state. Modern German philosophy, notably in Kant and Hegel, invented the fiction of a state that was universal in principle, defined as the rational organization of a community of free-thinking individuals submitted to the universality of a principle (the Law), in relation to which the particularity of states was merely an accident of fact, marking their imperfection or perversity.[39] The state and reason were in this way made to enter into a curious exchange: realized reason was identified with the de jure state, and the state was identified as the becoming of reason.[40]

But just as there is no universal subject, neither is there a universal state. The critique of the subject in Deleuze is necessarily linked to a critique of the state apparatus and of modes of thought that wed the question of politics (and therefore ethics) to the destiny of the state. Since processes of subjectivation always take place within concrete social assemblages, one of the aims of the *Capitalism and Schizophrenia* project, as its title indicates, is to elaborate a general typology of various social assemblages and their corresponding processes of subjectivation.[41] The theoretical core of the project is derived from the theory of synthesis put forward by Kant in the first *Critique* (categorical, hypothetical, disjunctive), which Deleuze and Guattari reformulate into a theory of passive syntheses (connective, convergent, arithmetic, disjunctive).[42] The result is a typology of four basic types of social assemblages: (1) so-called *primitive* societies (and their modern equivalents), which effect syntheses of connection in segmented codes and territories, according to supple lines of filiation and alliance, and have specific mechanisms that ward off the formation of a centralized state; (2) *state* apparatuses, which effect syntheses of convergence, forcing local codes to converge on a single center according to various mechanisms of capture or overcoding; (3) nomadic *war machines*, which effect an arithmetic synthesis capable of occupying and distributing themselves over a smooth space and are by nature external to the state; and finally (4) *capitalism*, which effects a disjunctive synthesis between labor and capital and effectively decodes the codes and overcodings of previous formations.[43] None of these formations exists in a pure form; each type simply seeks to mark out the consistency of a concept and is valid only to the degree that it provides a critical tool for analyzing concrete assemblages and modes of existence, which are by definition mixed states requiring a "microanalysis" of the syntheses and lines they actualize.[44] The state is one social type among others, with its own history, its own complex relations with other social formations, and its own processes of capture, unification, and totalization. Modes of existence, as degrees of power, are determined by their affects, that is, by the lines of synthesis of the concrete social assemblage in which they exist. Deleuze and Guattari write: "The pursuits we call by various names — schizoanalysis, micropolitics, pragmatism, diagrammatics, rhizomatics, cartography — have no other object than the study of these lines, . . . to study their dangers, to mark their mixtures as well as their distinctions."[45]

2. *How is a mode of existence evaluated?* The first ethical question concerning the determination of modes leads directly into the second question: How does one evaluate modes of existence thus determined? This, one might say, is the ethical task properly speaking, and it is here that Deleuze and Foucault have come under criticism, even from sympathetic readers, for their apparent inability (or refusal) to put forward normative criteria of judgment, leading critics to caricature the political consequences of such a philosophy as everything from an "infantile leftism" to "neo-conservative."[46] What does it mean to evaluate modes of existence according to purely immanent criteria?

If modes of existence are defined as a degree of power (the capacity to affect and to be affected), then they can be evaluated in terms of the manner in which they come into possession of their power. From the viewpoint of an ethology of humans, Spinoza distinguishes between two types of affections: *passive* affections, which originate outside the individual and separate it from its power of acting; and *active* affections, which are explained by the nature of the affected individual and allow it to come into possession of its power. To the degree that a body's power of being affected is filled by passive affections, this power itself is presented as a *power of being acted upon;* conversely, to the degree that a body manages to fill (at least partially) its power of being affected by active affections, this capacity will be presented as a *power of acting.* For a given individual, its capacity to affect and be affected (its degree of power) remains constant and is constantly filled, under continuously variable conditions, by a series of affects and affections, while the power of acting and the power of being acted upon vary greatly, in inverse ratio to each other. But in fact this opposition between passive and active affections is purely abstract, for *only the power of acting is, strictly speaking, real, positive, and affirmative.* Our power of being acted on is simply a *limitation* on our power of acting and merely expresses the degree to which we are separated from what we "can do."[47]

It is this distinction that allows Spinoza to introduce an "ethical difference" between various types of modes of existence. In Spinoza, an individual will be considered "bad" (or servile or weak or foolish) who remains cut off from its power of acting, who remains in a state of slavery or impotence; conversely, a mode of existence will be called "good" (or free or rational or strong) that exercises its capacity for being affected in such a way that its power of acting increases, to the point where it produces active affections and adequate ideas. For Deleuze, this is the point of convergence that unites Nietzsche and Spinoza. It is never a matter of judging degrees of power quantitatively: the smallest degree of power is equivalent to the largest degree once it is not separated from what it can do. It is rather a question of knowing whether a mode of existence, however small or great, can deploy its power, increasing its power of acting to the point where it goes to the limit of what it "can do."[48] Modes are no longer "judged" in terms of their degree of proximity to or distance from an external principle but are "evaluated" in terms of the manner by which they "occupy" their existence: the intensity of their power, their "tenor" of life.[49]

What an ethics of immanence will criticize, then, is not simply modes of thought derived from base modes of existence but anything that *separates* a mode of existence from its power of acting. This is the second positive task of an immanent ethics. When Spinoza and Nietzsche criticize transcendence, their interest is not merely theoretical or speculative (to expose its fictional or illusory status) but rather practical and ethical: far from being our salvation, *transcendence expresses our slavery and impotence at its lowest point.*[50] This is why Foucault could interpret *Anti-Oedipus* as a book of ethics, insofar as it attempted to diagnose the contemporary mechanisms of "microfascism" — in psychoanalysis and elsewhere — that cause us to desire the very things that dominate and exploit us and that cause us to fight *for* our servitude as stubbornly as though it were our salvation. At the same time, the book attempted to set forth the concrete conditions under which a mode of existence can come into possession of its power, in other words, how it can become *active*. This leads us to a third question.

3. *What are the conditions for the creation of new modes of existence?* How are modes of existence capable of being created actively rather than merely being determined passively? This question follows directly from the second, insofar as the creation of new modes of existence can only occur on the condition that modes are capable of *affecting themselves*. This is the thread that unites the minor tradition of ethical thought that Deleuze draws upon: the Stoics, as Pierre Hadot has shown, thought of ethics as an *askesis*, an affect of the self upon itself, whose end was a self-transformation;[51] Spinoza, after defining a mode by its capacity for being affected, sought to define the means by which to render possible the attainment of active affections and adequate ideas; and Nietzsche discovered the artistic operation of the will to power as the invention of new "possibilities of life," a transvaluation of the value-positing element. This question of auto-affection is the object of some of Deleuze's most difficult and penetrating passages, such as those describing Spinoza's emphasis on the need for common notions in creating active affections and attaining blessedness, or the final chapter of *Nietzsche and Philosophy*, where Deleuze charts out the transvaluation of negation into affirmation, reactive into active.[52]

The study of variations in these creative or productive processes of subjectivation is the third positive task posed by Deleuze's conception of ethics. Foucault, for his part, suggested in *The Use of Pleasure* that the relation of a mode to itself could be analyzed, historically, from the point of view of four aspects or rubrics: (1) *ethical substance* (ontology), which designates the material element of ourselves that is deemed to be relevant to our ethical conduct and open to transformation (feelings, intentions, desires, etc.); (2) *mode of subjection* (deontology), which designates the means by which one is incited to recognize what one considers to be one's "ethical" obligations (for example, in relation to a divine Law, a cosmological order, a rational rule, an aesthetic form); (3) *ethical work* (ascetics), which designates the "self-forming activity" that one exerts upon oneself (self-examination, meditation, confession, exercise, diet, the following of exemplary role models, and so on); and (4) *telos* (teleology), which designates the goal or mode of being toward which this ethical activity of auto-affection is directed.[53] Here again, such a history of modes of auto-affection, which Foucault attempted to inaugurate, must be sharply distinguished from a history of moral codes, since it would map out the complex terrain and conditions in which new modes of existence appeared that were fundamentally irreducible to these codes.

Finally, for both Deleuze and Foucault, the aim of these typological and historical investigations is always borne upon the present: What is our present situation? What are our own modes of existence, our possibilities of life or processes of subjectivation (which are irreducible to our moral codes)? How and in what places are new modes of existence produced? It may be that the creators of new modes of existence are the "noble" (Nietzsche) or the "rational" (Spinoza) or the aestheticized existence of the "free man" (Foucault) or "minorities" (in the Deleuzian sense of this term).[54] One cannot know in advance, and these foci of creation change with different social assemblages. Deleuze has offered one such analysis of our present formation in an essay entitled "Post-script on the Societies of Control."[55] If Foucault spoke of societies of *discipline*, and their principal techniques of enclosure (prisons, hospitals, schools, factories, barracks, families), Deleuze suggests that we are now entering into societies of *control*, which no longer operate by enclosure (hence the crisis facing each of these institutions) but, as Paul Virilio has shown, by processes of continuous control and instantaneous communication.[56] Forms of resistance and delinquency have thereby changed accordingly: the strikes and "sabotage" of the nineteenth century have given way to piratings and the introduction of viruses of the late twentieth century. What may become increasingly important in the future, Deleuze suggests, are modes of existence that are able "to create vacuoles of noncommunication, circuit breakers, so we can elude control."[57] But as Deleuze likes to insist, one can never predict in advance where these loci of experimentation will occur; one can only be attentive to the unknown that is knocking at the door.

The primary consequence of a differential conception of ethics perhaps lies in its change of orientation away from the universal and toward the *singular* and away from the historical toward the *actual*. One does not seek universals in order to judge but singularities that are capable of creating, of producing the new. "When Foucault admires Kant for having posed the problem of philosophy, not in relation to the eternal but in relation to the Now, he means that the object of philosophy is not to contemplate the eternal, nor to reflect on history, but to diagnose our actual becomings."[58] History thinks in terms of the past, present, and future; but if history in this way surrounds and delimits us, it nonetheless does not tell us who we are, but what we are in the process of differing ourselves from. When Foucault wrote on disciplinary societies, or on Greek and Christian modes of subjectivation, he did so in order to find out in what ways we are *no longer* disciplinary, are *no longer* Greeks or Christians, and are becoming other. This difference between the present and the actual, for Deleuze, is much more important than the difference between the present and the past. The present is what we are and, for that reason, what we are already ceasing to be; the actual is not what we are but rather what we are becoming, what we are in the process of becoming. History, in other words, is what separates us from ourselves and what we have to traverse in order to think ourselves; whereas the actual is the formation of the new, the emergence of what Foucault called our "actuality."[59] To diagnose the becomings in each present that passes is the task that Nietzsche assigned to the philosopher as a physician, "the physician of civilization," or the inventor of new modes of existence. To act against the past, and therefore on the present, in favor (one hopes) of a time to come: such, for Deleuze, is the task of the philosopher. This time to come is not the future of history but the Now that is distinguished from every present; it is not an instant but a becoming, the "actual" or the "untimely," the conditions for the production of the New. "This is perhaps the secret," concludes Deleuze, "to make something exist, and not to judge. If it is so distasteful to judge, this is not because everything is equally valid, but on the contrary because everything that is worthy can only create and distinguish itself by defying judgment."[60]

These three questions concerning the determination, evaluation, and creation of modes of existence serve to demarcate the problematics and tasks of a purely immanent ethics. In rejecting the idea of a transcendental subject, it seeks to define the immanent processes of subjectivation that determine variable modes of existence. In refusing all forms of transcendence, it evaluates the differences between these modes of existence on the basis of purely immanent criteria of power. Finally, in rejecting universals, it analyzes the present in terms of the conditions it presents for the production of the singular, that is, for the creation of new modes of existence.

Notes

1. Michel Foucault, foreword to Gilles Deleuze and Félix Guattari, *Anti-Oedipus: Capitalism and Schizophrenia*, trans. Robert Hurley, Mark Seem, and Helen R. Lane (New York: Viking, 1977), xiii.

2. See Monique Canto-Sperber, "Pour la philosophie morale," *Le débat* 72 (November–December 1992): 40–51.

3. See Foucault's introduction to *The Use of Pleasure*, trans. Robert Hurley (New York: Random House, 1985), 3–32, where he explains the reformulation of the project.

4. Gilles Deleuze, *Negotiations: 1972–1990*, trans. Martin Joughin (New York: Columbia University Press, 1995), 135: "Everything tended toward the great Spinoza-Nietzsche identity" (translation modified). For Deleuze's analyses, see *Nietzsche and Philosophy*, trans. Hugh Tomlinson (New York: Columbia University Press, 1981) (original: 1962); and *Expressionism in Philosophy: Spinoza*, trans. Martin Joughin (New York: Zone Books, 1990) (original: 1968).

5. Deleuze, *Nietzsche and Philosophy*, 1. For the distinction between "morality" and "ethics," see Deleuze, *Negotiations*, 100, 113–14. *Règles facultatives* is a term Deleuze adopts from the sociolinguist William Labov to designate "functions of internal variation and no longer constants"; see Deleuze, *Foucault*, trans. Seán Hand (Minneapolis: University of Minnesota Press, 1988), 147n.18.

6. At best, the Spinozistic and Nietzschean critiques have been accepted as negative moments, exemplary instances of what must be fought *against* and rejected in the ethico-moral domain. See, for example, Alasdair MacIntyre, *After Virtue: A Study in Moral Theory*, 2d ed. (Notre Dame, Ind.: University of Notre Dame Press, 1984), who, for his part, summarizes the contemporary ethical options in the chapter title "Aristotle or Nietzsche?" ("The defensibility of the Nietzschean position turns *in the end* on the answer to the question: was it right in the first place to reject Aristotle?" [117]).

7. Gilles Deleuze, *Critique et clinique* (Paris: Minuit, 1993), 168.

8. Gilles Deleuze, "Qu'est-ce qu'un dispositif?" in *Michel Foucault, philosophe* (Paris: Seuil, 1989), 189.

9. Deleuze, *Critique et clinique*, 171.

10. Gilles Deleuze, *The Fold: Leibniz and the Baroque*, trans. Tom Conley (Minneapolis: University of Minnesota Press, 1993), 73 (translation modified).

11. Gilles Deleuze and Félix Guattari, *What Is Philosophy?* trans. Hugh Tomlinson and Graham Burchell (New York: Columbia University Press, 1994), 74.

12. Deleuze, *Nietzsche and Philosophy*, 89–90. See Immanuel Kant, *Critique of Practical Reason*, trans. Lewis White Beck (Indianapolis: Bobbs-Merrill, 1956), §§7, 31–32: the consciousness of the moral Law is a fact, "not an empirical fact, but the sole fact of pure reason, which by it proclaims itself as originating law."

13. Friedrich Nietzsche, *On the Genealogy of Morals*, trans. Walter Kaufman (New York: Random House, 1967), preface, §§6, 20; essay 3, §§24, 153.

14. Deleuze, *Nietzsche and Philosophy*, 1.

15. For the critical points that follow, see Gilles Deleuze, *Masochism: Coldness and Cruelty*, trans. Jean McNeil (New York: Zone Books, 1989), chap. 7, "Humor, Irony, and the Law," 81–90. See also his analyses in *Kant's Critical Philosophy: The Doctrine of the Faculties*, trans. Hugh Tomlinson and Barbara Habberjam (Minneapolis: University of Minnesota Press, 1984).

16. Deleuze, *Critique et clinique*, 46.

17. Gilles Deleuze and Félix Guattari, *Kafka: Toward a Minor Literature*, trans. Dana Polan (Minneapolis: University of Minnesota Press, 1986), 44–45.

18. Sigmund Freud, *Civilization and Its Discontents*, trans. James Strachey (New York: W. W. Norton and Co., 1961), 72–73.

19. Deleuze, *Masochism*, 86–90. "Perversion" plays an important role in Deleuze's writings as a specific type of mode of existence that retains a positivity of its own.

20. See Gilles Deleuze, *Difference and Repetition*, trans. Paul Patton (New York: Columbia University Press, 1994), 5–8.

21. For Deleuze's analysis of the slave and the priest as modes of existence, see *Nietzsche and Philosophy*, "From *Ressentiment* to the Bad Conscience," 111–45. Deleuze provides a useful summary of his interpretation in *Nietzsche* (Paris: Presses Universitaires de France, 1965), 17–41.

22. Deleuze, *Nietzsche and Philosophy*, 142.

23. Gilles Deleuze and Félix Guattari, *Anti-Oedipus*, trans. Robert Hurley, Mark Seem, and Helen R. Lane (New York: Viking Press, 1977), 215; emphasis added.

24. Deleuze, *Critique et clinique*, 158.

25. Gilles Deleuze and Félix Guattari, *A Thousand Plateaus*, trans. Brian Massumi (Minneapolis: University of Minnesota Press, 1987), 376.

26. Deleuze, *Critique et clinique*, 160. For Deleuze's analysis of the second *Critique*, see *Kant's Critical Philosophy*, chap. 2, 28–45.

27. Deleuze and Guattari, *What Is Philosophy?* 73.

28. Deleuze's analysis of this tradition is found in his two-volume *Cinema*, where he draws a parallel between the philosophy of Pascal and Kierkegaard and the films of Bresson and Dreyer. See Gilles Deleuze, *The Movement-Image*, trans. Hugh Tomlinson and Barbara Habberjam (Minneapolis: University of Minnesota Press, 1986), 114–16; and *The Time-Image*, trans. Hugh Tomlinson and Robert Galeta (Minneapolis: University of Minnesota Press, 1989), 176–79.

29. Friedrich Nietzsche, *Will to Power*, trans. Walter Kaufman and R. J. Hollingdale (New York: Random House, 1967), §§83, 51–52.

30. Gilles Deleuze, *Empiricism and Subjectivity*, trans. Constantin V. Boundas (New York: Columbia University Press, 1991), 87.

31. See Deleuze, *Difference and Repetition*, 86–87.

32. See Deleuze's formulations of "the ethical question" in Spinoza in *Expressionism in Philosophy: Spinoza*: (1) Of what affections are we capable? What is the extent of our power? (226); (2) What must we do to be affected by a maximum of joyful passions? (273); and (3) How can we come to produce active affections? (246).

33. Nietzsche, *Will to Power*, §§532, 289; see also §§489, 270.

34. On the distinction between "arborescent" and "rhizomatic" models of thought, see Deleuze and Guattari, *A Thousand Plateaus*, 3–25. For Spinoza's critique of the Aristotelian tradition, see Gilles Deleuze, *Spinoza: Practical Philosophy*, trans. Robert Hurley (San Francisco: City Lights, 1988), 44–48, and idem, *Expressionism in Philosophy: Spinoza*, 277–78.

35. See Spinoza, *Ethics*, book 3, pro 3, scholium, in *The Collected Works of Spinoza*, trans. Edwin Curley (Princeton, N.J.: Princeton University Press, 1985), 495: "No one has yet determined what a body can do." This clause is repeated like a motif in several of Deleuze's books.

36. Deleuze, *Critique et clinique*, 161.

37. On these points, see Gilles Deleuze, *Périclès et Verdi: La philosophie de François Châtelet* (Paris: Minuit, 1988), 14–17.

38. See Michel Foucault, *The History of Sexuality*, vol. 2, *The Use of Pleasure*; and vol. 3, *The Care of the Self*, trans. Robert Hurley (New York: Pantheon, 1986). The

fourth volume of the series, *Les aveux de la chair* (The confessions of the flesh), was
written but never published.

39. This is particularly true of a certain Hegelianism of the right that still dominates political philosophy and weds the destiny of thought to the state (Alexandre
Kojève and Eric Weil in France, Leo Strauss and Allan Bloom in America). On this
score, see Jacques Derrida, *Spectres de Marx* (Paris: Galilée, 1993), 98–100, where Derrida critiques one of the most recent avatars of this trend, Francis Fukuyama, and
Fukuyama's book *The End of History and the Last Man*.

40. Modern thought thus found itself subordinated to an image of thought derived
from the legislative and juridical organization of the state, leading to the prevalence, in
political philosophy, of such categories as the "republic" of free spirits, the "tribunal"
of reason, the "rights" of man, the consensual "contract," "inquiries" into the understanding (method, recognition, question and response, judgment), and so on. On these
themes, see Deleuze and Guattari, *A Thousand Plateaus*, 374–80.

41. See Deleuze and Guattari, *Anti-Oedipus* and *A Thousand Plateaus*.

42. Immanuel Kant, *Critique of Pure Reason*, trans. Norman Kemp Smith (London:
Macmillan, 1929), A323/B379.

43. *Anti-Oedipus* analyzes "primitive" societies, the state, and capitalism (139–271);
A Thousand Plateaus adds to this an analysis of the war machine (351–423), and in an
essential chapter entitled "Apparatus of Capture" (424–73), it attempts to lay out in
specific terms the complex relations between these various typologies.

44. See Deleuze, *Negotiations*, 86.

45. Gilles Deleuze and Claire Parnet, *Dialogues*, trans. Hugh Tomlinson and Barbara Habberjam (New York: Columbia University Press, 1987), 125, and Deleuze and
Guattari, *A Thousand Plateaus*, 277.

46. On "infantile leftism," see Michael Walzer, "The Politics of Michel Foucault,"
in *Foucault: A Critical Reader*, ed. David Couzens Hoy (New York: Basil Blackwell,
1986), 51. On "neoconservatism," see Jürgen Habermas, *The Philosophical Discourse of
Modernity* (Cambridge, Mass.: MIT Press, 1988).

47. Deleuze analyzes all these distinctions in detail in *Expressionism in Philosophy:
Spinoza*, especially in chap. 16, "The Ethical Vision of the World," 255–72; see also
Spinoza: Practical Philosophy, entry on "Power," 97–104.

48. See Deleuze, *Difference and Repetition*, 41.

49. See Deleuze and Guattari, *What Is Philosophy?* 74: "There is not the slightest
reason for thinking that modes of existence need transcendent values by which they
could be compared, selected, and judged relative to one another. There are only immanent criteria. A possibility of life is evaluated through itself in the movements it
lays out and the intensities it creates on a plane of immanence: what is not laid out or
created is rejected. A mode of existence is good or bad, noble or vulgar, complete or
empty, independently of Good or Evil or any transcendent value: there are never any
criteria other than the tenor of existence, the intensification of life."

50. For instance, in a famous text, which in some respects parallels Nietzsche's analyses in the *Genealogy of Morals*, Spinoza showed how the notion of the Law arose
among the Hebrews from a misunderstanding of affective relations. When God for-
bade Adam to eat the fruit of the Garden of Eden, he did so because he knew it
would affect Adam's body like a poison, decomposing its constitutive relation. But
Adam, unable to perceive these affective relations, mistook the prohibition for a *com-*

mandment, the effect of decomposition as a *punishment*, and the word of God as a *Law* (see Spinoza, letter 19, to Blijenbergh, in *Collected Works*, 357–61). On the important question, Can there be inherently evil modes of existence? see Deleuze's article, "The Letters on Evil (Correspondence with Blyenbergh [Blijenbergh])," in *Spinoza: Practical Philosophy*, 30–43.

51. Pierre Hadot, *Philosophy as a Way of Life*, ed. Arnold I. Davidson (Cambridge, Mass.: Blackwell, 1995), esp. 81–125. See also Gilles Deleuze, "On the Moral Problem in Stoic Philosophy," in *The Logic of Sense*, trans. Mark Lester with Charles Stivale, ed. Constantin V. Boundas (New York: Columbia University Press, 1990), 142–53.

52. See *Expressionism in Philosophy: Spinoza*, chaps. 17–19, pp. 273–320; and *Nietzsche and Philosophy*, chap. 5, pp. 147–98.

53. See Foucault, *Use of Pleasure*, 25–30.

54. For Deleuze and Guattari's development of the concept of the "minor," see *A Thousand Plateaus*, 105–6, 291–92, 469–73; and *Kafka*, chap. 3.

55. Gilles Deleuze, "Post-script on the Societies of Control," in *Negotiations*, 177–82.

56. See Paul Virilio's analyses in *Speed and Politics*, trans. Mark Polizzotti (New York: Semiotext[e], 1986).

57. Deleuze, *Negotiations*, 175.

58. Deleuze and Guattari, *What Is Philosophy?* 112 (translation modified).

59. On these Foucauldian themes, see Deleuze's analyses in his *Foucault*, 115–19, as well as the important passage in *What Is Philosophy?* 111–13.

60. Deleuze, *Critique et clinique*, 169.

Another Always Thinks in Me

Aden Evens, Mani Haghighi, Stacey Johnson, Karen Ocaña, and Gordon Thompson

Freedom and Problem

Our problem is freedom. It is what Gilles Deleuze would call a "true problem," and it brings about the solution it deserves. In fact, the solution to the problem of freedom is its exercise. But let the word "solution" stand in quotation marks: as Bergson has shown, problems may have solutions, but these solutions do not dissolve the problematic nature of true problems. True problems remain problematic, even when solved. What do we mean by "true problems"? For Deleuze, the truth of a problem is measured by its capacity to insist, persist, and return. This constitutes the extrabeing of a problem. A true problem is an Idea, a virtual multiplicity or structure. "Virtual" and "Ideal" express not that the problem is unreal, for it is absolutely real, but rather that it has the being of a problem: *to be solved.* A problem desires its solution; it *is* the desire for its solution. It is not so much that problems move but that they *are* the movements toward their solutions. The virtuality of a problem indicates just this potency, this power of movement from virtual to actual. And this important power of actualization makes the phenomenal world. In *Difference and Repetition,* Deleuze emphasizes that the problem

> takes place in time not between one actual term, however small, and another actual term, but between the virtual and its actualization — in other words, it goes from the structure to its incarnation, from the conditions of a problem to the cases of solution, from the differential elements and their ideal connections to actual terms and diverse real relations which constitute at each moment the actuality of time.[1]

The problem is this progressive movement, the power to make actual, but it does not expend itself in exerting this power. It maintains its virtuality, persisting as virtual even in its actual solution. Undiminished by its incarnation, the potency of a problem is its ability to exceed materiality, even as it makes the material world. It is a capacity to create representations and yet by its very excess to evade their capture. True problems move of their own accord, diving and resurfacing in order to escape the hooks cast by propositional language. By contrast, propositions themselves can do no more than bob up and down with the ripples on the surface, the residual solutions that float as evidence of slippery and powerful subaquatic problems. For language, a problem is always "the one that got away."

Freedom as Problem

Freedom is just such a problem. It actualizes itself in every movement, and it would not, therefore, be incorrect to conclude that movement is the solution to the problem of freedom. But this would invite misunderstanding. We should rather say that movement is the actualization of freedom-*as-problem*, that is, the actual process of freedom problematizing itself. The distinction is important because the rigorous characterization of freedom-as-problem in *Difference and Repetition* has little to do with the traditional philosophical debates over the "problem of freedom." For this reason, we find it necessary here to introduce the term *freedomdum*. As the cogitandum is the power of thought, and the sentiendum the power of sensation, so the freedomdum is the transcendental, ideal, and virtual element of freedom, the very power of movement. Although it does not exist apart from its actualization, freedomdum, as the power of every movement, is conceptually distinct from the movements in which it is actualized. In particular, it is conceptually distinct from the movement *of its own* actualization, the becoming-free that is true *Freedom*. Freedomdum is the being of freedom, its degree zero of signification, and it is thus distinguishable from freedom itself, which is always a movement, a becoming-free. Insofar as they direct the flow of problems from virtual to actual, however, both freedomdum and freedom are radically different from the false problem of free will that is a merely conscious, and therefore disposable, phenomenon.

Freedom is in every movement, and movement always begins in the virtual. Therefore, freedom is a passage, or a passing through, from virtual to actual; it is the movement of actualization. It is a perpetually contorting dynamism, from problem to solution and from abstract to concrete. Because it is the movement in every movement, the power of freedom is a pure power, and it is this purity that makes freedom unique among problems. It is the power of power that folds back on itself and carries itself to the nth degree. In Deleuze's words, "[F]reedom has [a] physical sense: 'to detonate' an explosive, to use it for more and more powerful movements."[2] The problem explodes like something abrupt, brutal, and revolutionary.

The Problem of Unfreedom

But why call this actualizing movement "freedom"? After all, it has been given
other names. In *Bergsonism,* for example, Deleuze aligns it with élan vital. In
the context of the discussion so far, we have not justified our preference for the
term "freedom," while we could easily put forward reasons why it is insufficient or inappropriate. It appears at this point that there is no *trick* to freedom,
and this is a crucial problem. How could freedom, as the dynamism of every
movement, the power of every power, fail to manifest itself always and everywhere? If freedom perpetually generates and affirms itself, then how is it that
powerlessness can become manifest? Where could powerlessness begin, and
how could it remain powerlessness? Here it may seem that we have deval-
ued the importance of freedom by seeing signs of it all around. If freedom
is everywhere, how can we talk about the *"problem* of freedom" and mean
anything at all?

But just where freedom seemed to lose its potency, and hence its prob-
lematicity, it has already reasserted itself as a problem. Its new problematic
might better be called the "problem of unfreedom." The problem of unfreedom poses a series of questions already asked by Spinoza and Reich. It is also
a question to which Deleuze often returns:

> Why are [people] proud of their own enslavement? . . . Why is it so difficult not
> only to win but to bear freedom?[3]

> Why do people fight *for* their servitude as stubbornly as though it were their
> salvation? . . . [T]he astonishing thing is not that some people steal or that others
> occasionally go out on strike, but rather that all those who are starving do not
> steal as a regular practice, and all those who are exploited are not continually out
> on strike.[4]

Clearly, despite the superabundance of freedom on the ontological level,
we haven't got the hang of it in the social field. This is a problem that
the "free will versus determinacy debate" has failed to address. Neither the
self-determinism of the centered subject nor the pious resignation of God's
servants answers the question, How can we love fascism?

Free Will as False Problem

Following Spinoza and Nietzsche, Deleuze attempts to make freedom a purely
positive power. To do this, it is essential to make a clear distinction between
freedom as positivity, on the one hand, and "free will," on the other. In effect, it is necessary to "liberate" freedom from the determinations of the will.
According to the doctrine of free will, agents can determine their own actions by making choices. Free will thus involves the agent in a false game
of determination: the power of determination is mistaken for the measure of
freedom. The architectonics of free will is therefore inherently despotic, and

the philosophy that theorizes it, inevitably a state-philosophy: the alleged determinator of destiny is identified as the freest man, while the affirmer of chance is dismissed as the nonchalant and passive bystander in the game of determination. The negative power of free will lies precisely in its capability to mask the essential indeterminacy of all becomings; and it is for this reason that state-philosophy in general, and the philosophy of free will in particular, thrive on the generation and cultivation of stupidity. As a mask, however, the face of free will can only articulate a static and frozen expression. It posits a false subjective force disconnected from its creative capabilities. Commenting on Nietzsche's important assertion that "there is no 'being' behind doing," Deleuze writes:

> We create grotesque representations of force and will, we separate force from what it can do, setting it up in ourselves as "worthy" because it holds back from what it cannot do, but as "blameworthy" in the thing where it manifests precisely the force that it has. We split the will in two, inventing a neutral subject endowed with free will to which we give the capacity to act and refrain from action.[5]

In this way, the projection of freedom as free will on the plane of consciousness amounts to a mere representation. This, as we have seen, abstracts freedom from itself (that is, from movement) and neutralizes its positive force. The subject is postulated, in Nietzsche's words, to facilitate "the sublime self-deception that interprets weakness as freedom."[6] Clearly, then, the elimination of the neutral subject is not the elimination of agency. Rather, as we shall see, it is the prerequisite for agency[7] to affirm and be free. The postulation of free will simultaneously marks the birth of the subject and the rejection of affirmation. And so, self-deception and stupidity remain the only strategies with which the game of determination can be kept from derailing.

Freedom as pure positivity, in contrast, does not have the determination of a specific goal as its function. On the contrary, its function amounts to a pure affirmation of chance; it is the affirmation of the absolute indeterminacy of the dice throw. Whereas the postulation of free will implies the falsehood of a passive, neutral subject, the affirmation of indeterminacy marks a positive dynamism: "The undetermined is not a simple imperfection in our knowledge or a lack in the object: it is a perfectly positive, objective structure which acts as a focus or horizon within perception."[8] Rather than a passive resignation in the face of indeterminate results, the affirmation of the dice throw actively engages not only the content of destiny but also the indeterminacy that gives rise to it. The problem of unfreedom, therefore, must be understood first of all as a problem of negativity, a failure to affirm. The futile obsession to determine the content of destiny becomes the primary force behind the manifestation of powerlessness; crucially, however, this obsession always carries within it the seeds of its own demise. As such, the problem of unfreedom can be identified as the negative effect of what we earlier called the ontological superabundance of freedom. Before we explore the affirmative strategies of unmasking this negativity we must first map its generation.

The Genesis of the Negative

Traditional dialectics identifies the negative as the driving force behind affirmation, thus positing affirmation as an *effect* of negation: "It is as though Difference were evil and already negative, so that it could produce affirmation only by expiation — that is by assuming at once both the weight of that which is denied and negation itself."[9] But Deleuze has a radically different conception of the negative. In *Difference and Repetition*, the negative is presented as a trace rather than a driving force or a motor: it is a residual ripple on the turbulent surface, while the turbulence itself is the mark of freedom moving. As such, negation does not *generate* affirmation as the product of a dialectical apparatus but rather *follows* it, as the foam floating on waves:

> Negation is difference, but difference seen from its underside, seen from below. Seen the right way up, from top to bottom, difference is affirmation. This proposition, however, means many things: that difference is an object of affirmation; that affirmation itself is multiple; that it is creation but also that it must be created, as affirming difference, as being difference in itself.... Negation results from affirmation: this means that negation arises in the wake of affirmation or beside it, *but only as the shadow of the more profound genetic element* — of that power or "will" which engenders the affirmation and the difference in the affirmation.[10]

Difference is an object of affirmation, and affirmation is an object of itself. Here lies the absolute profundity of affirmation: it is at once subject *and* object of its own desire while it propels difference. We have seen how negation, as a posterior structure trailing the movement of affirmation, functions as a mask: it folds back on itself to cover over the movement that generates it. This movement of folding back attempts to congeal the primary differential movement into a static determinable form. As such it manages to pose the negative problem of unfreedom. It is for this reason that we read freedom as a movement of unmasking. But there is more to freedom than just that: it is also a process of cartography, an inscription of the turbulence of chance in thought.

The Introduction of the Unthought into Thought

Like any true problem, freedom is an Idea, a virtual and potent structure. For this reason, Deleuze often talks about Problem-Idea complexes made up of differential elements and relations that subsist in virtuality. Because the

virtual is extrapropositional and subrepresentative, and because it does not resemble the propositions in which it is actualized, Deleuze distinguishes two
affirmations, the primary, "causal" affirmation that generates difference and
produces, as a residue or excess, the secondary, "effective" affirmation. This
second affirmation, which is propositional, affirms the differences it has actualized. Freedom moves in-between these two affirmations, one virtual, the
other actual; one unconscious and extralinguistic, the other representational
and propositional:

> [T]he entire positivity of Ideas is developed between the affirmations of chance
> (imperative and decisive questions) and the resultant affirmations to which these
> give rise (decisive resolutions or cases of solution). The game of the problematic
> and the imperative has replaced that of the hypothetical and the categorical; the
> game of difference and repetition has replaced that of the Same and represen-
> tation. The dice are thrown against the sky, with all the force of displacement
> of the aleatory point, with their imperative points like lightning, forming ideal
> problem-constellations in the sky. They fall back to Earth with all the force of
> the victorious solutions which bring back the throw.[11]

The movement from problem to solution, that is, the movement of freedom, is the throw of the dice. The phenomenal world is determined by this
throw, but the throw itself is an affirmation of indeterminacy and chance, limited by no determination and subject to no external rules. The dice are thrown
from a purely virtual and ideal aleatory point that is freedomdum. In the terms
of differential calculus, the curve that moves among the singular points of a
diagram to join them does not move in an infinitesimally small gap, but rather
in a nonspatial site defined by difference in itself. The generation of ideas
as conjunctions of singular points, as well as the actualization of a virtual potency, both presuppose an ideal, nonspatial movement. This movement cannot
be represented in an image of thought. Thus, the passage from the undetermined to determination does not take place over a spatiotemporal continuum,
but all at once, with the jolt of a sign: every movement is a sudden explosion
of the virtual upon the actual. The explosion of actualization also implies a
movement of individuation: it differentiates reality into phenomena that are
the stuff of conscious thought: "[T]he diagram, in so far as it exposes a set
of relations between forces, is not a place but rather a 'non-place': it is a place
only of mutation. Suddenly things are not perceived or propositions articulated in the same way."[12] Every determination is a crossing of a gap from
virtual to actual: this gap is the site of the problem; it is the problematic. Yet
to cross it, as we have said, is not to move in space or time. Determination itself does not take place *in* space and time simply because every determination
is a determination *of* space and time. Rather than its a priori determinations,
the space and time of a problem are its ideal footprints.

We have seen that problems in general, and freedom in particular, move
in ideal sites that are nonspatiotemporal. These movements in turn determine

the actual spatiotemporal characteristics of cases of solution. To open thought to these movements is to go beyond representation; it is to introduce into thought its own transcendental instance, its untimely here and now. And so to think freedom is to think the unthought: actualization overflows and backlogs, creating an excess in the virtual. The introduction of freedom into thought, which produces the primary affirmation, makes thought double back on itself: thinking the unthought regenerates a positive and creative freedom, the freedom of the new mutant.

The ideal-problematic passage from virtuality to actuality is often described in terms of a violence or an aggression of thought. For Deleuze, "every thought becomes an aggression."[13] Freedom flashes when extreme intensity foists itself upon a body, deterritorializing thought, transforming it and giving it the power to escape. Overloaded, thought can only think what is not thought, can only think what is new. Only such an intense aggression allows thought to open itself up to the unthought, though intensity and aggression must never be confused with carelessness, annihilation, or abolition. When thought is overtaken by intensities that approach suddenly and from blindspots and that warp the time and space around them, when thought is too full to digest its content, but rumbles and churns in overfull intensity, then thought can no longer contain itself or separate itself from its content. Thinking the unthought, thought mutates and *becomes* the unthought.

This mutation undermines and overwhelms all identity, even that of thought itself. The movement of thought, the movement of freedom in thought, presupposes a fracture in the thinking agent: the I must split to give thought room. In order for the agent, the I, the it, the bird, the dice, the stone to start thinking, they become *touchstones,* flying-stones, or skipping-stones skimming the waves: they are becoming cormorant, growing wings, fishingbirds flying high and low, transcendent and immanent, grappling or battling with their prey. The result is a conjunction of flows in which the hunter and the prey can no longer be distinguished from each other: for the bird, hunting is a becoming-fish, and the fish is always a part of the bird-assemblage. As flying objects, the thinking agents must dive into the undetermined turbulence of the waves; they must throw themselves into chance. To wait for calm waters, to cheat the indeterminacy of chance, is to risk starvation.

Chance and Destiny

As a movement that rejects both aspects of the game of determination (that is, free will and determinacy), freedom *uses* chance without trying to *master* it; it affirms chance without trying to win it; *it really lets go.* And so, the chance-destiny inscribed by the dice throw has a Dionysian character: it is "not a probability distributed over several throws but all chance at once; not a final, desired, willed combination, but the fatal combination, fatal and loved, *amor fati*."[14]

As we have seen, Deleuze follows Nietzsche in positing two aspects for each throw of the dice: the dice that are thrown (to the sky) are the same, and yet distinguishable from, the dice that fall back (on the earth). The throwing of the dice is the affirmation of indeterminacy from the aleatory point. The falling back of the dice constitutes a different sort of affirmation; it affirms the actualization of freedom, the organization of singular points in their concrete positions on the diagram, and the generation of the cases of solution. The dice thrown affirm the *indeterminacy* of destiny, while the dice falling back affirm its *content*. These in turn correspond to the two aspects of freedom that we have distinguished here as freedomdum (the *being* of freedom-as-problem) and freedom (the *becoming*-dynamic of freedom). "The dice throw affirms becoming and it affirms the being of becoming."[15] It is this double affirmation of pure chance that we have in mind when we speak of freedom as a force that carries itself to the nth degree.

Unfreedom implies that the game of dice has been played badly. The game is played badly if the players pretend not to be playing (reserving the right to play only for a determining God, craving to be eaten by God), or if they try to cheat chance by second-guessing it (fixing the game in an attempt to internalize divinity, craving to eat God). The idea, however, is neither to be subservient to Gods nor to become a Human-God, but rather to metamorphose into *personne* or a "semi-divine being":

> The question that continually returns is . . . the following. If the forces within man compose a form only by entering into a relation with forms from the outside, with what new forms do they now risk entering into a relation, and what new form will emerge that is neither God nor Man? This is the correct place for the problem which Nietzsche called '*der Übermensch*.'[16]

The being of *Übermensch* is implicated in a power to make decisions. In *Bergsonism*, Deleuze makes this explicit when he writes that "true freedom lies in a power to decide, to constitute problems themselves. And this 'semi-divine' power entails the disappearance of false problems as much as the creative upsurge of true ones."[17] In *Difference and Repetition* he goes on to say that "problems are inseparable from a power of decision, a *fiat* which, when we are infused by it, makes us semi-divine beings."[18] But this power is not our own. That we are infused with a power of decision does not mean that we select our imperatives or that our questions emanate from the I. We are not the authors of our destiny. Even "the gods themselves are subject to the . . . sky-chance."[19] This is why theft is primary to thought: because "another always thinks in me, another who must also be thought."[20] The power of decision is realized in the thought of these others. This is not a power that we own; it is not a power that *can* be owned. It is only available in theft. We must steal our freedom.

And in this labor, agency assumes its paradoxical aspect, for "when it comes down to it, you are all alone, and yet you are like a conspiracy of criminals. You are no longer an author, you are a production studio, you have never been more populated."[21] Agency, therefore, is a doubling of an outside-population within oneself, or rather, it is the creation of a self through a folding-in of an outside pack. I drink the ocean; my mouth opens; and a whole chorus sings.

The Problem of Creativity

The dice throw is an ideal game with thought as its playground. ("Ideas are the problematic combinations which result from throws.")[22] As such, it may seem that the game of chance and freedom is played in thought alone and nowhere else. Deleuze implies as much when, in *The Logic of Sense*, he writes:

> The ideal game of which we speak cannot be played by either man or God. It can only be thought as nonsense. But precisely for this reason, it is the reality of thought itself and the unconscious of pure thought.... [O]nly thought finds it possible *to affirm all chance and to make chance into an object of affirmation*. If one tries to play this game other than in thought, nothing happens; and if one tries to produce a result other than the work of art, nothing is produced. This game is reserved then for thought and art. In it there are nothing but victories for those who know how to play, that is how to affirm and ramify chance, instead of dividing it *in order to* dominate it, *in order to* wager, *in order to* win.[23]

The affirmation of chance takes place as the production of thought, though thought itself is located in a space unmarked by the presence of either man or God: it is a thought from the *outside*. For this reason, the double affirmation of thought and art as the prerequisites for the exercise of freedom does not suggest a solipsistic interiority: to think freely is always to think the outside, as a fold, thought is a doubling of the unthought within a body. As such, this doubling can never be

> the projection of the interior; on the contrary, it is the interiorization of the outside. It is not the doubling of the One, but a redoubling of the other.... It is never the other who is the double in the doubling process, it is a self that lives me as the double of the other: I do not encounter myself on the outside, I find the other in me.[24]

The presence of the outside within thought, and the determination of the phenomenal world through the actualizing movement of thought, form the double movement of Deleuze's "transcendental empiricism." Thought is never a merely virtual potency detached from its actualization; rather, it is always an actualization of a virtuality; it is at once transcendent and immanent. By the same token, "a problem always has the solution it deserves," while the solution always carries within it the problem in its persisting virtuality. And so, we could say that the virtual and the actual, or the problem and its solution, are in a relation of *parallelism*.

In *Spinoza: Practical Philosophy,* Deleuze discusses Spinoza's thesis of parallelism between the mind and the body: "One seeks to acquire a knowledge of the powers of the body," he writes, "in order to discover, *in a parallel fashion,* the powers of the mind that elude consciousness."[25] The movements of thought are always on the level of the body, and the actions of the body are in themselves always thought. The falling back of the dice is the threshold that brings thought to the body. This embodiment is the insistence, persistence, and return of art to life. For as Deleuze has written, "[T]here is no other aesthetic problem than that of the insertion of art into everyday life."[26]

It would be misleading to think of art as the manifestation of thought in the external world because the virtuality of thought persists and insists even in its actualized form. Instead, we must say that art is the free movement of the unthought in its envelopment of thought: it is the freeing of thought. Every instance of the unthought's free movement is an instance at which art is actualized. In this way, the problem of freedom once again reasserts itself in yet another new form. This new problematic might be called the "problem of aesthetic creativity." The problem of creativity suggests a whole new series of questions already posed by Nietzsche and Bergson. It is also a problem that Deleuze strongly associates with the last volumes of Foucault's writing. This new return of the problem of freedom through the notion of creativity by no means suggests a return to a subject-centered agency:

> [Creative emotion] no longer has anything to do with an individual who contests or even invents, nor with a society that constrains.... [It is] precisely a cosmic Memory, that actualizes all the levels at the same time, that liberates man from the plane or the level that is proper to him, in order to make him a creator, adequate to the whole movement of creation.... It is the genesis of intuition in intelligence. If man accedes to the open creative totality, it is therefore by acting, by creating, rather than by contemplating.[27]

The genesis of intuition in intelligence, or the introduction of the unthought into thought, is therefore to be distinguished from mere contemplation. Instead, true thought always amounts to the extension of thought into action. For Deleuze, real thinking is inseparable from acting, and true action is always a free movement of creativity:

> Art ... connects the tableau of cruelty with that of stupidity, and discovers underneath consumption a schizophrenic clattering of the jaws, and underneath the most ignoble destructions of war, still more processes of consumption. It aesthetically reproduces the illusions and mystifications which make up the real essence of this civilisation, in order that Difference may at last be expressed with a force of anger which is itself repetitive and capable of introducing the strangest selection, even if this is only a contraction here and there — in other words, a freedom for the end of a world.[28]

Notes

1. Gilles Deleuze, *Difference and Repetition*, trans. Paul Patton (New York: Columbia University Press, 1994), 183.

2. Gilles Deleuze, *Bergsonism*, trans. Hugh Tomlinson and Barbara Habberjam (New York: Zone Books, 1988), 107.

3. Gilles Deleuze, *Spinoza: Practical Philosophy*, trans. Robert Hurley (San Francisco: City Lights, 1988), 10.

4. Gilles Deleuze and Félix Guattari, *Anti-Oedipus: Capitalism and Schizophrenia*, trans. Robert Hurley, Mark Seem, and Helen R. Lane (Minneapolis: University of Minnesota Press, 1983), 29.

5. Gilles Deleuze, *Nietzsche and Philosophy*, trans. Hugh Tomlinson (New York: Columbia University Press, 1983), 23.

6. Friedrich Nietzsche, *On the Genealogy of Morals*, trans. Walter Kaufmann and R. J. Hollingdale (New York: Vintage, 1989), 46.

7. By agency, we do not mean an originary source of change, but rather a locus of transformation, a place where change takes place.

8. Deleuze, *Difference and Repetition*, 169.

9. Ibid., 53.

10. Ibid., 55.

11. Ibid., 283–84.

12. Gilles Deleuze, *Foucault*, trans. Seán Hand (Minneapolis: University of Minnesota Press, 1986), 85.

13. Deleuze, *Difference and Repetition*, xx.

14. Deleuze, *Nietzsche and Philosophy*, 27.

15. Ibid., 25.

16. Deleuze, *Foucault*, 130.

17. Deleuze, *Bergsonism*, 15.

18. Deleuze, *Difference and Repetition*, 197.

19. Ibid., 199.

20. Ibid., 199–200.

21. Gilles Deleuze and Clair Parnet, *Dialogues*, trans. Hugh Tomlinson and Barbara Habberjam (New York: Columbia University Press, 1987), 9.

22. Deleuze, *Difference and Repetition*, 198.

23. Deleuze, *The Logic of Sense*, trans. Mark Lester, ed. Constantin V. Boundas (New York: Columbia University Press, 1990), 60.

24. Deleuze, *Foucault*, 98.

25. Deleuze, *Spinoza: Practical Philosophy*, 18.

26. Deleuze, *Difference and Repetition*, 293.

27. Deleuze, *Bergsonism*, 111.

28. Deleuze, *Difference and Repetition*, 293.

Select Bibliography
Compiled by Timothy S. Murphy and Daniel W. Smith

A complete bibliography of Deleuze's works, by Timothy S. Murphy, can be found in *Deleuze: A Critical Reader*, ed. Paul Patton (Oxford: Blackwell, 1996), 270–300.

Principal Books by Deleuze

1952

With André Cresson. *David Hume: Sa vie, son oeuvre, avec un exposé de sa philosophie*. Paris: Presses Universitaires de France.

1953

Empirisme et subjectivité: Essai sur la nature humaine selon Hume. Paris: Presses Universitaires de France. English translation: *Empiricism and Subjectivity: An Essay on Hume's Theory of Human Nature*, trans. Constantin V. Boundas (New York: Columbia University Press, 1991), with a new preface by Deleuze.

1962

Nietzsche et la philosophie. Paris: Presses Universitaires de France. English translation: *Nietzsche and Philosophy*, trans. Hugh Tomlinson (New York: Columbia University Press, 1983), with a new preface by Deleuze.

1963

La philosophie critique de Kant: Doctrine des facultés. Paris: Presses Universitaires de France. English translation: *Kant's Critical Philosophy: The Doctrine of the Faculties*, trans. Hugh Tomlinson and Barbara Habberjam (Minneapolis: University of Minnesota Press, 1984), with a new preface by Deleuze.

1964

Marcel Proust et les signes. Paris: Presses Universitaires de France. The second edition, *Proust et les signes* (1970), includes an additional chapter, "La machine littéraire." The third edition (1976) adds a new conclusion, "Présence et fonction de la folie, l'arraignée." English translation (of 2d ed.): *Proust and Signs,* trans. Richard Howard (New York: George Braziller, 1972).

1965

Nietzsche: Sa vie, son oeuvre, avec un exposé de sa philosophie. Paris: Presses Universitaires de France.

1966

Le Bergsonisme. Paris: Presses Universitaires de France. English translation: *Bergsonism,* trans. Hugh Tomlinson and Barbara Habberjam (New York: Zone Books, 1988), with a new afterword by Deleuze.

1967

Présentation de Sacher-Masoch. Paris: Minuit. English translation: *Masochism,* trans. Jean McNeil (New York: Zone Books, 1989).

1968

Différence et répétition. Paris: Presses Universitaires de France. English translation: *Difference and Repetition,* trans. Paul Patton (New York: Columbia University Press, 1994), with a new preface by Deleuze.
Spinoza et le problème de l'expression. Paris: Minuit. English translation: *Expressionism in Philosophy: Spinoza,* trans. Martin Joughin (New York: Zone Books, 1990).

1969

Logique du sens. Paris: Minuit. English translation: *The Logic of Sense,* trans. Mark Lester with Charles Stivale, ed. Constantin V. Boundas (New York: Columbia University Press, 1990).

1970

Spinoza: Textes choisis. Paris: Presses Universitaires de France. 2d ed.: *Spinoza: Philosophie pratique* (Paris: Minuit, 1981), includes three new chapters. English translation (of 2d ed.): *Spinoza: Practical Philosophy,* trans. Robert Hurley (San Francisco: City Lights, 1988).

1972

With Félix Guattari. *Capitalisme et schizophrénie.* Vol. 1, *L'Anti-Oedipe.* Paris: Minuit. English translation: *Anti-Oedipus: Capitalism and Schizophrenia,* trans. Robert Hurley, Mark Seem, and Helen R. Lane (New York: Viking Press, 1977).

1975

With Félix Guattari. *Kafka: Pour une litterature mineure.* Paris: Minuit. English translation: *Kafka: Toward a Minor Literature,* trans. Dana Polan (Minneapolis: University of Minnesota Press, 1986).

1977

With Claire Parnet. *Dialogues.* Paris: Flammarion. English translation: *Dialogues,* trans. Hugh Tomlinson and Barbara Habberjam (New York: Columbia University Press, 1987), with a new preface by Deleuze.

1980

With Félix Guattari. *Capitalisme et schizophrenie.* Vol. 2, *Mille plateaux.* Paris: Minuit. English translation: *A Thousand Plateaus: Capitalism and Schizophrenia,* trans. Brian Massumi (Minneapolis: University of Minnesota Press, 1987).

1981

Francis Bacon: Logique de la sensation. Paris: Éditions de la Différence. 2d, rev. ed., 1984. English translation (of 2d ed.): *Francis Bacon: The Logic of Sensation,* trans. Daniel W. Smith (London: Verso Books, 1998).

1983

Cinema-1: L'image-mouvement. Paris: Minuit. English translation: *Cinema 1: The Movement-Image,* trans. Hugh Tomlinson and Barbara Habberjam (Minneapolis: University of Minnesota Press, 1986), with a new preface by Deleuze.

1985

Cinéma-2: L'image-temps. Paris: Minuit. English translation: *Cinema 2: The Time-Image,* trans. Hugh Tomlinson and Robert Galeta (Minneapolis: University of Minnesota Press, 1989).

1986

Foucault. Paris: Minuit. English translation: *Foucault,* trans. Seán Hand (Minneapolis: University of Minnesota Press, 1988).

1988

Le pli: Leibniz et le baroque. Paris: Minuit. English translation: *The Fold: Leibniz and the Baroque,* trans. Tom Conley (Minneapolis: University of Minnesota Press, 1993).

1990

Pourparlers 1972–1990. Paris: Minuit. English translation: *Negotiations 1972–1990,* trans. Martin Joughin (New York: Columbia University Press, 1995).

1991

With Félix Guattari. *Qu'est-ce que la philosophie?* Paris: Minuit. English translation: *What Is Philosophy?* trans. Hugh Tomlinson and Graham Burchell (New York: Columbia University Press, 1994).

1993

Critique et clinique. Paris: Minuit. English translation: *Essays Critical and Clinical,* trans. Daniel W. Smith and Michael A. Greco (Minneapolis: University of Minnesota Press, 1997).

Articles, Interviews, and Prefaces

1945

"Description de la femme: Pour une philosophie d'Autrui sexuée." *Poésie* 45, no. 28 (October–December): 28–39.

1946

"Du Christ à la bourgeoisie." *Espace:* 93–106.
"Dires et profils." *Poésie* 47, no. 36 (December): 68–78.
"Mathèse, science et philosophie." Introduction to *Études sur la Mathèse ou anarchie et hiérarchie de la science,* by Jean Malfatti de Montereggio, ix–xxiv. Paris: Éditions du Griffon d'Or.

1947

Introduction to *La religieuse,* by Denis Diderot, vii–xx. Paris: Éditions Marcel Daubin.

1953

Introduction to *Instincts et institutions,* edited by Gilles Deleuze, viii–xi. Paris: Hachette.

1954

"Jean Hyppolite, 'Logique et existence.'" Book review. *Revue philosophique de la France et de l'étranger* 144, nos. 7–9 (July–September): 457–60.

1956

"Bergson 1859–1941." In *Les philosophes célèbres,* edited by Maurice Merleau-Ponty, 292–99. Paris: Éditions d'Art Lucien Mazenod.
"La conception de la différence chez Bergson." *Les etudes Bergsoniennes* 4:77–112.
"'Descartes, l'homme et l'oeuvre,' par Ferdinand Alquié." Book review. *Cahiers du sud* 43, no. 337 (October): 473–75.

1959

"Sens et valeurs" (on Nietzsche). *Arguments* 15:20–28. Reprinted in revised form in *Nietzsche et la philosophie.*

1961

"Lucrèce et le naturalisme." *Études philosophiques* 1:19–29. Reprinted in revised form as an appendix to *Logique du sens.*
"De Sacher-Masoch au masochisme." *Arguments* 21:40–46.

1962

"250ᵉ anniversaire de la naissance de Rousseau. Jean-Jacques Rousseau, précurseur de Kafka, de Céline et de Ponge." *Arts* 872 (6–12 June): 3.

1963

"L'idée de genèse dans l'esthétique de Kant." *Revue d'esthétique* 16, no. 2 (April–June): 113–36.
"Mystère d'Ariane" (on Nietzsche). *Bulletin de la société français d'études nietzschéennes* (March): 12–15. Reprinted in *Philosophie* 17 (winter 1987): 67–72. A revised version of this essay later appeared in *Magazine littéraire* 298 (April 1992): 21–24, and was included in *Critique et clinique.*
"Raymond Roussel ou l'horreur du vide." Book review of *Raymond Roussel,* by Michel Foucault. *Arts* (23 October).
"Unité de 'A la recherche du Temps perdu.'" *Révue de metaphysique et de morale* 4 (October–December): 427–42. Reprinted in revised form in *Marcel Proust et les signes.*

1964

"Il a été mon maître" (on Sartre). *Arts* (28 October–3 November): 8–9. Reprinted in Jean-Jacques Brochier, *Pour Sartre* (Paris: Éditions Jean-Claude Lattès, 1995), 82–88.

1965

"Pierre Klossowski ou les corps-langage." *Critique* 214:199–219. Reprinted in revised form as an appendix to *Logique du sens*.

1966

"Gilbert Simondon, 'L'individu et sa genèse physico-biologique.'" Book review. *Revue philosophique de la France et de l'étranger* 156, nos. 1–3 (January–March): 115–18.

"L'homme, une existence douteuse." Book review of *Les mots et les choses*, by Michel Foucault. *Le nouvel observateur* (1 June): 32–34.

"Philosophie de la série noire" (on hard-boiled detective fiction). *Arts & loisirs* 18 (26 January–1 February): 12–13. Reprinted in *Roman* 24 (September 1988): 43–47.

"Renverser le Platonisme." *Revue de métaphysique et de morale* 71, no. 4 (October–December): 426–38. Reprinted in revised form as an appendix to *Logique du sens*.

1967

"Conclusions: Sur la volonté de puissance et l'éternel retour." In *Cahiers de Royaumont: Philosophie #VI: Nietzsche*, 275–87. Paris: Minuit.

"L'éclat de rire de Nietzsche." Interview with Guy Dumur. *Le nouvel observateur* (5 April): 40–41.

Introduction to *La bête humaine*, by Émile Zola. In *Oeuvres complètes*, edited by Henri Mitterand, vol. 6, pp. 13–21. Paris: Cercle du livre précieux. Reprinted in revised form as an appendix to *Logique du sens* and as the foreword to the Gallimard edition of *La bête humaine* (Paris, 1977), 7–24.

"La méthode de dramatisation." *Bulletin de la société française de philosophie* 61, no. 3 (July–September): 89–118.

"Mystique et masochisme." Interview with Madeleine Chapsal. *La quinzaine littéraire* 25 (1–15 April): 12–13.

"Une théorie d'Autrui (Autrui, Robinson et le pervers)" (on Michel Tournier's *Vendredi*). *Critique* 241:503–25. Reprinted in revised form as an appendix to *Logique du sens* and as a postface to Tournier's *Vendredi ou les limbes du Pacifique* (Paris: Gallimard, 1972), 257–83.

With Michel Foucault. General introduction *Le gai savoir, et fragments posthumes*, by F. Nietzsche, i–iv. Paris: Gallimard.

1968

"A propos de l'édition des oeuvres complètes de Nietzsche." Interview with Jean-Noël Vuarnet. *Les lettres françaises* 1223 (28 February–5 March): 5, 7, 9.

"Le schizophrène et le mot" (on Carroll and Artaud). *Critique* 255–256 (August–September): 731–46. English translations: "The Schizophrenic and Language: Surface and Depth in Lewis Carroll and Antonin Artaud," in *Textual Strategies: Perspectives in Poststructuralist Criticism*, edited by J. Harari (Ithaca, N.Y.: Cornell University Press, 1979), 277–95, and in *Literature and Psychoanalysis*, edited by E. Kurzweil and W. Phillips (New York: Columbia University Press, 1983).

1969

"Gilles Deleuze parle de la philosophie." Interview with Jeannette Columbel. *La quinzaine littéraire* 68 (1–15 March): 18–19.

"Spinoza et la méthode générale de M. Gueroult." Book review of *Spinoza*, vol. 1, by Martial Gueroult. *Revue de metaphysique et de morale* 74, no. 4 (October–December): 426–37.

1970

"Faille et feux locaux: Kostas Axelos." *Critique* 26, no. 275 (April): 344–51.

"Un nouvel archiviste." Book review of *L'archaeologie du savoir*, by Michel Foucault. *Critique* 274 (March): 195–209. Published as a separate volume by Fata Morgana (1972). Reprinted in revised form in Deleuze's *Foucault*. English translation: "A New Archivist," in *Theoretical Strategies*, by Stephen Muecke, edited by Peter Botsman (Sydney: Local Consumption, 1982).

"Proust et les signes." *La quinzaine littéraire* 103 (1–15 October): 18–21. Extract from "La machine littéraire," an essay added in the second edition of *Proust et les signes*.

"Schizologie." Preface to *Le schizo et les langues*, by Louis Wolfson. Paris: Gallimard. Reprinted in revised form in *Critique et clinique*.

With Félix Guattari. "Le synthèse disjonctive." *L'arc* 43 (issue entitled: *Klossowski*): 54–62. Reprinted in revised form in *L'Anti-Oedipe*.

1971

With Michel Foucault, Denis Langlois, Claude Mauriac, and Denis Perrier-Daville. "Questions à Marcellin." *Le nouvel observateur* (5 July): 15.

1972

"Appréciation" (of Jean-François Lyotard's *Discours, figure*). *La quinzaine littéraire* 140 (1 May): 19.

"Ce que les prisonniers attendent de nous . . ." (on the Groupe d'Information sur les Prisons). *Le nouvel observateur* (31 January): 24.

"Gilles Deleuze présente Hélène Cixous ou l'écriture stroboscopique." Book review of *Neutre*, by Hélène Cixous. *Le monde*, 11 August, 10.

"Hume." In *Histoire de la philosophie*, edited by François Châtelet. Vol. 4, *Les lumières*, 65–78. Paris: Hachette. Reprinted in *La Philosophie*, edited by François Châtelet, vol. 2, *De Galilée à Jean-Jacques Rousseau* (Verviers, Belgium: Marabout, 1979), 226–39.

"Joyce indirect." *Change* 11:54–59. The article is an assemblage, by Jean Paris, of previously written texts by Deleuze on Joyce.

"'Qu'est-ce que c'est, tes "machines désirantes" a toi?'" Introduction to "Sainte Jackie, Comedienne et Bourreau," by Pierre Bénichou. *Les temps modernes* 316 (November): 854–56.

"A quoi reconnait-on le structuralisme?" In *Histoire de la philosophie*, edited by François Châtelet. Vol. 8, *Le XXe siècle*. Paris: Hachette. Reprinted in *La philosophie*, edited by François Châtelet, vol. 4, *au XXe siècle* (Verviers, Belgium: Marabout, 1979), 293–329.

"Trois problèmes de groupe." Foreword to *Psychanalyse et transversalité*, by Félix Guattari. Paris: François Maspero, i–xi. Reprinted as "Pierre-Félix," *Chimères* 23 (summer 1994): 7–21. English translation: "Three Group Problems," translated by Mark Seem, *Semiotext(e): Anti-Oedipus* 2, no. 3 (1977): 99–109.

With Félix Guattari. "Sur capitalisme et schizophrénie." Interview with Catherine Backès-Clément. *L'arc* 49 (issue entitled: *Deleuze*). Reprinted in 1980, 47–55. Also reprinted in *Pourparlers 1972–1990*.

With Félix Guattari. "Capitalismo e schizofrenia." Interview by Vittorio Marchetti. *Tempi moderni* 12:47–64. Reprinted in *Una tomba per edipo* (1974): 339–56. English translation: "Capitalism and Schizophrenia," in *Chaosophy*, by Félix Guattari, translated by Jarred Becker (New York: Semiotext[e], 1995), 75–92.

With Félix Guattari. "Deleuze et Guattari s'expliquent...." Interview with Maurice Nadeau, Raphaël Pividal, François Châtelet, Roger Dadoun, Serge Leclaire, Henri Torrubia, Pierre Clastres, and Pierre Rose. *La quinzaine littéraire* 143 (16–30 June): 15–19. English translation: "In Flux," in *Chaosophy*, by Félix Guattari, translated by Jeanine Herman (New York: Semiotext[e], 1995), 93–117.

With Jean-Paul Sartre, Simone de Beauvoir, Claude Mauriac, Jean-Marie Domenach, Hélène Cixous, Jean-Pierre Faye, Michel Foucault, and Maurice Clavel. "On en parlera demain: Les dossiers (incomplets) de l'écran." *Le nouvel observateur* (7 February): 25.

With Michel Foucault. "Les intellectuals et le pouvoir." *L'arc* 49 (issue entitled *Deleuze*): 3–10. Reprinted in 1980. English translation: "Intellectuals and Power," in *Language, Counter-memory, Practice*, by Michel Foucault, translated by Donald F. Bouchard and Sherry Simon (Ithaca, N.Y.: Cornell University Press, 1977), 205–17. Also published in *Telos* 16 (summer 1973): 103–9.

1973

"Lettre à Michel Cressole." *La quinzaine littéraire* 161 (April 1): 17–19. Also in *Deleuze*, by Michel Cressole (Paris: Éditions Universitaires, 1973), 107–18. Reprinted in *Pourparlers 1972–1990*.

"Pensée nomade" (and ensuing discussion). In *Nietzsche aujourd'hui?* Vol. 1: *Intensités* (Paris: 10/18), 105–21. English translation: "Nomad Thought" (without discussion), in *The New Nietzsche: Contemporary Styles of Interpretation,* edited and translated by David B. Allison (Cambridge, Mass.: MIT Press, 1977), 142–49.

"Présence et fonction de la folie dans la recherche du Temps perdu." *Saggi e richerche di letteratura francese* 12, n.s. (Rome): 381–90. Later published as the conclusion to *Proust et les signes* (3d ed., 1976).

"Sex-pol en acte." In *Grande Encyclopédie des Homosexualités: Trois milliards de pervers.* Special issue of *Recherches* 12 (March): 28–31.

With Félix Guattari. "Bilan-programme pour machines désirantes." *Minuit* 2 (January): 1–25. Reprinted as an appendix to the second edition of *L'Anti-Oedipe* (1972). English translation: "Balance Sheet-Program for Desiring-Machines," in *Chaosophy,* by Félix Guattari, translated by David L. Sweet (New York: Semiotext[e], 1995), 119–50.

With Félix Guattari. "Deleuze et Guattari." Interview. In *C'est demain la veille,* edited by M.-A. Burnier, 137–61. Paris: Seuil. English translation: "Capitalism: A Very Special Delirium," in *Chaosophy,* by Félix Guattari, translated by David L. Sweet (New York: Semiotext[e], 1995), 53–73.

With Félix Guattari. "14 Mai 1914: Un seul ou plusieurs loups?" *Minuit* 5 (September): 2–16. Reprinted in revised form in *Mille plateaux.* English translation: "May 14, 1914: One or Several Wolves?" translated by Mark Seem *Semiotext[e]* (title of edition: *Anti-Oedipus* 2, no. 3 [1977]).

With Félix Guattari. "Le nouvel arpenteur: Intensités et blocs d'enfance dans 'Le château.'" *Critique* 319 (December): 1046–54. Reprinted in revised form in *Kafka: Pour une littérature mineure.*

With Gérard Fromanger. *Fromanger, le peintre et le modèle.* Paris: Baudard Alvarez. Contains "Le froid et le chaud" by Deleuze and reproductions of a series of Fromanger's paintings.

1974

Preface to *L'apres-mai des faunes,* by Guy Hocquenghem, 7–17. Paris: Grasset.

With Félix Guattari. "28 novembre 1947: Comment se faire un corps sans organes?" *Minuit* 10 (September): 56–84. Reprinted in revised form in *Mille plateaux.* English translation: "How to Make Yourself a Body without Organs," translated by Suzanne Guerlac, *Semiotext(e)* 4, no. 1 (1981).

1975

"Deux régimes de fous." In *Psychanalyse et sémiotique: Actes du colloque de Milan,* 165–70 (Paris: 10/18).

"Ecrivain non: Un nouveau cartographe." Book review of *Surveillir et punir,* by Michel Foucault. *Critique* 343 (December): 1207–27. Reprinted in revised form in *Foucault.*

"Schizophrénie et société." In *Encyclopaedia universalis,* vol. 14. Paris: Encyclopaedia Universalis, 733–35.

With Jean-François Lyotard. "A propos du departement de psychanalyse à Vincennes." *Les temps modernes* 342 (January): 862–63. English translation: "Concerning the Vincennes Psychoanalysis Department," in *Political Writings,* by Jean-François

Lyotard, translated by Bill Readings and Kevin Paul Geiman (Minneapolis: University of Minnesota Press, 1993), 68–69.
With Roland Barthes and Gerard Genette. "Table ronde." *Cahiers de Marcel Proust,* n.s., 7:87–115.

1976

"Avenir de linguistique." Preface to *L'Aliénation linguistique,* by Henri Gobard, 9–14. Paris: Flammarion. Simultaneously published as "Les langues sont des bouillies où des fonctions et des mouvements mettent un peu d'ordre polémique," *La quinzaine littéraire* (1–15 May): 12–13.
"Gilles Deleuze fasciné par *'Le Misogyne.'*" Book review of Alain Roger's novel. *La quinzaine littéraire* 229 (16–31 March): 8–9.
"Nota dell'autore per l'edizione italiana." *Logica del senso.* Milan: Feltrinelli, 293–95.
"Trois questions sur *Six fois deux*" (on Godard's television films). *Cahiers du cinéma* 271:5–12. Reprinted in *Pourparlers 1972–1990.*
With Félix Guattari. *Rhizome: Introduction.* Paris: Minuit. Reprinted in revised form in *Mille plateaux.* English translation: "Rhizome," translated by Paul Foss and Paul Patton, *I and C* 8 (1981). Also in *On the Line,* by Deleuze and Guattari, translated by John Johnston (New York: Semiotext[e], 1983).

1977

"A propos des nouveaux philosophes et d'un problème plus général." *Minuit* 24, supplement (5 June). Reprinted in *Recherches* 30 (issue entitled *Les untorelli*) (November 1977): 179–84, and in *Faut-il brûler les nouveaux philosophes?* (Paris: Nouvelles Éditions Oswald, 1978), 186–94. Excerpts also appeared in *Le monde,* 19–20 June 1977, 19, under the title "Gilles Deleuze contre les 'nouveaux philosophes.'"
"Ascension du social." Postface to *La police des familles,* by Jacques Donzelot, 213–20. Paris: Minuit. English translation: "The Rise of the Social," preface to *The Policing of Families,* by Jacques Donzelot, translated by Robert Hurley (New York: Pantheon, 1979), ix–xvii.
"Le juif riche" (on Daniel Schmid's film *L'ombre des anges*). *Le monde,* 18 February, 26. Reprinted in *Daniel Schmid,* edited by Irène Lambelet, 93–95 (Lausanne: Éditions l'âge d'homme, 1982).
"Nous croyons au caractère constructiviste de certaines agitations de gauche" (petition concerning the Italian Left). *Recherches* 30 (issue entitled *Les untorelli*) (November): 149–50.
With Félix Guattari. "Le pire moyen de faire l'Europe" (on Klaus Croissant and the Baader-Meinhof Group). *Le monde,* 2 November, 6.
With Félix Guattari. *Politique et psychanalyse.* Alençon: Des Mots Perdus. The book includes two articles by Deleuze: "Quatre propositions sur le psychanalyse" and "L'interpretation des énoncés" (with Félix Guattari, Claire Parnet, and André Scala). English translations: "Four Propositions on Psychoanalysis," translated by Paul Foss, and "The Interpretation of Utterances," translated by Paul Foss and

Meaghan Morris, in *Language, Sexuality, and Subversion,* edited by Foss and Morris (Darlington, Australia: Feral Press, 1978), 135–40, 141–58.

1978

"Deux questions" (on drug use). In ... *où il est question de la toxicomanie,* by François Châtelet et al. Alençon: Des Mots Perdus, unpaginated.
"Les Gêneurs" (on the Palestinians). *Le monde,* 7 April.
"Philosophie et Minorité." *Critique* 34, no. 369 (February): 154–55.
"La plainte et le corps." Book review of *L'Absence,* by Pierre Fedida. *Le monde,* 13 October.
"Spinoza et nous" (and ensuing discussion). *Revue de synthèse* 3, nos. 89–91 (January–September): 271–78. Reprinted in revised form in *Spinoza: Philosophie pratique.*
With Carmelo Bene. *Sovrapposizioni.* Milan: Feltrinelli. French publication: *Superpositions* (Paris: Minuit, 1979). Contains "Un manifeste de moins," by Deleuze, 85–131. English translation: "One Manifesto Less," in *The Deleuze Reader,* edited by Constantin V. Boundas, translated by Alan Orenstein (New York: Columbia University Press, 1993), 204–22.
With Fanny Deleuze. "Nietzsche et Paulus, Lawrence et Jean de Patmos." Preface to *Apocalypse,* by D. H. Lawrence, 7–37. Paris: Balland. Reprinted in revised form in *Critique et clinique.*

1979

"Ce livre est littéralement une preuve d'innocence." Book review of *Marx au-delà de Marx,* by Antonio Negri. *Le matin de Paris,* 13 December, 32.
"En quoi la philosophie peut servir à des mathématiciens, ou même à des musiciens — même et surtout quand elle ne parle pas de musique ou de mathématiques." In *Vincennes ou le désir d'apprendre,* edited by Jean Brunet et al., 120–21. Paris: Éditions Alain Moreau.

1980

"8 ans après: Entretien 1980." Interview with Catherine Clément. *L'arc* 49 (issue entitled *Deleuze*) (rev. ed.): 99–102.
"'Mille plateaux' ne font pas une montagne, ils ouvrent mille chemins philosophiques." Interview with Christian Descamps, Didier Eribon, and Robert Maggiori. *Libération,* 23 October. Reprinted in *Pourparlers 1972–1990.*
With François Châtelet. "Pourquoi en être arrivé là?" Interview on the Université de Paris — VIII/Vincennes, by J. Gene. *Libération,* 17 March, 4.
With François Châtelet and Jean-François Lyotard. "Pour une commission d'enquête" (on Vincennes). *Libération,* 17 March, 4.

1981

"Peindre le cri." *Critique* 408 (May): 506–11. Extract from *Francis Bacon: Logique de la sensation.*

"La peinture enflamme l'écriture." Interview with Hervé Guibert. *Le monde,* 3 December, 15. English translation: "What Counts Is the Scream," *The Guardian,* 10 January 1982.

1982

"Les Indiens de Palestine." Interview with Elias Sanbar. *Libération,* 8–9 May, 20–21.

"Lettre à Uno sur le langage." *Gendai shisō (La revue de la pensée aujourd'hui)* (Tokyo) (December): 50–58. Translated into Japanese by Kuniichi Uno.

Preface to *L'Anomalie sauvage: Puissance et pouvoir chez Spinoza,* by Antonio Negri, translated by François Matheron, 9–12. Paris: Presses Universitaires de France.

With Kuniichi Uno. "Exposé d'une poétique rhizomatique." *Gendai shisō (La revue de la pensée aujourd'hui)* (Tokyo) (December): 94–102. Translated into Japanese by Kuniichi Uno.

1983

"L'abstraction lyrique." *Change international* 1:82. Extract from *L'image-mouvement.*

"Cinéma-1, première." Interview with Serge Daney. And "Le philosophe menuisier." Interview with Didier Eribon. *Libération,* 3 October, 30–31.

"Godard et Rivette." *La quinzaine littéraire* 404 (1 November): 6–7. Reprinted in revised form in *L'image-temps.*

"'La photographie est déjà tirée dans les choses.'" Interview with Pascal Bonitzer and Jean Narboni. *Cahiers du cinéma* 352 (October): 35–40. Reprinted in *Pourparlers 1972–1990.*

"Portrait du philosophe en spectateur." Interview with Hervé Guibert. *Le monde,* 6 October, 1, 17.

Preface to the English translation of *Nietzsche and Philosophy.* Translated by Hugh Tomlinson, ix–xiv. New York: Columbia University Press.

With Jean-Pierre Bamberger. "Le pacifisme aujourd'hui." Interview by Claire Parnet. *Les nouvelles* (15–21 December): 60–64.

1984

"Books" (on Francis Bacon). Translated by Lisa Liebmann. *Artforum* (January): 68–69. Text related to *Francis Bacon: Logique de la sensation.*

"On Four Poetic Formulas Which Might Summarize the Kantian Philosophy." In *Kant's Critical Philosophy: The Doctrine of the Faculties,* translated by Hugh Tomlinson and Barbara Habberjam, vii–xiii. Minneapolis: University of Minnesota Press. French publication: "Sur quatre formules poétiques qui pourraient résumer la philosophie kantienne," *Philosophie* 9 (1986): 29–34. Reprinted in revised form in *Critique et clinique.*

"Grandeur de Yasser Arafat." *Revue d'études Palestiniennes* 10 (winter): 41–43.

"Lettre à Uno: Comment nous avons travaillé à deux." *Gendai shisō (La revue de la pensée aujourd'hui)* (Tokyo) 12, no. 11/9: 8–11. Translated into Japanese by Kuniichi Uno.

"Le temps musical." *Gendai shisō (La revue de la pensée aujourd'hui)* (Tokyo) 12, no. 11/9: 294–98. Translated into Japanese by Kuniichi Uno.
With Félix Guattari. "Mai 68 n'a pas eu lieu." *Les nouvelles* (3–10 May): 75–76.
With François Châtelet and Félix Guattari. "Pour un droit d'asile politique un et indivisible." *Le nouvel observateur* 1041 (October): 18.

1985

"Il etait une étoile de groupe" (on François Châtelet). *Libération*, December 27, 1–22.
"Le philosophe et le cinéma." Interview by Gilbert Calbasso and Fabbrice Revault d'Allonnes. *Cinéma* 334 (18–24 December): 2–3. Reprinted in *Pourparlers 1972–1990*.
"Les plages d'immanence." In *L'art des confins: Mélanges offert à Maurice de Gandillac*, edited by Annie Cazenave and Jean-François Lyotard, 79–81. Paris: Presses Universitaires de France.
Untitled interview with Antoine Dulaure and Claire Parnet. *L'autre journal* 8 (October): 10–22. Reprinted as "Les Intercesseurs," in *Pourparlers 1972–1990*.

1986

"Boulez, Proust et les temps: 'Occuper sans compter.'" In *Eclats/Boulez*, edited by Claude Samuel, 98–100. Paris: Centre Georges Pompidou. English translation: "Boulez, Proust and Time: 'Occupying without Counting'" translated by Timothy S. Murphy, *Angelaki* (issue entitled *The Love of Music*) 3, no. 2.
"Le cerveau, c'est l'écran." Interview with A. Bergala et al. *Cahiers du cinéma* 380 (February): 25–32.
"'Fendre les choses, fendre les mots.'" *Libération*, 2 September, 27–28. And "Michel Foucault dans la troisième dimension." *Libération*, 3 September, 38. Two-part interview with Robert Maggiori. Reprinted in *Pourparlers 1972–1990*.
"The Intellectual and Politics: Foucault and the Prison." Interview with Paul Rabinow and Keith Gandal. *History of the Present* 2 (spring): 1–2, 20–21.
"Optimisme, pessimisme et voyage: Lettre à Serge Daney." Preface to *Ciné journal*, by Serge Daney, 5–13. Paris: Cahiers du cinéma. Reprinted in *Pourparlers 1972–1990*.
"Le plus grand film irlandais" (on Samuel Beckett's *Film*). *Revue d'esthétique*: 381–82. Reprinted in revised form in *Critique et clinique*.
"Sur le régime cristallin." *Hors cadre* 4: 39–45. Reprinted in *Pourparlers 1972–1990*.
"La vie comme une oeuvre d'art." Interview with Didier Eribon. *Le nouvel observateur* 1138 (4 September): 66–68. Expanded version published in *Pourparlers 1972–1990*.

1987

With Félix Guattari. Preface to *Mille piani: Capitalismo e schizofrenia*, translated by Giorgio Passerone, xi–xiv. Rome: Bibliotheca Biographica.

1988

"Un critère pour le baroque." *Chimères* 5 no. 6:3–9. Reprinted in *Le pli: Leibniz et le baroque.*

"Foucault, historien du present." *Magazine littéraire* 257 (September): 51–52.

"La pensée mise en plis." Interview with Robert Maggiori. *Libération,* 22 September, i–iii. Reprinted in *Pourparlers 1972–1990.*

Périclès et Verdi: La philosophie de François Châtelet. Paris: Minuit.

"'A Philosophical Concept....'" Translated by Julien Deleuze. *Topoi* 7, no. 2 (September): 111–12. Reprinted in *Who Comes after the Subject?* edited by E. Cadava (New York: Routledge, 1991). French translation: "Un concept philosophique," translated by René Major after loss of French original, *Cahiers confrontation* 20 (winter 1989): 89–90.

"Signes et événements." Interview with Raymond Bellour and François Ewald. *Magazine littéraire* 257 (September): 16–25. Reprinted *Pourparlers 1972–1990.*

1989

"Bartleby, ou la formule." Postface to *Bartleby, Les iles enchantées, Le campanile,* by Herman Melville, translated by Michèle Causse, 171–208. Paris: Flammarion. Reprinted in revised form in *Critique et clinique.*

"Lettre à Réda Bensmaïa." *Lendemains* 14, no. 53:9. Reprinted in *Pourparlers 1972–1990.*

Preface to the English edition of *Cinema 2: The Time-Image,* translated by Hugh Tomlinson and Robert Galeta, xi–xii. Minneapolis: University of Minnesota Press.

"Qu'est-ce qu'un dispositif?" (and ensuing discussion). In *Michel Foucault philosophe, Rencontre internationale Paris 9, 10, 11 janvier 1988,* 185–95. Paris: Seuil. English translation: "What Is a Dispositif?" In *Michel Foucault Philosopher,* translated by Timothy J. Armstrong (New York: Routledge, 1992), 159–68.

"Re-présentation de Masoch." *Libération,* 18 May, 30. Reprinted in revised form in *Critique et clinique.*

"Les trois cercles de Rivette." *Cahiers du cinéma* 416 (February): 18–19.

1990

"Avoir une idée en cinéma: Á propos du cinéma des Straub-Huillet." In *Hölderlin, Cézanne,* by Jean-Marie Straub and Danièle Huillet, 65–77. Lédignan: Éditions Antigone.

"Les conditions de la question: Qu'est-ce que la philosophie?" *Chimères* 8 (May): 123–32. Reprinted in revised form in *Qu'est-ce que la philosophie?* English translation: "The Conditions of the Question: What Is Philosophy?" translated by Daniel W. Smith and Arnold I. Davidson, *Critical Inquiry* 17, no. 3 (spring 1991): 471–78.

"Le devenir révolutionnaire et les créations politiques." Interview with Toni Negri. *Futur antérieur* 1 (spring): 100–108. Reprinted in *Pourparlers 1972–1990.*

Letter-preface to *Sahara: L'esthétique de Gilles Deleuze,* by Mireille Buydens, 5. Paris: Vrin.

"Post-scriptum sur les sociétés de contrôle." *L'autre journal* 1 (May). Reprinted in *Pourparlers 1972–1990.*

With Pierre Bourdieu, Jérôme Lindon, and Pierre Vidal-Naquet. "Adresse au gouvernement français" (on Operation Desert Shield). *Libération,* 5 September, 6.

1991

Preface to *Les temps capitaux,* vol. 1: *Récits de la conquête du temps,* by Éric Alliez, 7–9. Paris: Éditions du Cerf. English translation: Foreword to *Capital Times: Tales from the Conquest of Time,* by Éric Alliez, translated by Georges Van Den Abbeele (Minneapolis: University of Minnesota Press, 1995), xi–xiii.

Preface to *La Linea astratta: Pragmatica dello stile,* by Giorgio Passerone, translated by Giorgio Passerone, 9–13. Milan: Edizioni Angelo Guerini.

With Félix Guattari. "'Nous avons inventé la ritornelle.'" Interview with Didier Eribon. *Le nouvel observateur* 12–18 (September): 109–10.

With Félix Guattari. "Secret de fabrication: Deleuze-Guattari: Nous Deux." Interview with Robert Maggiori. *Libération,* 12 September, 17–19. Reprinted in *La Philosophie au jour le jour,* by Robert Maggiori (Paris: Flammarion, 1994), 374–81.

With René Scherer. "La guerre immonde" (on the Persian Gulf War). *Libération,* 4 March, 11.

1992

"Remarques" (on Plato). In *Nos Grecs et leurs modernes: Les stratégies contemporaines d'appropriation de l'antiquité,* edited by Barbara Cassin, 249–50. Paris: Seuil. Reprinted in revised form in *Critique et clinique.*

With Samuel Beckett. *Quad et autre pièces pour la télévision, suivi de L'Épuisé.* Paris: Minuit. Contains four pieces by Beckett and "L'Épuisé" by Deleuze, 55–112. English translation: "The Exhausted," translated by Anthony Uhlmann, *SubStance* 78 (1995): 3–28; a revised version of this translation is included in *Essays Critical and Clinical.*

1993

The Deleuze Reader. Edited by Constantin V. Boundas. New York: Columbia University Press. This volume consists entirely of previously published texts, though some appear in English for the first time.

Letter-preface to *Variations: La philosophie de Gilles Deleuze,* by Jean-Clet Martin, 7–9. Paris: Éditions Payot.

"Pour Félix" (on Guattari's death). *Chimères* 18 (winter): 209–10.

1994

"Désir et plaisir" (on *La volonté de savoir,* by Michel Foucault). *Magazine littéraire* 325 (October): 59–65. English translation: "Desire and Pleasure," in *Foucault and His*

Interlocutors, ed. Arnold I. Davidson, translated by Daniel W. Smith (Chicago: University of Chicago Press, 1997).
"Sept dessins." *Chimères* 21 (winter): 13–20.

1995

"L'immanence: Une vie...." *Philosophie* 47 (1 September): 3–7.
"Le 'Je me souviens' de Gilles Deleuze." Interview with Didier Eribon. *Le nouvel observateur* 1619 (16–22 November): 50–51.

1996

"L'actuel et le virtuel." Parts 1 and 2. Published as an appendix to the Livre de Poche edition of *Dialogues*, by Deleuze and Claire Parnet, 177–85. Paris: Flammarion. A portion of this text was published as "Extrait du dernier texte écrit par Gilles Deleuze," *Cahiers du cinéma* 497 (December 1995): 28.

Appeals and Petitions Signed by Deleuze (Partial List)

1971

"Appel aux travailleurs du quartier contre les réseaux organisés de racistes appuyés par le pouvoir" (against anti-Algerian violence). Circulated after 27 November 1971. Unpublished but cited in Didier Eribon, *Michel Foucault* (Paris: Flammarion, 1989), 254.

1972

"Appel contre les bombardements des digues du Vietnam par l'aviation U.S." (against U.S. aerial bombardment of dikes in Vietnam). *Le monde*, 9–10 July, 5.

1973

"Sale race! Sale pédé!" (against the firing of politically active homosexuals from faculties). *Recherches* 12 (*Grande encyclopédie des homosexualités: Trois milliards de pervers*) (March): reverse of optional cover sheet.

1976

"Plusieurs personnalités regrettent 'le silence des autorités françaises'" (against human rights violations in Iran). *Le monde*, 4 February, 4.
"L'appel du 18 joint" (for the legalization of marijuana). *Libération*, 18 June, 16.

1977

"A propos d'un procès" (against imprisonment for statutory rape). *Le monde*, 26 January, 24.

"A propos de *L'Ombre des anges:* Des cinéastes, des critiques et des intellectuels protestent contre les atteintes à la liberté d'expression" (against restrictions on freedom of expression in cinema). *Le monde*, 18 February, 26.

"Un appel pour la révision du code pénal à propos des relations mineurs-adultes" (against imprisonment for statutory rape). *Le monde*, 22–23 May, 24.

"L'appel des intellectuels français contre la répression en Italie" (against repression of extreme leftist groups by the PCI [Partie Communiste Internationale]). *Recherches* 30 (issue entitled *Les untorelli*) (November): 149–50.

1980

"Appel à la candidature de Coluche" (encouraging comedian Coluche to run for president of France). *Le monde*, 19 November, 10.

1981

"Appeal for the Formation of an International Commission to Inquire about the Italian Judiciary Situation and the Situation in Italian Jails." Organized in January 1981. Cited in Antonio Negri, *Marx beyond Marx* (Brooklyn, N.Y.: Autonomedia, 1991), 238. Text available from the Texas Archives of Autonomist Marxism, c/o Harry Cleaver, Department of Economics, University of Texas at Austin, Austin, TX 78712–1173.

"Un appel d'écrivains et de scientifiques de gauche" (in support of Solidarity and Polish autonomy). *Le monde*, 23 December, 5. Also printed, in abridged form, in *Le matin de Paris*, 21 December 1981, 9.

"Appel des intellectuels européens pour la Pologne" (against detention of militants in Poland). *Libération*, 30 December, 36.

1982

"Un million pour la résistance Salvadorienne" (against Reagan administration intervention in El Salvador). *Le matin de Paris*, 5 February, 1.

1983

"Des intellectuels préparent un Livre blanc en faveur des inculpés" (on the "Coral" affair, concerning unfounded accusations of child molestation). *Le monde*, 22 January, 12.

1984

"Les QHS en Italie: Les familles des détenus alertent l'opinion européene" (against the Italian "special prisons" for accused terrorists). *Libération*, 6 June, 10.

"Pour un droit d'asile politique un et indivisible" (on the right to political asylum). *Le nouvel observateur* 1041 (October): 18.

1989

"La veuve d'Ali Mécili va déposer plainte contre X...pour forfaiture" (against the deportation of a murder suspect for reasons of "public order"). *Le monde,* 5 December.

Contributors

Bernardo Alexander Attias is an assistant professor of speech communication in the College of Arts, Media, and Communication at the California State University, Northridge. His work is at the interstices of rhetorical studies, cultural studies, and theories of communication and technology, with special emphasis on histories of sexuality, international political economy, and theories of racial formation.

Jonathan L. Beller is currently a Research Fellow in History of Consciousness at the University of California, Santa Cruz. His essays include "The Spectatorship of the Proletariat," "Desiring the Involuntary," and "City of Television." He also writes on film and painting for the *Manila Chronicle.*

Bruno Bosteels is an assistant professor in the Department of Romance Languages and Literatures at Harvard University. He is currently completing *After Borges: States of Criticism and Theory.* He is also cotranslator of Gianni Vattimo's *The Secularization of Philosophy.* The study of Félix Guattari is part of a larger theoretical project, tentatively titled "Confabulations: Critical Theory from Adorno to Žižek."

Gilles Deleuze (1925–95) taught philosophy at the University of Paris VIII, Vincennes-St. Denis. His final work, *Critique et clinique,* has recently been translated into English by Daniel W. Smith and Michael A. Greco as *Essays Critical and Clinical* (Minnesota, 1997).

Aden Evens is a Ph.D. candidate in the Department of East Asian Studies at McGill University. He is the author of "Sound Ideas," published in *Canadian Review of Comparative Literature.*

Gary Genosko is an independent researcher, writer, and editor. He is the author of *Baudrillard and Signs, Undisciplined Theory* and the editor of *The Guattari Reader.* He has recently completed work on his forthcoming book, *McLuhan and Baudrillard: The Masters of Implosion,* and is embarking on a three-volume edited collection entitled *Critical Assessments: Deleuze and Guattari.*

Mani Haghighi lives in Tehran and Toronto. He is the Persian translator of Michel Foucault's *Ceci n'est pas une pipe* and has edited an anthology of postmodern texts, *The Aporia of Signs.*

Michael Hardt is an assistant professor in the Literature Program at Duke University. He is the author of *Gilles Deleuze: An Apprenticeship in Philosophy* (Minnesota, 1993) and coauthor with Antonio Negri of *Labor of Dionysus: A Critique of the State-Form* (Minnesota, 1994).

Kevin Jon Heller is currently a criminal-defense attorney in Los Angeles. He graduated from Stanford Law School in 1996 and is a Ph.D. candidate in literature at Duke University. Heller has published essays on Michel Foucault, Theodor Adorno, postmodern architecture, and criminal conspiracies.

Eugene W. Holland is an associate professor of French and comparative studies at the Ohio State University. He is the author of *Baudelaire and Schizoanalysis: The Sociopoetics of Modernism* and *Introduction to Schizoanalysis.*

John S. Howard is currently studying legal theory and constitutional interpretation at the School of Law, Saint Louis University. He has recently completed doctoral work and is the author of essays on literary theory, British romanticism and culture, and legal and literary hermeneutics. He is the author of a book-length study entitled *Romantic Dialectics and the Politics of the Subject.*

Stacey Johnson is a doctoral candidate in the graduate program in communications at McGill University. She is the coeditor, with Will Straw, Rebecca Sullivan, Gary Friedlander, and Gary Kennedy, of *Popular Music, Style, and Identity.*

Eleanor Kaufman is a Mellon Postdoctoral Fellow at Cornell University. She is currently working on a study of the laudatory French philosophical essay that focuses on Georges Bataille, Maurice Blanchot, Gilles Deleuze, Michel Foucault, and Pierre Klossowski.

Samira Kawash is an assistant professor in the Department of English at Rutgers University. She is the author of *Dislocating the Color Line: Identity, Hybridity, and Singularity in African American Narrative.*

Brian Massumi is an Australian Research Council fellow based at the Humanities Research Centre of the Australian National University. He is the author of *A User's Guide to Capitalism; Schizophrenia: Deviations from Deleuze and Guattari; First and Last Emperors: The Body of the Despot and the Absolute State* (with Kenneth Dean); and *The Critique of Pure Feeling* (forthcoming).

Timothy S. Murphy is a lecturer in the Department of English at the University of California, Los Angeles. He is the author of *Wising Up the Marks: The*

Amodern William Burroughs, as well as essays on modern and contemporary fiction and theory.

Karen Ocaña has an M.A. from McGill University. She is the author of "Synthetic Authenticity," a thesis on Angela Carter, Gilles Deleuze, and Félix Guattari, and "Permutating Crash."

Bryan Reynolds is a lecturer on the Committee on Degrees in History and Literature at Harvard University. He is currently working on a book entitled *Becoming Criminal: Transversal Power and Cultural Dissidence in Early Modern England.* He has published essays in *Appendx, The Upstart Crow, Theatre Journal,* and *Social Semiotics.*

Daniel W. Smith is an assistant professor of philosophy at Grinnell College. He has translated Gilles Deleuze's *Essays Critical and Clinical* (with Michael A. Greco; Minnesota, 1997) and *Francis Bacon: The Logic of Sensation,* as well as Pierre Klossowski's *Nietzsche and the Vicious Circle.*

Gordon Thompson is a potter and an independent scholar living in Toronto.

Index